Morphological Length and Prosodically Defective Morphemes

OXFORD STUDIES IN PHONOLOGY AND PHONETICS

GENERAL EDITORS:
Andrew Nevins, *University College London*, Keren Rice, *University of Toronto*

ADVISORY EDITORS: Stuart Davis, *Indiana University*, Heather Goad, *McGill University*, Carlos Gussenhoven, *Radboud University*, Haruo Kubozono, *National Institute for Japanese Language and Linguistics*, Sun-Ah Jun, *University of California, Los Angeles*, Maria-Rosa Lloret, *Universitat de Barcelona*, Douglas Pulleyblank, *University of British Columbia*, Rachid Ridouane, *Laboratoire de Phonétique et Phonologie, Paris*, Rachel Walker, *University of Southern California*

Morphological Length and Prosodically Defective Morphemes

EVA ZIMMERMANN

OXFORD
UNIVERSITY PRESS

OXFORD
UNIVERSITY PRESS

Great Clarendon Street, Oxford, OX2 6DP,
United Kingdom

Oxford University Press is a department of the University of Oxford.
It furthers the University's objective of excellence in research, scholarship,
and education by publishing worldwide. Oxford is a registered trade mark of
Oxford University Press in the UK and in certain other countries

© Eva Zimmermann 2017

The moral rights of the author have been asserted

First Edition published in 2017

Impression: 1

Published in the United States of America by Oxford University Press
198 Madison Avenue, New York, NY 10016, United States of America

British Library Cataloguing in Publication Data
Data available

Library of Congress Control Number: 2016953471

ISBN 978-0-19-874732-1

Printed in Great Britain by
Clays Ltd, St Ives plc

Contents

Series preface

Oxford Studies in Phonology and Phonetics provides a platform for original research on sound structure in natural language within contemporary phonological theory and related areas of inquiry such as phonetic theory, morphological theory, the architecture of the grammar, and cognitive science. Contributors are encouraged to present their work in the context of contemporary theoretical issues in a manner accessible to a range of people, including phonologists, phoneticians, morphologists, psycholinguists, and cognitive scientists. Manuscripts should include a wealth of empirical examples, where relevant, and make full use of the possibilities for digital media that can be leveraged on a companion website with access to materials such as sound files, videos, extended databases, and software.

This is a companion series to Oxford Surveys in Phonology and Phonetics, which provides critical overviews of the major approaches to research topics of current interest, a discussion of their relative value, and an assessment of what degree of consensus exists about any one of them. The Studies series will equally seek to combine empirical phenomena with theoretical frameworks, but its authors will propose an original line of argumentation, often as the inception or culmination of an ongoing original research programme.

In this book, Eva Zimmerman investigates a phenomenon known as morphological length manipulation, or instances where segmental length alternations (e.g. vowel shortening or lengthening) rely on morphological information. She proposes that all morphological derivation is at its root additive. Writing in the theory of Prosodically Defective Morphemes, Zimmermann ably demonstrates how to derive apparently non-concatenative morphology from the affixation of prosodically defective morphemes. She further extends the proposal to subtractive length manipulation, where the prosodically defective integration of morphemes can result in non-realization of underlying phonological elements when they 'usurp' a prosodic node from their base that they lack underlyingly. All variation in such patterns thus derives from the underlying prosodic structure of defective morphemes and constraints that regulate their integration. This timely monograph provides a large dataset of length-alternation phenomena that is typologically balanced and representative. Zimmermann's elegant approach does justice to the complexity of the topic and provides a solid foundation for researchers who are interested in exploring this central aspect of the phonology-morphology interface.

Andrew Nevins
Keren Rice

Acknowledgements

This book is based on the dissertation I defended in 2014 at Leipzig University. While the main claim remains the same, the book differs substantially from the thesis, both in structure and some specific argumentations and analyses. I would like to thank my supervisors Nina Topintzi and Stuart Davis, not only for their helpful criticisms and comments on the original PhD thesis, but also for their support and encouragement for the plan to turn it into a book. I'm also very grateful to Andrew Nevins and Keren Rice, the series editors, for their support and excellent suggestions on the original manuscript.

The grounding of this book is the joint work I did with Jochen Trommer over the years: his influence on this book and his support while writing it can hardly be overestimated and I am deeply grateful.

Most parts of this work were presented at various conferences or in different colloquia during the last few years and I am thankful for all the the input and criticisms I received at, for example, several Old World Conferences in Phonology and Manchester Phonology Meetings. To name just a few people to whom I am indebted for many helpful comments and discussions over the years: John Alderete, Eric Baković, Ricardo Bermúdez-Otero, Chuck Cairns, Laura Downing, Caroline Féry, Gunnar Hansson, Sharon Inkelas, Pavel Iosad, Junko Ito, Larry Hyman, Yuni Kim, Björn Köhnlein, Marc van Oostendorp, Jaye Padgett, Douglas Pulleyblank, and Sharon Rose.

I also want to express my deep gratitude to the people at the Department of Linguistics at Leipzig University. The amount of constructive criticism, valuable input, support, and enthusiasm for all sorts of linguistic challenges I encountered over the years has been very impressive and I want to thank Andreas Opitz, Anita Steube, Anke Himmelreich, Barbara Stiebels, Daniela Henze, Doreen Georgi, Fabian Heck, Gereon Müller, Jochen Trommer, Martin Salzmann, Peter Staroverov, Philipp Weisser and Sandhya Sundaresan.

I worked on this book while holding research associate positions funded by the German Research Association (DFG) and I gratefully acknowledge this funding (project 'Hierarchy Effects in Kiranti and Broader Algic' (TR 521-3) and project 'Featural Affixes: The Morphology of Phonological Features' (TR 521/6-1)). I'm also thankful for the financial support of the Fulbright Commission and the Free State of Saxony that granted me a 'Landesstipendium'.

List of glosses, abbreviations, and symbols

Glosses

1, 2, 3	first, second, and third person
1>3	first person acting on third person
2>3	second person acting on third person
2<->3	second person acting on third person or vice versa
ABL	ablative
ACC	accusative
AFF	affirmative
ALL	allative
ANT	anticipatory
BEN	benefactive
BFR	category buffer
COMPL	completive
CONT	continuative
CT	change of topic
DETA	detailed action
DPST	deductive past
DUB	dubitative
F	feminine
FUT	future
IMPF	imperfect
INF	infinitive
IR	interrogative
NMLZ	nominalizer
O	object
PASS	passive
PL	plural
PST	past
REV	reversive
S	subject
SF	stem formative

Sɢ	singular
Sᴍʟꜰ	semelfactive
Sᴛᴀᴛ	stative
Sᴜʙᴏʀᴅ	subordinate
Tᴏᴘ	topic
Vʙ	verbalizer

Abbreviations

Affr	Affricate
C	Consonant
CL	Compensatory Lengthening
CT	Cophonology Theory
Fric	Fricative
Gem	Gemination
H	high tone
IO	Input–Output (relation)
L	low tone
MLM	Morphological Length-Manipulation
NoCr	NoCrossingCondition
NKK	NoKickingCondition
OO	Output–output (relation)
OT	Optimality Theory
PDM	Prosodically Defective Morphemes
RMO	RecoverableMorphemeOrderPrinciple
S	Segment
SSM	Southern Sierra Miwok
TAF	Transderivational Antifaithfulness
V	Vowel
VL	Vowel lengthening

Symbols

☛	empirically correct but wrongly suboptimal under the given ranking
☞	the winning candidate
↯	excluded by GEN
μ	mora
σ	syllable
Φ	foot
ω	prosodic word

1

Introduction

In this book, the phenomenon of Morphological Length-Manipulation is investigated and it is argued that it is best analysed in a theoretical framework termed 'Prosodically Defective Morphemes': if all possible prosodically defective morpheme representations and their potential effects for the resulting surface structure are taken into account, instances of length-manipulating non-concatenative morphology and length-manipulating morpheme-specific phonology are predicted. The argumentation in this book is hence in line with the general claim that all morphology results from combination and that non-concatenative exponents arise from an 'enriched notion of affix that allows the inclusion of autosegmental tiers' (Stonham, 1994: 27). Although this position has been defended various times for specific phenomena, it has rarely been discussed against the background of a broad typological survey. In contrast to most existing claims, the argumentation in this book is based on a representative data set for attested morphological length-manipulating patterns in the languages of the world that serves as a basis for the theoretical arguments. It is argued that alternative accounts suffer from severe under- and overgeneration problems if one tests them against the full range of attested phenomena.

Before an overview of this book is presented in section 1.3, the phenomenon of Morphological Length-Manipulation (MLM) is introduced and defined in section 1.1 and it is discussed why it is interesting and challenging from a theoretical perspective in section 1.2.

1.1 Morphological Length-Manipulation

1.1.1 Additive MLM

Segment lengthening and epenthesis are common phonological strategies to optimize the phonological structure of a surface form. In Hixkaryana, for example, we find an instance of iambic lengthening ensuring that all vowels in even-numbered, non-final syllables in a string of CV-syllables are long. Examples are given in (1-a) where two morphemes are shown in different morphological contexts and different vowels surface as long depending on the number of syllables preceding the base. In (1-a-i), the second vowel of the stem/hananɨhɨ/ is long if it surfaces in the second syllable,

Morphological Length and Prosodically Defective Morphemes. First edition. Eva Zimmermann.
© Eva Zimmermann 2017. First published 2017 by Oxford University Press.

whereas it is short if it surfaces in the third syllable (Derbyshire, 1979, 1985; Hayes, 1995). In Kuuku-YaʔU, on the other hand, an intervocalic consonant following a main-stressed vowel is geminated (Thompson, 1976; Hayes, 1995; McGarrity, 2008; Bye and de Lacy, 2008). The language employs a default-to-opposite stress system where main stress is on the rightmost long vowel if there is one (1-b-ii) and otherwise on the initial syllable (1-b-i). The gemination can hence be interpreted as a strategy to ensure that the main-stressed syllable is heavy (=bimoraic).

(1)   *Segment lengthening*
    a. *Vowel lengthening in Hixkaryana*   (Hayes, 1995: 206)

	UNDERLYING	SURFACE	
i.	ki—hananɨhɨ—no	khanaːnɨhno	'I taught you'
	mɨ—hananɨhɨ—no	mɨhaːnanɨhno	'you taught him'
ii.	owto—hona	owtohoːna	'to the village'
	tohkurʲe—hona	tohkurʲeːhona	'to Tohkurye'

    b. *Consonant lengthening in Kuuku-YaʔU*   (McGarrity, 2008: 58+64)

	UNDERLYING	SURFACE	
i.	pama	pámːa	'Aboriginal person'
	waliʔi	wálːiʔi	'spotted lizard'
	kacinpinta	kácːinpinta	'female'
	mukana	múkːana	'big'
ii.	wiːmumu	wíːmumu	'large number of ants'
	mumaːɲa	mumáːɲa	'rub'

The examples in (2), on the other hand, show contexts where an additional non-underlying segment is realized. In Mohawk (2-a), an additional /e/ surfaces if a consonant is expected to directly follow a single sonorant or a /ʔ/ (Michelson, 1983; Piggott, 1995).[1] And in Selayarese (2-b), an additional /ʔ/ surfaces between two identical vowels that are otherwise expected to be adjacent (Mithun and Basri, 1986; Lombardi, 2002). It can be seen that adding vowel-initial suffixes or vowel-final prefixes[2] can trigger /ʔ/-insertion (2-b-i). If two adjacent non-identical vowels are expected to surface, no epenthesis surfaces (2-b-ii).

(2)   *Phonologically motivated insertion*
    a. *Vowel insertion in Mohawk*   (Piggott, 1995: 292)

UNDERLYING	SURFACE	
k—runju—s	kerúnjus	'I sketch'
ʌ—k—r—ʌ—ʔ	ʌkerʌʔ	'I will put it into a container'
te—k—rik—s	tékeriks	'I put them together'
ʌ—k—arat—ʔ	ʌkárateʔ	'I lay myself down'
ro—kut—ot—ʔ	rokútoteʔ	'he has a bump on his nose'

[1] The pattern of vowel epenthesis in Mohawk is far more complex and involves more contexts. See, for example, Piggott (1995).
[2] Note that only the relevant morpheme boundaries are marked in the examples.

b. *Consonant insertion in Selayarese*   (Mithun and Basri, 1986: 242)

	UNDERLYING	SURFACE	
i.	amal:i−i	amal:i?i	'(s)he bought'
	a?liŋka−a	a?liŋka?a	'I walked'
	ku−uraɲi	ku?uraɲi	'I accompany him'
ii.	amal:i−a	amal:ia	'I bought'
	a?liŋka−i	a?liŋkai	'(s)he walked'
	ku−inuɲi	kuinuɲi	'I drink it'

The four processes in (1) and (2) apply in a certain phonological context and receive a straightforward phonological explanation: vowel lengthening in Hixkaryana (1-a) is an instance of iambic lengthening that ensures that every stressed vowel is long, consonant gemination in Kuuku-Ya?u (1-b) ensures that all main-stressed syllables are heavy, vowel insertion in Mohawk avoids illicit consonant clusters (2-a), and consonant epenthesis in Selayarese (2-b) avoids two adjacent identical vowels.

Now let's take a look at the data in (3), from the Pama-Nyungan language Gidabal (Geytenbeek and Geytenbeek, 1971; Kenstowicz and Kisseberth, 1977). As in the Hixkaryana data in (1-a), a length alternation for vowels can be observed that surface as short in one context and long in another. However, there is a crucial difference to the patterns in (1) and (2), namely the fact that the length alternation in Gidabal cannot be explained by referring only to phonological structure. Stress in Gidabal is on the first syllable and on syllables containing long vowels; the vowel lengthening in (3) hence applies not in all stressed positions. And even more crucially, short final vowels are attested in non-imperative forms in the same phonological contexts. If the structure /gida/ were under some interpretation more marked than /gida:/ and final vowel lengthening were a general phonological process of Gidabal, we would expect this lengthening to apply in the non-imperative as well. The same holds for the reverse analysis that /gida:/ is the underlying form and /gida/ the phonologically more unmarked form—a short vowel would be expected in the imperative form.

In contrast, the length alternation is bound to morphological contexts: Whereas verbs end in a short final vowel in their non-imperative form, the final vowel of the imperative form is always long.[3]

---

[3] It is clear that a detailed understanding of the phonology and morphology of a language is necessary to be sure that such instances are indeed morphologically triggered and not phonologically predictable. For reasons of space, such a detailed background information is not given for all the languages discussed here. The reader is referred to the Appendix for some more facts about all the languages discussed in the following. The transcription of the data is standardized to IPA in most cases and hence often deviates from the original source; see again the Appendix for details. The sources for all data in this book are given in the line above all examples. The page where the examples can be found is given either there or in the same line as the example. If more than one source is listed, the respective sources are abbreviated with the first/the first two letters of the author(s) before the page number.

(3) *Vowel lengthening in Gidabal*   (Geytenbeek and Geytenbeek, 1971: 21–24)

BASE		IMPERATIVE
gida	'to tell'	gida:
ma	'to put'	ma:
jaga	'to fix'	jaga:
ga:da—li—wa	'to keep on chasing'	ga:daliwa:

In fact, we can find morphologically induced counterparts to all four operations discussed so far. In Shoshone (Numic) (4a), the durative aspect for verbs is marked by geminating the medial consonant of the verb stem (a pattern common in many other Numic languages, see, for example, Crum and Dayley, 1993; Haugen, 2008; McLaughlin, 1982).[4] In the data from Upriver Halkomelem (Salishan) (4-b), the continuative form of verbs realizes the additional sequence /hɛ/ before the stem. A closer look at the data reveals that this is in fact only one of four predictable allomorphs to realize the continuative; most of them add additional segments or length to the initial syllable. The /hɛ/-insertion in (4-b) can hence reasonably be analysed as epenthesis (see section 5.3.1 for more details). Finally, in Shizuoka Japanese, emphatic adjective formation involves one of three length-manipulating operations, among them insertion of an additional nasal segment that surfaces as homorganic to an adjacent consonant (4-c-i) (Davis and Ueda, 2002, 2005, 2006). Realization of this segment alternates predictably with vowel- and consonant lengthening (4-c-ii, iii) and can hence—absolutely parallel to the argumentation for Upriver Halkomelem above— reasonably analysed as epenthesis (see section 2.1.1 for some more details).

(4) a. *Consonant gemination in Shoshone*   (Crum and Dayley, 1993: 94)

STEM		DURATIVE
nɨmi	'travel'	nɨm:i
maka	'feed'	mak:a
taikʷa(h)	'speak'	taik:ʷa
ɨkʷi(')	'smell'	ɨk:ʷi
hapi(')	'lie (down)'	hap:i
jɨkʷi(')	'say'	jɨk:ʷi

b. *Vowel (and consonant) epenthesis in Upriver Halkomelem*   (Galloway, 1993)

NON-CONTINUATIVE		CONTINUATIVE		
máq'ət	'swallow sth.'	həmq'ət	'swallowing sth.'	60
wə́q'ʷ	'drown, drift downstream'	həwq'ʷ	'drowning'	273
jə́q'əs	'file'	héjq'əs	'filing'	61
lə́qəm	'dive'	hélqəm	'diving'	61

---

[4] Note that the superscript '(h)' and '(')' notate the common Numic 'final features': certain morphemes trigger a change (nasalizing, preaspirating, doubling) on a following consonant.

c. *Consonant epenthesis in Shizuoka Japanese*   (Davis and Ueda, 2005: 3)

	BASE		EMPHATIC FORM
i.	hade	'showy'	hande
	ozoi	'terrible'	onzoi
	nagai	'long'	naŋgai
	karai	'spicy'	kanrai
ii.	katai	'hard'	katːai
	osoi	'slow'	osːoi
iii.	zonzai	'impolite'	zoːnzai
	supːai	'sour'	suːpːai

As in Gidabal, there is no context for these operations that can be determined by phonological factors alone. In contrast, they are all crucially bound to contexts that can be characterized by a specific morpho-syntactic information that is not marked by affixation of segmental material. Given that the absence of a segment is taken to be the length zero, all these examples have in common that the length of a segment is affected in some way, hence they are instances of 'length-manipulation'. In Gidabal and Shoshone, a short segment alternates with a long one (S → Sː), and in Upriver Halkomelem and Shizuoka Japanese, a zero segment alternates with a segment (ø → S).

The example in (5) is yet different from the data in (4) since an additional segmental affix is present in the context where a segmental lengthening operation applies. Affixation of the reversive suffix /−i/ in Wolof (Atlantic) results in gemination of a preceding stem consonant (5-a). The examples in (5-b) show that phonologically similar suffixes do not trigger the length-manipulation. This is especially apparent since the two suffixes are homophonous and only the reversive /−i/ triggers degemination whereas the base is realized unchanged[5] before the inchoative suffix /−i/. As before, the phonological context alone is insufficient to account for the length-alternation but crucial reference to the morpho-syntactic category is necessary. In contrast to the examples in, (3)–(4), however, the morphological category in question is also marked by a segmental affix.

---

[5] Note that there are additional vowel changes for some stems. It is concluded in Ka (1994) that those 'stem vowel changes are a morphologized phenomenon' (p. 96). If those changes are indeed instances of morpheme-specific phonology, an analysis assuming floating vocalic features would nicely account for those facts and would perfectly be in line with the PDM claim defended here. Since we are only concerned with the MLM, these changes are ignored in the following.

(5) *Gemination in Wolof*   (Ka, 1994: 87, 88)

    a. BASE   REVERSIVE

ub	ubːi	'to open'
teg	tegːi	'to remove'
lem	lemːi	'to unfold'
lal	lalːi	'to take off (a sheet)'

    b. BASE   INCHOATIVE

takː	tekːi	'to untie'
gəmː	gimːi	'to open eyes'

In the following, instances such as the gemination in Wolof are termed *Additive Affixation*: a segmental affix triggers an additional length-manipulating operation. The patterns in (3)–(4) where the manipulation of segment length alone is the sole marking for a certain morpho-syntactic context, on the other hand, are termed *Addition*. The latter is standardly assumed to be an instance of non-concatenative morphology where a morphological information is not marked by the addition of segmental material but some operation that, for example, manipulates the sub- or suprasegmental structure of the base (for discussion and a definition see, for example, Bye and Svenonius, 2012). The former phenomenon is termed 'morphologically conditioned phonology' (Anttila, 2002), the 'dominance effect' of certain affixes (Alderete, 2001*a*), or 'morpheme-specific phonology' (Pater, 2009) since a phonological operation applies only in the context of adding of a certain segmental affix. Additive Affixation and Addition are what is termed additive *Morphological Length-Manipulation* in the following: lengthening or addition of segments is bound to a specific morpho-syntactic context and cannot be explained with reference to the phonological context alone.

1.1.2 *Subtractive MLM*

In all the examples discussed so far, the length of a segment was affected in an additive way: a segment became longer or a whole segment was added. The logical counterpart to these patterns are processes that affect the length of a segment in a subtractive way. In the domain of purely phonologically triggered processes, it is not difficult to come up with examples that show the subtractive mirror image of the additive phonological processes given in (1) and (2).

In Yokuts (Yokuts-Utian), for example, a process of vowel shortening can be observed (6-a). Long vowels in closed syllables are illicit in the language and whenever an underlyingly long vowel is expected to surface in a closed syllable, vowel shortening applies (Newman, 1932; Noske, 1985; Archangeli, 1991). And in Diola-Fogny (Sapir, 1969; Kager, 1999*b*; McCarthy, 2008*b*), we see a process of consonant deletion (6-b). Illicit consonant clusters in Diola-Fogny are avoided via deletion of a consonant.

(6)   *Phonologically motivated shortening*

    a. *Vowel shortening in Yokuts* (Archangeli, 1991: 239)

UNDERLYING	SURFACE	
taːn—sit	tansit	'will go toward'
doːs—hat'—iːn	doshot'en	'will want to tell'
taːwt̥—aː—al	tawt̥al	'might kill'
taxaː—t	taxat	'was brought'

    b. *Consonant deletion in Diola-Fogny* (Sapir, 1969: 17)

UNDERLYING	SURFACE	
lɛt—ku—jaw	lɛkujaw	'they will not go'
na—manj—manj	namamanj	'he knows'
ɛ—rɛnt—rɛnt	ɛrɛrɛnt	'it is light'

As for segment lengthening and segment insertion, morphologically triggered counterparts to these shortening and deletion operations are attested as well. And quite parallel to the distinction into Addition and Additive Affixes, a distinction into *Subtraction* and *Subtractive Affixes* can be made. In Yine (Maipurean), vowels directly preceding certain suffixes are systematically deleted (7-a). This vowel deletion is no regular phonological process of the language but only triggered by an arbitrary class of suffixes that share no obvious common feature in terms of their semantics or phonology. The latter fact is apparent since pairs of homophonous suffixes exist where one suffix triggers deletion (e.g. nominalizing /—nu/) and the other does not (e.g. anticipatory /—nu/). Examples of non-triggering suffixes are given in (7-a-ii) and to facilitate reading, the morpho-syntactic meaning is added as index to the homophonous pairs of suffixes. The operation of segment deletion is hence bound to specific morphological contexts that are marked by certain segmental suffixes. Quite parallel to Additive Affixation, this is termed an instance of Subtractive Affixation. Subtractive Affixes like these vowel-deletion triggering affixes in Yine are always underlined in this book. In Wolof (Atlantic), the causative suffix /—al/ triggers degemination of a preceding long consonant (Ka, 1994; Bell, 2003) (7-b-i).[6] As the vowel deletion in Yine, this degemination is not phonologically predictable. This is most apparent in the data (7-b-ii) where it can be seen that the homophonous benefactive suffix /—al/ does not trigger degemination. The degemination is hence an instance of MLM, more concretely of Subtractive Affixation. Interestingly, the data in (5) showed us that the language also employs Additive Affixation. As discussed in some more detail in section 3.2.2, such a coexistence of additive and subtractive MLM in one language is not uncommon and follows straightforwardly in the theory of *Prosodically Defective Morphemes* (=PDM) proposed in this book.

---

[6] Some pairs of singleton–geminate alternations in Wolof are not entirely regular. The geminate /pː/, for example, always alternates with the singleton continuant /f/. An alternation that is not unexpected in this example since the stop /p/ is impossible intervocalically (Ka, 1994).

In the Chadic language Hausa (Hayes, 1990; Wolff, 1993; Smirnova, 1985; Schuh, 1989; Newman, 2000; Jaggar, 2001; Crysmann, 2004; Álvarez, 2005), the formation of a proper noun from a common noun involves only shortening of a final long vowel (7-c). In Canela Krahô (Macro-Ge), on the other hand, segment deletion[7] can be observed that is not accompanied by addition of a segmental affix (Popjes and Popjes, 2010). Non-realization of the base-final consonant forms finite verbs from infinite bases (7-d). That the process can not reasonably be analysed as insertion is apparent since the consonant quality of the putative inserted final consonant is not predictable. Non-realization of the final consonant is hence the only exponent for a certain morpho-syntactic category in Canela Krahô.

(7) *Morphological subtractive operations*
   a. *Morphological vowel deletion in Yine*   (Matteson, 1965)

	UNDERLYING	SURFACE		
i.	neta—ja	netja	'I see there'	M36
	pawata—maka	pawatmaka	'I would have made a fire'	M74
	çema—çe—ta	çemçeta	'to have never, never heard'	M79
	homkahita—ka$_{PASS}$	homkahitka	to be followed'	M80
	tsapo—ta$_{DETA}$	tsapta	'to have repeated cramps'	M87
ii.	tçiɾika—ka$_{SMLF}$	tçiɾikaka	'to ignite'	M85
	nika—ta$_{SF}$	nikata	'to terminate'	M88

   b. *Morphological consonant shortening in Wolof*   (Ka, 1994: 96, 97)

	BASE		CAUSATIVE	
i.	seg:	'to filter'	segal	'to press oily products'
	son:	'to be tired'	sonal	'to tire, bother'
	top:	'to follow'	tofal	'to add'
	sed:	'to be cold'	seral	'to cool'
	muc:	'to be safe'	musəl	'to save'
ii.	BASE		BENEFACTIVE	
	bət:	'to pierce'	bət:al	'to pierce for'
	dug:	'to enter'	dug:əl	'to enter for'

   c. *Morphological vowel shortening in Hausa*   (Schuh, 1989: 38)

PROPER NOUN		COMMON NOUN	
marka:	'height of rainy season'	marka	'name of woman born at this time'
ba:ko:	'stranger'	ba:ko	'man's name'
baki:	'black'	baki	'Blackie'
kuma:tu:	'cheeks'	kuma:tu	'name of so. with fat cheeks'

---

[7] For theoretical reasons that are discussed in section 2.2.2, 'deletion' in the present framework is in fact 'non-realization'. Both terms are used in free variation.

d. *Morphological consonant deletion in Canela Krahô*

(Popjes and Popjes, 2010: 192)

LONG		SHORT
ihkulan	'(so.) kills it'	ihkula
tɔn	'(so.) makes it'	tɔ
ihkah:ɯl	'(so.) whips it'	ihkah:ɯ
katɔl	'he arrives'	katɔ

The patterns in (7) all have in common that a process that is crucially bound to a certain morpho-syntactic context reduces the length of a segment: it becomes shorter (S: → S) or remains completely unrealized (S → ø).

1.1.3 A definition of the phenomenon

The examples of Addition, Subtraction, Additive Affixation, and Subtractive Affixation discussed in the previous sections 1.1.1 and 1.1.2 in fact illustrate the full range of what is taken to be Morphological Length-Manipulation (=MLM) in the following. This empirical area is a subset of what is termed 'morphologically conditioned phonology' in Inkelas (2014) where an insightful study and empirical overview of similar phenomena at the phonology–morphology boundary is given.

The different patterns of MLM can be classified with at least three relevant parameters. For one, either an additive (ø → S or S → S:) or a subtractive (S → ø or S:→ S) length-manipulating operation has applied. Secondly, the length-manipulation targets either a vowel or a consonant.[8] A cross-classification of these differences results in eight basic length-manipulation operations that are summarized in (8) together with the terms used throughout the book.

(8) *Morphological length-manipulating operations*

	Additive		Subtractive	
	S → S:	ø → S	S: → S	S → ø
Vowel	Vowel lengthening	Epenthesis	Vowel shortening	Deletion
Consonant	Gemination		Degemination	

---

[8] Deletion and epenthesis can target more than one segment and some patterns delete/insert a segmental string CV, hence target a consonant and a vowel at the same time. It is abstracted away from these complex patterns for now.

Together with the difference between non-concatenative morphology (=Addition and Subtraction) and morpheme-specific phonology (=Additive and Subtractive Affixes), a typology of sixteen possible patterns of MLM arises. Most of them are attested in the languages of the world and all these different types are discussed and analysed throughout this book. In (9), an example for every pattern in one language is listed, some of which were illustrated above.

(9)   *16 Morphological length-manipulating patterns*

	Addition	Additive Affix
Vowel lengthening	1 Gidabal	2 Bukusu
Gemination	3 Shoshone	4 Pulaar
Vowel epenthesis	5 Southern Sierra Miwok	6 Arbizu Basque
Consonant epenthesis	7 Shizuoka Japanese	8 Standard Japanese
	Subtraction	**Subtractive Affix**
Vowel shortening	9 Oromo	10 Kashaya
Degemination	11 ???	12 Wolof
Vowel deletion	13 Lardil	14 Yine
Consonant deletion	15 Canela Krahô	16 West Greenlandic

For only one of the sixteen expected patterns of MLM, could no convincing attested instance be found, namely degemination as a non-concatenative operation. However, this might receive a straightforward independent explanation in the fact that geminate consonants are cross-linguistically more marked than singleton consonants. The lack of an example for pattern 11 is hence taken as an accidental gap.

In this book, a unified theoretical account of all these types of MLM is proposed. As is shown in detail in the following chapters, the difference between Additive/Subtractive Affixation and Addition/Subtraction is irrelevant for most parts of the theoretical analysis and the different terms are used merely to facilitate the empirical description of data. This follows the insight in the detailed study in Inkelas (2014) where MLM falls under a subset of the phenomena discussed there as 'morphologically conditioned phonology'.

The empirical aim of this book is to provide a representative data collection of attested instances of MLM. Such an empirical base allows us to make a strong argument for a specific theoretical framework that predicts all attested patterns and excludes imaginable patterns that are generally unattested. For such an empirical survey that backs up a theoretical claim, one needs a clear definition of the empirical phenomenon in question which is as theory-neutral as possible. A first definition of morphological length-manipulating *operations* that summarizes the preceding discussion is given in (10).

(10) *Morphological length-manipulating operations*
      Two output forms A and B are related via a length-manipulating operation iff
      a. one form is morphologically derived from the other,
          (i.e. the morpho-syntactic features expressed by the two forms are in a subset-
          superset relation)
      and
      b. there is a segmental length difference between both forms, i.e. either
          (i) or (ii) applies,
          (i)   a segment in A is longer than its correspondent in B
                (=*Long-Short-Alternation*),
          (ii) a segment is present in A but not in B that is not part of the
                underlying representation of the morphemes in A
                (=*Segment-Zero-Alternation*),
      and this segmental length difference cannot be explained in purely phono-
      logical terms.

It is clear that the definition is not completely theory-neutral. The identification of an
MLM operation requires a morphological analysis both in terms of expressed morphological and/or semantic features and in terms of segmentation into morphemes.[9]

This definition, however, only allows us to identify surface alternations that can
be described as morphologically triggered length-manipulations, it is not sufficient
for unambiguously relating a morphological context with one MLM *pattern*. For an
illustration of this problem, let's briefly consider examples of MLM in Leggbo and
Upriver Halkomelem.

Progressive formation in Leggbo involves addition of the suffix /−i/ in addition to
two processes of gemination that apply to the first and the second base consonant as
can be seen in (11) (the pattern discussed and analysed in detail in section 6.2.4.1).
According to the definition in (10), these two gemination processes are two MLM
operations. However, both of them are unambiguously associated with one morpheme
and an analysis is hence preferably where both operations are part of the same MLM
pattern, triggered in the same morphological context or by the same morpheme.

---

[9] Especially the issue of segmentation into morphemes is a task far from being trivial and is notoriously
biased by the analyst (for a general discussion of this subsegmentation problem see, for example, Bank and
Trommer (to appear) or Bank and Trommer (2015)). In the following, the segmentation into morphemes
follows the one given in the descriptive sources in most cases. However, since the distinction into Addition-
Additive Affix and Subtraction-Subtractive Affix is not relevant for the general logic of the present analysis,
the morpheme segmentation problem is not crucial for the arguments made in this book.

(11) *Progressive in Leggbo: Gemination*   (Hyman, 2009: 16)

BASE		PROGRESSIVE
bal	'to remove oil/palmnut'	bːalːi
dum	'to bite'	dːumːi
kum	'to pierce, stab'	kːumːi
vɔŋ	'to want, look for'	fɔŋːi
sɛŋ	'to go'	sɛŋːi

On the other hand, it is possible that different instances of MLM apply in the same morphological context and the choice between them is phonologically predictable given the structure of the base.

An example is the continuative formation in Upriver Halkomelem that is analysed in detail in section 5.3.1. Two of the four allomorphs that form the continuative are given in (12): vowel lengthening and reduplication of an initial CV sequence. The choice between the allomorphs in Upriver Halkomelem is predictable given the phonological structure of the base: when the base starts with a glottal consonant, vowel lengthening surfaces (12-a) and when the base starts with a non-glottal consonant and has a full stressed vowel in the initial syllable, reduplication can be observed (12-b). Since one of the allomorphs is a Long-Short-Alternation, the pattern is part of the MLM data sample.

(12) *Continuative allomorphy in Upriver Halkomelem*   (Galloway, 1993)

a. *Vowel lengthening*

NON-CONTINUATIVE		CONTINUATIVE		
ʔíməç	'walk'	ʔíːməç	'walking'	66
ʔíχət	'scrape sth./so.'	ʔíːχət	'scraping sth./so.'	67
hílt	'roll sth. over'	híːlt	'roll sth. over'	67
hákʷəç	'use sth.'	háːkʷəç	'using sth.'	270

b. *Reduplication*

NON-CONTINUATIVE		CONTINUATIVE		
q'ísət	'tie sth.'	q'íq'əsət	'tying sth.'	68
p'étθ	'sew'	p'ép'ətθ	'sewing'	266
t'éjəq'	'get angry'	t'ét'əjəq'	'getting angry'	136
jíq	'fall (of snow)'	jíjəq	'falling (of snow)'	135

Continuative formation in Upriver Halkomelem shows hence different MLM operations in complementary distribution that mark the same morphological category and should reasonably be analysed as a single MLM pattern.

A definition of MLM pattern hence takes into account the possibility of multiple MLM operations that constitute a single MLM pattern: either those operations are in complementary distribution since they are phonologically predictable allomorphs for a morpheme or they are expected to cooccur as part of a more complex MLM. The definition in (13), of course, does not exclude that the set of M_x only contains a single MLM operation. As will becomes clear in the following chapters, this is in fact the most frequent default pattern of MLM.

(13)   *MLM pattern, preliminary*

A set M_x of MLM operations M_1–M_n constitutes a pattern of MLM iff their context of application is bound to the presence of the same morpho-syntactic features.

With this definition of MLM pattern in mind, let's return to the definition for MLM operation given in (10). There are in fact several apparent MLM phenomena that are not or only under special circumstances part of the MLM data sample presented here. This is mainly due to the fact that for several processes, the decision whether they are instances of MLM or not hinges to a certain degree on their theoretical implementation. A second important consideration is the (partial) exclusion of MLM operations for which extensive empirical and theoretical discussions already exist and which straightforwardly follow under the general framework of PDM.

One of these MLM operations is reduplication. It increases the number of segments if one compares a base and its reduplicated form and hence should be considered an instance of MLM. Even more so since the theoretical significance of (empty) prosodic nodes in the analyses for reduplication has been discussed extensively over the last few decades (see, for example, Marantz (1982), or McCarthy and Prince (1986/1996) et seq.). On the other hand, the added segments could be interpreted as being already present in the underlying base since they are copies of existing base segments. For the data sample that is the basis for the theoretical arguments in this book, reduplication is disregarded for most parts. This choice is motivated by two main points. *First*, reduplication is a far more well-studied phenomenon than the remaining segmental-lengthening operations. There are a lot of comprehensive studies about attested reduplication phenomena and their theoretical account (for literature and discussion see, for example, Spaelti, 1997; Raimy, 2000; Hurch, 2005; Samuels, 2010; Saba Kirchner, in press). And, *second*, it is trivially necessary to restrict the number of relevant data to a reasonable size if one claims to have a representative sample for a specific phenomenon. Reduplication is hence only included in the data sample and discussed throughout this book if it is one phonologically predictable allomorph in a morphological context where a Long-Short-Alternation can be found in other phonological contexts.

Another note is in order regarding morphological epenthesis as instance of MLM. Given the reasoning above, a process of segment insertion is expected as counterpart to segment deletion as an instance of length-manipulating morphology. And indeed it is argued here that such cases exist (see the description of Upriver Halkomelem in (4-b)). On the other hand, it is clear that they are hard to identify based on surface observations about the paradigms in a language. This follows from the simple fact that on the surface, nothing distinguishes underlying segments that are assumed to be part of the lexical representation of a morpheme from epenthetic segments. If more segments are present in a morphologically more complex form than in its base, the default assumption would presumably be that an affix consisting of segments was added. One criterion to distinguish underlying from epenthetic segments could be the fact that epenthetic segments in a language have either an unmarked default value or a quality that depends partially or completely on the quality of neighbouring segments (for discussion see, for example Hall, 2011). However, this criterion only allows us to exclude segments that are not epenthetic, it does not allow the reverse conclusion that all instances of unmarked default segments or segments that underwent harmony are epenthetic. Quite parallel to reduplication, morphological epenthesis is hence only included as an instance of MLM into the data sample if it alternates phonologically predictable with a Long-Short-Alternation.

In addition, instances that are standardly described as templatic morphology are generally excluded. The best-known example is probably Semitic morphology but there are also instances of templatic morphology attested in, for example, Southern Sierra Miwok, a language that is discussed in this book in some detail since it also exhibits non-templatic morphological lengthening patterns. The exclusion of templatic length-manipulation also excludes many instances of subtractive morphology, namely truncation.[10] All instances of morphological deletion considered in the following are hence instances where the deleted portion can be characterized prosodically, not instances where words are stripped down to a certain fixed size. It is clear that under the general account of PDM, it is expected that templatic morphology follows in principle from the same mechanism. Templatic morphology is nevertheless excluded for two reasons which are very similar to the reasonings that led to an exclusion of most reduplication patterns. *First*, claims that templatic morphology follows from adjusting a base to a certain prosodic category have been made elsewhere (for discussion and literature see, for example, McCarthy and Prince, 1994*b*) and, *second*, these phenomena have received considerably far more attention in the (theoretical) literature (see, for example, McCarthy, 1981; McCarthy and Prince, 1986/1996, 1990; Bensoukas, 2001; Ussishkin, 2003, 2005; Bye and Svenonius, 2012) and this book aims to focus on an area where the empirical base is less clear.

---

[10] Following the distinction into truncation and subtraction developed in Arndt-Lappe and Alber (2012).

These above discussed restrictions are included in the revised definition of MLM pattern in (14). In contrast to the definition in (13), all phonologically predictable allomorphs for a morpheme are counted as one MLM pattern. In addition, templatic morphology is completely excluded and epenthesis and reduplication alone are not sufficient to define a pattern of MLM. It is clear that this definition still leaves space for interpretation and the restriction 'no prosodic restriction on the number of syllables or segments holds for all bases' is presumably not a sufficient characterization for all templatic patterns excluded here. A straightforward example is the broken plural formation in Arabic that has been argued not to be 'templatic' in this sense but is nevertheless excluded (see, for example, McCarthy, 1983*b*; McCarthy and Prince, 1990; McCarthy, 2000*a*) mainly to avoid a reimplementation of existing analyses for a well-known phenomenon that already follow the general logic of the account proposed here.

(14)   *MLM pattern, revisited*
       A set M_x of MLM operations M_1–M_n constitutes a pattern of MLM iff
       a. their context of application is bound to the presence of the same morpho-syntactic features, and
       b. one MLM operation in M_x is a Long-Short-Alternation (10-b-i), and
       c. no prosodic restriction on the number of syllables or segments holds for all bases that results from the application of M_1 to M_x.
          (If no such restriction holds in the rest of the language.)

Given this definition, it is clear that a language can have different patterns of MLM, either in different morphological contexts or as lexically marked allomorphs for the same morpheme. Aymara, for example, which is discussed in detail in section 4.2 employs four different MLM patterns: Addition, Subtraction, Additive Affixes, and Subtractive Affixes and all these different patterns are associated with different morphological contexts. On the other hand, in Murle, two different Subtraction patterns coexist in the same morphological context. In this Kwa language (for an analysis, see sections 3.2.2.2 and 3.2.3), two productive plural formations involve non-realization of base-final material (Arensen, 1982; Haspelmath, 2002). As can be seen in (15), either the base-final consonant or the base-final VC sequence remains unrealized. The choice between these two allomorphs realizing the same morphological feature is unpredictable and hence must be lexically marked—according to the definition in (14); two Subtraction patterns are thus listed for Murle in the data sample.

(15)   *Subtraction in Murle: plural formation*   (Arensen, 1982: 40–43)

	Base		Plural
a.	keloc	'flea'	kel
	ziza:coc	'termite'	ziza:c
	cinotot	'moustache'	cinot
	mininit	'spirit'	minin

> b. bawot   'goat'   bawo
>   zoːc   'foot'   zɔː
>   idiŋ   'meat'   idi
>   korton   'anthill'   korto

Given this definition of MLM patterns, a representative data sample was conducted that serves as the empirical base for the theoretical argumentation in this book. In chapter 6, this data sample is described in more detail and the crucial empirical generalizations about attested and unattested MLM patterns are summarized. This discussion is located after the theoretical discussion of PDM since the ultimate goal is to show that this theoretical framework is able to predict all and only the attested patterns of MLM. Consequently, the theoretical background assumptions and the PDM account of MLM is discussed in chapters 2 to 5 before we return to the complete picture of attested MLM patterns.

1.2 MLM as a challenge for theoretical accounts

The most obvious challenge that MLM poses for any theoretical account is the existence of subtractive MLM (Martin, 1988; Mel'cuk, 1991; Anderson, 1992; Dressler, 2000; Steins, 2000; Inkelas, 2014) since it apparently undermines the common background assumption that morphology is additive (for example, Bye and Svenonius, 2012). Or as Inkelas (2014) puts it: 'Subtractive morphology has served as the strongest argument that morphological constructions are, at least in some cases, processual, in the sense that they cannot be analyzed by means of the addition of a morpheme' (p. 64). In this book, the claim originally made in Trommer and Zimmermann (2014) (see also Trommer, 2011*a*) is extended that this assumption can indeed be maintained and that the affixation of prosodic nodes might result in subtractive MLM as well as in additive MLM. For this first attempt to reduce subtractive non-concatenative operations to simple affixation, the coexistence of additive and subtractive MLM patterns in a single language is a new challenge. This point and especially the problems for the original Generalized Mora Affixation account in Trommer and Zimmermann (2014) is addressed in section 3.2.2 (see especially 3.2.2.1) where several languages are discussed where additive and subtractive MLM patterns coexist.

The existence of morpheme-specific phonology as the application of phonological processes that are only triggered by the presence of some morpheme is another challenge for theoretical accounts of phonology. From a standpoint of theoretical economy and restrictiveness, it is clear that a theory is preferable where the different modules of the grammar do not have direct access to all information of other modules (formulated for the phonology as the 'Indirect Reference Hypothesis' in, for example, Inkelas, 1990). The challenge is hence to account for morpheme-specific phonology in a theory where the phonology has no direct access to specific morphological information.

In addition, a unified account for the non-concatenative morphology and morpheme-specific phonology (see the discussion in 1.1.3) is desired. Mainly because in the domain of MLM, the same generalizations and restrictions about frequency and non-existing patterns hold in both domains. The theory of PDM is exactly such a unified theoretical account to non-concatenative morphology and morpheme-specific phonology involving length-manipulations that predicts this parallel behaviour in a straightforward manner.

A crucial generalization about MLM in the data sample concerns the possible base positions that can be affected by MLM in the languages of the world. A pattern of MLM always affects one specific base position and only a restricted set of base positions can be affected by MLM, absolutely parallel to the findings for segmental infixation in Yu (2007). In chapter 7, the most prominent OT-alternatives to non-concatenative morphology and/or morpheme-specific phonology are summarized that all over-generate in this respect (namely REALIZEMORPHEME-based account, Cophonology Theory, morpheme-specific constraints, and Transderivational Antifaithfulness; see section 7.1 for an introduction).

1.3 Structure of the book

Chapter 2: The theory of Prosodically Defective Morphemes   The theoretical background for the theory of PDM is presented. PDM is based on the simple insight that if all possible prosodically defective morpheme representations and their potential effects on the phonological structure are taken into account, instances of length-manipulating non-concatenative morphology and length-manipulating morpheme-specific phonology are predicted. The chapter begins with discussing previous accounts which argue that the affixation of prosodic nodes may result in specific MLM phenomena in a certain language. Later, the concrete theoretical background assumptions for the proposed theory of PDM are presented. It is an optimality-theoretic system based on containment for phonological primitives and association lines. New theoretical assumptions are made about the linearization of morphemes that in particular implement a severe restriction on the ordering possibilities of morphemic prosodic nodes. This theory correctly predicts that MLM operations can only affect a restricted set of base positions. As an independent argument for containment theory, the issue of opacity problems in the domain of MLM and the solution containment offers are discussed. Finally, a first general overview is given of how this theory accounts for all MLM patterns.

Chapter 3: Subtractive MLM and Prosodically Defective Morphemes   This chapter discusses how the theory of PDM accounts for instances of subtractive MLM—the empirical phenomenon that is notoriously challenging for the claim that morphology is additive. Two general mechanisms inside PDM can predict subtractive MLM: usurpation of moras and the defective integration of morphemic prosodic nodes. Usurpation can arise if a segment underlyingly lacks a mora and 'usurps' it from a neighbouring segment that is hence deprived of it (16-a). In the second scenario, a prosodic node that is underlyingly not integrated into the higher/lower prosodic structure is affixed to a base and remains defectively integrated in the output (16-b). Given the standard assumption that only elements properly integrated under the highest prosodic node of the prosodic hierarchy are visible for the phonetics, this affix node and everything it dominates remain phonetically uninterpreted.

(16)   *PDM and subtractive MLM*
        a. *Morpheme-specific vowel deletion in Yine*

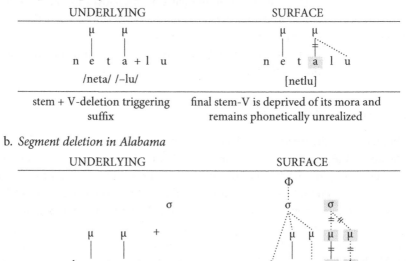

Both these mechanisms are discussed in detail in this chapter and it is shown how all attested types of subtractive MLM in the representative data set fall out from the theory. The upshot is that subtractive morphology is purely epiphenomenal and involves addition of a (prosodically defective) morpheme. A crucial prediction of PDM is that subtractive and additive MLM should easily coexist in one language. It is shown that this prediction is indeed borne out.

Chapter 4: Prosodically Defective Morphemes and blocking   This chapter investigates the predictions that arise in the theory of PDM if multiple prosodically defective morphemes interact with each other. In particular, such interactions predict blocking of MLM: one prosodically defective morpheme bleeds the effect of another. Those effects are indeed borne out. For one, there are instances where several morphemes in a language are lexically marked exceptions to an MLM process. This can follow, it is shown, if those morphemes are prosodically defective themselves. A very interesting instance of such an effect can be found in Aymara where a so-called 'rescuer morpheme' exists whose only surface effect is to block an expected MLM pattern. A detailed case study for Aymara is presented in this chapter and it is shown how such a complex pattern of MLM falls out under the theory of PDM. On the other hand, there are cases where allomorphy between different MLM processes can be found and this alternation can not be predicted given the phonological form of the morphemes in question. It is shown that again the exceptional behaviour of some morphemes in the presence of a triggering prosodically defective morpheme follows if those morphemes themselves are prosodically defective. The chapter hence strengthens the role of phonological representation and shifts the burden of various (apparently morphological) idiosyncratic lexical information to the phonological representation of the morphemes in question.

Chapter 5: Morpheme contiguity   One new constraint family argued for in this book are constraints ensuring a 'morph-contiguous' projection of prosodic nodes. It is argued that the phonological representation of a morpheme strives to be contiguous across different tiers, i.e. phonological elements affiliated with one morpheme avoid being dominated by a phonological element that is affiliated with another morpheme. In the simplest case, this results in classic CONTIGUITY effects of the sort that there is no interleaving: a prosodic affix node is, for example, preferably only realized at the absolute edge of its base. In the first section, it is shown how different patterns of phonologically predictable allomorphy involving MLM follow from such a preference. In addition, this constraint type allows us to solve a general opacity problem that OT-accounts assuming floating prosodic nodes face. The relevant constraint demanding morph-contiguous mora licensing ensures that an epenthetic mora is inserted in contexts where a vowel would otherwise only be dominated by a mora with a different morphological affiliation. This constraint not only solves an opacity problem of OT, it also predicts an interesting typology of languages where all or only some vowels undergo morphological lengthening. As is shown with several examples, this typology is indeed borne out. Special attention is paid to a detailed case study of long epenthesis in Southern Sierra Miwok that poses a particular problem for alternative accounts. A final effect that is addressed in this chapter concerns additive MLM that follows from the affixation of prosodic feet. This is particularly interesting since it extends the mechanism of affixed 'floating' prosodic nodes from moras to elements higher in the prosodic hierarchy and hence generalizes this theoretical mechanism. If an affix-foot strives to dominate as few base segments as possible, epenthesis and/or lengthening can be predicted in order to fill the foot with enough prosodic weight to be well-formed but to avoid integration of more base segments than absolutely necessary. It is shown how this mechanism predicts interesting cases of non-concatenative allomorphy in the domain of MLM.

Chapter 6: The complete empirical picture of MLM and the linearization of morphemes   This chapter presents the representative data set of MLM phenomena which was the base for all the preceding theoretical arguments and discusses the empirical generalizations about (un)attested MLM patterns one can draw from this data set. After giving some general background information about the data set and how it is genetically and areally balanced, the discussion of empirical generalizations mainly focusses on the positions in the base that are possible and frequent targets for MLM operations. Two main generalizations hold for the MLM patterns in the data set: MLM patterns show a strong edge bias and are far more frequently attested at the right edge of their base than on the left edge. Both these generalizations follow straightforwardly from adopting the claim that MLM results from affixation. The dispreference for infixation and the preference for suffixes that is well-established for segmental affixes then predicts these generalizations about MLM patterns. How the locality restriction for MLM follows from the theoretical assumptions about morpheme linearization, and especially the assumption of the RecoverableMorphemeOrderCondition proposed in this book account for all the attested MLM patterns and excludes unattested non-local ones, is shown in detail. Special attention is paid to some interesting case studies of multiple MLM operations found in one morphological context. Since the theory of PDM predicts the existence of multiple prosodic nodes in the representation for a single morpheme (on the same/different tier and affixed to the same/different edge of their base), such patterns are straightforwardly expected.

Chapter 7: A critical review of alternative accounts   Whereas the previous chapters argued that the framework of PDM, implemented in containment-based OT, is able to predict all and only the attested instances of MLM in the languages of the world, this chapter argues that it is also preferable over alternative accounts both in terms of theoretical economy and empirical coverage. The most important existing theoretical OT alternatives are introduced which includes analyses for which it has been claimed that they are able to account for non-concatenative morphology in general and/or length-manipulation in specific: Transderivational Antifaithfulness (Alderete, 2001*b*, *a*), a REALIZE MORPHEME-based theory (Kurisu, 2001), Cophonology Theory (Inkelas and Zoll, 2007), and lexically indexed constraints (Pater, 2009). It is shown that all these four accounts suffer from severe over- and/or undergeneration problems if they are tested against the full typology of attested MLM patterns. An additional and more general argument against the alternative accounts is based on theoretical economy: the introduction of powerful new mechanisms adopted in all these alternative accounts is unnecessary at least in the domain of MLM. The independently motivated primitives of the prosodic organization together with the assumption that prosodically defective structures exist and might have crucial consequences for the surface interpretation for segments allows us to predict all attested patterns of MLM.

2

The theory of Prosodically Defective Morphemes

In this chapter, the theoretical background for the analyses in this book is presented. Before the framework of *Prosodically Defective Morphemes* (=PDM) is defined, an overview of existing claims in the line of reasoning pursued in this book is given, namely claims that MLM is the result of simple concatenation of morphemes (section 2.1).

The necessary theoretical background for the unified theory of PDM is presented in section 2.2. One central theoretical assumption is containment (section 2.2.2). It is emphasized at various points in the theoretical discussion that the analyses presented for subtractive MLM inside PDM are only possible in an OT system where deletion is impossible but elements may remain invisible for the phonetic interpretation. Closely related is the assumption of morphological colours (section 2.2.3) that will become crucial in the proposed extension of morpheme contiguity to dominance relations in a prosodic tree (discussed in chapter 5). Another crucial background assumption concerns the linearization of morphemes that is argued to be severely restricted by the inherent impossibility of metathesis in containment and by the newly proposed RecoverableMorphemeOrderCondition, discussed in section 2.2.6. How these theoretical background assumptions interact in the framework termed PDM and predict different patterns of MLM is sketched in section 2.2.7.

2.1 Previous accounts: MLM as an epiphenomenon

There are two general approaches to non-concatenative morphology: it is either stated that these phenomena cannot follow in the regular phonology and/or morphology and morpheme-specific (word-formation) rules (Matthews, 1974; Anderson, 1992; Stump, 2001) or constraints (Kurisu, 2001; Horwood, 2001) are assumed, or the view is defended that non-concatenative morphology is epiphenomenal and follows from the affixation of phonological primitives that are independently motivated (Lieber, 1992; Stonham, 1994; Saba Kirchner, 2010; Trommer, 2011a; Bermúdez-Otero, 2012; Bye and Svenonius, 2012). A term summarizing this latter line of research arguing that non-

Morphological Length and Prosodically Defective Morphemes. First edition. Eva Zimmermann.
© Eva Zimmermann 2017. First published 2017 by Oxford University Press.

concatenative morphology is epiphenomenal is 'Generalized Nonlinear Affixation' (Bermúdez-Otero (2012), extending the term 'Generalized Mora Affixation' in Trommer and Zimmermann (2010)). For mutation, these primitives of the phonological theory are the subsegmental phonological features that are independently motivated as target and context of phonological rules (Akinlabi, 1996; Wolf, 2007). For length-manipulation, the relevant phonological primitives are necessarily suprasegmental and hence the prosodic nodes. The framework of PDM is crucially based on exactly this argumentation and can be understood as yet another generalization of the 'Generalized Nonlinear Affixation' framework that not only takes affixes consisting of floating prosodic nodes into account but also, for example, morpheme representations where segments lack an association with a higher prosodic node underlyingly.

The second empirical domain termed 'morpheme-specific phonology' above has not been discussed as extensively as non-concatenative morphology in the domain of length-manipulations and all approaches I am aware of crucially rely on morpheme-specific mechanisms (for example, Alderete, 2001b; Pater, 2009; Finley, 2009). In the following subsections, existing accounts of MLM are summarized that are in line with the theory of PDM defended in this book.

2.1.1 Mora affixation

Since the influential paper by Hayes (1989) where it is argued that segmental quantity is encoded on a non-segmental tier, the mora is one standard means to represent the quantity of segments and/or syllables (for an overview and literature see, for example, Broselow et al., 1997; Szigetvári, 2011; Davis, 2011b). A standard nonlinear representation of segmental length is given in (1), based crucially on the adoption of moras: short vowels are dominated by one mora, long vowels by two moras, short coda consonants are either dominated by a mora or directly associated with the syllable node, and geminate consonants are dominated by a mora and associated with the following onset position as well (Hyman, 1985; McCarthy and Prince, 1986/1996; Hayes, 1989).[1]

(1)   *Segmental length in terms of moras*

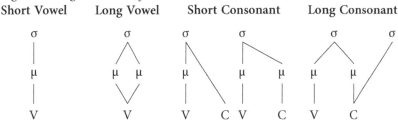

---

[1] This is only a summary of the most basic insights of segmental length representation. Especially the representation of geminates is often rather controversial and a structure where consonantal length is represented in terms of the number of segmental root nodes has been proposed as the more adequate model for geminates in several languages (see, for example, Selkirk, 1991; Tranel, 1991; Ringen and Vago, 2011). In section 2.2, a more detailed discussion and introduction of prosodic nodes and the prosodic hierarchy is given.

These autosegmental representations allow an intriguing representation for morphemes that are expressed only by lengthening a segment: they are represented as a mora. In the following, such prosodic nodes that are assumed to be affixed, hence are (part of) the underlying representation for a morpheme, are termed *morphemic*. The first analysis that proposes that additive MLM results from affixing a mora can be found in Lombardi and McCarthy (1991). Since then, numerous other analyses have followed that argue for mora affixation in different languages. In this section, the general logic of these existing mora affixation accounts is discussed, the facts they capture and the potential problems they have. It is concluded that there are two major problems with all existing mora affixation accounts in standard OT: one of them is the more or less prominent problem of 'opaque mora assignment' in standard OT (see section 2.2.4), the other is a locality problem.

The mora affixation analysis proposed in Lombardi and McCarthy (1991) accounts for morphological lengthening in Choctaw, Alabama, Balangao, and Keley-i and it is implemented inside the framework of prosodic circumscription (Lombardi and McCarthy, 1991; McCarthy and Prince, 1990; McCarthy, 2000a). Prosodic circumscription theory crucially assumes that bases can be recursively delimited to certain prosodically defined portions resulting in an 'outparsed' portion and a 'remainder'. Both these parts can then be targeted by further (morphological) operations like 'prefix mora'. In the analysis of medial gemination in Choctaw, for example, a mora affix is prefixed to a base form that is created by making the first mora of the base extraprosodic (see section 5.3.3 for an account of Choctaw).

The first mora affixation analysis inside the framework of OT is the proposal in Samek-Lodovici (1992) that analyses the morphological lengthening in Keley-i and Alabama. Two constraint (types) are crucial in this OT analysis for mora affixation: a constraint demanding that the affixed mora must be realized (2-a), i.e. integrated into the base, and constraints demanding that the mora strives to be realized at the leftmost/rightmost edge of their base (2-b, c) (Samek-Lodovici, 1992: 6, 10). For these constraints, Samek-Lodovici (1992) defines that a 'syllable unit is *affected* by the moraic affix iff it directly dominates the affix mora or if it dominates directly or indirectly the segment directly dominated by the affix mora' (Samek-Lodovici, 1992: 10).[2]

(2)   a. PARSM   Avoid unparsed moras.

   b. LEFT   One violation for each syllable intervening between the left edge and the first syllable *affected* by the affix.

   c. RIGHT   One violation for each syllable intervening between the right edge and the first syllable *affected* by the affix.

---

[2] A point that remains unclear in the analysis in Samek-Lodovici (1992) is whether 'LEFT' and 'RIGHT' are sensitive to 'affix moras' in general or whether these constraints are marked for being sensitive to specific morphemes. In a language where a μ-prefix and a μ-suffix exist, the latter would obviously be necessary.

Tableau (3) illustrates the logic of this approach with the data of morphological vowel lengthening in Gidabal (chapter 1, (3)). Undominated PARSM ensures that an affix mora cannot remain unassociated as in (3-a) and undominated RIGHT ensures that the additional mora must be associated with the rightmost vowel, excluding candidate (3-c).

(3) *Final vowel lengthening in Gidabal*

μ μ μ | | + g i d a	PARSM	RIGHT	LEFT

a.   μ   μ μ
      | | |
     g i d a
	*!		

☞ b.   μ   μ μ
      | |⁄
     g i d a
			*

c.   μ μ   μ
     ＼| |
     g i d a
		*!	

The constraints LEFT and RIGHT are necessary since it is assumed that mora affixes can in principle be realized anywhere in the word and phonological well-formedness constraints select the optimal realization for a particular base. The morphological gemination in the Austronesian language Keley-i, it is argued, is evidence for such an analysis since either a base-initial or a base-medial consonant is geminated, the choice being determined by phonological well-formedness constraints. That this claim is apparently empirically incorrect and Samek-Lodovici's interpretation of the Keley-i data is flawed is discussed in detail in Zimmermann and Trommer (2013) where it is argued that the surface effect of a gemination process that is realized in different positions of its base is in fact the result of two different gemination processes targeting different base positions. This claim is based mainly on the simple fact that words exist where gemination in both positions surfaces. However, it has to be noted that the empirical base for the Keley-i discussion is rather doubtful: Samek-Lodovici (1992) bases his argumentation on a very short sketch of Keley-i morphology in Hohulin and Kenstowicz (1979)—apparently the only source and a rather scarce empirical base where hardly any morphological or phonological background facts are given. In contrast to the original claim made in Samek-Lodovici (1992), it is argued here that the generalization that prosodic nodes can in principle 'wander inside' their base overgenerates. This issue is addressed in particular in chapter 6 where the empirical generalizations apparent in the data sample of MLM are discussed. In the present framework, affix moras are hence severely restricted in their ability to be realized in different base positions.

Following Samek-Lodovici's proposal, several mora affixation analyses have been proposed inside OT that are very similar to this original account. Examples where additive MLM is analysed as mora affixation are the analyses for Shizuoka Japanese in Davis and Ueda (2005) and Davis and Ueda (2002), for Saanich in Davis and Ueda (2006) and Bye and Svenonius (2012), for Alabama in Grimes (2002), for Choctaw in Grimes (2002), for Limburg Dutch in van Oostendorp (2005), for Diegueño in Wolf (2007) and Topintzi (2008b), for Dinka in Flack (2007b), for Korean in Yoon (2008), for Hiaki and Tawala in Haugen and Kennard (2008), for Huallaga Quechua in Saba Kirchner (in press), and for Kwa'kwala in Saba Kirchner (in press, 2007) and Saba Kirchner (2010).

As in the account in Samek-Lodovici (1992), all these OT analyses assume some constraint ensuring that the affix mora is realized, e.g. MAX-μ_i 'Realize the imperfective mora' (Grimes, 2002: 7) or *FLOAT-μ (Wolf, 2007: 316).[3] The question where this additional mora is realized in its base is not explicitly discussed in most of these accounts. The analyses that deal with this matter all follow the logic of Samek-Lodovici's original account in assuming that the base mora is in principle free to be associated with any base segment but is restricted by a constraint like ALIGN-L(μ_{EMPH},WD) (Davis and Ueda, 2005: 4) forcing it to the left or right edge of its base (Davis and Ueda, 2005; Grimes, 2002; Topintzi, 2008b). In all these analyses, the edge-orientation of the affix mora can hence be less important than phonological markedness or faithfulness[4] and the mora is in principle able to be realized in a non-edge position of its base. As is argued in chapter 6, this logic of a floating mora that can leave its edge position to be realized in a more unmarked position seriously overgenerates and makes several empirical mispredictions.

A final interesting claim for mora affixation that results in an instance of non-concatenative morphology is the analysis for Paiwan reduplication in Bye and Svenonius (2012). In this Austronesian language, the intensive is formed via a suffixed reduplicant that copies either a CVCV or a CVC sequence (Chen, 2006; Yeh, 2008). The important insight is that the reduplicant is bimoraic in both contexts. Bye and

---

[3] To be precise, nearly all these approaches would need in fact two constraint types: one demanding that every (affix) mora is realized in the output and one demanding that a mora in the output must be integrated in the prosodic structure. This follows since these approaches are all implemented in correspondence-theoretic OT where non-realization of an element that is present in the input is in principle possible. In contrast, the analysis in Samek-Lodovici (1992) is based on containment and consequently no deletion of elements that are underlyingly present is possible. These details are hardly ever discussed and a general MAX constraint is assumed in most analyses ensuring that the affix mora is present and completely integrated into the structure.

[4] For example, in Grimes (2002), faithfulness to the weight of the final syllable is high-ranked and lengthening of the penultimate syllable is predicted in Alabama.

Svenonius (2012) thus assume that the representation for the intensive contains two morphemic moras that are suffixed. In this book, further evidence is added for that claim that multiple prosodic nodes can be (part of) morphemes (see section 6.2.4).

And then there are various examples where mora affixes are assumed to capture empirical generalizations but where no explicit analysis is presented. Examples are Stonham (2007) on the non-concatenative allomorphy in Saanich, Hardy and Montler (1988*a*, *b*) on segmental lengthening in Alabama,[5] Brown (2003) on pre-lengthening suffixes in Southern Sierra Miwok, Paster (2010) on morphological lengthening in Asante Twi, and Álvarez (2005) who mentions Huallaga Quechua, Hausa, and Slovak and gives an extensive discussion of morphological vowel lengthening in Guajiro.

One major argument for this prevalence of mora affixation accounts in the decades after the moraic tier as standard representation for segmental length was introduced, is the fact that they elegantly predict instances of non-concatenative morphology simply from affixing phonological elements. What can alternatively be analysed as the result of morphological word-formation or readjustment rules can hence follow in a purely phonological account. Another main argument for mora affixation comes from non-concatenative allomorphy, i.e. the situation where different non-concatenative operations apply in phonologically predictable contexts to realize the same morpheme. If the different non-concatenative operations result in additional prosodic weight for a syllable, a mora affixation analysis is a straightforward account to explain such data. An example for such a pattern can be found in the Shizuoka dialect of Japanese (Davis and Ueda, 2002, 2005, 2006). The emphatic adjective in Shizuoka Japanese is marked via lengthening of the first vowel if the initial syllable is closed (4-a), via insertion of a (homorganic) nasal consonant if the first syllable is open and the consonant following the first vowel is a voiced consonant (4-b), and via gemination of the consonant following the first vowel if this consonant is voiceless and the first syllable is open (4-c).

(4) *Non-concatenative allomorphy in Shizuoka Japanese*   (Davis and Ueda, 2005: 3)

	BASE	EMPHATIC FORM	
a.	*Vowel lengthening*		
	zonzai	zoːnzai	'impolite'
	supːai	suːpːai	'sour'
	onzukutai	oːnzukutai	'ugly'
	kandarui	kaːndarui	'languid'

---

[5] Although they do not use the term 'mora' but rather state that the 'morpheme is merely an empty timing slot' (p. 405).

b. *Nasal insertion*

hade	hande	'showy'
ozoi	onzoi	'terrible'
nagai	naŋgai	'long'
karai	kanrai	'spicy'

c. *Consonant gemination*

katai	katːai	'hard'
osoi	osːoi	'slow'
kitanai	kitːanai	'dirty'
atsui	atːsui	'hot'

The crucial observation in Davis and Ueda (2002, 2005) and Davis and Ueda (2006) is now that all these three different strategies add prosodic weight to the first syllable: it is light in the normal adjective form but heavy in the emphatic adjective. The straightforward analysis for the Shizuoka Japanese emphatic adjective formation and similar patterns of length-manipulation is therefore the affixation of a morphological mora. In their analysis, an undominated morpheme-specific faithfulness constraint MORPHR-μ_E 'The emphatic morpheme μ_e must be realized' (Davis and Ueda, 2002: 9) ensures that the affix mora is integrated into the prosodic structure of its base and a morpheme-specific ALIGN-L constraint forces the mora to be realized at the left edge. This constraint is violated whenever the mora is associated with a syllable that is not the first in the word. The choice between the three different non-concatenative allomorphs follows from the ranking of the faithfulness constraints penalizing one of the three operations to realize the affix mora and general markedness constraints. DEP-N penalizing insertion of an epenthetic nasal consonant and *GEM penalizing geminate consonants are both dominated by *LV penalizing long vowels. In principle, nasal insertion and gemination are hence the preferred strategies to realize the affix mora. On the other hand, *CC penalizing complex syllable margins, NO-NT penalizing nasals adjacent to voiceless consonants, and NO-VG penalizing voiced geminates are taken to be undominated in Shizuoka Japanese and make certain realization strategies for the morphemic mora impossible for certain bases. More specifically, *CC excludes nasal insertion for bases starting with a closed syllable (5-iii-b) whereas NO-NT excludes nasal insertion for bases with a voiceless consonant following the first vowel (5-ii-b). NO-VG, finally, excludes gemination for bases with a voiced consonant following the first vowel (5-i-c). The tableaux in (5) summarize this analysis given by Davis and Ueda.

(5) *Mora affixation in Davis and Ueda (2002) et. seq.*

	ALIGNL	NoVG	NoNT	*CC	*LV	DepN	*GEM
i. Nasal Insertion							
a. h a d e					*!		
☞ b. h a n d e						*	
c. h a d e			*!				*
d. h a d e	*!				*		
ii. Gemination							
a. k a t a i					*!		
b. k a n t a i			*!			*	
☞ c. k a t a i							*
iii. Vowel lengthening							
☞ a. z o n z a i					*		
b. z o n n z a i				*!		*	
c. z o n z a i		*!					*

This argumentation that the affixation of a mora may result in different surface effects in different phonological contexts in a single language has been applied to other instances of non-concatenative allomorphy as well: to the allomorphy between CV-reduplication, insertion of an epenthetic /ʔ/ coda, and CV metathesis in Saanich (Grimes, 2002; Davis and Ueda, 2006; Stonham, 2007; Zimmermann, 2009; Bye and Svenonius, 2012), to consonant gradation in North Saami (Bals Baal et al., 2012), and to the allomorphy between nasal insertion and vowel lengthening in Standard Japanese (Davis and Ueda, 2002).

The preceding discussion shows that the claim that moras can be (part of) a morpheme representation is by no means new and has been proposed for various phenomena by now. However, there are two major problems with the general logic of mora affixation in a standard model of correspondence-theoretic OT. For one, there is a serious opacity problem resulting from the simple fact that Richness of the Base predicts that mora affixes are expected to attach to bases without an underlying mora. An affixed mora has only an additive effect if it is *added* to the moraic structure of its base, it cannot have any lengthening effect if it is realized instead of a mora whose insertion is predictable from general well-formedness demands. This issue and the solution to this problem argued for in this book is discussed in detail in section 2.2.4.

A second problem is the fact that in all these accounts, the affix mora is in principle free to be associated with any base segment. Its localization in the base is only restricted by violable constraints as, for example RIGHT/LEFT in Samek-Lodovici (1992) (see (2)). If one recalls that the moras in these contexts are representations for affixes, this line of reasoning is reminiscent of the phonological displacement account to segmental infixation (Moravcsik, 1977; Prince and Smolensky, 1993/2002; Stemberger and Bernhardt, 1998; Halle, 2003; Horwood, 2002; Klein, 2005). It is argued here that affix moras and prosodic morphemes in general are highly restricted in their possibilities to be linearized in their base, quite parallel to the arguments Yu (2007) gives for a restrictive theory of segmental infixation. The background assumptions about linear ordering of morphemic prosodic nodes are given in section 2.2.6 and the general picture of linearization sites for prosodic affixes is presented in chapter 6.

2.1.2 Syllable and foot affixation

If the mora as the smallest prosodic entity is a possible morpheme, the assumption that other prosodic constituents are possible morphemes as well is a natural and perhaps even expected extension of already established mechanisms. The assumption of a morphemic syllable can be understood as one consequent way of implementing the insight that prosodic elements like syllables are the relevant units in truncatory or reduplicative morphologies (Weeda, 1992; McCarthy and Prince, 1986/1996; et seq.). Rather than restricting the mapping of base material to such a syllable template by additional rules or constraints to determine, for example, the exact size of a reduplicant, integration of material under a morphemic node and its integration into the overall prosodic structure follows in the PDM account from simple parsing constraints demanding full prosodic integration for all elements.

Examples for analyses assuming the affixation of morphemic syllables can be found in the influential proposal on reduplication in Marantz (1982), but also in more recent analyses in Saba Kirchner (2010) and Bermúdez-Otero (2012). In the latter account, reduplication in Tangale is argued to follow from affixing a 'prosodic treelet comprising a syllable node dominating a nuclear mora and an onset position occupied by a featureless root node' (Bermúdez-Otero, 2012: 57). The affix syllable in this account is hence prespecified for being a light syllable with an obligatory onset. In the stratal OT system presented there, the base to which the syllable affix attaches to is already supplied with a syllable structure on its own. The affix syllable cannot simply dominate base segments since this would result in a fusion with existing syllable structure and fatal violations of UNIFORMITY. In Saba Kirchner (2010), reduplication in Samala is analysed as the effect of syllable affixation. In contrast to the reduplication in Tangale, Samala reduplication follows from affixing a heavy syllable that already contains two moras. The realization of the additional prosodic structure is consequently ensured via MAX-μ. The analysis is based on the assumption of stratal OT as well. In a standard parallel OT system, the same opacity problem arises that was already discussed for moras: for an input where no underlying syllable is present, the affix syllable is simply assumed to dominate base material and hence no surface effect is predicted. In the present account, this opacity problem is solved by the adoption of the constraint family ensuring morph-contiguous prosodic structure (see section 2.2.3).

An analysis assuming the affixation of a morphemic foot is proposed in the account van Oostendorp (2012) gives for the past tense formation in Modern Greek. Stress in the past tense is always on the antepenultimate syllable and even triggers augmentation of an additional vowel in case this syllable is not underlyingly present. This pattern is predicted, it is argued, if '[p]ast [t]ense in Modern Greek is a stress marker only, i.e. a segmentally empty foot' (van Oostendorp, 2012: 1173). The fixed position of this foot is ensured by ALIGN constraints. How its realization is enforced is not explicitly discussed in van Oostendorp (2012). At first glance, it seems rather peculiar to assume 'floating feet' since feet are only projections and should be impossible on their own without any material they dominate. However, moras are projections as well. And if a theory allows floating moras to exist without any segment they dominate, nothing at all would prohibit floating feet that do not dominate anything underlyingly (van Oostendorp, 2007c).

2.1.3 *Subtraction by affixation?*

In the preceding sections 2.1.1 and 2.1.2, analyses where the affixation of a prosodic node has been argued to result in some kind of additive length-manipulation were discussed: vowel lengthening, gemination, reduplication, and/or epenthesis. An apparently obvious challenge to the claim that all MLM results from affixing prosodic nodes is the existence of subtractive length-manipulation that was introduced and illustrated in section 1.1.2 with examples from Yine, Wolof, Hausa, and Canela Krahô. In this section, some analyses arguing that defectively integrated prosodic nodes that were affixed to a base can indeed result in subtractive MLM are presented.

In Kiparsky (1991), the concept of catalexis as counterpart to extrametricality is introduced. In his definition, extrametrical prosodic nodes are inaccessible for phonological rules and principles and are erased from the structure (see also, for example, Inkelas, 1990). Catalectic prosodic nodes, on the other hand, are empty prosodic categories that are added and are accessible for the phonology. They do not dominate an element lower on the prosodic hierarchy but are integrated under a higher prosodic node. The most pervasive argument for such structures is the fact that they allow us to eliminate degenerate feet from metrical theory and hence allows us to adopt the bimoraic foot as universal word minimality requirement. In languages with subminimal monomoraic words, a catalectic mora at the right edge of the word could then be assumed. Such an analysis makes some predictions about the cooccurrence of subminimal words and final stress in rightwards trochaic systems: If a language with a rightward-trochaic stress system has subminimal words, it allows catalexis and secondary stress is predicted on final odd-numbered syllables. If, however, a rightwards trochaic system does not allow subminimal words, catalexis is excluded and no secondary stress on final odd-numbered syllables is expected (Kager, 1999*a*: 270). As Kiparsky (1991) and Kager (1999*a*) argue, these predictions are borne out. In addition, the possibility of 'catalexis as morpheme' is discussed in Kager (1999*a*). It is argued that instances of stress shifting morphemes might result from affixing a prosodic node that is catalectic in the resulting representation. An example presented comes from the Austronesian language Toba Batak where lexical stress is either on the penultimate or ultimate syllable. Some morphemes are now only expressed via stress shift from the penultimate to the ultimate syllable (for example, /lápu/ 'to smear' → /lapú/ 'be smeared' (Kager, 1999*a*: 13)). Such a pattern follows if the passive morpheme is analysed as a morphemic syllable that remains catalectic in the output as is illustrated in (6). In this structure, the foot is well-formed since it dominates two syllables and stress is realized in this trochaic system on the final syllable.

(6)   *Catalexis in Toba Batak: stress shifting morpheme in Kager (1999a)*

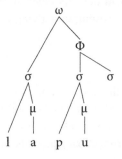

Another effect of a catalectic morphemic prosodic node is discussed in Seiler (2008). An analysis for plural formation in Taubergrund German (7) is presented that is based on a morphemic mora as representation for the plural. Crucially, this morphemic mora is dominated by a syllable in the output but does not dominate a segment, hence is a catalectic mora. This second mora in the representation for the consistently monosyllabic bases makes now an otherwise expected vowel lengthening process to avoid subminimal words obsolete. Since vowel lengthening is absent in the plural but not in the singular where the (morphemic) catalectic mora is not part of the structure, the plural is apparently formed from the singular via shortening. In Seiler's analysis, however, the plural form results from the absence of an otherwise expected phonological rule. The structures in (8) illustrate his analysis of catalexis that blocks an expected phonological rule.

(7)   *'Shortening' in Taubergrund German*   (Heilig, 1898: 78)

SINGULAR		PLURAL
riːs	'crack'	ris
fiːʃ	'fish'	fiʃ
ʃniːds	'cut'	ʃnids
fleːk	'blot'	flek
diːʃ	'table'	diʃ
ʃdriːk	'rope'	ʃdrik

(8)   *Plural formation as catalectic mora affixation*

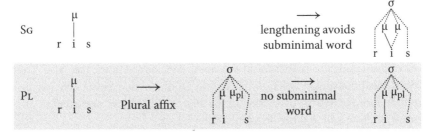

In Trommer and Zimmermann (2014) (see also Trommer, 2011a), finally, other logically possible types of defectively integrated prosodic structure are investigated with respect to their predictions for subtractive non-concatenative morphology. Their analyses rely on the concept of defective integration of moras, i.e. configurations where an association with a dominating and/or a dominated element is missing for a mora. More concretely, the representations in (9) are assumed to result in Subtraction. In the catalectic structure in (9-a) (termed 'hanging mora' in Trommer and Zimmermann (2014)), a morphemic mora is dominated by a syllable node but does not dominate a segment. Since a syllable that dominates four moras is a prosodically marked structure, the additional integration of the morphemic mora results in deassociation of one of the underlying association lines between the vowel and one mora. In (9-b), on the other hand, a morphemic mora does dominate a segment but it is not dominated by a syllable node (a 'drifting mora' in Trommer and Zimmermann, 2014). Given that elements must only have one root node and cannot be dominated by two highest prosodic nodes, the underlying association of the segment with a mora is marked as invisible. And since only elements that are dominated by the highest prosodic node are phonetically interpreted, this segment remains unrealized at the surface. Both structures in (9) have in common that one mora remains unrealized but they differ in the surface effect this mora subtraction has: in (9-a), vowel shortening results and in (9-b), segment deletion results. Note that these effects are not necessarily bound to the specific configurations in (9): a hanging mora could also result in segment deletion and vice versa. For ease of readability, the affixed morphemic nodes are circled. The depiction in (9) also introduces a convention used throughout this book: elements that remain uninterpreted by the phonetics are marked with a grey background and 'phonetically invisible' association lines are crossed out. These notions are introduced and defined in more detail in section 2.2.2.

(9) *Subtraction in Trommer and Zimmermann (2014)*
     a. *Shortening, a hanging μ*   b. *Deletion, a drifting μ*

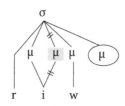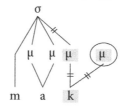

Patterns that are analysed in these terms in Trommer and Zimmermann (2014) are vowel shortening in Taubergrund German, Päri, and Anywa (see also Trommer, 2011a), final consonant deletion in Tohono O'odham, and vowel deletion in Lardil and Modern Hebrew. A discussion of the analysis for Anywa presented in Trommer (2011a) is discussed in more detail in section 3.2.1.4.

In this book, this general argumentation that defective prosodic structure can result in subtractive non-concatenative morphology is adopted but extended in two respects. *First*, the mechanism of mora-usurpation is proposed that is predicted in a containment-based system if underlying elements lack an association with a higher prosodic node. And *second*, the predictions made from defectively integrating morphemic prosodic nodes higher in the hierarchy than the mora are discussed. The argumentation in Trommer and Zimmermann (2014) is only based on moras and shows that many MLM patterns follow from the full or defective integration of moras. This claim is extended here and it is argued that all kinds of subtractive MLM are predicted if one takes into account the full range of prosodic nodes and their possible (defective) integration into a base. Even more, it is argued in section 3.2.2.1, that the analysis in terms of defective mora integration in Trommer and Zimmermann (2014) is problematic at least for Lardil and Tohono O'odham. Both languages employ an instance of additive MLM as well that is best analysed as the result of mora affixation— an intriguing account that becomes apparently impossible given their assumption that morphemic moras are defectively integrated in these languages. In the PDM account, the coexistence of additive and subtractive MLM that results from the affixation of morphemic prosodic nodes is indeed possible if the morphemic prosodic nodes are on different tiers of the prosodic hierarchy.

Another major difference to the proposal in Trommer (2011*a*) is the assumption of a parallel OT system whereas Egalitarian stratal OT is adopted in Trommer (2011*a*). The most crucial consequence from this assumption is that every morpheme is optimized prior to concatenation and that all morpheme representations contain only one (prosodic) root node. This allows us to solve various opacity problems standard parallel OT faces. However, this assumption also excludes various analyses proposed here. It makes mora usurping morphemes discussed in section 3.1 impossible and also the presence of multiple morphemic nodes in one morpheme representation (see section 6.2.4) or an additional morphemic node in the representation of an otherwise segmental morpheme.

2.1.4 Lack of prosodic nodes in the input

In the preceding section, existing analyses where the affixation of prosodic nodes is argued to result in some type of MLM were summarized and sketched. A second relevant background assumption for the theory is the fact that segments that lack prosodic structure underlyingly may also trigger MLM. We hence turn from cases where there is 'too much' prosodic structure in the input to cases where 'too little' prosodic structure is underlyingly present.

An intriguing analysis based on the assumption that non-existent prosodic structure results in some length-manipulating surface effect can be found in Yearley (1995) for Russian jer vowels (for similar arguments, see also Spencer, 1986; Rubach, 1986; Szypra, 1992). These vowels that alternate with zero in certain contexts are a well-known phenomena that can be found in all Slavic languages (for literature and discussion see, for example, Scheer, 2011). The examples in (10) show that some vowels /e/ and /o/ in Russian are not realized on the surface if they are followed by a CV sequence and the following vowel is not a jer vowel itself. Jer vowels can occur in stems or affixes of all types.

(10) *Russian jer vowels*   (Rubach, 1986; Yearley, 1995)

kusok	'piece' (Nom.Sg)	kuska	'piece' (Gen.Sg)	Y533
den'	'day' (Nom.Sg)	dn'a	'day' (Gen.Sg)	Y533
koren	'root' (Nom.Sg)	korna	'root' (Acc.Sg)	R249
ogon	'fire' (Nom.Sg)	ogna	'fire' (Acc.Sg)	R249
žog	'burned' (M.Pst)	žgla	'burned' (F.Pst)	Y533

Crucially now, not all instances of /e/ and /o/ alternate with zero in Russian as can be seen in (11) where /e/ and /o/ in two stems are realized irrespective of whether the stem is followed by a CV sequence or not.

(11)   *'Normal' vowels*   (Yearley, 1995: 533)
       mesto   'place' (Nom.Sg)   mest   'place' (Gen.Sg)
       rabota 'work' (Nom.Sg)   rabot   'work' (Gen.Sg)

Since there are two different vowels alternating with zero in Russian, an alternative analysis that this involves epenthesis is implausible. The quality of the inserted 'epenthetic' vowel as /e/ or /o/ would be unpredictable under such an analysis. We must therefore conclude that certain vowels are lexically marked for undergoing this type of vowel–zero alternation. In Yearley's analysis, this lexical difference between vowels reduces to the simple contrast of whether a vowel is underlyingly associated with a mora or not. Jer vowels in Yearley's analysis are vowels that lack a mora underlyingly, hence an epenthetic mora must be inserted in order to realize these vowels. However, this insertion induces a violation of faithfulness constraints preserving the underlying mora structure. Such a violation is only tolerated if the unfaithful operation helps to avoid higher-ranked phonological markedness considerations, more concretely the demand to avoid complex codas in Russian. For example, in the suffix-less nominative form /koren/ 'root' in (10), the jer vowel is realized since otherwise the illicit form */korn/ would result.

A somewhat similar analysis based on the assumption that a vowel that lacks a mora can result in MLM can be found in the analysis Stiebels and Wunderlich (1999) provide for second stems in Hungarian (Kenesei et al., 1998; Stiebels and Wunderlich, 1999; Siptár and Törkenczy, 2000; Abrusan, 2005; Grimes, 2010). *First*, it is important to distinguish three classes of suffixes, termed class I–III in Stiebels and Wunderlich (1999). Class I suffixes are consonant-initial in all contexts and class II suffixes are vowel-initial in all contexts. Class III suffixes now alternate between a vowel- and a consonant-initial form, depending on the base that precedes them. These differences are summarized in (12).

(12)   *Three suffix types in Hungarian*   (Stiebels and Wunderlich, 1999: 255)

			'stone'	'bush'	'door'	'wine'
I.	C-initial	Dat	køː–nek	bokor–nak	ajtoː–nak	bor–nak
II.	V-initial	Causal–Final	køː–eːrt	bokor–eːrt	ajtoː–eːrt	bor–eːrt
III.		1.Pl.Poss	køv–ynk	bokr–unk	ajtoː–nk	bor–unk

Second, there are some bases that have a so-called 'second stem', a modified base form that occurs before class III suffixes. The stems that have such a second stem are either nouns or verbs and it is phonologically and morphologically not predictable whether a stem alternates before a class III suffix or not. Some examples for second stem formations in Hungarian are given in (13). In principle, the class III suffixes trigger either non-realization of a preceding stem vowel (13-a) or shortening of an underlyingly long vowel (13-b). Additional 'metathesis' in (13-c) avoids a coda /h/ that is generally illicit in Hungarian and epenthesis in (13-d) an illicit vowel cluster.[6] The examples on the left-hand side are only given as a comparison: these are stems without a second stem that do not undergo any alternation if preceded by a class III suffix. It can be seen that the stems are phonologically quite similar. Note that the additional vowel changes observable in the suffixes are a consequence of vowel harmony in Hungarian.

(13)   *Second stems in Hungarian*   (Stiebels and Wunderlich, 1999: 273–281)
           a. Vowel deletion   *c. Vowel deletion & metathesis*

		>second stem<		>second stem<	
		'bush'	'edge'	'fluff'	'guffaw'
	Nom	bokor	perem	kø:	nø:
I.	Dat	bokor—nak	perem—nek	pehej—nek	røhej—nek
II.	Caus—Fin	bokor—e:rt	perem—e:rt	pehej—e:rt	røhej—e:rt
III.	Pl	bokr—ok	perem—ek	pejh—ek	røhej—ek
	1.Pl.Poss	bokr—unk	perem—ynk	pejh—ynk	røhej—ynk
	N-A	bokr—os	perem—es	pejh—es	røhej—es

           b. Vowel shortening   *d. Vowel shortening &*
                                                  epenthesis of /v/

		>second stem<		>second stem<	
		'bird'	'teacher'	'stone'	'woman'
	Nom	mada:r	tana:r	kø:	nø:
I.	Dat	mada:r—nak	tana:r—nak	kø:—nek	nø:—nek
II.	Caus-Fin	mada:r—e:rt	tana:r—e:rt	kø:—e:rt	nø:—e:rt
III.	Pl	madar—ak	tana:r—ok	køv—ek	nø:—ek
	1.Pl.Poss	madar—unk	tana:r—unk	køv—ynk	nø:—nk
	N-A	madar—as	tana:r—os	køv—es	nø:—s

Stiebels and Wunderlich (1999) provide an analysis that is based on the assumption that the second stem has an underlyingly floating mora and that type III suffixes lack a mora underlyingly for their vowel. Crucially, their account is based on the assumption that the second stem (with the floating mora) is a separate allomorph that is lexically stored for certain stems. This implements the intuition that 'these stems are selected just in those cases where the noun combines with suffixes that have an initial "non-moraic" vowel' (Stiebels and Wunderlich, 1999: 253). In their

---

[6] In addition, some stems undergo a change of vowel quality. Since the aim of this book are patterns of MLM, these additional facts are ignored in the following and the reader is referred to Stiebels and Wunderlich (1999) where an intriguing analysis for these facts in terms of floating features is given.

analysis, the choice between different (lexically stored) allomorphs for a morpheme is hence optimized together with the general phonological optimization of a form. This allows them to capture their generalization that the two 'cracked' representations 'select for each other' (Stiebels and Wunderlich, 1999: 268). The general logic of this analysis is hence similar to the analysis in Yearley (1995): an underlyingly mora-less vowel triggers MLM. Both analyses are thus expected consequences from the general claim that prosodically defective morpheme representations may result in MLM. In section 3.1.4, a slightly modified analysis for Hungarian second stems is presented that is based on this basic logic but is implemented in standard OT and without the need to optimize the choice between lexically stored allomorphs for a morpheme.

2.1.5 Summary: previous accounts

The important claims of the analyses and proposals discussed in the preceding subsections can be summarized with the three crucial assumptions in (14).

(14)   *MLM as epiphenomenon*
   a. Morphemic prosodic nodes can be fully integrated and result in additive MLM.
   b. Morphemic prosodic nodes can be integrated defectively and result in subtractive MLM.
   c. Underlying segments that are not dominated by a prosodic node may result in MLM.

And these assumptions in fact already summarize all the relevant representations and configurations assumed for a unified analysis of MLM. Most of the proposals discussed above are analyses for a specific type of non-concatenative morphology or morpheme-specific phonology. To show that the claims in (14) implemented in a specific version of OT are in fact sufficient to account for all instances of MLM is the aim of this book.

   Although there are some programmatic claims that non-concatenative morphology is epiphenomenal (Bye and Svenonius, 2012; Bermúdez-Otero, 2012), a unified theoretical analysis for the whole range of relevant phenomena based on a representative empirical data set has not been proposed so far. The most comprehensive analysis in these terms that I am aware of is Trommer (2011a) where the complex pattern of Western Nilotic morphology is analysed. However, an exhaustive picture of one empirical domain (Western Nilotic) is given there, whereas the aim of this book is to present a typology of related phenomena in a diversity of languages.

2.2 The theoretical framework of PDM

In this book, existing claims that MLM is epiphenomenal are pursued, extended, and an argument is made for the framework summarized as the theory of *Prosodically Defective Morphemes* (=PDM). 'Prosodically defective' refers to a prosodically incomplete structure where a prosodic node is not dominated or does not dominate another prosodic node. Two very general types of 'prosodically defective morphemes' hence exist: a morpheme representation can be prosodically defective in the input or in the output. That representations can be prosodically defective in the input is a necessary consequence of Richness of the Base. In fact the majority of morpheme representations considered in theoretical work are prosodically defective in this sense. Only a morpheme representation properly integrated under a prosodic word node would be 'prosodically complete'.

And that representations can be prosodically defective in the output is a necessary consequence of an OT system where the constraints ensuring prosodic layering are violable.

(15)   *A morpheme representation is prosodically defective . . .*

    a. *in the input if . . .*

        it contains phonological elements (¬PrWd) that are not dominated by a node higher on the prosodic hierarchy, and/or

        it contains prosodic nodes (¬segments) that do not dominate a node lower on the prosodic hierarchy.

    b. *in the output if . . .*

        it contains phonological elements (¬PrWd) that are not phonetically visibly dominated by a node higher on the prosodic hierarchy, and/or

        it contains prosodic nodes (¬segments) that do not phonetically visibly dominate a node lower on the prosodic hierarchy.

The existence of defective morpheme representations of one or the other type in (15) is hence in principle already acknowledged in most OT systems. What differentiates the current proposal from most previous work is that underlyingly defective morpheme representations (15-a) are taken to potentially give rise to surface phenomena like MLM. Underlyingly defective structure is hence not completely neutralized to prosodically complete structure in all contexts. The claim that prosodically defective underlying morpheme representations can predict MLM crucially relies on the assumption of Richness of the Base stating that the input into the grammar is universal and unrestricted (Prince and Smolensky, 1993/2002; McCarthy and Prince, 1995; Kager, 1999*b*). It is argued throughout this book that different types of defective or underspecified input representations result in MLM and hence that any restriction excluding defective structures from the input is not only unnecessary but makes a straightforward account of theoretically challenging phenomena impossible.[7]

---

[7] In principle, this assumption is compatible with the assumption in, for example, Inkelas (1995) or Bermúdez-Otero (1999) that Lexicon Optimization restricts the possible inputs. They argue that all predictable structure that is non-contrastive in a language is lexically stored. Underspecification or 'defective' structure is therefore only a possible input if its output alternates in a language. Under the present account, it is simply argued that more structural differences result in output alternations than is standardly assumed.

The main claim defended here is hence that the defective structures in input and/or output defined in (15) together with the containment-based OT system introduced in the following sections provide a unified account for MLM phenomena as the result of concatenating morphemes. PDM is based mainly on the three very basic assumptions listed in (16).

(16)   *Basic theoretical assumptions: Defective Prosodic Morpheme representations*
      a. The nodes of the prosodic hierarchy exist as independent phonological elements.
      b. The constraints ensuring prosodic layering/penalizing floating prosodic nodes are bidirectional.
      c. An OT system based on coloured containment.

A first sketch of the central prosodic configurations that are relevant for such an argumentation is given in (17) with some abstract symbols representing tiers of the prosodic hierarchy. In (17-a), a prosodic node is added and is fully integrated into the structure of its base, i.e. it is associated with a higher element and dominates a lower element. (17-b) and (17-c) are two defective integrations where a node is added to a structure but an association with a lower (17-b) or a higher (17-c) node is missing. (17-d) finally is a structure where a node is fully integrated into the structure and this new association triggers deassociation of an underlying node to its higher structure.

(17)   *Basic configurations in PDM*

a. Full Integration	b. Defective Integration I	c. Defective Integration II	d. Usurpation

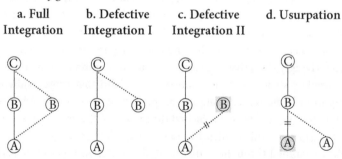

In addition, different combinations of these basic configurations can coexist in one language. Two brief examples are given in (18) where two possible combinations of full and defective integration are illustrated. For one, it is possible that a morphemic node is not integrated in some contexts (18-a-i), but fully integrated in others (18-a-ii). And on the other hand, it is possible that a morphemic node on tier n is fully integrated (18-b-i) whereas a new node on another tier is only defectively integrated (18-b-ii).

(18) *Combinations of basic configurations in one grammar*
  a. **Full vs. defective integration**   b. **Full vs. defective integration**
       in different contexts   **on different tiers**

  i. Context I   ii. Context II   i.   ii.

These combinations of defective integrated structures are predicted by grammars possible in the containment-based OT system adopted here and it is argued that their expected surface configurations are indeed attested in the patterns of MLM in the languages of the world.

The following subsections introduce all relevant theoretical background assumptions and constraint types relevant for the analyses presented in the following chapters. In subsection 2.2.2 and 2.2.3, the two central assumptions of containment and morphological colours resulting in a 'coloured containment' OT system are introduced. The solution containment offers to opacity problems can be taken as an independent argument for this theory; a point that is briefly discussed in subsection 2.2.4. Subsection 2.2.5 briefly presents the assumptions and theoretical implementation for reduplication assumed in the following discussion.

And in subsection 2.2.6, the assumptions about linear ordering of morphemes and possible realization points for morphemic prosodic nodes are presented that are especially relevant for the discussion of the empirical generalizations about attested MLM patterns in chapter 6. Finally, a first overview of the representations that are predicted in the theory of PDM and how they account for MLM is given in subsection 2.2.7.

As a starting point, some necessary background assumptions about the organization into prosodic structure are given in subsection 2.2.1.

2.2.1 *Avant: prosodic structure and Richness of the Base*

The most basic background assumption for the theory of PDM are the prosodic nodes, organized in the prosodic hierarchy. The assumption of the prosodic hierarchy as an abstract, non-segmental structure had its origin in the insight of prosodic phonology that stress is not a segmental feature but a nonlinear property (Liberman and Prince, 1977; Hayes, 1995). With the development of Prosodic Morphology, these primitives of the phonological theory became relevant for the morphology as well (McCarthy and Prince, 1986/1996: et seq.). This is the first standard assumption this book is based on: the prosodic nodes exist as entities of their own and only elements properly integrated under the highest prosodic node of the prosodic hierarchy

(19) are visible for the phonetics (=Stray Erasure, McCarthy, 1979; Steriade, 1982; Itô, 1988).

(19)   *Prosodic hierarchy*   (Nespor and Vogel, 1986)

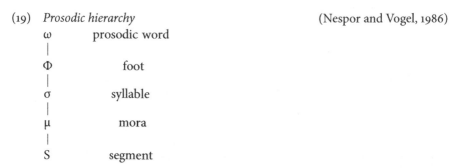

In an OT system where Richness of the Base ensures that there are no restrictions about the possible input structures, it is clear that some constraints must ensure that the phonological representations conform to this hierarchy. Constraints of this type have been proposed several times, for example, as HEADEDNESS (Selkirk, 1995), as (biconditional) PROJECT (X,Y) (van Oostendorp, 1995), as PARSE-INTO-X where X stands for a node on the prosodic hierarchy (Spaelti, 1994; Itô and Mester, 2009), or as LICENSE-X (Kiparsky, 2003). The logic of most of these constraint systems is to start at the segmental level and require proper parsing on all higher levels. The claim of PDM is now that defective output structures where this prosodic integration is incomplete should be taken into account as well since they predict attested surface effects. It is therefore assumed that PARSE constraints are bi-directional in the sense that two constraints about proper parsing exist for every pair of prosodic nodes on tier n and tier n–1: one demanding that a node on tier n ($\neq\omega$) must be dominated by a node on tier n+1, and one demanding that a node on tier n ($\neq$S) must dominate a node on tier n–1. For the moraic tier, for example, the two general constraints (20) are relevant where 'Do' abbreviates 'dominates' and 'DD' 'is dominated by'.

(20)   a. μ-Do-S   Assign a violation mark for every μ that does not dominate a segment.
       b. μ-DD-σ Assign a violation mark for every μ that is not dominated by a σ.

The constraint scheme in (20) is assumed to exist for all pairs of prosodic nodes on tier n and on tier n–1, but also for relations between nodes on tier n and tier n–2/n+2 relations. This is necessary since by now it has been shown that the assumption of a strict layering of prosodic nodes in the hierarchy in (19) (Nespor and Vogel, 1986; Selkirk, 1986) is too strict and the assumption of weak layering is more adequate (Itô and Mester, 2003; Kiparsky, 2003). The assumption of weak layering opens up the possibility of extraprosodic elements (Prince and Smolensky, 1993/2002; Hyde,

2011). A high-ranked constraint μ-DD-Φ, for example, can become relevant in a language with extrasyllabic but moraic consonants. If integration of a mora under a syllable is blocked for some reasons, the mora is at least forced to be integrated under a prosodic foot. Note that if syllabification and more general integration into prosodic structure follows from constraints in the format of (20), Weight-by-Position (Hayes, 1989; Sherer, 1994; Zec, 1995; Rosenthall and van der Hulst, 1999) is ensured by a constraint C-DD-σ demanding that every consonant is dominated by a mora.

2.2.2 Containment

No literal deletion   The main claim defended in this book is that prosodically defective morphemes may result in MLM. This implies that the difference between an underlyingly incomplete and complete prosodic structure is not necessarily neutralized to the same complete prosodic structure in the output. The theoretical assumption that straightforwardly implements such a situation where underlying distinctions are preserved, is the principle of containment. The containment-based OT system adopted throughout this book has been termed 'Coloured Containment' and is in most parts identical to the system proposed in Trommer and Zimmermann (2014) and Trommer (2011*a*). As is argued in this book, this assumption not only solves some general opacity problems of standard parallel OT, but naturally predicts configurations of defective prosodic integration in the output that are crucial in accounting for the full range of MLM. The assumption of containment was already present in the discussion of OT in Prince and Smolensky (1993/2002) but was rejected in favour of correspondence-theoretic OT (McCarthy and Prince, 1995: et seq.). Its original formulation given in (21) demands that the input is *contained* in the output and hence has no independent status in the model. In contrast to correspondence-theoretic OT (McCarthy and Prince, 1995), constraints in containment theory only evaluate one representation, namely the output.

(21)   *Containment*   (Prince and Smolensky, 1993/2002)
       Every element of the phonological input representation is contained in the output.

This assumption prohibits any literal deletion of structure. Elements can only lack a phonetic interpretation if they are not integrated under the highest prosodic node and are consequently phonetically 'invisible' (Prince and Smolensky, 1993/2002). Containment as assumed here goes even further and demands that the input must be *reconstructable* from the output at any time. Consequently, not only elements like segments or features underlie containment but association relations do as well

(Goldrick, 2000; van Oostendorp, 2006; Revithiadou, 2007; Trommer, 2011a; Trommer and Zimmermann, 2014). Association lines that are underlyingly present can never be deleted but can only remain phonetically 'invisible' if they are marked as uninterpretable for the phonetics. Consequently, there are four possible types of association lines, given in (22): Association lines that are underlyingly present and are phonetically visible in the output (22-a) (=notated as straight lines), underlying association lines that are marked as invisible (22-b) (=notated as lines that are crossed out), phonetically visible association lines that were not underlyingly present (22-c) (=notated as dotted lines), and epenthetic association lines that are marked as phonetically invisible (22-d) (=notated as dotted lines that are crossed out). Association lines that are part of the underlying representation of a morpheme are termed 'morphological' in the following.

(22)   *Marking conventions for different types of association lines*

Morphological association lines		Epenthetic association lines	
phonetically visible:	phonetically invisible:	phonetically visible:	phonetically invisible:
a. (A)—(B)	b. (A)≠(B)	c. (A)⋮(B)	d. (A)≠(B)

This typology of association lines is highly reminiscent of the association relations in Turbidity Theory (Goldrick, 2000; van Oostendorp, 2006; Revithiadou, 2007) where association lines are replaced with the two relations of projection and pronunciation. In Goldrick's original proposal of Turbidity Theory, the former denotes an abstract relationship between two elements and the latter denotes the output relation that is visible for the phonetics (Goldrick, 2000). A slightly different version of Turbidity Theory is proposed in Revithiadou (2007) (see also van Oostendorp, 2006, 2007b, 2008), where projection is assumed to represent underlying association relations. Given containment, projection lines can never change and will always represent underlying associations whereas pronunciation lines can be manipulated. An unfaithful mapping like deletion or spreading/shifting of elements hence leads to an imperfect match between these two relations. The typology in (22) that is also adopted in Zimmermann (2013b) actually unifies these two conceptions by assuming four possible association relations. A summary of the different conceptions and notational differences in the typology of association lines is given in the following table (23).

(23) *Different association relations*

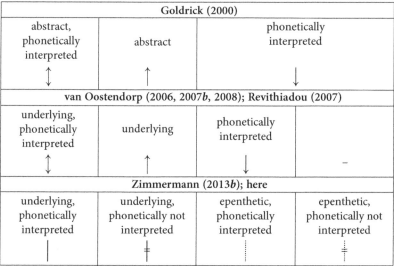

Goldrick (2000)			
abstract, phonetically interpreted ↕	abstract ↑	phonetically interpreted ↓	
van Oostendorp (2006, 2007b, 2008); Revithiadou (2007)			
underlying, phonetically interpreted ↕	underlying ↑	phonetically interpreted ↓	–
Zimmermann (2013b); here			
underlying, phonetically interpreted │	underlying, phonetically not interpreted ╪	epenthetic, phonetically interpreted ┆	epenthetic, phonetically not interpreted ╪

For every association line, it is hence clear whether it is phonetically invisible or not and whether it is epenthetic or underlyingly present. It is assumed that this status of association lines is evaluated by constraints penalizing inserted (24a) or phonetically invisible (24b) association lines, the pendants to correspondence-theoretic faithfulness constraints MAX and DEP for association lines.[8]

(24) a. $\ast\,\genfrac{}{}{0pt}{}{\mu}{S}$ Assign a violation mark for every inserted association line between a μ and a segment.

---

[8] It has been argued that general DEP-LINK-μ and DEP-μ constraints are potentially problematic for parallel OT and Richness of the Base since they predict unattested syllabification and weight contrasts (Bermúdez-Otero, 1999; Campos-Astorkiza, 2004). The solution proposed in Bermúdez-Otero (1999) (see also Bermúdez-Otero, 2001; Campos-Astorkiza, 2004; Campos-Astorkiza, 2003; Topintzi, 2006 and Topintzi (2010)) is a modified version of DEP-μ that takes into account the concept of positional μ-licensing (i).

(i) *Positional μ-licensing*   (Bermúdez-Otero, 1999: 48)
    A segment α is positionally μ-licensed by a μ_α if, and only if,
    a. α does not have an input correspondent linked to a μ, and
    b. α is immediately dominated by μ_α, and by μ_α only.

The constraint P-DEP-μ then only penalizes the insertion of non-positional moras, i.e. those moras that are not the only prosodic node directly dominating a segment. Insertion of predictable moras on short vowels or weight by position for coda consonants is thus not penalized by P-DEP-μ. However, it has been argued that there are indeed languages where syllabification is contrastive (Elfner, 2006) and hence DEP constraints for association lines and prosodic nodes are taken to be in principle unproblematic.

b. $*\begin{matrix} \mu \\ | \\ | \\ S \end{matrix}$ Assign a violation mark for every association line between a μ and a segment that is marked as phonetically invisible.

Now that we have a theory about possible association lines, a notion of phonetic visibility for all other phonological elements like segments, prosodic nodes, features, or tones follows straightforwardly. Those phonological elements are standardly taken to be phonetically invisible if they are not properly integrated under the highest prosodic word node (Prince and Smolensky, 1993/2002: 25). Since association lines can be marked as phonetically invisible, it is clear that a 'properly integrated' element that is visible for the phonetics implies that it is integrated under the highest prosodic node via phonetically visible association lines. A phonetically invisible association to an element X may hence have major consequences for all elements dominated by this element. In fact, the marking of an association line as phonetically invisible is taken to be the only operation that can apply in GEN to mark phonological structure as unrealized: phonological elements may remain phonetically invisible as a consequence of this simple operation. The definitions in (25) about phonetic (in)visibility of elements in the prosodic hierarchy define this relation between phonological structure and phonetic visibility.

(25)   *Principles of phonetic (in)visibility*
   a. Every association line linking a phonetically invisible element to a lower element is *phonetically invisible*.
   b. Every phonological element is *phonetically invisible* iff it is not associated to a higher prosodic node by a phonetically visible association line.

These assumptions make some predictions about impossible and possible prosodic structures. If the only association line of a prosodic element to a higher node is marked as phonetically invisible, the node itself remains phonetically invisible. Consequently (see (25-a)), the association lines that link it to lower prosodic nodes become phonetically invisible as well and so forth. For ease of readability, all phonetically invisible elements are marked with a grey background in the following. Some exemplifying structures are given in (26): For a structure where a syllable is underlyingly associated with a mora and that mora in turn to a vowel, only the four structures in (26-I) are possible (with respect to the determination of phonetic visibility). If the only association line linking the vowel to the mora is marked as phonetically invisible (26-b), the vowel is necessarily phonetically invisible as well since it is not dominated by a higher prosodic node via a phonetically visible association line. Similarly, if the association line between the syllable and the mora is marked as phonetically invisible (26-c), the mora is phonetically invisible and hence the association to the vowel and the vowel itself, too. And if the syllable is phonetically invisible (26-d), all the structure it dominates is phonetically invisible as well. For a structure where a vowel, two moras, and a syllable are present, however, more possibilities arise. The depictions in (26-II) list some of them. If the mora is phonetically invisible (26-g), the vowel is not necessarily phonetically invisible since it could be associated to the other mora by a phonetically visible association line. The structures in (26-III), on the other hand, are impossible since they violate one or both of the principles in (25). In (26-i), a vowel is taken to be phonetically interpreted although it is not dominated by a phonetically visible higher prosodic node. And in (26-j), a vowel is taken to be uninterpreted that is integrated under a higher prosodic node by a phonetically visible association line. In the following, structures excluded by GEN are marked with ⚡.

(26)   I. *Possible prosodic structures I*

II. *Possible prosodic structures II*

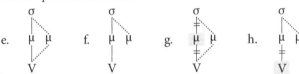

III. *Impossible prosodic structures*

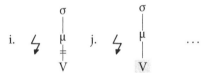

The pendant to correspondence-theoretic MAX constraints are hence constraints demanding that an element is phonetically visible. In order to avoid confusion with the correspondence-theoretic terminology, these constraints are termed PVIS (=Phonetically Visibility). An example is the constraint PVIS$_S$ (27) demanding phonetic visibility for segments. Given the principles for phonetic visibility (25), this requires a structure where every segment is dominated by a phonetically visible prosodic node through a phonetically visible association line.

(27)   PVIS$_S$ Assign a violation mark for every segment that is phonetically invisible.

Let's return to the parsing constraints in (20) once more. It is clear that the different types of association lines introduced in (22) are marked to different degrees. The unmarked association line is an underlying association relation that is phonetically visible. The other three types of association lines are marked since they are inserted and/or phonetically invisible and hence violate the constraint *μ........ S (24-a) or *μ —⊬— S (24-b). These different degrees of markedness are also relevant for the parsing constraints demanding prosodic integration in (20). It is assumed that they are split up into three versions, one demanding a phonetically visible association line (28-a)+(29-a), one demanding a phonetically visible or morphological association line (28-b)+(29-b), and one demanding an association by *some* kind of association (28-c)+(29-c). These parametrizations are marked with the indices 'p' for phonetically interpreted association lines and 'm' for morphological association lines. That constraints are sensitive to this distinction between, for example, a non-existent association line and a phonetically invisible association line is actually a prediction from containment and the fact that all underlying structure remains present even if it is phonetically invisible on the surface.[9] These PARSE constraints solve some notoriously difficult opacity problems and predict various types of defective prosodic integration. As is argued here, the surface effects predicted by those defective integrations are all attested.

(28) a. $\mu > Do_p > S$ — Assign a violation mark for every μ that does not phonetically dominate a segment.

  b. $\mu > Do_p^m > S$ — Assign a violation mark for every μ that does not phonetically or morphologically dominate a segment.

  c. $\mu > Do > S$ — Assign a violation mark for every μ that does not dominate a segment.

(29) a. $\mu < DD_p < \sigma$ — Assign a violation mark for every μ that is not phonetically dominated by a σ.

  b. $\mu < DD_p^m < \sigma$ — Assign a violation mark for every μ that is not phonetically or morphologically dominated by a σ.

  c. $\mu < DD < \sigma$ — Assign a violation mark for every μ that is not dominated by a σ.

In most of the following discussion, only the b. versions are relevant that are satisfied if a morphological or phonologically visible association line links two elements.

The building of prosodic structure in OT   In this book, the (full or defective) repair of underlyingly incomplete prosodic structure is the mechanism relevant for an account of MLM. Some standard markedness assumptions about possible prosodic

[9] This is an extension of the 'Cloning Hypothesis' assuming that all constraints exist in two versions, one referring only to phonetically visible structures and a less restrictive version referring to *any* information, irrespective of whether it is phonetically visible or not, see Trommer (2011a). In principle, all constraints hence exist in multiple versions, specified for different degrees of phonetic visibility and morphological affiliation. In most cases, only a single version of every constraint is relevant in the following analyses and the 'p' and 'm' indices referring to 'phonetically visible' and 'morphological' are not added for all constraints—it is clear from the respective definitions which structure they are sensitive to.

structures are hence necessary. For one, crossing association lines are standardly taken to be excluded (Goldsmith, 1976). In the containment-based OT system adopted here, a modified version of the NoCrossingCondition is assumed that only restricts phonetically visible association lines. Association lines that are both marked as phonetically invisible may hence cross.

(30) *A restriction on GEN: the* NoCrossingCondition *(=*NoCr*)*
      Association lines may not cross if one or both of them is phonetically visible. Whereas two association lines cross iff
      a. element X precedes element Y on tier n and element V precedes element W on tier n–x, and
      b. Y is associated with V and X with W.

Another restriction that is assumed to hold in GEN is the exclusion of a so called 'Kicking' configuration, illustrated in (32) where a node is newly associated with an element that was already underlyingly associated with a node of the same type and this latter node is in consequence forced to reassociate. From the perspective of the node X, this is a vacuous combination of processes since an association with a node is marked as invisible and a new association of a node of the same type is added.

(31) *A restriction on GEN: the* NoKickingCondition *(=*NKK*)*
      Given two nodes X and Y on tier n and two nodes W and Z on tier n–1:
      it is impossible to add an association line between X and W iff
      a. X is associated with Z by a morphological association line that is marked as invisible and
      b. Z is also associated with Y by an inserted association line.

(32) *Excluded Kicking configuration*

An additional standard assumption about the prosodic hierarchy adopted here is the fact that in the unmarked case, every node has only one highest prosodic node, i.e. has only one path to a prosodic node that is not dominated by a higher node. The class of constraints that ensure this prosodic well-formedness are given in (33). They exist for every element of the prosodic hierarchy; the two constraints that are relevant in the analyses below are (33-a) demanding only one root node for segments and (33-b) demanding only one root for moras.

(33) a. ONERT-S   Assign a violation mark for every phonetically visible segment dominated by more than one highest prosodic node (=a node that is not dominated by another node).

b. ONERT-μ   Assign a violation mark for every phonetically visible μ dominated by more than one highest prosodic node
(=a node that is not dominated by another node).

A more specific version of this constraint type are constraints demanding that an
element X on tier n strives to be dominated by only one element Y on tier n+1. The
most prominent and uncontroversial example for this constraint type is (34), mirroring the standard markedness constraint against long vowels. Given the principles
of phonetic (in)visibility (25), it follows that the vowel and the moras referred to in
(34) are necessarily phonetically visible as well since they are linked by a phonetically
visible association line.

(34) $*^\mu V^\mu$ Assign a violation mark for every vowel phonetically associated with more
than one μ.

Quite parallel, there are also constraints of the type (35) demanding that nodes strive to
dominate only one lower prosodic node. The example in (35) penalizes every instance
of a mora dominating more than one vowel phonetically. It is a version of NOSHAREDμ
in Broselow et al. (1997) and reminiscent of the proper bracketing condition in Nespor
and Vogel (1986).

(35) $*_V \mu_V$ Assign a violation mark for every μ that is phonetically associated to more
than one vowel.

This constraint is crucial for predicting the mechanism of mora-usurpation discussed
in detail in section 3.1.

2.2.3 *Morphological colours*

Morphological information in the phonology   One main advantage of PDM is the
fact that non-concatenative morphology and morpheme-specific phonology follow
from the same basic mechanism. A difference in the underlying prosodic specification
between two segmentally identical morphemes, for example, can hence predict that
one of them triggers morpheme-specific phonology and the other does not. Apparently lexical distinctions hence follow from different underlying representations and
any reference to specific morphological information is unnecessary in the phonology.
A version of the 'Indirect Reference Hypothesis' (Inkelas, 1990) is hence adopted that
restricts the ability of the phonology to refer to morpho-syntactic information. The
only morphological information the phonology has access to is whether two elements
are affiliated with the same morpheme or with different morphemes and whether
an element is not affiliated with any morpheme at all. In addition, the phonological
constraint system has access to the information whether material is affiliated with an
affix or a stem. That the phonology is sensitive to this morphological distinction is well

established (see the overviews in Urbanczyk (2011) or Trommer (2010) for discussion and literature). The former assumption is implicit in most analyses and explicitly formalized in the theory of morphological colours (van Oostendorp, 2003, 2008, 2006, 2007a; Revithiadou, 2007) that is adopted here. It is assumed that every morpheme has an underlying 'colour' and all phonological elements that are part of the underlying representation of this morpheme bear this colour. For reasons of typographical restrictions, morphemic affiliations are abbreviated with subscribed symbols in the following: $W_\circ$, $X_\bullet$, $Y_\square$, and $Z_\blacksquare$ respectively. In the majority of configurations that are discussed in the following, only two different morphemic affiliations ($X_\circ$ vs. $Y_\bullet$) are relevant, namely the affiliation of an affix and its base.

The morphological colour cannot be changed by the phonology and epenthetic elements hence lack a colour. The theory of morphological colours not only allows us to identify epenthetic material, it also allows us to detect whether two phonological elements belong to the same or two different morphemes. This information is essential for predicting derived environment effects and especially for the formulation of the constraint ALTERNATION (49) discussed below.

The pendant to correspondence-theoretic DEP are constraints termed COL!. An example is given in (36) where the constraint against epenthetic segments is formulated.

(36) COL!$_S$ Assign a violation mark for every segment not licensed by morphological colour.

An extension of COL! constraints adopted here are constraints demanding that prosodic nodes strive to dominate elements with a morphological colour. Examples are the constraints (37) demanding that every syllable must project at least one morphologically coloured mora (37-a) and every foot at least one morphologically coloured segment (37-b). The former predicts an interesting asymmetry in the analysis presented for Yine in section 3.1.1 where epenthetic moras are inserted for every consonant that is not prevocalic but insertion of an epenthetic mora is a marked strategy to supply an underlyingly mora-less vowel with a mora. And the latter makes crucial predictions in the analysis for non-concatenative allomorphy in Upriver Halkomelem discussed in section 5.3.1 where a morphemic foot is mainly filled with epenthetic or reduplicated material but must not *only* contain such colourless segments. In a sense, they are more general versions of the constraints against colourless material (36) in that they demand that prosodic nodes are not exclusively filled with epenthetic material, quite similar to HEAD-DEP in Alderete (1999).

(37) a. $^*\sigma$-COL!μ Assign a violation mark for every σ node that only dominates colourless μ's phonetically or morphologically.

b. *Φ-COL!S   Assign a violation mark for every Φ node that only dominates colourless segments phonetically or morphologically.

Such an OT framework adopting the assumptions of containment and morphological colours is termed 'coloured containment' in the following.

Morph-contiguous prosodic projection   Inside correspondence-theoretic OT, a class of constraints ensures that representations should be contiguous. In the version proposed in Landman (2002), these CONTIGUITY constraints require that a morpheme representation should be contiguous, i.e. neither deletion (violating (38-a)) nor insertion (violating (38-b)) should disrupt a morpheme representation. This predicts instances where deletion or epenthesis are tolerated at morpheme edges but never inside a morpheme. Lardil is discussed as an example for the former pattern and Chukchee as an instance of the latter in Landman (2002).

(38)   a. M-I-CONTIG   The portions of the input standing in correspondence and belonging to the same M form contiguous strings.

b. M-O-CONTIG   The portions of the output standing in correspondence and belonging to the same M form contiguous strings.

Assuming coloured containment, it is clear that those constraints can easily be reimplemented as in (39).

(39)   a. CNT$_{PVis}$ Assign a violation mark for every phonetically invisible segment S_O that is preceded and followed by phonetically visible segments A_O and B_O that belong to the same morpheme.

b. CNT$_{Lic}$ Assign a violation mark for every colourless segment S that is preceded and followed by phonetically visible segments A_O and B_O that belong to the same morpheme.

Here, it is now argued that this standard concept of morpheme CONTIGUITY needs to be extended in two respects. For one, linear contiguity must also be ensured across different tiers. More concretely, it is argued that the depiction (40-b) are instances where the linear contiguity of a morpheme is disrupted whereas the morphemes in (40-a) are linearly contiguous. In both structures, a morpheme $M_\bullet$ consisting of a morphemic mora is adjacent to a morpheme M_O that consists of the segmental string /C_O V_O C_O/. In (40-a), the morphemic mora is associated to the consonant C_O which is at the edge of the morpheme M_O. In (40-b), on the other hand, the morphemic mora is associated to a vowel V_O and hence a consonant C_O intervenes between the morpheme edge and the segment to which the mora associates. As is discussed in more detail in section 2.2.6, this structure is perfectly licit with respect to the principles of morpheme order and linearization. It represents, however, a discontiguous morpheme representation in the sense that the morpheme edges do not coincide: the affix $M_\bullet$ is realized 'within' morpheme M_O if one takes into account the whole prosodic structure.

(40) *Linear morpheme contiguity*
   a. *Morph-contiguous integration*   b. *A non-morph-contiguous structure*

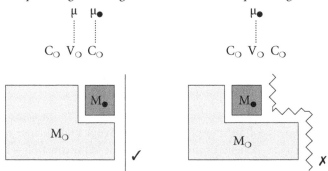

That the structure in (40-b) is dispreferred in contrast to (40-a) is predicted from the linear CONTIGUITY constraint (41) demanding that a morphemic prosodic node must dominate phonological elements at the edge of another morpheme. In section 5.1, it is argued that it correctly derives attested instances of phonologically predictable allomorphy triggered by morphemic moras or instances where the realization of a morphemic mora is blocked in certain contexts.

(41) CNT_M Assign a violation mark for every P_O on tier n that is associated to $x_\bullet$ on tier n–1 and $x_\bullet$ is preceded by element $w_\bullet$ and followed by element $z_\bullet$.

In addition to this linear CONTIGUITY across different prosodic tiers, it is argued that the concept of morpheme contiguity must be extended to vertical relations in a prosodic structure as well. The assumption underlying the concept of vertical morpheme contiguity is that the abstract depiction in (42-a) is the ideal prosodic integration with respect to morphological affiliation and the structures in (42-b) and (42-c) are marked structures. In (42-b), a morphological mora dominates a segment with a different morphological affiliation and in (42-c), a morphological syllable dominates two moras and an onset consonant with a different morphological affiliation.

(42) *Vertical morpheme contiguity*
   a.   b.   c.

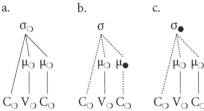

Constraints demanding vertical morpheme contiguity are of two types: they restrict the morphological affiliation of elements dominated by node X or the morphological affiliation of elements dominating node X. In the following, it is argued that both constraint types make correct predictions in the analyses of MLM.

In (43), two constraints are given demanding that a morphologically coloured prosodic node must not dominate elements with another morphological colour, formulated for the syllable in (43-a) and for feet in (43-b).

(43) a. $^*\sigma_O < S_\bullet$ Assign a violation mark for every σ_O that phonetically dominates a segment with another morphological colour $_\bullet$.

b. $^*\Phi_O < S_\bullet$ Assign a violation mark for every Φ_O that phonetically dominates a segment with another morphological colour $_\bullet$.

These constraints are closely related to standard CONTIGUITY in the sense that they demand that no elements of one morpheme must interrupt a dominance relation in the prosodic hierarchy of elements of another morpheme. If the constraints in (43) are high-ranked in a language and a morphemic prosodic node is affixed, it is predicted that this morphemic prosodic node avoids dominating base segments since they are affiliated with another morpheme. If the prosodic node must nevertheless be filled with segmental material, epenthesis and/or copying become optimal to fill the morphemic prosodic node. These constraints are hence crucial in the implementation of the general account that morphemic prosodic nodes offer for reduplication as discussed in 2.2.5. Specifically, (43-b) is relevant for the foot affixation analysis proposed for Upriver Halkomelem where a morphemic foot prefers to be filled with epenthetic or copied material.

In contrast to standard CONTIGUITY, they demand contiguity across the tiers of the prosodic hierarchy, not only between elements on one tier. Several related concepts and constraints demanding morphemic contiguity across tiers can be found in the literature. For one, the constraint MORPH-O-CONTIG ('The tokens of output structure affiliated with a given morpheme collectively span an uninterrupted interval.' (Wolf, 2007: 59)) is similar since it demands a contiguous morpheme representation; it is different since it refers to (linear) spans, not dominance relations. Another example for a related concept is MORPHOLOGICALSYLLABLEINTEGRITY demanding that all elements integrated under a syllable node should be in the morphological domain of that syllable (van Oostendorp, 2004) or TAUTOMORPHEMICITY demanding that morpheme and syllable boundaries should coincide (Crowhurst, 1994; Bickel, 1998).

An example for the predictions that $^*\sigma_O < S_\bullet$ (43-a) makes can be illustrated with the Diola-Fogny consonant deletion, already introduced above in section 1.1.2 (6-b) (Sapir, 1969; Kager, 1999b; McCarthy, 2008b). In this Atlantic language, a deletion process seems to be guided by the demand to achieve maximal isomorphism between syllable boundaries and morpheme boundaries. Consider the data in (44), where deletion of the first consonant in word-internal CC-clusters can be observed.

(44) *Consonant deletion in Diola-Fogny*   (Sapir, 1969: 17)

UNDERLYING	SURFACE	
lɛt−ku−jaw	lɛkujaw	'they won't go'
na−manj−manj	namamanj	'he knows'
ɛ−rɛnt−rɛnt	ɛrɛrɛnt	'it is light'

Kager (1999*b*) claims that the deletion is triggered by syllable well-formedness conditions (CODA-CONDITION). The fact that the first consonant is deleted and not the second one follows from the constraint (45) demanding alignment between morpheme and syllable boundaries. In a correct output form /lɛ.ku.jaw, all morpheme boundaries coincide with a syllable boundary whereas in an alternative candidate */lɛ.tu.jaw/, the segment of the first morpheme /lɛt/ is syllabified as onset of the following syllable and therefore misaligns the two boundaries.

(45)   ALIGN-   The left edge of every morpheme coincides with the left edge of a
       MORPH-L   syllable.

An alternative implementation that avoids reference to ALIGNMENT constraints is a solution that refers to the morphological affiliation of the prosodic structure. If syllable structure is underlyingly present, $^*\sigma_O < S_\bullet$ demands that the segmental material affiliated to one morpheme must not be syllabified under the syllable node of another morpheme. For the Diola-Fogny data, this predicts that */le.tu.jaw/ is excluded since /t/ is syllabified under the syllable node morphologically affiliated with another morpheme (/−ku/), briefly shown in (46).

(46)   *Consonant deletion in Diola-Fogny*

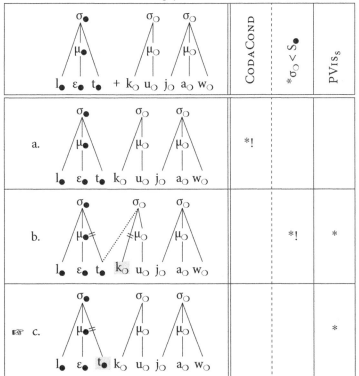

With respect to higher prosodic structure than the syllable, this constraint hence predicts a language where every morpheme projects its own prosodic word structure. A prediction that is indeed borne out in, for example, Diyari (Poser, 1989).

The constraints in (43) restrict the morphological affiliation of elements that are dominated by a higher prosodic node. The counterpart constraints restricting the morphological affiliation of elements that dominate some lower node are taken to be slightly different from the formulation in (43). It is not assumed that every element X_i associated with a prosodic node Y_j on tier n+1 necessarily constitutes a marked configuration. It is rather assumed that it is necessary to be licensed by *some* higher prosodic node that is not affiliated with another morphological colour. This implies that additional insertion of an epenthetic prosodic node can ensure a morph-contiguous prosodic projection for a segment dominated by a morphemic prosodic node. More concretely, the constraint (47) is proposed demanding that every element strives to be dominated either by a prosodic node that is affiliated with the same morpheme or by an epenthetic prosodic node. The subscript 'o' abbreviates the condition that the constraint is violated if the node in question is *only* dominated by elements with another morphological colour.

(47) Assign a violation mark for every vowel V that does not project a $^*V_O <_O \mu_\bullet$ morph-contiguous μ that bears the same morphological colour or no morphological colour at all.

The assumption of $^*V_O <_O \mu_\bullet$ not only solves a notoriously problematic instance of opaque mora projection for mora affixation analyses in standard OT (see the following section 2.2.4) but also predicts attested patterns of 'long epenthesis' in the contexts of morphological lengthening, discussed in detail in section 5.2.3. That long epenthesis is a severe problem for alternative accounts is shown in section 7.4. The constraint can be understood as a more specific version of a parsing constraint (20) that refers to the morphological affiliation of the involved elements and demands that every element project its 'own' prosodic structure. An apparently similar constraint is V-WT↑ that is defined as: '[a]ll vowels must project their own μ' (Goldrick, 2000: 3). It is proposed inside Turbidity Theory (see (23)) and demands a projection line between a vowel and a mora, hence an abstract structural relationship that is not necessarily phonetically interpreted. In the analysis of compensatory lengthening in Luganda in Goldrick (2000), V-WT↑ has the same effect that the parsing constraints (28) and (29) can predict in a containment-based system: an underlying vowel that is not realized on the surface can still project a mora and this mora is then associated with a phonetically visible host and results in lengthening. V-WT↑ is thus crucially different from $^*V_O <_O \mu_\bullet$ since it does not refer to morphological affiliation. Instances of opaque mora projection where a segment projects its *own* mora instead of only associating with a mora affiliated with a different morphological colour (see sections 2.2.4 and 5.2.3) can not be captured by V-WT↑.

Alternation In all the following analyses, it is taken for granted that a morphemic prosodic node must dominate material that is affiliated with another morpheme. This point can be illustrated with an example of Additive Affixation from Oromo (Heine, 1981; Owens, 1985; Stroomer, 1987; Ali and Zaborski, 1990; Lloret, 1991) where the suffix /−mihi/ triggers lengthening of a preceding vowel (/nama−mihi/ → /namaːmihi/ 'man' (negation)), quite similar to the /−i/ that triggers gemination in Wolof (see 1.1.1, (5)). It is assumed that this affix contains an additional morphemic mora in its representation as in (48-a). It is now apparent that this mora is always associated with segments that precede this affix, never with segments of that affix itself (48-b).

(48) *Additive Affix in Oromo*

a. Input   ☞**b. association with a base segment**

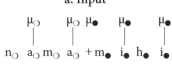   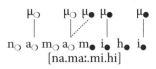

[na.maː.mi.hi]

*c. association with a suffix segment

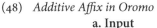

[namamiːhi]

A constraint that predicts this requirement is ALTERNATION (van Oostendorp, 2007a: 39) or the slightly different version STRICT ALTERNATION (van Oostendorp, 2012: 1176), both given in (49).

(49) a. ALTERNATION   If an association line links two elements of colour α, the line should also have colour α.

b. STRICT ALTERNATION   Association lines which could be underlying, must be underlying.

This constraint scheme easily predicts morphologically derived environment effects that arise since a new association line (∼spreading/assimilation) is only possible across morpheme boundaries. A classic example for a morphological derived environment effect is assibilation in Finnish (Kiparsky, 1993; Kula, 2008; Trommer, 2011b; Burzio, 2000, 2011). A sequence of /ti/ in Finnish is avoided via assibilation of the consonant. However, assibilation only applies across morpheme boundaries (50-a), the underlying initial sequence /ti/ in (50-b) is realized faithfully.

(50) *Assibilation in Finnish*   (Kula, 2008: 1339)

	UNDERLYING	SURFACE		
a.	halut−i	halusi		'wanted'
b.	tilat−i	tilasi	*silasi	'order' (3.Sg.Pst)

A possible autosegmental analysis for assibilation is to assume spreading of [–cont] from the vowel to the consonant (see, for example, Jurgec, 2012). A high-ranked ALTERNATION then predicts that such a new association line is only possible in (51-a) where the feature and the potential host are affiliated with different morphemes, never for an underlying /ti/ sequence as in (51-b).[10]

(51) *Morphologically derived environment effects: Finnish*   (Kula, 2008: 1340)
  a. Spreading possible   b. Spreading impossible

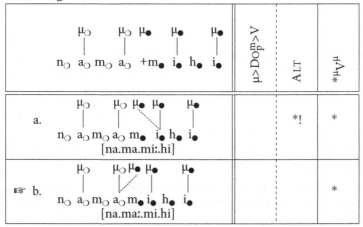

If we integrate an undominated ALTERNATION (=ALT) in our analysis for Oromo Additive Affixation, full integration of the morphemic mora will always result in lengthening of a preceding base segment, never lengthening of the suffix vowel. In candidate (52-a), an epenthetic and hence colourless association line links the suffix mora affiliated with ● to the suffix segment also affiliated with ●—a violation of ALTERNATION arises.

(52) *Additive Affixation in Oromo*

	n_O a_O m_O a_O $+m_●$ $i_●$ $h_●$ $i_●$	$\mu{>}Dom_P^m{>}V$	ALT	$*\mu_V^\mu$
a.	n_O a_O m_O a_O $m_●$ $i_●$ $h_●$ $i_●$ [na.ma.miː.hi]		*!	*
☞ b.	n_O a_O m_O a_O $m_●$ $i_●$ $h_●$ $i_●$ [na.maː.mi.hi]			*

If the demand that morphemic prosodic nodes must be associated with material affiliated with another morpheme is ensured by a violable constraint such as ALTER-NATION, it is predicted that a language should exist where it is low-ranked. In such a language, a morphemic node can in principle be associated with material affiliated

---

[10] A simplified feature-geometric representation is used where the feature [±cont] is simply associated with the IPA symbol for the segment. It also abstracts away from the discussion where features are associated in a feature-geometric representation and which features are 'able' to spread (see, for example, Clements, 1985; McCarthy, 1988; Rice and Avery, 1989; Clements and Hume, 1995).

with the same morpheme. If this intramorphemic association of the morphemic node is predicted in all contexts, the pattern is on the surface indistinguishable from an underlying representation where the morphemic node is associated underlyingly. Far more interesting is the prediction of ALTERNATION: a morphemic node prefers heteromorphemic association with elements affiliated with another morpheme but in case this is impossible, it is associated intramorphemically. An example for such an alternating additive MLM can be found in Dhaasanac (Tosco, 2001; Nishiguchi, 2007, 2009), a Cushitic language. In Dhaasanac, the plural affix /—am/ triggers gemination of a preceding base consonant as can be seen in (53-a). However, this gemination can only be observed for monosyllabic bases, never for polysyllabic bases—a blocking that is interesting in itself. Crucially now, in those contexts where gemination of a base segment is impossible, the vowel of the suffix surfaces as long (53-b).[11]

(53) *Alternating lengthening in Dhaasanac*   (Tosco, 2001: 87)

	SG		PL
a.	kur	'knee'	kurːam
	kór	'double-pointed fork'	korːam
	ʃar	'a kind of stick'	ʃarːam
b.	ʔarːoɲoɗ	'clearing-stick'	ʔarːoɲoɗaːm
	ʔoɲor	'black'	ʔoɲoraːm
	deger	'barren'	degeraːm

This can now be interpreted as a standard case of mora affixation: the Additive Suffixes are assumed to contain a morphemic mora. In case this mora cannot dock onto a base segment, it is associated with the suffix vowel under violation of $*^{\mu}V^{\mu}$. The underlying structures of this alternating lengthening pattern are given in (54).

(54) *Alternating lengthening in Dhaasanac*
    a. **Monosyllabic base:**   b. **Polysyllabic base:**
       base consonant lengthening   **affix vowel lengthening**

 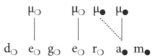

ALTERNATION is hence taken to be a violable constraint that allows alternating MLM as in Dhaasanac if it is low-ranked. In all following analyses involving morphemic prosodic nodes, however, any association alternatives where a morphemic prosodic node is associated with an element affiliated with the same morphological colour are not discussed and assumed to be excluded by high-ranked ALTERNATION.

---

[11] Additive Affixation in Dhaasanac is more complex than that and involves, for example, also gemination-triggering suffixes that do not show alternating vowel lengthening. How the existence of such exceptional non-alternating suffixes follows in a PDM account is discussed in section 4.1.1.

2.2.4 *Excursus I: opaque mora projection and coloured containment*

Before we turn to the concrete derivations of MLM in the framework of PDM, the consequences of the theoretical framework proposed so far for two notoriously diffi- cult opacity problems in standard OT are discussed. More concretely, it is shown how the assumption of morph-contiguous prosodic licensing (47) and of the containment principle that phonetically invisible structure is still accessible solves two layers of opaque mora projection.

It was already mentioned in section 2.1.1 that the implementation of mora affixation in standard parallel OT faces a potentially serious opacity problem. Affixation of a morphemic mora only results in an augmentation effect if the mora is added to an already existing moraic structure of its base and no surface effect is expected if the mora simply replaces a mora that is expected to be inserted for independent (syllabification) demands anyway. That short vowels are dominated by a mora is predictable and a non-contrastive information—moras on short vowels must hence not be part of the underlying representation given the assumption of Richness of the Base (Prince and Smolensky, 1993/2002). In (55), it is shown how the two processes of epenthetic mora insertion to supply underlyingly mora-less vowels with a mora and association of a morphological mora interact in a rule-based account to predict additive MLM correctly for underlyingly mora-less bases. The example is taken from Gidabal (see 1.1.1, (3)).

(55)   *Opaque μ-projection in the presence of a morphemic μ: a rule-based account*

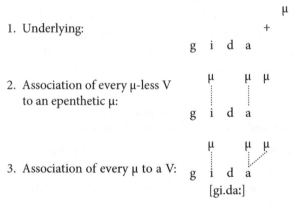

1. Underlying:

2. Association of every μ-less V to an epenthetic μ:

3. Association of every μ to a V:
   [gi.daː]

It is clear that the two rules (55-2) and (55-3) must apply precisely in this order to predict the correct outcome. With respect to the distinction into transparent and opaque rule interactions (Kiparsky, 1968, 1973; McCarthy, 2007b, a; Bakovic, 2011), summarized in (56), this means that rule (55-3) would bleed rule (55-2) if it applied first. The order in (55) is an instance of counter-bleeding and therefore an opaque rule interaction.

(56)   a. *Transparent rule interactions*
        (i) Feeding: A rule R_1 creates the context for the application of rule R_2.
        (ii) Bleeding: A rule R_1 destroys the context for the application of rule R_2.

b. *Opaque rule interactions*
 (i) Counter-feeding: A rule R_1 feeds rule R_2 but they apply in the order $R_2 \gg R_1$.
 (ii) Counter-bleeding: A rule R_1 bleeds rule R_2 but they apply in the order $R_2 \gg R_1$.

The tableau (57) illustrates this problem for a standard parallel OT system. Empirically, candidate (57-c) is optimal where the final vowel is associated with the morphemic mora *and* with an epenthetic mora. In an OT system where insertion of epenthetic elements is penalized by a DEP constraint (COL!$_\mu$ in the current framework), this candidate is expected to be harmonically bounded by candidate (57-d) where the morphemic mora is simply associated with the underlyingly mora-less vowel without an additional mora insertion.[12] Candidates (57-a) and (57-b) are given for completeness showing that insertion of an epenthetic mora is necessary in order to ensure that every vowel is dominated by a mora (excluding (57-a)) and that the morphemic mora must be associated with some segment (excluding (57-b)).

(57) *Opaque μ-projection in OT*

$\mu_\bullet$ + go io do ao	PVis$_V$	PVis$_\mu$	COL!$_\mu$
a. $\mu_\bullet$ go io do ao [gda]	*!		
b. μ μ $\mu_\bullet$ go io do ao [gi.da]		*!	**
☞ c. μ $\mu_\bullet$ go io do ao [gi.da]			*
☛ d. μ μ $\mu_\bullet$ go io do ao [gi.daː]			**!

[12] Even if one assumes the modified concept of P-DEP-μ (Bermúdez-Otero, 2001; Campos-Astorkiza, 2004, 2003; Topintzi, 2006, 2010) or rejects the assumption of DEP-μ completely (Bermúdez-Otero, 1999; Campos-Astorkiza, 2004), the harmonic bounding remains simply because long vowels are cross-linguistically marked.

The constraint $*V_O <_O \mu_\bullet$ (47) easily solves this opacity problem as shown in tableau (58). The problematic candidate (57-c)/(58-c) where the morphemic mora is associated with an underlyingly mora-less base vowel violates $*V_O <_O \mu_\bullet$ since the vowel is only dominated by a mora that bears another morphological colour. A possible repair that avoids a violation of $*V_O <_O \mu_\bullet$ is the insertion of an epenthetic mora as in candidate (58-d). In this winning structure, the final base vowel is dominated by a colourless mora and by a mora with a different morphological colour—the former ensures a morph-contiguous projection of prosodic nodes.

(58)   *Opaque μ-projection in OT: the effect of* $*V_O <_O \mu_\bullet$

$\mu_\bullet$ + $g_O \; i_O \; d_O \; a_O$	$*V_O <_O \mu_\bullet$	$V<DD_P^m <\mu$	$\mu>Do_P^m >V$	$CoL!_\mu$
c. $\mu \quad \mu_\bullet$ $g_O \; i_O \; d_O \; a_O$ [gi.da]	*!			*
☞ d. $\mu \quad \mu \; \mu_\bullet$ $g_O \; i_O \; d_O \; a_O$ [gi.daː]				**

Crucially now, opaque μ-projection is only required by $*V_O <_O \mu_\bullet$, a violable constraint. It is hence predicted that its effect can be overridden by higher-ranked constraints, most notably $CoL!_\mu$. In such a grammar, additive MLM triggered by affixation of a morphemic mora is predicted to affect only certain morphemes (=those with an underlying mora dominating the vowel in the scope of the morphological lengthening) while morphological lengthening is blocked in other morphological contexts (=where a vowel lacks a mora underlyingly). It is argued that this prediction is borne out and that languages exist where morphological lengthening is blocked for certain (lexically marked) morphological contexts. This is discussed in more detail in section 5.2 where the predictions of $*V_O <_O \mu_\bullet$ are investigated.

A related instance of opaque mora assignment in standard parallel OT has received considerably more theoretical interest, namely the opaque mora assignment in the context of compensatory lengthening (=CL). The standard view of CL as the preservation of a (coda or vowel) mora (Hayes, 1989) is notoriously hard to implement in a standard model of OT since moras on these elements are predictable and thus must not be underlyingly present. In (59) it is illustrated how mora assignment and CL interact in a rule-based account. The example is from Old French where /blazmer/ after consonant loss results in /blaːmer/ (Picard, 2004; Gess, 2011: 1514). Weight-by-position (Hyman, 1985; Zec, 1988; Rosenthall and van der Hulst, 1999) first assigns a mora to the coda consonants (59-2) and subsequent consonant deletion (59-3) then leaves the mora unassociated. In a next step (59-4), this otherwise floating mora is associated with the preceding vowel.[13]

(59) *Opaque μ-projection in CL contexts: a rule-based account*

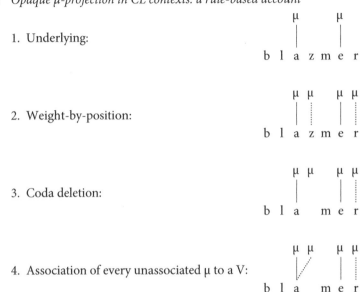

1. Underlying:

2. Weight-by-position:

3. Coda deletion:

4. Association of every unassociated μ to a V:

Again, such a derivation is highly problematic in standard parallel OT where any reference to intermediate steps such as (59-2) is impossible. Without such a reference, it remains mysterious why a consonant that is never realized on the surface projects a mora. Various analyses in different OT-frameworks have been proposed to account for the opacity of CL in OT: theories assuming some notion of intermediate derivation stages (for example the theory of enriched inputs (Sprouse, 1997), stratal OT (Kiparsky, 2011; Bermúdez-Otero, in preparation), the framework of Sympathy Theory (McCarthy, 2003*b*), OT-CC (McCarthy, 2007*c*; Shaw, 2009), or Harmonic Serialism (McCarthy, 2000*b*; Samko, 2011; Torres-Tamarit, 2012)), proposals that abandon the idea that CL is mora preservation (for example the assumption that CL is preservation of root nodes in Campos-Astorkiza (2003) or the preservation of segmental positions in Topintzi (2006, 2010)), through a concept of comparative faithfulness (Yun, 2006), and finally theories assuming Turbidity Theory (Goldrick, 2000). One of the main arguments for a containment-based system such as the one adopted throughout this book is in fact its ability to account for cases of opacity such as the ones sketched in (55) and (59) while maintaining a monostratal parallel system without any reference to intermediate derivation stages—a desired result given the original architecture of OT as a parallel system (Prince and Smolensky, 1993/2002). If a monostratal system is able to solve the opacity problem, it can therefore be taken as in principle superior to systems adopting some notion of ordered optimization.

---

[13] For ease of exposition, the short vowels are underlyingly associated with moras—these are phonologically predictable as well.

How this second area of opaque mora-projection also straightforwardly falls out in the present containment-based system is illustrated in (60) for the example in (59). The crucial insight is that a containment-based system predicts that elements that are not phonetically interpreted are still in the structure and can cause constraint violations. Phonologically predictable moras can consequently be required to dominate segments that remain phonetically unrealized. If the moras are in addition forced to dominate some segment in a phonetically visible way, CL is predicted. In the tableau (60) below, C<DD<μ demands that every consonant must be dominated by a mora.[14] Crucially now, this includes the 'coda' consonant /z/ although it remains unrealized on the surface, excluding candidate (60-a). Since the consonant must remain phonetically invisible, the association line linking the consonant to a mora is phonetically invisible. The constraint C<DD<μ is nevertheless satisfied since it only requires *some* association relation between a consonant and a mora. And if this additional mora is in the structure, $\mu>Do_p^m>S$ demands that it must dominate some segment in a phonetically visible way as well. Note that the tableau only illustrates the general logic and does not include a trigger for the consonant loss.[15]

(60)   *Opaque CL in containment-based OT*

		$*\mu\text{-Ons}$	Onset!	$\mu>Do_p^m>S$	C<DD<μ	$*\mu\text{......}S$
	μ μ │ │ b l a z m e r					
a.	μ μ μ │ │ ┊ b l a z m e r				****!	*
b.	μ μ μ μ │ ╪ │ ┊ b l a z m e r			*!	***	**
☞ c.	μ μ μ μ │╱╪ │ ┊ b l a z m e r				***	***

---

[14] This implementation of weight by position requires further mechanisms ensuring that not *all* consonants project moras: this simply follows from the joint effect of Onset! and *μ-Ons ensuring that consonants are preferably syllabified as onsets that are non-moraic.

[15] The process in fact is diachronic. Actually much of the data often discussed in the context of CL is diachronic. An example is the typology of CL in Gess (2011) where synchronic and diachronic instances of CL are not distinguished—a possible problem if one aims to base a theoretical discussion on this empirical data set since only synchronic processes are relevant for a theory about existing grammars (see also Topintzi, 2012).

This analysis actually mirrors the essential parts of the analysis that Goldrick (2000) gives for CL in Luganda in Turbidity Theory (see section 2.2.2 and especially (23) for a discussion on Turbidity Theory and the departures from it in the present system). This straightforward solution for a well-known opacity problem in standard parallel OT is taken as a strong independent argument for the assumption of containment.

2.2.5 Excursus II: copying as phonological repair operation

Although reduplication as MLM on its own is excluded from the present discussion (see section 1.1.3), several instances of reduplication are still in the data sample and are discussed in this book simply because reduplication sometimes alternates phonologically predictably with other MLM operations. Since it is assumed that phonologically predictable allomorphy results from affixing one exponent, the formal implementation of reduplication is highly relevant for the following theoretical discussion since it needs to be shown how one exponent is realized via a Long-Short Alternation in one context and via reduplication in other contexts.

Copying or 'reduplication' is taken to be a general phonological repair process comparable to epenthesis or deletion, a view explicitly proposed and discussed in the theory of Minimal Reduplication (Saba Kirchner, 2013, 2010). An alternative view is one where morphological copying and phonological 'echo-epenthesis' are argued to result from crucially different mechanisms (see, for example, Kawahara (2007)). In contrast, copying is taken to be one strategy to avoid marked structures that can result from phonological operations[16] or morphological concatenation in the theory of Minimal Reduplication. The latter case is what is called 'morphological reduplication' in Saba Kirchner (2010): it applies in the presence of empty prosodic nodes (=a marked structure). In that respect, the proposal is in fact very similar to the original proposal by Marantz (1982) that already emphasizes that reduplication pattens are 'normal affixation processes' (Marantz, 1982: 436). The reduplication affixes only lack segmental features and hence the base 'lends' its phonemic material to fill this otherwise empty structure. This is exactly the same general principle that underlies the theory of morphological reduplication in the theory of Minimal Reduplication. That empty skeletal positions as one possible representation for a reduplication-triggering morpheme are assumed in Marantz (1982) where Minimal Reduplication theory only assumes empty prosodic nodes, is not a crucial architectural difference and does not change the general logic of the account where reduplication fills the otherwise empty structure.

However, one important difference that sets the original proposal in Marantz (1982) and the Minimal Reduplication theory apart is that the former assumes that 'the only mechanism available to morphological theory to lend the stem's phonemic melody

---

[16] A process termed 'compensatory reduplication' or 'phonologically-driven reduplication' (see, for example, Yu, 2004: and references cited therein).

to a reduplicating affix is the copying "over" the reduplicating affix of the entire phonemic melody of the stem' (Marantz, 1982: 445). This is a very important difference since it excludes that the affixed (defective) material can be filled with anything but copied segments. Segmental lengthening or epenthesis can hence not be triggered by the very same mechanism of prosodic node affixation. In fact, one main empirical argument for the theory of Minimal Reduplication is the existence of languages where copying alternates with other types of non-concatenative exponence. An example is the continuative formation in Upriver Halkomelem where the non-continuative form of verbs is marked via reduplication, vowel lengthening, epenthesis, or stress shift (see section 5.3.1). Other examples can be found in Hiaki (Molina, 1999; Haugen, 2005, 2008; Harley and Leyva, 2009; Saba Kirchner, 2010), Kwak'wala (Saba Kirchner, 2010; Bermúdez-Otero, 2012), or Afar (Bye and Svenonius, 2012) where copying of segments alternates predictably with epenthesis. The theory of Minimal Reduplication straightforwardly predicts such patterns since the empty prosodic structure is not bound to a specific repair such as copying: it simply must be filled with segmental content and the languages choose between the different strategies the phonology employs to provide additional material in a specific phonological context. These patterns where reduplication alternates predictably with other strategies to supply additional prosodic weight are not only problematic for the original account in Marantz (1982) but also for the standard OT-account for reduplication that is based on an abstract empty RED morpheme and Faith-BR constraints ensuring identity between base and reduplicant (McCarthy and Prince, 1995). As Saba Kirchner (2010) puts it, reduplication in these accounts is seen as a 'phonological goal' which 'makes it difficult to account for cases where a single morpheme triggers reduplication in some words, but some other processes in other words' (p. 112).

A second main argument for the unified theory of Minimal Reduplication is its theoretical economy and elegance by abandoning any phonological mechanisms specific to a certain morphological process.[17] The only necessary assumption is the existence of prosodic nodes as representations for morphemes and copying as one phonological strategy to fill these nodes with segmental material.

The theoretical implementation of copying in containment theory adopted here is taken to be based on an operation that creates identical copies of segments. The only information that is not copied is the morphological affiliation. Copying hence introduces elements that were not underlyingly present and are colourless. Any change in the copied portion consequently violates standard constraints preserving underlying phonological structure. That base and reduplicant are similar/identical is hence a necessary consequence since they are identical instances of underlying elements. The

---

[17] An example for such an arbitrary mechanism is the standard correspondence-theoretic mysterious RED morpheme that triggers reduplication by establishing a new correspondence relation between base and reduplicant (McCarthy and Prince, 1995).

original segment and its copied counterpart are assumed to be linked by a structural relation that allows us to count the distance between the two. It is proposed that this relation is in fact a horizontal association line that links segments in a string. The inventory of possible association relations is hence enriched to include associations between elements on the same tier. In the present containment-theoretic system where inserted association lines that remain invisible for the phonetic interpretation exist for independent reasons, such an abstract relation is easily possible. Copying is hence different from epenthesis since the new colourless elements are associated to another segment via a horizontal association line. In the illustrating example in (61), copying applies to realize a morphemic mora. In the following, the simplified notation in (61-b) is used for copied elements.

(61) *Simplified notation for elements licensed by OO correspondence*
   a. *Copying introduces horizontal association lines*   b. *Abbreviated as:*

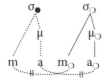

The constraints penalizing epenthesis and copying are taken to be in a Paninian relationship: COL!$_S$ in (36) (repeated in (62-a)) requires that segments bear a morphological colour (=they are neither inserted nor copied) and LIC!$_S$ in (62-b) requires that segments are either morphologically coloured or are linked to another output segment (=they are not epenthetic).[18] The constraint penalizing copying as an operation manipulating the phonological structure is the constraint (62-c) penalizing segments linked via phonetically invisible association lines. Locality restrictions for copying (for an overview see, for example, Kawahara (2004)) follow easily in such a system from constraints against segments crossed by association lines ('Assign a violation mark for every segment x that is preceded by segment y and followed by segment z and y and z are associated.'). This mechanism of vertical association is conceptually similar to string-internal correspondence argued for in Walker (2000a), Walker (2000c), and Hansson (2001).

(62) a. COL!$_S$ Assign a violation mark for every segment not licensed by morphological colour.

   b. LIC!$_S$ Assign a violation mark for every segment neither licensed by morphological colour nor by association to another segment.

   c. *▢   Assign a violation mark for every pair of segments x and y that are associated via a phonetically invisible association line.

---

[18] The two constraints are hence not ranked with respect to each other in most tableaux. Only indirect ranking arguments are possible between constraints in a stringency relation since they never conflict with each other (McCarthy, 2008a: 65–67).

2.2.6 *The linearization of morphemic prosodic nodes*

The central claim in this book is that MLM results from affixation of prosodically defective morphemes and that this has major consequences for the question of where in the word an MLM operation is expected.

In the domain of segmental affixes, the theoretical analyses about the placement of morphemes can be roughly distinguished between two major theories:[19] *Phonological Dislocation* and *Morphological Pivot Affixation*. Approaches assuming phonological dislocation take it for granted that affixes are prefixed or suffixed to a base but may dislocate from this edge position inside their base to optimize the phonological structure (Moravcsik, 1977; Prince and Smolensky, 1993/2002; Stemberger and Bernhardt, 1998; Halle, 2003; Horwood, 2002; Klein, 2005). Although some infixation patterns indeed optimize the phonological structure and hence follow naturally under a phonological dislocation account, there are a number of striking counterexamples to the claim that dislocation is phonologically optimizing (for a discussion see, for example Fitzpatrick, to appear; Yu, 2007; Inkelas, 2014). The alternative is to reject any phonological dislocation for affixes. This strong claim is made in the Morphological Pivot Affixation theory (Yu, 2002, 2007) where it is assumed that infixation as a situation where an affix is realized inside its base follows since affixes are prefixed or suffixed to specific base positions (='pivots') and these pivots are potentially inside the base. A crucial feature of pivot theories is that the set of pivots is strictly limited. The exhaustive list of pivots that are assumed in Yu (2007) is given in (63) (for a slightly different inventory of anchor points see Fitzpatrick, to appear).

(63)   *Possible pivots for segmental affixes*   (Yu, 2007)
   a. **Initial pivot**
      (i)   First consonant/onset
      (ii)   First vowel/nucleus
      (iii) First syllable

   b. **Final pivot**
      (i)   Final vowel/nucleus
      (ii)   Final syllable

   c. **Prominence pivot**
      (i)   Stressed syllable
      (ii)   Stressed vowel/nucleus

In addition, it is explicitly assumed that affixes cannot be dislocated to optimize the phonological structure, an assumption that is in principle independent from the pivot affixation claim. In Yu (2003), generalized alignment constraints formalize the linearization subcategorization requirements of affixes and the universal fixed ranking

---

[19] The following summary is based on the discussion in Zimmermann and Trommer (2013).

hierarchy M ≫ P stating that no phonological (markedness) constraint may ever outrank those morphological constraints implements that phonological dislocation is impossible. In Yu (2007), generalized alignment constraints are assumed inside sign-based morphology: the subcategorization requirements of morphemes are part of the sign and hence inviolable.

The empirical survey in this book confirms that the landing sites for morphemic prosodic nodes triggering length-manipulation are restricted in a way absolutely parallel to segmental affixes and show a strong edge-bias. This parallel behaviour of segmental affixes and morphemic prosodic nodes is expected from a diachronic per-spective given the fact that many instances of morphemic prosodic nodes originated from purely segmental affixes. In Arbizu Basque (Hualde, 1990, 1991; van de Weijer, 1992; Artiagoitia, 1993; Hualde and Ortiz de Urbina, 2003; Hualde, 2012), for example, an Addition pattern in the future (/esan/ → /esaːn/ 'say' (Fᴜᴛ), (Hualde, 1990: 285)) can diachronically be explained as the result of regular intervocalic consonant loss after suffixation (/esanen/ → /esaen/) and subsequent total vowel assimilation of the adjacent non-identical vowel. This interpretation receives support from neighbouring dialects where apparent intermediate stages of this development are attested (e.g. /esain/ Hualde, 1990). Similarly, in Lango (Noonan, 1992; Okello, 2003), several vowel-initial morphemes trigger gemination of a preceding consonant (/gwôk/ → /gwôk: à lótɕə̀ 'the man's dog' (Noonan, 1992: 154, 156)) that historically were consonant-initial and gemination resulted from cluster simplification; a productive process that is still active in Lango. However, the historical origin of MLM is not discussed in this book, mostly because it is irrelevant for the language learner who has no access to these facts. That only a limited set of possible landing sites for prosodic affixes are available must hence be hard wired into the grammar.

As was already discussed in 2.1.1, hardly any of the alternative accounts to length-manipulation facts based on mora affixation aim to derive locality restrictions. This is mainly due to the simple fact that most of the analyses only deal with one or several related instances of MLM and no general claim about existing patterns is made. A first general account about the linearization of mora affixes is made in Zimmermann and Trommer (2013) where Yu's pivot affixation theory is extended to mora affixation in a stratal OT system.

In contrast, the linearization theory put forth here is implemented in a parallel system acknowledging the fact that certain bases may lack underlying prosodic structure. The two basic assumptions are that, *first*, GEN is restricted by the principle demanding that the underlying order of morphemes must be recoverable on all tiers of the phonological representation and that, *second*, every affix may contain a morphemic colour index. As is argued below, these assumptions allow a unified account for the restricted possibilities of segmental and non-segmental affixes to be realized in/affect non-edge positions of their base. The theory hence captures the empirical observation that all types of affixes are always realized in a fixed position with respect to their base and are only realized in a very limited set of possible base positions that can roughly be characterized with an edge bias.

Before we turn to the theoretical implementation of morpheme linearization, let's briefly concentrate on the challenge posed for morpheme linearization in a parallel OT-model as soon as morphemic prosodic nodes are taken into account, not only segmental affixes. Consider the example in (64) where the morphemic mora in Gidabal is suffixed to a base that underlyingly lacks any moras. It was argued above in (58) that high-ranked $*V_O <_O \mu_\bullet$ could ensure in the present system that every base vowel projects an epenthetic mora in this case in order to ensure morph-contiguous prosodic structure. However, this only ensures that some vowel is lengthened in such a configuration, it is not clear *which* vowel is lengthened. One of the inherent principles (and advantages) of autosegmental phonology is the fact that elements are only ordered to elements on the same tier. For our example, this means that a suffixed mora is linearly ordered to all elements on the moraic tier but if there are no other elements underlyingly on its tier, it cannot violate any linearization statements and nothing can favour the structure (64-a) over (64-b). The structure in (64-b) does not involve any 'reordering' that is inherently impossible in containment, but insertion of epenthetic elements.

(64) *Mora suffixation in Gidabal*

Input		Candidates

In a derivational OT system like stratal OT (Kiparsky, 2000; Bermúdez-Otero, in preparation), this problem can be solved. In Egalitarian Stratal OT (Trommer, 2011a; Bermúdez-Otero, in preparation), it is assumed that all independent morphological objects (=not part of other morphological objects) undergo phonological evaluation at every stratum (Trommer, 2011a: 72). Crucially, this includes an evaluation of the lexical array, hence of all morphemes prior to morphological concatenation. In Gidabal, for example, this pre-optimization step would ensure that all morphemes are equipped with moras at the point where a mora affix is added. A 'suffixed' affix mora can therefore be forced to follow all base moras.

In contrast, a solution couched in a parallel OT model is proposed here. Two terms need to be defined before the theoretical implementation for morpheme linearization is given. In the following, *morpheme* refers to a meaning paired with n exponents and *exponent* refers to a phonological representation that is marked for being a prefix or a suffix and the possibility to be marked for a certain lexical class. Given this definition, every morpheme can consist of more than one exponent. Either different exponents can be marked for attaching to different classes of morphemes (=lexically marked allomorphy) or exponents differ in being a suffix or a prefix and cooccur (=extended exponence). A straightforward instance of the latter are circumfixes as, for example, the German past participle formation that involves prefixing /gə—/ and suffixing /—t/ for several verbs (/maxn̩/ → /gəmaxt/ 'make' (Hall, 2000: 542)). Given this definition, phonologically predictable allomorphy is taken to result from one single exponent whose surface realization is determined by the general phonological processes and requirements of the language.

(65)   a. *Morpheme*
          A meaning paired with a set S of n exponents where different members of S
          are either
          (i)   marked for different lexical classes
          or
          (ii)   marked for different base edges (prefix or suffix).

       b. *Exponent*
          A set S of phonological elements p_a, p_b, . . ., p_x that all share the same
          morphological colour and where all pairs p_a and p_b (in S) on the same tier
          are ordered to each other.

An important part of the definition of exponent in (65) is that all phonological elements that are part of this exponent and are on the same phonological tier, are ordered to each other. Given the containment-based system adopted here, reordering of phonological elements is generally impossible. In containment, 'there is no way to mark that two segments have changed their order' (van Oostendorp, 2006: 20)[20] and phonological elements that precede/follow each other underlyingly must preserve this order in the phonology. The first generalization that phonological dislocation is generally impossible is hence in principle already implicit in the theoretical framework. The second step in determining the absolute order of phonological elements follows from the order of morphological exponents with respect to each other. Given that all exponents are either prefixed or suffixed to their base (65-a), they are hence ordered with respect to the morpheme that immediately follows (for a prefix) or precedes them (for a suffix). The abstract morphological structure in (66-a) where two prefixes and suffixes are added to a stem hence corresponds to the ordering relations

---

[20] All surface 'reorderings' must therefore be a product of non-parsing and insertion. See Zimmermann (2009) for a detailed discussion of metathesis and containment.

in (66-b): prefix$_1$ precedes stem$_x$, suffix$_1$ follows stem$_x$, prefix$_2$ precedes prefix$_1$, and suffix$_2$ follows suffix$_1$.

(66)   *Order of exponents with respect to their base*
    a. Prfx$_2$– Prfx$_1$– stem$_x$ –Sfx$_1$ –Sfx$_2$
    b. M$_1$ ≪ M$_2$ ≪ M$_3$ ≫ M$_4$ ≫ M$_5$

It is crucial to note that the linearity conditions discussed so far do not yet imply an ordering between phonological elements on the same tier that belong to different exponents. This ordering is taken to be restricted by the RMO (67) that ensures that the order of phonological elements on the prosodic and segmental tier reflect the order of exponents while still allowing a minimal amount of interleaving at exponent edges. The RMO crucially relies on the notion that elements 'reflect' exponents. For one, every element that is part of the underlying representation of an exponent, hence bears its affiliation, trivially reflects this exponent. In addition, elements also reflect the morphological colour of all elements they dominate.

(67)   *Restriction on GEN:* RecoverableMorphemeOrderCondition
    (=RMO)
    The order of two exponents must be recoverable on all tiers.
    a. A prosodic node **reflects** a exponent $_\bigcirc$ iff it bears morphological colour $_\bigcirc$ or it dominates an element that bears morphological colour $_\bigcirc$.
    b. Exponent order M$_\bigcirc$ ≪ M$_\bullet$ (M$_\bigcirc$ precedes M$_\bullet$) is **recoverable** on tier n iff there is no element P on tier n that reflects M$_\bigcirc$ and follows an element Q on tier n that reflects M$_\bullet$ but not M$_\bigcirc$.
    c. Exponent order M$_\bigcirc$ ≫ M$_\bullet$ (M$_\bullet$ follows M$_\bigcirc$) is **recoverable** on tier n iff there is no element R on tier n that reflects M$_\bullet$ and precedes an element S on tier n that reflects M$_\bigcirc$ but not M$_\bullet$.

The principle hence demands that no portion of a prefix must follow an element of its base (67-a) and no portion of a suffix must precede an element of its base (67-b). The consequences of this restriction are illustrated in (68) with some possible and impossible structures given the exponent order M$_\bigcirc$ ≫ M$_\bullet$, hence an instance of suffixed exponent M$_\bullet$. In order to ease the readability, the morphological colours that are reflected by each prosodic node are listed underneath it within small boxes. On the segmental tier, the order M$_\bigcirc$ ≫ M$_\bullet$ is reflected in all configurations since all segments affiliated with M$_\bigcirc$ always precede all segments affiliated with M$_\bullet$. In (68-a), the morphemic mora affiliated with exponent M$_\bullet$ is associated with the final base vowel. The penultimate mora hence reflects the morphological colour of exponent M$_\bigcirc$ and M$_\bullet$ since it bears the latter underlyingly and dominates a segment that is affiliated with the former. The order M$_\bigcirc$ ≫ M$_\bullet$ is reflected on all tiers. In (68-b), the morphemic mora dominates an epenthetic element and hence only reflects the affix colour M$_\bullet$. It is not followed by any mora reflecting exponent $M_\bigcirc$ and hence no problem for the $\mathbb{RMO}$ arises. In (68-c), a morphemic mora affiliated with exponent $M_\bullet$ is associated with the final vowel of the base and precedes the final base mora. This morphemic mora reflects the exponents $M_\bigcirc$ and $M_\bullet$ since it is affiliated with the latter and dominates segments affiliated with the former. The final base mora, on the other hand, only reflects exponent $M_\bigcirc$ since it is affiliated with this exponent and only dominates segments associated with this same exponent as well. This is hence an instance where an element only reflecting $M_\bullet$ precedes an element only reflecting $M_\bigcirc$ and is consequently illicit given the exponent order $M_\bigcirc \gg M_\bullet$ and the $\mathbb{RMO}$. In (68-d), the morphemic mora affiliated with $M_\bullet$ dominates an epenthetic segment and hence only reflects exponent $M_\bullet$. Since it is followed by a base mora that only dominates segments affiliated with $M_\bigcirc$, another structure excluded by the $\mathbb{RMO}$ arises.

(68)   *Exponent order: $M_\bigcirc \gg M_\bullet$*

    a. *Possible vowel lengthening*

    c. *Impossible vowel lengthening*

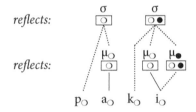

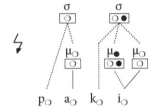

    b. *Possible C-epenthesis*

    d. *Impossible C-epenthesis*

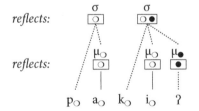

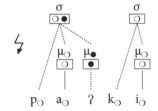

Note that the definition in (67) is not defined exclusively over phonetically visible association lines. The restriction is hence also crucial for morphemic prosodic nodes that are only associated with their base by a phonetically invisible association relation, more concretely defectively integrated morphemic prosodic nodes.

So far, the assumption of the $\mathbb{RMO}$ (67) prohibits any infixation for morphemic prosodic nodes and ensures that they can only be realized at the edge of their base. This assumption is obviously too restrictive. Not only is the effect of infixation well attested for segmental affixes (see the discussion above), it will become clear in the empirical discussion of MLM throughout this book that morphemic prosodic nodes can be 'infixing' as well. The crucial assumption that allows a restricted ability of being realized 'inside' another exponent follows from the assumption of colour indices.

A colour index is assumed to be an abstract element in the phonological representation that only and exclusively consists of morphological affiliation information on a specific phonological tier. If it is part of the representation of an exponent, it basically functions as a placeholder for a phonological element on this tier. Colour indices are morphological information and hence uninterpretable for the phonology. It is thus an inviolable restriction on GEN that it cannot generate a structure with an empty colour index. The only strategy available to GEN to get rid of empty colour indices is the operation of index fusion, defined in (69). An empty colour index can only and exclusively fuse with an element on the same tier. This might potentially result in an element with two morphological affiliations.

(69) *An operation in GEN: Index fusion*
Every empty colour index $_\bigcirc$ must fuse with an element on the same tier:
$X_\bullet + _\bigcirc \rightarrow X_{\bigcirc\bullet}$

The existence of colour indices and the mechanism of colour fusion extends the possible landing sites for affixes as is illustrated in (70) for a morphemic mora. A morphemic mora with an additional colour index that is suffixed to its base is predicted to be realized in an 'infixing' position preceding the final mora dominating base material. The final base mora undergoes index fusion and bears now the two colour indices of both exponents $M_\bigcirc$ and $M_\bullet$. From this it follows that the exponent order $M_\bigcirc \gg M_\bullet$ is reflected on the moraic tier although the affix mora is not realized as the final mora of the resulting word. The structures (70-c, d) are illustrations for impossible structures. In (70-c), the morphemic mora is realized in a position too far away from its edge and one mora only dominating stem material and hence reflecting only $M_\bigcirc$ follows the affix mora. In (70-d), index fusion has failed to take place. Since colour indices are not interpretable for the phonology, this structure is also illicit.

(70) *Exponent order: $M_\bigcirc \gg M_\bullet$*
Input

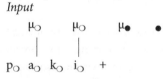

a. *Possible vowel lengthening*   c. *Impossible vowel lengthening*

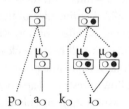   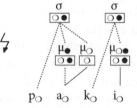

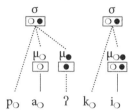

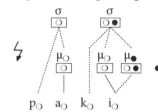

The assumption of colour indices as elements in the phonological representation is an apparently major departure from Consistency of Exponence, namely the assumption that elements can not change their morphological affiliation (McCarthy and Prince, 1993*b*, 1994*a*). There have been claims that consistency of exponence is indeed violable in, for example, Walker and Feng (2004) and Lubowicz (2010). However, it has to be emphasized that the existence of colour indices does not at all imply that GEN can freely change the morphological affiliation of phonological elements. It simply enriches the inventory of phonological objects with a morphological affiliation without a phonological object.

Consistency of exponence is particularly important for theories relying on a version of REALIZEMORPHEME that demands that some phonological element of a morpheme must be realized in the output (van Oostendorp, 2007*a*). Such a constraint is in fact obsolete in the theory of PDM since all its effects are predicted from constraints demanding realization and hence prosodic integration of phonological elements.

One constraint for which the existence of colour indices has major consequences is ALTERNATION. An element that undergoes index fusion is now affiliated with this morphological colour and hence an association to elements with the same morphemic affiliation induces a violation of ALTERNATION. This in fact can mirror the effects of affixing two morphemic prosodic nodes of the same type (i.e. $/-\mu_{oo}/$ instead of $/-\mu_o$ $\mu_o/$)—a prediction that is undoubtedly borne out. A more subtle and very interesting prediction arising for the linearization of morphemic nodes as a result of additional ALTERNATION violations in the presence of a colour index is discussed in an analysis for Balangao in section 6.2.4.3.

And most crucially, colour indices are restricted by the principles in (71) allowing only one colour index at the edge of an exponent. These restrictions in fact replace the list of possible affixation pivots assumed in Yu (2007) or Fitzpatrick (to appear). They hence have no theory-internal motivation but are purely empirically motivated: they predict all and only the attested effects of exponent linearization observed on all tiers of the phonological representation.

(71) *Morphemic Colour Indices*
    a. Every exponent has maximally one colour index on the morphologically outwards edge.
       (=suffixing exponents can end in a colour index and prefixing exponents can begin with a colour index.)

b. A colour index must be licensed by a phonological element that directly precedes or follows it on the same tier.

c. Colour indices are uninterpretable for the phonology.

In (70), it was shown how a morphemic mora with such a colour index can result in an infixing mora that is realized as the penultimate mora of its base.

In (72), it is shown how some of the infixation patterns discussed in Yu (2007) for segmental affixes result from colour indices in the morpheme representation. Interestingly, the segmental pivots for infixation in Yu (2007) are always specified for being a consonant or a vowel. Affixation can hence target the initial or final vowel but never simply the initial or final segment. For the colour index approach, it is hence assumed that 'segmental' colour indices exist on the C-place or V-place tier as in (72). The $\mathbb{RMO}$ is taken to evaluate all possible (sub-)segmental tiers and if the exponent order is recoverable on at least one, the principle is satisfied. Infixation after the first consonant in, for example, Mlabri (Yu, 2007) hence follows if a colour index exists on the C-place tier that fuses with the C-place node of the initial base consonant (72-a). That the exponent order is reflected on the (sub-)segmental C-place tier is sufficient to satisfy the $\mathbb{RMO}$. It is clear that no problem for the $\mathbb{RMO}$ arises on higher prosodic tiers since the prosodic nodes reflect the morphemic affiliation of all the elements they dominate. The initial syllable, for example, hence reflects both morpheme colours $M_{\bigcirc}$ and $M_{\bullet}$. It is interesting that many of the infixation patterns that illustrate the set of affix pivots in Yu (2007) are instances of reduplication. For the colour index theory advocated here, copying on the segmental level does not create a potential problem for the $\mathbb{RMO}$ simply because the copied segments have no morphemic colour on their own (see the discussion in section 2.2.5).

Infixing reduplication is hence in most cases simply analysable as affixation of morphemic prosodic nodes that are potentially followed or preceded by a colour index. An example is infixing CV-reduplication in Ineseño Chumash (72-b) that surfaces before the final syllable in (one possible) analysis given in Yu (2007). The exponent in question is assumed to be prefixed to its base and to consist of a morphemic syllable followed by a colour index on the syllable tier. This colour index fuses with the final syllable dominating base material (either an underlying syllable or an epenthetic one as in (72-b)) which hence reflects the exponents $M_{\bigcirc}$ and $M_{\bullet}$. The affix syllable is realized preceding this syllable and segments are copied in order to fill the morphemic syllable node with segmental material. Since these copied segments do not bear any morphological colour, this syllable only reflects the morpheme colour $M_{\bullet}$. Since it is not followed by a syllable node that exclusively reflects the stem exponent $M_{\bigcirc}$, the structure is perfectly licit for the $\mathbb{RMO}$.[21]

---

[21] The containment-based system also allows that affixes have underlying nodes on tiers that will remain phonetically unrealized but ensures that the exponent order is recoverable in the phonological structure. The segmental infixation in Alabama cited in Yu (2007), for example, involves infixation of a

(72) *Segmental infixation and colour indices*
  a. *Pivot: Suffix to the first consonant (e.g. Mlabri)*

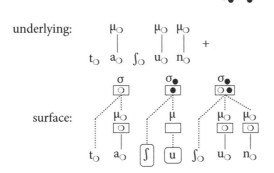

The illustrations in (72) show that the colour index approach is well-suited for infixation patterns where one phonological element on a tier is 'skipped' by an affix. However, Yu (2007) also lists infixation patterns where the parts 'skipped' by the infix are variable. This holds, for example, for affixes that are realized before the first vowel as in Toratan agent voice formation /empo/ → /m–empo/ 'sit' and /lompuq/ → /l–um–ompuq/ 'go out' (Yu, 2007: 92). A colour index on the C-place tier could account for the infixation in /l–um–ompuq/ but not for the initial realization in /m–empo/ where the colour index has no chance to fuse with a consonant since none precedes the initial base vowel. Fusion of the putative consonantal colour index with the second base consonant is impossible given that this would result in either exponent-internal reordering of the colour index or a structure violating the RMO. A last resort option must hence be that a colour index can fuse with the licensing phonological element following/preceding it. This repair is then taken to violate an OT-constraint against two identical morphological affiliations on one element.

consonantal affix /l/ after the first vowel. In the colour index approach, such a pattern is only possible if the affix contains a colour index on the V-place tier—which in turn involves a V-place node dominating the consonant. In containment theory, this V-place node will always remain in the phonological structure even if straightforward constraints about possible feature combinations will ensure that this node is never phonetically realized.

Attested patterns of prefixation to the initial vowel face an even more serious problem. Future research will show whether all the segmental infixation patterns discussed in Yu (2007) can successfully be reanalysed via colour indices or whether different mechanisms are necessary to account for segmental and non-segmental infixation. The aim of this book is primarily a theoretical claim about the linearization of non-segmental affixes. For those, it is argued in detail in chapter 6, the predictions made by the colour index approach and the $\mathbb{R}\mathbb{M}\mathbb{O}$ restricts the predicted patterns successfully to the attested instances of MLM.

2.2.7 *Putting the pieces together: the predictions of PDM*

To sum up the preceding discussion, (73) lists all operations that are possible in GEN.

(73)   *GEN can* ...
      a. ... mark association lines as phonetically invisible.
      b. ... insert colourless association lines.
      c. ... insert colourless phonological elements.
      d. ... copy underlying phonological elements.
      e. ... fuse colour indices on tier n with elements on tier n.

In addition, GEN is negatively restricted since the resulting candidates may not violate the restrictions in (74).

(74)   *GEN cannot create structures* ...
      a. ... that do not obey the $\mathbb{N}\mathbb{o}\mathbb{C}\mathbb{r}$, see (30).
      b. ... that do not obey the $\mathbb{N}\mathbb{K}\mathbb{K}$, see (31).
      c. ... that do not obey the $\mathbb{R}\mathbb{M}\mathbb{O}$, see (67).
      d. ... that contain a coloured index, see (71).

In this section, a first abstract overview of the configurations predicted in an OT system based on the assumptions discussed so far are given. The theory of PDM is crucially based on the claim that structures can be prosodically defective. It follows from Richness of the Base that prosodically defective structures are possible inputs. Furthermore, given the definition of 'prosodically defective' above, in fact nearly every morpheme representation assumed is prosodically defective. The interesting claim pursued here is simply that some of the prosodic structure that an input representation lacks or has too much can have (length-manipulating) effects on the surface structure. And that structures can be prosodically defective in the output is another necessary consequence of an OT system and the simple fact that the constraints ensuring prosodic layering are violable. In the OT system adopted here, two assumptions even increase the possibilities of defective output structures: *first*, the parsing constraints demanding prosodic layering are bidirectional (see (28)/(29)), and, *second*, the assumption of containment and the adoption of three markedness levels of prosodic integration (22).

The tableau (75) illustrates the possible relations between prosodically complete/defective underlying forms and resulting surface structures for the level syllable—mora—segment.[22] Two prosodically complete morphological structures (75-i, iii) and three underlyingly prosodically defective structures (75-ii, iv, v) are given and their possible mappings to different surface forms. They all employ different violation profiles with respect to the parsing constraints demanding that a mora must dominate a vowel and the constraints penalizing insertion and non-realization of association lines between a mora and a vowel.

(75) *Complete and defective prosodic output structures (no competition!)*

underlying	surface		$\mu > Do_P > S$	$\mu > Do_P^m > S$	$\mu > Do > S$	$*\mu \cdots S$	$*\mu \!-\!\!\!+\! S$
i. complete	→ complete	σ|μ|V					
ii. defective	→ complete	σ|μ⋯V				*	
iii. complete	→ defective	σ|μ‡V	*				*
iv. defective	→ defective	σ|μ‡V	*	*		*	
v. defective	→ defective	σ|μ	*	*	*		

---

[22] This illustration simplifies matters since only prosodic nodes up to the syllable level are given. Although we know the that the syllable is properly integrated under the highest prosodic node (=since it is phonetically visible), higher prosodic nodes could very well be defectively integrated.

Note that this is not a proper OT-tableau but a mere summary of constraint violations: these output structures cannot be generated from the same input since they have different morphological structures. In (75-i) and (75-ii), all three types of parsing constraints are satisfied and hence these are examples of complete prosodic structures in the output. The vowel and the mora in (75-i) are underlyingly associated and phonetically visible in the output and in (75-ii), a phonetically visible association line is inserted to link the mora to a vowel. In (75-iii), a morphological association line between the mora and a vowel is marked as phonetically invisible under violation of $*\mu \dashv\!\!\!- S$ and $\mu > Do_p > S$ and in (75-iv), an inserted association line between the mora and a vowel is marked as phonetically invisible under violation of $*\mu \cdots\cdots S$, $m > Do_p > S$, and $\mu > Do_p^m > S$. In (75-v), finally, no association line between the mora and a vowel is present and all three parsing constraints are violated.

The crucial interplay relevant for the (non-)repair of underlyingly prosodically defective structures is hence the one between the parsing constraint $X > Do_p > Y$ and the constraints penalizing insertion of epenthetic association lines. In the following, the most relevant prosodically defective morpheme representations are summarized and it is shown how they may result in different types of MLM. To highlight the fact that these configurations can in principle exist on all tiers of the prosodic hierarchy, the structures are illustrated with abstract symbols.

Full integration of morphemic prosodic nodes   The most relevant type of prosodically defective morpheme that results in MLM are morphemic prosodic nodes: prosodic nodes that lack an association to a higher and lower node underlyingly. The most straightforward effect of a morphemic prosodic node is its full integration in the prosodic structure of the base resulting in additive MLM, mirroring, for example, a standard mora affixation account as in (3). The tableau (76) shows that ranking $Ⓑ < DD_p^m < Ⓒ$ and $Ⓑ > Do_p^m > Ⓐ$ above the constraints penalizing epenthetic association lines $* Ⓒ \cdots\cdots Ⓑ$ and $* Ⓑ \cdots\cdots Ⓐ$ predict full phonetically visible integration of a morphemic node.

Defective integration of morphemic nodes   If now one or both of the constraints against epenthetic association lines is ranked above the corresponding parsing constraints demanding that the morphemic node must be dominated by a higher node and must itself dominate a lower node , then defective integration is predicted. Either an association with a lower node is missing (77) (termed 'hanging' in Trommer and Zimmermann, 2014) or an association with a higher prosodic node is missing (78) (termed 'drifting' in Trommer and Zimmermann, 2014). Candidates a. where the morphemic node remains completely unassociated are obviously 'defective', too. However, this structure does not make any interesting predictions for the surface interpretation. Since the morphemic node lacks any (phonetically interpretable or phonetically invisible) association relation to the prosodic structure, this structure is in principle not different from a structure where the morphemic prosodic node is absent.[23] It is consequently not discussed in the following. The prosodically defective surface structures predicted in (77) and (78), however, can have serious effects on the surface interpretation.

(76) *Full integration of prosodic nodes*

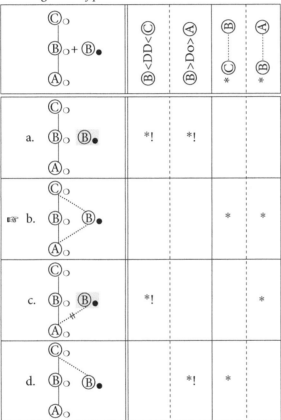

[23] The one exception can be found in the domain of tone. One standard representation for downstep is to assume a floating/completely unassociated L-tone between two H-tones (Pulleyblank, 1986; Paster and Kim, 2011). In the domain of length, however, autosegmental elements that are not integrated into the prosodic structure are not predicted to have any phonetic effect.

(77) *Defective integration I*

		B<DD<C	A ... *B	B>Do>A	B ... *C
	Cₒ / Bₒ + B / Aₒ				
a.	Cₒ / Bₒ (B•) / Aₒ	*!		*	
b.	Cₒ / Bₒ ⋯ B• / Aₒ		*!		*
c.	Cₒ / Bₒ ⋯ B• / Aₒ	*!	*!		
☞ d.	Cₒ ⋯ / Bₒ B• / Aₒ			*	*

(78) *Defective integration II*

		B<Do<A	B ... *C	B>DD>C	B ... *A
	Cₒ / Bₒ + B• / Aₒ				
a.	Cₒ / Bₒ (B•) / Aₒ	*!		*	
b.	Cₒ / Bₒ B• / Aₒ		*!		*
c.	Cₒ / Bₒ ⋯ B• / Aₒ			*	*
☞ d.	Cₒ ⋯ / Bₒ B / Aₒ	*!	*!		

Usurpation   In a usurpation grammar, the prosodically defective structure is a node on the lowest level of the hierarchy that lacks an association with a higher prosodic node. Since the parsing constraint $A<DD_p^m<B$ is undominated, an association with a higher prosodic node must be added. Interestingly now, the grammar could prevent that an epenthetic node is inserted with which the node can be associated. In (79), this alternative repair is prohibited by Col!ᵦ excluding candidate (79-b). The only chance that the node has to be dominated by a higher prosodic node could then be the insertion of an association line that links it to a higher prosodic node that was underlyingly present. And this association results in a structure where two lower prosodic nodes are associated with the same higher prosodic node, a configuration that must be repaired by marking the underlying association line to this higher node as invisible. The winning candidate in this 'usurpation' configuration is (79-c). A node n that lacks an underlying association with a higher node n+1 usurps this node from another element m that is associated with n+1 underlyingly. The relevant constraint penalizing the double association of one node with two lower nodes is assumed to be $*^\mu V^\mu$. In the following, usurpation is hence taken to be only possible for segments that usurp moras since $*^\mu V^\mu$ has no counterparts on higher prosodic levels.

(79) *Usurpation*

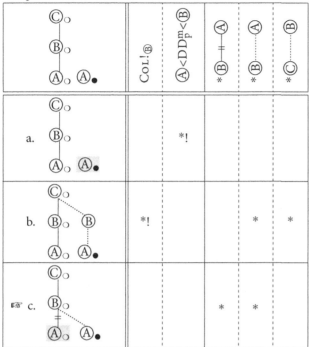

This briefly illustrates how the constraint system adopted here derives the basic configurations that might result in MLM. As was already mentioned above and illustrated in (18), combinations of these basic patterns are predicted to exist in languages as well. Throughout this book, various analyses are presented that show that the effects of these basic and combined patterns are indeed attested in the MLM patterns of the world.

The table (80) systematically summarizes where in the chapters 3 to 5 the major patterns of PDM are discussed. Three basic configurations are distinguished: the full integration of different morphemic prosodic nodes (80-1), defective integration of different morphemic nodes (80-2), and the lack of a prosodic node in the representation of a morpheme (80-3). A summarizing discussion with respect to the linearization of MLM patterns is given in chapter 6. A crucial assumption of the PDM account is that the prosodically defective morpheme representations are not restricted to a certain tier: morphemic prosodic feet and even prosodic word nodes are expected to exist as representations for morphemes. It is hard to imagine how the effect of the latter could result in a MLM that is not templatic, hence no analysis relying on the affixation of morphemic prosodic word nodes is discussed.[24]

(80)   *Prosodically defective morphemes in this book: overview*

1.	Full integration of a morphemic:		
		μ	Additive MLM: §5.1, §5.2, §5.3.3
			Exceptional non-undergoer: §4.1.2, §4.2
		σ	Additive MLM: §5.3.3, §6.2.4.3, §6.2.4.4
		Φ	Additive MLM (=non-concatenative allomorphy): §5.3
2.	Defective integration of a morphemic:		
		μ	Subtractive MLM: §3.2.1, §3.2.3
		σ	Subtractive MLM: §3.2.2, §3.2.3
3.	Morpheme underlyingly lacks a:		
		μ	Subtractive Affixation: §3.1
			Exceptions to additive MLM: §4.1.1, §5.2.2
		σ	Lexical allomorphy for subtractive MLM: §4.3

---

[24] That an effect very similar to the one predicted from morphemic prosodic word nodes indeed exists, was argued in Zimmermann and Trommer (2012) for the domain of blend formation. The crucial generalization about blend or portmanteau formation in Spanish is that the resulting new portmanteau word combines properties of two source words: the segmental structure of one source word and the prosodic structure (=length and stress) of the source word that is the morphological/semantic head of the construction (as in /pánsa/ 'belly' + /sàntaklós/ → /pànsaklós/ 'potbellied Santa Clause', (Zimmermann and Trommer, 2012: 235)). Such a pattern now follows if all segmental structure must be integrated under the prosodic structure of the morphological head of the construction—since there is not enough prosodic 'space' for all segmental material, deletion of segments results.

3

Subtractive MLM and Prosodically Defective Morphemes

Subtractive MLM can follow from two general mechanisms in the PDM framework: mora usurpation and defective integration of morphemic prosodic nodes. In section 3.1, the mechanism of mora usurpation is introduced and its predictions for the typology of MLM are discussed. It is shown how Subtractive Affixes can trigger mora usurpation that can result in all types of subtractive MLM operations: deletion or shortening for vowels or consonants and also phonologically predictable allomorphy between different subtractive MLM operations. Section 3.2 then turns to the second mechanism that predicts subtractive MLM, namely the defective prosodic integration of morphemic prosodic nodes. An especially interesting prediction of the proposed framework is the coexistence of additive and subtractive MLM in the same language. Such patterns and how they emerge in the theory of PDM are discussed in 3.2.2. Section 3.4 summarizes the analyses for subtractive MLM inside the framework of PDM.

3.1 Mora usurpation

The theory of PDM predicts a configuration best termed 'mora usurpation': an underlyingly mora-less vowel usurps the mora associated with a preceding segment and this segment in turn becomes shorter or phonetically invisible. In (1), a central usurpation configuration is illustrated: $V_\bullet$ underlyingly lacks a mora and associates to $\mu_\bigcirc$. Consequently, the underlying association of $V_\bigcirc$ to $\mu_\bigcirc$ is marked as phonetically invisible and hence the vowel remains unrealized since it lacks a phonetically visible prosodic integration. Vowel $V_\bullet$ can hence be said to have 'usurped' the mora and hence the prosodic integration of $V_\bigcirc$.

(1) *Mora usurpation*

$$\mu_\bigcirc \qquad\qquad\qquad \mu_\bigcirc$$

$$V_\bigcirc\ C_\bigcirc\ +\ V_\bullet \quad\rightarrow\quad V_\bigcirc\ C_\bigcirc\ V_\bullet$$

Morphological Length and Prosodically Defective Morphemes. First edition. Eva Zimmermann.
© Eva Zimmermann 2017. First published 2017 by Oxford University Press.

As is discussed in detail below, the prediction of mora usurpation is crucially bound to the assumption of containment and unexpected under a correspondence-theoretic OT system. It is shown in detail in the following subsections that mora usurpation patterns in different languages differ with respect to the question of whether only consonants, only vowels, or both segment types can be affected and whether segments can only be shortened, only be deleted, or both (in different contexts). The general mechanism of mora usurpation is introduced in a detailed case study of vowel deletion in Yine in section 3.1.1 before brief discussions of vowel shortening in Huallaga Quechua 3.1.2, degemination in Wolof 3.1.3, and alternation between vowel shortening and deletion in Hungarian 3.1.4 are added. All analyses of mora usurpation are summarized in 3.1.5.

3.1.1 *Vowel deletion in Yine*

Yine (formerly: Piro) is a Maipurean language[1] spoken mainly in the Peruvian Amazon by around 3,000 speakers (Urquía Sebastían and Marlett, 2008). The present investigation of the Yine facts is based mainly on the grammar by Matteson (1965), but also on Matteson (1954), Nies (1986), and the theoretical discussions in Lin (1987, 1993, 1997a, b, 2005) and Pater (2009). The relevant MLM in Yine is an instance of Subtractive Affixation and was already briefly introduced in section 1.1.2. Certain suffixes in the language trigger deletion of a preceding vowel that is unexpected from regular phonological processes of the language. In (2), it can be seen that every vowel that is predicted to precede such a Subtractive Suffix (=always underlined) is systematically absent[2] irrespective of whether this vowel is part of the stem (2-a) or a suffix (2-b).[3]

---

[1] The term 'Maipurean' (instead of 'Arawakan' that is used in the AUTOTYP classification (Bickel and Nichols, ongoing)) follows Payne (1991); Campbell (1997) and Urquía Sebastían and Marlett (2008) among others.

[2] There are additional interactions of the morpheme-specific vowel deletion with consonant deletion and compensatory lengthening that are ignored in the following. For one, three-consonant clusters are only possible as the result of prefixation in Yine but are illicit otherwise. If morpheme-specific vowel deletion is expected to create this illicit structure, the vowel deletion process is blocked and the Subtractive Suffixes are added without any surface effect (/terka−lu/ → /terkalu/ 'she washes it', (Matteson, 1965: 36)). In addition, consonant deletion applies whenever certain obstruents are expected to be adjacent. Vowel deletion sometimes feeds this consonant deletion process that in turn triggers compensatory lengthening (e.g. /nika−ka/ → /niːka/ 'he is eaten', (Matteson, 1965: 28)). For more details and literature see Zimmermann (2011) and Zimmermann (2013b) where an analysis for the interesting obstruent cluster restrictions and the interaction with opaque compensatory lengthening can be found respectively.

[3] Note that the sources for the Yine data do not always give a full segmentation into bare stem and all affixes. For example, the prefixes are not always marked as morphemes of their own.

(2) *One Subtractive Suffix: One vowel deletion…*   (Matteson, 1965; Pater, 2009)

a. *… of a stem vowel*

pawata—<u>maka</u>	pawatmaka	'I would have made a fire'	M74
neta—<u>ja</u>	netja	'I see there'	M36
neta—<u>lu</u>	netlu	'I see him'	M36
walapu—<u>ni</u>	walapni	'the past summer'	M97
çema—çe—ta	çemçeta	'to have never, never heard'	M79
ñomkañita—<u>ka</u>	ñomkañitka	'to be followed'	M80
ñeneka—<u>sa</u>	ñeneksa	'to distribute'	M88

b. *… of a suffix vowel*

meji—wa—<u>lu</u>	mejiwlu	'celebration'	P6
jona—ta—<u>na</u>—wa	jonatnawa	'to paint oneself'	P6
neta—nu—<u>lu</u>	netanru[4]	'I am going to see him'	M36
wujlaka—na—<u>lu</u>	wujlakanru	'we hit him'	M74
npinita—<u>maka</u>—lu	npinitmaklu	'I would have given medicine to him'	M74
rapnutja—pa—<u>no</u>	rapnutjapno	'in order that he repay me'	M74

The Subtractive Suffixes form an arbitrary class and have no obvious semantic or morpho-syntactic feature in common. In addition, no phonological property distinguishes these suffixes from suffixes that do not trigger vowel deletion in Yine. This is apparent since pairs of homophonous suffixes exist where one is a Subtractive Suffix and the other is not. Examples for this are given in (3). The data in (3-a) is particularly striking since not only are the two suffixes homonymous, but the two stems to which the different affixes attach are phonologically quite similar as well. Only the nominalizing suffix /—nu/ triggers deletion; the homophonous anticipatory suffix does not.

(3) *Subtractive Suffixes and homophonous suffixes*   (Matteson, 1965; Pater, 2009)

    a. i. hata—<u>nu</u>   hatnu   'light, shining'   P129
             shine—Nmlz

      ii. heta—nu   hetanu   'going to see'   P129
             see—Ant

    b. i. homkahita—<u>ka</u> homkahitka 'to be followed' M80
             follow—Pass

      ii. tçirika—ka   tçirikaka   'to ignite'   M85
             rub—Smlf

---

[4] The realization of /l/ as [r] after /n/ is predictable. In addition, the vowel /u/ is realized as [i] if it follows an /i/.

c. i. tsapo—<u>ta</u>   tsapta   'to have repeated cramps'   M87
    have.a.muscle.cramp—Det A
  ii. nika—ta   nikata   'to terminate'   M88
    eat—SF

Given a descriptive generalization like 'delete the vowel directly preceding a Subtractive Suffix', we would expect multiple deletion of vowels in contexts where multiple Subtractive Suffixes are present. However, as can be seen in the data in (4), this is not the case: only one vowel is deleted if multiple monosyllabic Subtractive Suffixes are adjacent.[5] Or to put it another way: Subtractive Suffixes never trigger deletion of a preceding monosyllabic Subtractive Suffix. The absence of multiple vowel deletion is in fact consistent with the general restriction that three-consonant clusters in the language are only possible as the result of prefixation, never as the result of vowel deletion. A form */nasukjlu/ is hence independently excluded.

Note that the final two examples in (4) show the interaction of some phonological processes of the language, namely vowel deletion, phonologically triggered consonant deletion, and compensatory vowel lengthening (see footnote 2).

(4) *Multiple Subtractive Suffixes = one vowel deletion*   (Matteson, 1965)
    nasuka—<u>ja</u>—<u>lu</u>   nasukjalu   'I fled from him'   41
    maçnaka—<u>ni</u>—<u>lu</u>   maçnakniɾi   'he is unfortunately disobedient' 117
    ḥaluka—<u>ka</u>—<u>lu</u>—ɾu   ḥaluːkaluɾu   'that can be desired'   224
    kawa—<u>kaka</u>—<u>ka</u>—na   kawkaːkana   'bathe themselves'   144

A final relevant context is an exceptional non-undergoer suffix that resists vowel deletion consistently if followed by a Subtractive Suffix. A discussion and analysis of this additional data is postponed to section 4.1.2.

Morpheme-specific vowel deletion in Yine in the framework of PDM results from a defective phonological representation for the Subtractive Suffixes. More specifically, it is argued that Subtractive Suffix vowels lack a mora underlyingly. Vowel deletion is then predicted if the constraint ranking of the language ensures that this defective structure is not simply neutralized on the surface by inserting an epenthetic mora. Since every vowel must be dominated by at least one mora in order to be integrated into the phonological structure, a mora-less vowel 'searches' for a mora it can be associated with. Its best chance to get associated with a mora in Yine is to be associated with the mora of the preceding vowel and this results in a situation where the underlying association of the mora with its vowel becomes uninterpretable.

---

[5] There are two exceptions to this generalization. In /kna—mtasa—çe—<u>kaka</u>/ 'lanky' (Matteson, 1965: 158) and in /pto—tsotaçi—çi—<u>ḥima</u>/ a little bit' (Matteson, 1965: 172), two Subtractive Suffixes are added and two vowels are deleted (resulting in /knamtaːçkaka/ and /ptotsotaːçĥima/). However, it is striking that these two examples are taken from the exemplifying Yine texts in Matteson (1965) and are not explicitly mentioned or discussed in the description. The generalizations about morpheme-specific vowel deletion are hence based on the examples given in (4) and these two cases are taken as rare exceptions.

The implementation of this intuition in the present containment-based OT-framework consists of three main ingredients. *First*, the vowel is forced to be associated with a mora due to the parsing constraint in (5-a). *Second*, the mora-less vowel can only be associated with the mora of the preceding vowel since insertion of an epenthetic mora is penalized by $^*\sigma$-Col!μ demanding that every syllable must be licensed by at least one morphologically coloured mora (see (37-a) in section 2.2.3, repeated in (5-b)).[6] Underlyingly mora-less vowels hence strive to be associated with an underlying mora. Given that association lines may never cross (=NoCr, see section 2.2.2, (30)), the only available mora is now the one dominating the preceding vowel. *Third*, this association with the preceding mora results in a structure where one mora is linked to two vowels phonetically. This prosodically marked structure is excluded by the markedness constraint $^*{}_V{}^\mu{}_V$, defined in section 2.2.2, (35), repeated in (5-c).

(5)   a. $V{<}DD^m_P{<}\mu$ Assign a violation mark for every μ that is not phonetically or morphologically dominated by a σ.

   b. $^*\sigma$-Col!μ Assign a violation mark for every σ node that only dominates colourless μ's phonetically or morphologically.

   c. $^*{}_V{}^\mu{}_V$ Assign a violation mark for every μ that is phonetically associated with more than one vowel.

A violation of (5-c) can be avoided if the underlying association line of the doubly-linked mora is marked as phonetically invisible. Since the vowel preceding the Subtractive Suffix then lacks any phonetically visible integration into the prosodic structure, it is not realized under violation of PVis$_V$.[7]

Tableau (6) illustrates mora usurpation for an example where the Subtractive Suffix /−lu/ 'him' triggers deletion of the stem-final vowel in /neta/ 'to see'. Recall that all phonetically invisible elements (=not properly integrated) are highlighted in grey for ease of exposition. In candidate (6-a), the affix vowel /u/ is left without any prosodic integration.[8] The fatal violation for this candidate is the violation of $V{<}DD^m_P{<}\mu$ since

---

[6] That $^*\sigma$-Col!μ penalizes insertion of an epenthetic mora in order to realize the underlyingly mora-less vowel and not the more general Col!μ follows from facts about syllabification in Yine. Following the analysis in Lin (1997*b*), it is taken for granted that all consonants that are not prevocalic are extrasyllabic but moraic in Yine resulting in what is called a 'minor syllable' by Lin (1998). The reader is referred to Matteson (1965); Lin (1997*b*) and Lin (1998) for a detailed discussion of the phonetic and phonotactic evidence for this claim. Under this assumption, an interesting asymmetry arises in Yine: epenthetic moras are inserted to license extrasyllabic consonants that are not prevocalic but are never inserted to allow realization of the underlyingly mora-less vowel. This asymmetry is straightforwardly predicted from $^*\sigma$-Col!μ, a constraint demanding licensing of a syllable with a morphologically coloured mora, similar to the vertical morpheme Contiguity constraints discussed in chapter 5.

[7] See the formulation of the general constraint against phonetically invisible segments PVis$_S$ (27) in section 2.2.2. That this constraint is sensitive to the distinction between consonants and vowels is introduced in McCarthy and Prince (1995) as the distinction into Max-V and Max-C.

[8] This candidate is only fully faithful up to the moraic level. Higher prosodic structure like syllables or the prosodic word node is excluded which is obviously added to parse the output correctly.

the vowel is not dominated by a mora via a phonetically visible or morphological association line. In candidate (6-b), the affix vowel is associated with an inserted epenthetic mora but this option to provide the affix vowel with a mora is excluded by high-ranked $*\sigma\text{-Col!}\mu$ since the syllable node only dominates the epenthetic mora and no morphologically coloured mora. The affix vowel therefore has no other chance than to be associated with the preceding stem mora (6-c-e).

(6) *Mora usurpation*

	Input: $\mu_O\ \mu_O$ over $n_O\ e_O\ t_O\ a_O$ + $l_\bullet\ u_\bullet$	$V{<}DD^m_p{<}\mu$	$*_V{}^{\mu}{}_V$	$*\sigma\text{-Col!}\mu$	$PVIs_V$
a.	$\mu_O\ \mu_O$ — $n_O\ e_O\ t_O\ a_O\ l_\bullet\ u_\bullet$ · [ne.ta.l°]	*!			*
b.	$\mu_O\ \mu_O\ \mu$ — $n_O\ e_O\ t_O\ a_O\ l_\bullet\ u_\bullet$ · [ne.ta.lu]			*!	
c.	$\mu_O\ \mu_O$ — $n_O\ e_O\ t_O\ a_O\ l_\bullet\ u_\bullet$ · [ne.ta.lu]		*!		
☞ d.	$\mu_O\ \mu_O$ — $n_O\ e_O\ t_O\ a_O\ l_\bullet\ u_\bullet$ · [ne.t°.lu]				*
e.	$\mu_O\ \mu_O$ — $n_O\ e_O\ t_O\ a_O\ l_\bullet\ u_\bullet$ · [ne.ta.l°]	*!			*

However, if the stem mora integrates the affix vowel, it cannot phonetically dominate its original vowel (candidate (6-c)) as well because this violates $*_V{}^{\mu}{}_V$. Since the constraint only penalizes two phonetically visible association lines between a mora and two vowels, a straightforward repair to avoid a violation of $*_V{}^{\mu}{}_V$ is to mark one of the two association lines as phonetically invisible. Marking the epenthetic association line as phonetically invisible as in candidate (6-e), however, introduces yet again the violation of $V{<}DD^m_p{<}\mu$ that was hoped to be avoided by inserting the additional association line. The constraint $V{<}DD_p^m{<}\mu$ is only satisfied if a phonetically visible or a morphological association line links every vowel to a mora, it is not satisfied by an inserted phonetically invisible association line. It must hence be the underlying association line between the mora and the vowel that is marked as phonetically invisible as in candidate (6-d). This candidate finally wins the competition since it avoids the illicit double-linked mora and every vowel is associated with a mora.[9]

The comparison between the candidates (6-a) and (6-d) nicely illustrates the key logic of usurpation that is only possible in containment theory. In both candidates, PV_{IS_V} is violated once since one vowel remains invisible (the affix vowel /u/ in (6-a) and the stem vowel /a/ in (6-d)). The crucial difference between the structures is the integration of material into the prosodic structure. Whereas the unrealized affix vowel in (6-a) is truly floating and not integrated into the structure by any association line, the unparsed stem vowel in (6-d) is at least integrated by a phonetically invisible association line. The constraint $V{<}DD_p^m{<}\mu$ therefore prefers the structure (6-d), where no vowel is completely unassociated. Usurpation therefore crucially relies on ranking $V{<}DD_p^m{<}\mu$, ${}^*{}_V\mu_V$, and ${}^*\sigma\text{-}\textsc{Col!}\mu$ above PV_{IS_V}. That ${}^*\sigma\text{-}\textsc{Col!}\mu$ is not ranked in the same high stratum as ${}^*{}_V\mu_V$, and $V{<}DD_p^m{<}\mu$ will become evident in the following discussion, especially in tableau (7).

In contexts where multiple monosyllabic Subtractive Suffixes are adjacent, only one vowel is deleted (see the data in (4)). This is straightforwardly expected from this analysis based on mora usurpation: Vowel deletion only results if an underlyingly mora-less vowel of a Subtractive Suffix usurps the mora to which a preceding vowel was underlyingly associated. In a structure like /nasuka—ja—lu/ (4), only the first affix vowel /a/ is preceded by a vowel that is underlyingly associated with a mora. The second affix vowel /u/ is preceded by a Subtractive Suffix and simply has no chance to usurp any mora that was underlyingly present. Tableau (7) shows how this single vowel deletion follows from the assumptions about mora usurpation made so far. Candidate (7-a) leaves both underlyingly mora-less vowels mora-less and incurs two fatal violations $V{<}DD_p^m{<}\mu$. Mora usurpation for the first of the two mora-less vowels applies in candidate (7-b). This candidate is suboptimal since it still leaves one vowel without a mora. What one might term 'multiple usurpation' can be found in (7-c) where both underlyingly mora-less vowels are associated with the preceding underlying mora. However, this results once again in a prosodically ill-formed structure where one mora is phonetically associated with two vowels. The winning candidate is therefore (7-d) where the second underlyingly mora-less is

---

[9] Recall that syllabification in Yine ensures that any consonant that cannot be syllabified as single onset to a phonetically visible vowel must be licensed by an extrasyllabic mora (see footnote 6). In the following tableaux, these consonantal moras are omitted to ease the readability of the depictions. In the transcription, moraic extrasyllabic consonants are notated as C^∂. Crucially, the inserted moras that license those consonants do not violate ${}^*\sigma\text{-}\textsc{Col!}\mu$ since they are not dominated by a syllable but a higher prosodic node.

supplied with an inserted mora. The violation of $*\sigma$-COL!μ is tolerated in this case since there is no better way to supply both mora-less vowels with a mora.

(7)   *Two Subtractive Suffixes: one non-realized vowel*

$\mu_\bigcirc$ $\cdots$ k$_\bigcirc$ a$_\bigcirc$ + j$_\bullet$ a$_\bullet$ + l$_\square$ u$_\square$	V<DD$_\text{p}^\text{m}$<μ	$*_\text{v}\mu_\text{v}$	$*\sigma$-COL!μ	PVIs$_\text{v}$
a. $\mu_\bigcirc$ $\cdots$ k$_\bigcirc$ a$_\bigcirc$ j$_\bullet$ a$_\bullet$ l$_\square$ u$_\square$ [na.su.ka.j°.l°]	*!*			**
b. $\mu_\bigcirc$ $\cdots$ k$_\bigcirc$ a$_\bigcirc$ j$_\bullet$ a$_\bullet$ l$_\square$ u$_\square$ [na.su.k°. ja.l°]	*!			**
c. $\mu_\bigcirc$ $\cdots$ k$_\bigcirc$ a$_\bigcirc$ j$_\bullet$ a$_\bullet$ l$_\square$ u$_\square$ [na.su.k°.ja.lu]		*!		*
☞ d. $\mu_\bigcirc$ μ $\cdots$ k$_\bigcirc$ a$_\bigcirc$ j$_\bullet$ a$_\bullet$ l$_\square$ u$_\square$ [na.su.k°.ja.lu]			*	*

A possible structure where both Subtractive Suffixes usurp an underlying mora is given in (8). The first of the two Subtractive Suffixes usurps the penultimate base mora and the second Subtractive Suffix usurps the final base mora. This structure is excluded in the PDM model both by the NoCr and the RMO that restrict GEN. The final stem mora reflects both the morphological affiliation of the stem$_\bigcirc$ and of the second Subtractive Suffix$_\square$ whereas the penultimate base mora reflects the stem$_\bigcirc$ and the first Subtractive Suffix$_\bullet$. A mora affiliated with the first Subtractive Suffix$_\bullet$ hence precedes a mora that is affiliated with the stem$_\bigcirc$ but not the first Subtractive Suffix$_\bullet$. The RMO is therefore violated with respect to the exponent order stem$_\bigcirc$ ≫ Subtractive Suffix$_\bullet$ in (8).

Note that for this investigating of exponent order on the moraic tier, the consonantal moras that were excluded in all preceding depictions (see footnote 6) are given for completeness as well. As can be seen, the presence of a mora dominating the consonant /k/ makes usurpation of the preceding vowel impossible since that would necessarily result in crossing association lines (see section 2.2.2, (30)).

(8) *Excluded multiple usurpation*

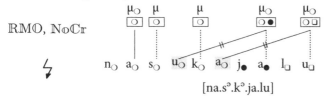

[na.sᵒ.kᵒ.ja.lu]

As was already discussed above, double vowel deletion in such a context is independently excluded since a consonant cluster as in */naskjalu/ is illicit. However, an account that implements the descriptive generalization that every Subtractive Suffix triggers deletion of a preceding vowel and where the absence of multiple vowel deletion is only due to phonological cluster restrictions faces the additional complication that it needs to be determined which of the two vowels is deleted. In a parallel OT account as in Pater (2009), both deletion options /nasukjalu/ and */nasukajlu/ are equally good. Both avoid a violation of the markedness constraint against illicit clusters and both violate the morpheme-specific ALIGN(SFX;C) constraint (see section 7.2.4 for more details) that is responsible for vowel deletion in this account. It is not clear which independently motivated constraint would reasonably decide between the two.

3.1.2 *Vowel shortening in Huallaga Quechua*

A second subtractive MLM pattern that can be predicted from mora usurpation is vowel shortening. An example for such a subtractive MLM can be found in Huallaga Quechua (Weber, 1947, 1996; Adelaar, 1984; Adelaar and Muysken, 2004). Huallaga is a variety of Quechua that makes a phonemic distinction between short and long vowels. An example for a minimal pair is /piʃi/ 'urinate' vs. /piʃiː/ 'lacking cause' (Weber, 1947: 451). Some suffixes now shorten a preceding long vowel as can be seen in (9). Again, Subtractive Suffixes are underlined. Although Huallaga Quechua exhibits phonological vowel shortening in order to avoid long vowels in closed syllables, most of the vowel shortenings in (9) are not phonologically predictable simply because nearly all of the shortened vowels surface in an open syllable.[10] Example (9-c) illustrates the additional process of phonological vowel shortening in the underlyingly long

---

[10] In some cases, it is highly plausible that the suffix in question once began with two consonants and hence vowel shortening was phonologically motivated at an earlier stage of language development. This is especially evident since some of the suffixes still begin with a consonant cluster in related dialects. For example, /−ra/ Pst in Huallaga Quechua corresponds to /−rqa/ in other dialects (Weber, 1947: 467). However, these synchronic facts are unavailable for a language learner and the vowel shortening must nevertheless receive a theoretical account in the synchronic grammar.

vowel of the Subtractive Suffix that becomes short since it is followed by a consonant syllabified as coda. The example in (10) shows that the Subtractive Suffixes have no surface effect if they are preceded by a short vowel.

(9)   *Subtractive Suffixes in H. Quechua: vowel shortening*   (Weber, 1947: 468)

    a. miku—jka:—ʃa—:—ta
        eat-Impf-Subord-1-O
        mikujkaʃa:ta
        'that which I ate'

    b. qoja:—pa:—ka:kU—n
        abide-Ben-Compl-3
        qojapaka:kun
        'he stays over the expected time, he overstays his welcome'

    c. melana:—pa:—n
        disgust-Ben-3
        melanapan
        'it is disgusting to him'

    d. tsara:—ra:—ra-n
        have-Stat-Pst-3
        tsarararan
        'he had it (in his possession)'

(10)   *Subtractive Suffixes in H. Quechua: no effect for short vowels*   (Weber, 1996: 150)
    ajwa—ra—n
    go-Pst-3
    ajwaran
    'went'

In all these examples, the Subtractive Suffix directly precedes a vowel, either a short or long one. This is straightforwardly expected since there are very few morphemes that end in a consonant and verbal roots are always vowel-final in Huallaga Quechua (Weber, 1947: 455). We can hence conclude that the Subtractive Suffix triggers non-realization of a mora that is associated with a directly preceding vowel if this does not result in non-realization of that vowel. This latter condition explains why no surface effect can be found for the short vowel in (10): non-realization of the only mora dominating a short vowel would leave this vowel without any prosodic integration and it would hence become unrealized.

It is argued that such an effect is also predicted from the mechanism of mora usurpation. As in Yine, it is assumed that the initial vowel of the Subtractive Affixes happens to lack a mora underlyingly. This mora-less vowel then usurps the underlying mora of a preceding long vowel. That mora usurpation is blocked if a short vowel precedes a Subtractive Affix follows from ranking PVis$_V$ above Col!$_\mu$. In those contexts, mora epenthesis instead of vowel-deletion is predicted. This is actually a crucial difference to the analysis for the vowel deletion in Yine where the reverse ranking COL!$_\mu$ above PVIS$_V$ predicts that vowel deletion is the preferred strategy to supply the mora-less vowel with a mora.[11] The tableaux in (11) show the analysis for mora usurpation in Huallaga Quechua. If a long vowel precedes the underlyingly mora-less vowel of a Subtractive Suffix (11-i), usurpation of the second underlying mora is possible without violating high-ranked PVIS$_V$ as in candidate (11-i-c). Insertion of an epenthetic mora in candidate (11-i-d) is therefore excluded by higher-ranked COL!$_\mu$. If, however, the Subtractive Suffix precedes a base with a short vowel in its last syllable as in (11-ii), then usurpation is impossible. It results in a fatal violation of PVIS$_V$ in candidate (11-ii-b) and insertion of an epenthetic mora as a last resort to supply the mora-less vowel with a mora becomes optimal in candidate (11-ii-c).

(11) *Mora usurpation in Huallaga Quechua*
   i. *Vowel shortening*

	V<DD^m_P<μ	PVIS$_V$	*V$^\mu_V$	COL!$_\mu$	*μ+S
a. [tsa.raːr]	*!	*!			
b. [tsa.raː.ra]				*!	
☞ c. [tsa.ra.ra]					*
d. [tsa.raː.ra]				*!	

[11] There are no underlyingly long vowels in Yine and all surface long vowels are the result of compensatory lengthening after C-deletion (Matteson, 1965: 31). A comparable vowel shortening effect of underlyingly long vowels is hence not expected in Yine.

ii. Preservation of short vowels

$\mu_\circ$ $\mu_\circ$ / $a_\circ$ $j_\circ$ $w_\circ$ $a_\circ$ + $r_\bullet$ $a_\bullet$	V<DD$^{m}_{p}$≺μ	PVIs$_v$	*V$^\mu_v$V	Col!$_\mu$	*μ_v + S
a. $\mu_\circ$ $\mu_\circ$ / $a_\circ$ $j_\circ$ $w_\circ$ $a_\circ$ $r_\bullet$ $a_\bullet$ [aj.war]	*!	*!			
b. $\mu_\circ$ $\mu_\circ$ / $a_\circ$ $j_\circ$ $w_\circ$ $a_\circ$ $r_\bullet$ $a_\bullet$ [aj.wra]		*!			*
☞ c. $\mu_\circ$ $\mu_\circ$ μ / $a_\circ$ $j_\circ$ $w_\circ$ $a_\circ$ $r_\bullet$ $a_\bullet$ [aj.wa.ra]				*	

3.1.3 Degemination in Wolof

A third subtractive MLM operation predicted from the mechanism of mora usurpation is degemination under the assumption that geminates are underlyingly moraic consonants (Davis, 2011a). Such a pattern is borne out in the Subtractive Affixation in Wolof, an Atlantic language (Ka, 1994; Bell, 2003). In Wolof, length is contrastive for vowels and consonants; the only restriction being that only a subset of consonants can be geminated (stops, nasals, liquids, and glides). Syllables can be either CV(VC) or CV(CC) where the final CC is either a geminate or a nasal followed by a voiceless stop. This restriction on the maximal syllable is evidence that geminates are indeed weight-contributing in Wolof and that trimoraic syllables are generally illicit (Bell, 2003).[12]

---

[12] An interesting problem with this analysis is the stress pattern of Wolof. In most contexts, main stress is on the first syllable; only if the second syllable contains a long vowel and the first syllable a short vowel, is the second syllable stressed. Since geminates are ignored by this rule, this seems to contradict the claim that they contribute to syllable weight. Bell (2003) proposes that this asymmetry follows if one assumes that only vocalic moras are counted for determining the stress. In contrast, it is argued here that the facts are easily predicted by a constraint about prosodic well-formedness. The constraint *$^\Phi$S$^\Phi$ demands that no segment is associated with two feet, excluding a structure where a foot is associated with two syllables if the first contains a geminate (ii-b). It is a more specific version of the ONERT constraints (see 2.2.2, (33)) penalizing not two highest prosodic nodes but two higher prosodic nodes of a certain type.

(i) *$^\Phi$S$^\Phi$ Assign a violation mark for every segment associated with a foot via two paths of association lines.

It was already shown in the introducing example (5) that Wolof employs an instance of additive MLM since some suffixes in Wolof trigger gemination of a preceding consonant. That the language also exhibits the reverse morpheme-specific phonological process was also already shown in the introduction with the data in section 1.1.1: some suffixes are always accompanied by degemination of a preceding long final consonant. An example is the causative suffix /−al/ (12-a). The data in (12-b) shows that final non-geminate consonants and long vowels surface without any change preceding /−al/. That this is an arbitrary feature of certain suffixes can easily be illustrated with the data in (12-c) where the homophonous non-subtracting suffix /−al/ 'inchoative' attaches to verb stems without triggering any change on the preceding base segments.

(12)   *Subtractive Suffixes and degemination in Wolof*

(Ka, 1994: 96, 97; Bell, 2003: 9)

a.	seg:	'to filter'	segal	'to press oily products'	(+causative /−al/)
	son:	'to be tired'	sonal	'to tire, bother'	
	dug:	'to come into'	dugǝl	'to introduce'	
	bǝt:	'to pierce'	bǝtǝl	'to make pierce'	
b.	bax	'to boil'	baxal	'to make boil'	
	fen	'to lie'	fenal	'to make lie'	
	be:s	'to be new'	be:sal	'to make new'	
c.	bǝt:	'to pierce'	bǝt:al	'to pierce for'	(+benefactive /−al/)
	dug:	'to enter'	dug:ǝl	'to enter for'	

An analysis for degemination in Wolof is given in Bell (2003) that is based on the assumption of morpheme-specific constraints: specific affixes select for an LL foot. In contrast, the present analysis avoids the assumption of morpheme-specific constraints[13] and assumes that the trigger for the degemination is a defective structure in the suffixes themselves; they contain an underlyingly mora-less vowel that usurps the underlying mora of a preceding segment. The crucial difference to the vowel shortening pattern in Huallaga Quechua is that long vowels in Wolof are realized as such before the Subtractive Suffix and only geminate consonants are shortened. In addition to ranking PVIs$_V$ above COL!$_\mu$, a constraint preserving the moraic count of vowels is therefore crucial. In the present theoretical framework, this is the constraint *μ ⊣⊢ V preserving underlying association lines between vowels and moras.

(ii)   *A violation of* *$^\Phi$S$^\Phi$*

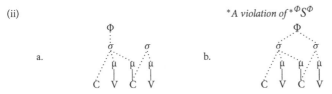

The tableaux in (13) illustrate the Wolof ranking for the three relevant contexts. If a geminate consonant precedes a Subtractive Suffix as in (13-i), mora usurpation is predicted to be optimal and the underlyingly moraic consonant is consequently syllabified as singleton onset, not as geminate (13-i-b). If, however, the consonant preceding the Subtractive Suffix is short (13-ii), the only mora the mora-less vowel could usurp is the mora associated with the preceding vowel. Usurpation as in (13-ii-b) and (13-iii-b) hence necessarily results in non-realization of an association line between a vowel and a mora and is excluded by high-ranked $*\mu$ ⊣⊢ V. In addition, this would result in non-realization of a vowel in case the preceding vowel is short (13-ii). Mora epenthesis instead of mora usurpation hence becomes optimal in (13-ii-c) and (13-iii-c). In contrast to the rankings in Huallaga Quechua and Yine, it is not $*_V\mu_V$ that triggers usurpation but the more general $*_s\mu_s$ that penalizes association of a mora to two segments.

The crucial difference to mora usurpation in Yine and Huallaga Quechua is hence that only moras underlyingly associated with consonants can be usurped: a straightforward prediction from a constraint system where constraints against phonetically invisible structure are sensitive to the distinction into vowels and consonants.

(13) *Mora usurpation in Wolof*
  i. *Degemination*

$\mu_{\circ}\ \mu_{\circ}$ $s_{\circ}\ e_{\circ}\ g_{\circ}$ + $a_{\bullet}\ l_{\bullet}$	$V<DD^m_p<\mu$	$PVis_V$	$*\mu$ ⊣⊢ V	$*_s\mu_s$	$CoL!_\mu$	$*\mu$ ⊣⊢ s
a. $\mu_{\circ}\ \mu_{\circ}$ $s_{\circ}\ e_{\circ}\ g_{\circ}\ a_{\bullet}\ l_{\bullet}$ [seg:l]	*!	*!				
☞ b. $\mu_{\circ}\ \mu_{\circ}$ $s_{\circ}\ e_{\circ}\ g_{\circ}\ a_{\bullet}\ l_{\bullet}$ [segal]						*
c. $\mu_{\circ}\ \mu_{\circ}\ \mu$ $s_{\circ}\ e_{\circ}\ g_{\circ}\ a_{\bullet}\ l_{\bullet}$ [seg:al]					*!	

ii. *No effect for short vowels*

μ_O | $b_O\ a_O\ x_O\ +\ a_\bullet\ l_\bullet$	V<DD^m_P<μ	PVis$_V$	*μ+V	*S$^\mu_S$	Col!μ	*S+μ
a. μ_O | $b_O\ a_O\ x_O\ a_\bullet\ l_\bullet$ [baxl]	*!	*!				
b. μ_O $\neq$ ⋯ $b_O\ a_O\ x_O\ a_\bullet\ l_\bullet$ [bxal]		*!	*!			*
☞ c. $\mu_O\quad \mu$ | $b_O\ a_O\ x_O\ a_\bullet\ l_\bullet$ [baxal]					*	

iii. *No effect for long vowels*

$\mu_O\ \mu_O$ V $b_O\ e_O\ s_O\ +\ a_\bullet\ l_\bullet$	V<DD^m_P<μ	PVis$_V$	*μ+V	*S$^\mu_S$	Col!μ	*S+μ
a. $\mu_O\ \mu_O$ V $b_O\ e_O\ s_O\ a_\bullet\ l_\bullet$ [be:sl]	*!	*!				
b. $\mu_O\ \mu_O$ $\neq$ $b_O\ e_O\ s_O\ a_\bullet\ l_\bullet$ [besal]			*!			*
☞ c. $\mu_O\ \mu_O\quad \mu$ V $b_O\ e_O\ s_O\ a_\bullet\ l_\bullet$ [be:sal]					*	

3.1.4 *Vowel shortening or deletion in Hungarian*

Now we turn to a more complex instance of subtractive MLM that was already briefly discussed in section 2.1.4, namely second stem formation in Hungarian (Kenesei et al., 1998; Stiebels and Wunderlich, 1999; Abrusan, 2005; Grimes, 2010). Recall that certain lexically marked stems in Hungarian show an alternative form resulting from a subtractive MLM if they precede a so-called class III suffix (Stiebels and Wunderlich, 1999). These type III suffixes are an arbitrary class of suffixes that may trigger alternations on the preceding base, illustrated in (14) with the plural suffix /−Vk/.[14] (14-a) shows that short vowels in the final syllable of the base are deleted and (14-b) shows that long vowels are shortened. The crucial difference to the Subtractive Affixation patterns discussed above is the fact that the stems preceding such a type III suffix do not predictably or necessarily undergo subtractive MLM. They are arbitrarily marked for whether they undergo MLM or not as shown in (14-c) where examples of (phonologically very similar) stems are given that do not undergo vowel shortening or deletion when preceding a type III suffix. For stems that show subtractive MLM, however, the allomorphy between vowel shortening and deletion is predictable: long vowels shorten and short vowels delete.[15] These class III suffixes are taken to be Subtractive Suffixes in the following.

(14)   *Hungarian*   (Stiebels and Wunderlich, 1999: 273–285)

a.	bokor−V̲k̲	bokrok	'bushes'
	terem−V̲k̲	termek	'halls'
	borju−V̲k̲	borjak	'calves'
b.	madaːr−V̲k̲	madarak	'birds'
c.	perem−V̲k̲	peremek	'edges'
	tanaːr−V̲k̲	tanaːrok	'teachers'

The first crucial part of the analysis is identical to the mora usurpation analyses given above: it is assumed that the class III suffixes are underlyingly mora-less and usurp the underlying mora of a preceding vowel. Tableaux (15-i) and (15-ii) show how the same ranking proposed for Yine easily predicts that a Subtractive Suffix in Hungarian is forced to usurp the underlying mora a preceding vowel is associated with: either this is the only mora of the vowel and deletion results or it is one of two moras and vowel shortening arises. The interesting difference to the analyses discussed in sections 3.1.1–3.1.3 for Yine, Huallaga Quechua, and Wolof is hence that the mora

---

[14] The vowel quality is determined by the preceding vowels.

[15] The pattern is actually more complex and involves, for example, also lowering of vowels for some secondary stems. This typology of shortening and deleting stems is also a simpler classification than the one given in, for example, Stiebels and Wunderlich (1999). Stems that undergo vowel shortening are further subdivided into v-stems and simple shortening stems. And some stems that undergo deletion of a vowel additionally 'metathesize' in order to avoid an illicit coda consonant (see section 2.1.4). Since the present account only aims to derive the MLM, these details are ignored for now and the reader is referred to the detailed discussion and analysis in Stiebels and Wunderlich (1999).

usurpation has different surface effects depending on the phonological structure of the preceding base. This alternation is a straightforward prediction of the PDM analysis employed here where the Subtractive Suffixes trigger non-realization of a mora.

(15) *Mora usurpation in Hungarian*
   i. *Vowel deletion*

$b_O o_O k_O o_O r_O$ + $o_\bullet k_\bullet$	V<DDᵖᵐ<μ	*VμV	CoL!μ	PVisᵥ	*μ+s
a. $b_O o_O k_O o_O r_O$ $o_\bullet k_\bullet$ [bokork]	*!			*	
☞ b. $b_O o_O k_O o_O r_O$ $o_\bullet k_\bullet$ [bokrok]				*	*
c. $b_O o_O k_O o_O r_O$ $o_\bullet k_\bullet$ [bokorok]			*!		

   ii. *Vowel shortening*

$m_O a_O d_O a_O r_O$ + $a_\bullet k_\bullet$	V<DDᵖᵐ<μ	*VμV	CoL!μ	PVisᵥ	*μ+s
a. $m_O a_O d_O a_O r_O$ $a_\bullet k_\bullet$ [mada:rk]	*!			*	
☞ b. $m_O a_O d_O a_O r_O$ $a_\bullet k_\bullet$ [madarak]					*
c. $m_O a_O d_O a_O r_O$ $a_\bullet k_\bullet$ [mada:rak]			*!		

A second crucial part of the analysis is an implementation of the fact that only certain stems show this MLM alternation and other stems don't have a second stem form. We return to that issue in section 4.1.2 where the exceptional non-undergoer suffixes of Yine are also analysed.

3.1.5 Summary: mora usurpation

The following table (16) summarizes all the patterns for which a mora usurpation analysis was proposed. It was shown how mora usurpation triggers either vowel deletion (as in Yine), vowel shortening (as in Huallaga Quechua), degemination (as in Wolof), or an allomorphy between vowel deletion and shortening (as in Hungarian). This full range of operations where a mora-sized portion of the base is subtracted is exactly what is predicted from the mechanism of mora usurpation. And the allomorphy between different mora-subtracting operations in Hungarian is additional evidence for an autosegmental account and against an alternative account where length is subtracted on the segmental tier. Two different operations (vowel deletion and vowel shortening) would be necessary under such an alternative account.

(16)   *Mora usurpation analyses: summary*

   3.1.1   **Yine**   → Non-realization of the final V

$$\begin{array}{cc} \mu_{\circ} & \mu_{\circ} \\ | & \nparallel \cdots \\ \end{array}$$
$$n_{\circ}\ e_{\circ}\ t_{\circ}\ a_{\circ}\ l_{\bullet}\ u_{\bullet}$$
$$[\text{ne.t}^{\circ}.\text{lu}]$$

   3.1.2   **Huallaga Quechua**   → Shortening of the final V

$$\begin{array}{cc} \mu_{\circ} & \mu_{\circ}\mu_{\circ} \\ | & \vee\!\!\!\nparallel \cdots \\ \end{array}$$
$$\text{ts}_{\circ}\ a_{\circ}\ r_{\circ}\ a_{\circ}\ \ r_{\bullet}\ a_{\bullet}$$
$$[\text{tsa.ra.ra}]$$

   3.1.3   **Wolof**   → Shortening of a final C

$$\begin{array}{cc} \mu_{\circ} & \mu_{\circ} \\ | & \nparallel \cdots \\ \end{array}$$
$$s_{\circ}\ e_{\circ}\ g_{\circ}\ a_{\bullet}\ l_{\bullet}$$
$$[\text{segal}]$$

   3.1.4   **Hungarian**   → Shortening or non-realization of a final V

$$\begin{array}{cc} \mu_{\circ} & \mu_{\circ} \\ | & \nparallel \cdots \\ \end{array}\qquad\begin{array}{cc} \mu_{\circ} & \mu_{\circ}\mu_{\circ} \\ | & \vee\!\!\!\nparallel \cdots \\ \end{array}$$
$$b_{\circ}\ o_{\circ}\ k_{\circ}\ o_{\circ}\ r_{\circ}\ o_{\bullet}\ k_{\bullet}\qquad m_{\circ}\ a_{\circ}\ d_{\circ}\ a_{\circ}\ r_{\circ}\ a_{\bullet}\ k_{\bullet}$$
$$[\text{bokrok}]\qquad\qquad\qquad[\text{madarak}]$$

The general mechanism of mora usurpation predicts that, *first*, only the non-realization of an underlyingly present mora can be enforced, and that, *second*, usurpation can only be triggered by the presence of an affix containing a segment that strives to be dominated by a mora. This first prediction is particularly striking for the mora usurpation analysis for Yine where it correctly accounts for the blocking of multiple vowel deletion in the context of multiple Subtractive Suffixes. An account that derives this blocking only from phonotactic constraints faces the complication that some independent mechanism must determine which one of the two expected vowel deletion operations is blocked. The second prediction implies that a mora-less consonant could in principle also trigger mora usurpation in a language where consonants are forced to be moraic. However, a plausible instance of a consonant triggering mora usurpation could not be found. Taking into account that the mechanism of mora usurpation can be characterized as marked and hence harder to learn since it implies that an abstract defective representation is deduced that triggers a surface effect on neighbouring phonological elements, this general rareness and the absence of consonant-triggered mora usurpation is not surprising.

3.2 Defective integration of morphemic prosodic nodes

Mora usurpation as discussed in section 3.1 is triggered by a defective underlying representation for certain morphemes: they lack an underlying mora. In this section, we turn to the second main mechanism that predicts subtractive MLM inside PDM: the defective integration of morphemic prosodic nodes. The configurations that are central in the following discussion are the ones in (17): a morphemic prosodic node is affixed (a mora in (17-a) and a syllable in (17-b)) and must dominate some element on a lower tier but is not integrated under a higher prosodic node in a phonetically visible way. More concretely, the morphemic mora in (17-a) must minimally dominate a segment but is not dominated by a syllable and the morphemic syllable in (17-b) must minimally dominate a mora but is not integrated under a foot node. Since the morphemic nodes lack any phonetically visible integration under a higher node, they remain phonetically invisible. All elements they dominate remain phonetically invisible as well if they lack any additional phonetically visible integration under another higher node.

(17)   *Defectively integrated morphemic nodes*
        a.   b.

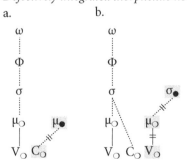

In sections 3.2.1.3 and 3.2.1.4, yet another possible type of defective integration of morphemic prosodic nodes and its effect for MLM is discussed, namely structures where a morphemic prosodic node lacks an association to a lower node but is integrated under a higher prosodic node. However, since the majority of MLM analyses in the following are based on the configurations in (17), they are introduced in some more detail here. The constraints that are relevant for predicting these defective prosodic structures in containment theory are given in their abstract version in (18).

(18)   *Constraints relevant for predicting defectively integrated morphemic nodes*

a. Ⓑ>Do>Ⓐ

Assign a violation mark for every Ⓑ that does not dominate an Ⓐ.

b. Ⓑ<DD$_p^m$<Ⓒ

Assign a violation mark for every Ⓑ that is not phonetically or morphologically dominated by a Ⓒ.

c. * Ⓒ·······Ⓑ

Assign a violation mark for every inserted association line between a Ⓒ and a Ⓑ.

d. * Ⓒ··^{Af}··Ⓑ

Assign a violation mark for every inserted association line between a Ⓒ and a Ⓑ if one or both is an affix element.

e. ONERT-Ⓐ

Assign a violation mark for every phonetically visible Ⓐ dominated by more than one highest prosodic node.
(=a node that is not dominated by another node).

Tableau (19) illustrates a defective integration of a morphemic node on tier B. This node Ⓑ is forced to dominate an element on tier A due to high-ranked Ⓑ>Do>Ⓐ (18-a). The parsing constraint demanding that it must be dominated by a higher node on tier C Ⓑ<DD$_p^m$<Ⓒ (18-b), however, is outranked by the constraint * Ⓒ·······Ⓑ (18-c) penalizing an epenthetic association line between an element on tier B and an element on tier C, excluding candidate (19-b) where the morphemic node is completely integrated into the prosodic structure. Constraints against epenthetic association lines are hence crucial in all the following analyses of defective prosodic integration since they block full integration of a morphemic node in most contexts. In many of the following analyses, the relevant constraint against epenthetic association lines is, however, only sensitive to affix material (18-d); it hence does not block all integration of (epenthetic) prosodic nodes. Finally, ONERT-Ⓐ (18-e) excludes a structure like the one in (19-c) where the phonetically visible node Ⓐ is dominated by two highest prosodic nodes: via a phonetically invisible association line to the morphemic prosodic node Ⓑ and via a phonetically visible association line to an underlying node Ⓑ. If the node Ⓐ remains phonetically invisible, this violation is avoided since ONERT-Ⓐ is defined in terms of phonetically visible segments. This repair is shown in candidate (19-d) where every underlying integration of this element into higher prosodic structure is marked as phonetically invisible. Note that the containment assumption is crucial to predict such a configuration: the parsing constraint

Ⓑ>Do>Ⓐ is satisfied if every node Ⓑ dominates a node Ⓐ via *some* association line, including a phonetically invisible one. This can be seen in the contrast between candidates (19-a) and (19-c): although the morphemic node does not dominate a lower node Ⓐ in a phonetically visible way in either of the candidates, node Ⓑ dominates a node Ⓐ at least via a phonetically invisible association line in candidate (19-d) and hence avoids a violation of Ⓑ>Do>Ⓐ. This is absolutely parallel to the containment-based logic of mora usurpation that is crucially based on the constraint V<DD<μ that is satisfied by *any* association of a vowel to a mora.

(19) *Defective integration of prosodic nodes I*

Ⓒ∘ Ⓑ∘ + Ⓑ• Ⓐ∘	Ⓑ>Do>Ⓐ	*Ⓑ⋯Ⓒ	OneRt-Ⓐ	Ⓑ<DDᵖᵐ<Ⓒ	*Ⓐ⋯Ⓑ
a. Ⓒ∘ / Ⓑ∘ Ⓑ• / Ⓐ∘	*!			*	
b. Ⓒ∘ / Ⓑ∘ Ⓑ• / Ⓐ∘		*!			*
c. Ⓒ∘ / Ⓑ∘ Ⓑ• / Ⓐ∘			*!	*	*
☞ d. Ⓒ∘ / Ⓑ∘ Ⓑ• / Ⓐ∘				*	*

In the following sections, the predictions of morphemic prosodic nodes that are defectively integrated into their base are discussed: morphemic moras in section 3.2.1 and morphemic syllables in section 3.2.2. Section 3.2.3 focusses on the interesting phenomenon of different lexically marked Subtraction allomorphs in one morphological context and shows how the PDM approach accounts for it. As will become clear throughout this discussion, defective integration of morphemic prosodic nodes can predict instances of Subtraction and Subtractive Affixes through the very same mechanism (in the same sense as full integration of morphemic prosodic nodes can predict either Additive Affixation or Addition). This is in fact an interesting difference to the mechanism of mora usurpation discussed in section 3.1 that is crucially bound to the presence of segmental material and hence can only predict instances of Subtractive Affixes.

3.2.1 *Defective mora integration*

3.2.1.1 Vowel deletion in Mauritian Creole and Modern Hebrew   If a mora is defectively integrated in the sense that it is not dominated by a higher prosodic node but must dominate some element lower on the prosodic hierarchy, all the elements that the mora dominates can be predicted to remain unrealized. The most straightforward prediction made from a defective mora integration is hence the non-realization of a vowel, dominated by the morphemic mora.

Morphological vowel deletion is attested in, for example, Mauritian Creole (Henri and Abeillé, 2008; Sye, 2009). Many verbs in Mauritian Creole surface in a so-called 'short form' in contexts where the verb is followed by a complement. As can be seen in the examples in (20), the final vowel of the verb remains unrealized in the short form of the verbs. Sometimes, this vowel deletion is accompanied by phonologically motivated consonant deletion to avoid final consonant clusters.

(20) *Subtraction in Mauritian Creole*   (Henri and Abeillé, 2008: 3+5)

Base	Short form	
vini	vin	'come'
mãze	mãz	'eat'
koze	koz	'speak'
zete	zet	'throw'
reste	res	'stay'

A detailed morphological analysis is necessary to determine the exact meaning of this morpheme that presumably realizes some agreement features (see for more details Sye, 2009), but this is irrelevant for the present purpose. Relevant is the representation assumed for the morpheme in question that is taken to be a morphemic mora. This morphemic mora must dominate a segment due to μ>Do>S but cannot be integrated under a syllable node due to *σ...Af..μ.[16] The former constraint excludes candidate (21-a) that leaves the morphemic mora completely unintegrated and the

---

[16] And neither under higher prosodic structures like the foot or the prosodic word. In the following, it is implicitly assumed that these marked prosodic structures violating the strict layering of the prosodic hierarchy are excluded by further high-ranked constraints against epenthetic association lines as well. In the case of a morphemic mora, the relevant constraints are *$_\Phi$...Af..μ and *$_\omega$...Af..μ.

latter excludes candidate (21-b) where the morphemic mora is integrated under the syllable node since that adds an epenthetic association line between an affix mora and a syllable. Note that the fact that the morphemic mora is phonetically visible in candidate (21-b) tells us that it must be integrated under a syllable node via a phonetically visible association line in this structure. Since ONERT-S is high-ranked, it is also impossible that the segment remains phonetically visible if it is associated with the defectively integrated morphemic mora, excluding candidate (21-c). Non-realization of the segment dominated by the mora as in (21-d) is hence predicted.

(21)   *Morphemic mora and vowel deletion*

Input: $\mu_O \; \mu_O \; \mu_\bullet$ / $v_O \, i_O \, n_O \, i_O$ +	$\mu{>}\text{Do}{>}\text{V}$	$*\sigma..\text{Af}..\mu$	ONERT-S	PVIS$_v$
a. $\mu_O \; \mu_O \, \mu_\bullet$ / $v_O \, i_O \, n_O \, i_O$ [vini]	*!			
b. $\mu_O \; \mu_O \, \mu_\bullet$ / $v_O \, i_O \, n_O \, i_O$ [viniː]		*!		
c. $\mu_O \; \mu_O \, \mu_\bullet$ / $v_O \, i_O \, n_O \, i_O$ [vini]			*!	
☞ d. $\mu_O \; \mu_O \, \mu_\bullet$ / $v_O \, i_O \, n_O \, i_O$ [vin]				*

Note that it is irrelevant whether the input vowel adjacent to the morphemic mora is underlyingly associated with a mora or not. A possible input with a final mora-less vowel is still predicted to result in a non-realized final vowel, the only difference would be that the vowel is only associated with the morphemic mora. This is shown in tableau (22). ONERT-S prohibits in this context the insertion of an epenthetic mora that integrates the vowel into the prosodic structure in a phonetically visible way as in candidate (22-d) and segment deletion is again predicted.

(22)   *Morphemic mora and vowel deletion: underlyingly mora-less vowel*

$\mu\bullet$ $v_O\ i_O\ n_O\ i_O\ +$	$\mu{>}\mathrm{Do}{>}\mathrm{V}$	$*\sigma\mathinner{...}^{\mathrm{Af}}\mathinner{...}\mu$	$\mathrm{PVIs_C}$	$\mathrm{OneRt\text{-}S}$	$\mathrm{PVIs_V}$
a. $\mu\bullet$ $v_O\ i_O\ n_O\ i_O$	*!		*!*		**
b. $\mu\quad\mu\ \mu\bullet$ $v_O\ i_O\ n_O\ i_O$ [vini]	*!				
c. $\mu\quad\mu\bullet$ $v_O\ i_O\ n_O\ i_O$ [vini]		*!			
d. $\mu\quad\mu\ \mu\bullet$ $v_O\ i_O\ n_O\ i_O$ [vini]				*!	
☞ e. $\mu\quad\mu\bullet$ $v_O\ i_O\ n_O\ i_O$ [vin]					*

An apparent prediction from this line of reasoning is that affix moras should always remain unrealized, including those affix moras that happen to underlyingly dominate segments. Consider, for example, a hypothetical suffix /–taː/ in Mauritian Creole.[17] The vowel is underlyingly long and hence assumed to be dominated by two moras. Every integration of this affix vowel into a syllable would now result in two violations of $*\sigma\mathinner{...}^{\mathrm{Af}}\mathinner{.}\mu$. Since it was argued above that $\mathrm{PVIs_V}$ is ranked below $*\sigma\mathinner{...}^{\mathrm{Af}}\mathinner{...}\mu$, we could expect that no segmental affix segment underlyingly associated to a mora ever surfaces in the language, briefly shown in (23) with the ranking from (22). This prediction of the PDM system is not problematic in itself: a language without any overt segmental affixes can be predicted that is obviously well-attested. However, many of the languages analysed below do exhibit segmental affixes in addition to morphemic prosodic nodes that are argued to result in MLM.

---

[17] The descriptions in Henri and Abeillé (2008) and Sye (2009) do not list straightforward examples for affixes in Mauritian Creole. Since this point is of crucial importance to all the following analyses based on $*\sigma\mathinner{...}^{\mathrm{Af}}\mathinner{.}\mu$, we abstract away from this concrete language and its (non-)existing affixes for a moment.

(23) *An apparent misprediction: non-realization of moraic segmental affixes?*

	μ>DO>V	*σ..Af..μ	PVis$_C$	OneRt-S	PVis$_V$
☞ a. [vinit]					*
b. [vinita]		*!		*!	
☞ c. [vinita:]		*!*			

For those languages, it is crucial to note that in the present containment system, non-realization of a segment that was underlyingly associated to a mora always implies non-realization of the underlying association of that segment to its mora. Undominated *μ —#^{Af} S hence excludes this problematic candidate as is shown in (24). It is hence predicted in PDM that morphemic prosodic nodes that do not dominate any prosodic or segmental node can behave crucially differently from prosodic nodes that dominate another element.

(24) *Realization of moraic affix segments but defective integration of morphemic moras*

	*μ—#^{Af} S	μ>DO>V	*σ..Af..μ	PVis$_C$	OneRt-S	PVis$_V$
a. [vinit]	*!*					*
b. [vinita]	*!		*		*	
☞ c. [vinita:]			**			

Unless otherwise noted, this asymmetry between underlying moraic segments and morphemic moras is assumed in all the following analyses. The MLM accounts hence make no necessary prediction about the realization of segmental affixes.

Another example for morphological vowel deletion can be found in Modern Hebrew (Glinert, 1989; Sheffer, 1995; Bat-El, 2002) as one of three strategies to form the imperative. In contrast to the vowel deletion in Mauritian Creole, it is the first base vowel that remains unrealized, not the final vowel. Some examples are given in (25). Note that in (25-b), the initial onset remains unrealized as well as is predicted by regular phonological demands to avoid illicit three-consonantal clusters. An analysis for this pattern is in principle identical to the one proposed for Mauritian Creole. The crucial difference is only that the morphemic mora representing the imperative in Modern Hebrew is prefixed to its base, not suffixed.

(25)   *Imperatives in Colloquial Hebrew*   (Bat-El, 2002: 660)

	Masc		Fem		
	Fut	Imp	Fut	Imp	
a. *V-deletion*					
	ti—male	tmale	te—mali	tmali	'to fill'
	ti—kanes	tkanes	ti—kansi	tkansi	'to enter'
	ti—galgel	tgalgel	te—galgeli	tgalgeli	'to roll'
b. *CV-deletion*					
	ti—tfor	tfor	ti—tferi	tferi	'to saw'
	ti—gzor	gzor	ti—gzeri	gzeri	'to cut'
	tit—karev	tkarev	tit—karvi	tkarvi	'to approach'

3.2.1.2 *Consonant deletion in Canela Krahô and Mebengokre*   If, in contrast to the ranking in Mauritian Creole and Modern Hebrew, PVis$_V$ is ranked high but PVis$_C$ is in turn ranked relatively low, defective integration of a morphemic mora can also result in consonant deletion. An example for morphological consonant deletion can be found in the Macro-Ge language Canela Krahô (Popjes and Popjes, 2010). Nearly all verbs in Canela Krahô occur in two forms, termed 'short' and 'long'. The distribution of the two verb forms corresponds roughly to the distinction into non-finite (=long) and finite (=short) verbal contexts (Miestamo, 1973). For bases ending in a consonant (26-a), the short form is formed by non-realization of the final consonant. Vowel-final bases (26-b) show no alternation.

(26)   *Two verb forms in Canela Krahô*   (Popjes and Popjes, 2010: 192, 193)

	Long	Short	
a.	ihkulan	ihkula	'(so.) kills it'
	tɔn	tɔ	'(so.) makes it'
	ihkah:ɯl	ihkah:ɯ	'(so.) whips it'
	katɔl	katɔ	'he arrives'
b.	cupa	cupa	'fear it' (specified object)

The tableau (27) derives consonant deletion in Canela Krahô in the PDM framework. The ranking differs from the ranking for Mauritian Creole only in the position of PVis$_V$. Since it is ranked in the same high stratum as μ>Do>V and OneRt-S, non-realization of the final vowel as in (27-c) cannot become optimal.[18] In contrast, non-realization of the last consonant in candidate (27-e) wins the competition. Candidate (27-a) is excluded since the morphemic mora does not dominate any segment and candidate (27-b) since it integrates the mora in a phonetically visible way under violation of *σ…Af..μ. Candidate (27-d) is a structure where the final consonant is dominated by the phonetically invisible mora and is also integrated under the highest prosodic node. This can easily be deduced since the consonant is phonetically visible (=not marked with a grey background) and we hence know that it must be associated with the syllable node via a phonetically visible association relation; a structure that is excluded by OneRt-S.

High-ranked PVis$_V$ also ensures that vowel-final bases never undergo any change if the morphemic mora is added. The morphemic mora simply has no chance to associate to a segment since association to the final vowel induces a fatal violation of PVis$_V$ and association to a preceding consonant results in crossing association lines.

(27)   *Morphemic mora and consonant deletion*

		μ>Do>V	*σ…Af..μ	PVis$_V$	OneRt-S	PVis$_C$
a.	[katɔl]	*!				
b.	[katɔːl]		*!			
c.	[katl]			*!		
d.	[katɔl]				*!	
☞ e.	[katɔ]					*

---

[18] In Canela Krahô, vowel deletion is in fact blocked by independent phonotactic reasons since coda clusters are impossible in this language. However, since the present purpose is to illustrate the general logic and rankings relevant for defectively integrated morphemic moras, I abstract away from that.

Crucially now, this analysis does not presuppose that moraic consonants are allowed in the phonetically interpreted structure of this language. The markedness constraint $*C_\mu$ against moraic consonants can still be higher-ranked than $C<DD_p^m<\mu$ and $*\mu \dashv\!\!\!\!- S$. In this case, no consonant is ever predicted to project a mora in a phonetically visible way due to a constraint like WEIGHT BY POSITION (Sherer, 1994; Zec, 1995; Rosenthall and van der Hulst, 1999). Only in the contexts of a morphemic mora, a mora dominating a consonant becomes optimal as last resort to avoid non-realization of a vowel. In Canela Krahô, for example, there is no evidence for moraic codas since stress assignment is insensitive to whether syllables have codas or not (stress is on the final syllable in most contexts) and the language only allows (CC)V(V)C syllables, hence no geminates (Popjes and Popjes, 2010). This follows if $*C_\mu$ is ranked in the same stratum as PVis$_C$ in Canela Krahô whereas $C<DD_p^m<\mu$ and $*\mu \dashv\!\!\!\!- S$ are ordered in a lower stratum. Underlying moraic consonants are hence neutralized to non-moraic consonants for the phonetic interpretation.

Given that the consonant that remains unrealized after defective mora-integration is not expected to be moraic in the context without a defectively integrated mora, it is also possible that affixation of a morphemic mora may result in non-realization of an initial consonant even if the language in question does not allow the rare and marked structure of initial geminates. This is the case in, for example, Mebengokre, another Macro-Ge language where third person is marked by non-realization of the initial consonant (Salanova, 2004, 2007, 2011), shown in (28).

(28) *Subtraction in Mebengokre*   (Salanova, 2004: 15, 16)

BASE		3.Ps	1.Ps
ʤur	'pus'	ur	iʤur
ɲikra	'hand'	ikra	iɲikra
pɯtʌ	'to adopt'	utʌ	ipɯtʌ
jamak	'ear'	amak	ijamak
puʤu	'to hide'	uʤu	ipuʤu

The difference between Canela Krahô and Mebengokre is hence basically the same as the difference between Mauritian Creole and Modern Hebrew: in the former languages, a morphemic mora suffix triggers the relevant MLM whereas in the latter languages, a morphemic mora prefix is responsible for the non-realization of base segments.

3.2.1.3 *Vowel shortening in Mam*   Now we turn to a second type of MLM predicted from the defective integration of a morphemic mora, namely vowel shortening. The analysis also relies on a different type of defective integration: the morphemic prosodic node does not lack an association to a higher prosodic node but an association to a lower node. The analysis in the following is basically identical to the proposal made in Trommer and Zimmermann (2014) where the relevant configuration is termed 'hanging mora'.

In fact, the catalectic moras in Taubergrund German in the analysis of Seiler (2008) were already discussed as one instance of 'shortening' that results from mora affixation (see section 2.1.3). In the analysis presented in Seiler (2008), an affixed mora is integrated defectively in the structure and does not dominate a segment. Nevertheless, this mora is dominated by a syllable and hence its presence is sufficient to satisfy the bimoraic word minimality requirement. The apparent 'shortening' is hence the absence of an otherwise expected vowel lengthening that is phonologically motivated from a general word minimality restriction. This intriguing analysis is perfectly in line with all the assumptions made in the framework of PDM and would crucially be based on the constraint $*\mu...^{Af}...\varsigma$, the counterpart to $*\sigma...^{Af}...\mu$. 'True' vowel shortening in the sense that an underlying association of a mora with a vowel is marked as phonetically invisible can be predicted by defective mora integration as well. An example for morphological vowel shortening that is taken to result from affixing a morphological mora can be found in Mam, a Mayan language (England, 1983; Inkelas, to appear). This language has several instances of Subtractive Suffixes that trigger shortening of a preceding long vowel. Examples are given in (29-a). The data in (29-b) shows that no effect is obtained if the vowel preceding the Subtractive Affix is underlyingly short. It is important to know that the language also employs phonologically predictable vowel shortening since only one long vowel per word is allowed.[19] The suffixes in (29), however, all contain short vowels and hence are not predicted to trigger phonological vowel shortening (Inkelas, to appear).[20]

(29) *Subtractive Suffixes in Mam*   (England, 1983)

BASE		SUFFIXED FORM			
a. noːx	'fill'	noxna	'full'	(+participal /−na/)	126
juːp	'put out fire'	jupna	'put out'		126
toːq	'break'	toqna	'broken'		126
xaːw	'go up'	xawnaṣ	'up'	(+directional /−naṣ/)	131
eːl	'go out'	elnaṣ	'West'		131
oːk	'go in'	oknaṣ	'East'		131
qʼoːx	'anger'	qʼoxleʔn	'state of fighting'	(+abstract noun /−leʔn/)	121
b. kjim	'die'	kjimna	'dead'		126
kʼub	'go down'	kubʼnaṣ	'down'		131
kʼab	'wound'	kabʼleʔn	'wound'		121

---

[19] And in case two morphemes are concatenated that contain long vowels, morphological factors determine which one is shortened (England, 1983).

[20] It is a very reasonable hypothesis to assume that they contained long vowels in an earlier stage of the language and the process was phonologically motivated once. It is, however, purely morphological from a synchronic perspective.

An analysis for this vowel shortening based on morphemic mora affixation is given in (30). A morphemic mora is part of the underlying representation of the suffix /—na/. This morphemic mora has no chance to be associated with a segment due to high-ranked $*\mu...\underline{Af}...$ S but must be integrated under a syllable node due to high-ranked PVis_μ. Candidate (30-i-a) where the morphemic mora is not integrated and candidate (30-i-b) where the morphemic mora is fully integrated are therefore excluded (note that candidate (30-i-b) is impossible for independent reasons since the vowel is extralong—an unattested configuration in Mam). Insertion of an epenthetic syllable is one strategy to integrate the morphemic mora into the structure and hence satisfy $\text{PVis}_{\mu\text{-}Af}$ as in candidate (30-i-c). This, however, violates relatively high-ranked Col!_σ. Note that this does not imply that insertion of epenthetic syllables is generally impossible: high-ranked PVis_S predicts that as many syllables are inserted as necessary to integrate all underlying segments into the highest prosodic structure, hence making them phonetically interpretable. Syllable epenthesis is only excluded as a repair to provide morphemic moras with a syllable. An alternative that avoids this violation is a structure where the morphemic mora is associated with the syllable node that integrates the preceding base segments into the overall prosodic structure as in candidates (30-i-d) and (30-i-e). Since superheavy syllables dominating more than two moras in a phonetically visible way are excluded in Mam, this association makes an integration of both the base moras impossible. Candidate (30-i-e) finally wins the competition that integrates the affix mora defectively and phonetically integrates only one of the two underlying moras. This candidate only violates general PVis_μ since one base mora remains unrealized but avoids a violation of $\text{PVis}_{\mu\text{-}Af}$ since the morphemic affix mora is integrated. This analysis is thus based on the simple intuition that all moras strive to be integrated in a phonetically visible way and realization of affix moras is more important than realization of base moras.[21] Since only two moras can be integrated under one syllable node and syllable nodes cannot be inserted in order to ensure realization of moras, a competition arises if two base moras and one affix mora strive to be integrated under a single syllable node.

---

[21] This analysis predicts that long affix vowels preceding such a Subtractive Suffix are never shortened but surface as long. $\text{PVis}_{\mu\text{-}Af}$ would demand realization of all three affix moras present in such a context (=the two moras underlyingly dominating the vowel and the morphemic affix mora) and is hence not sufficient to decide which moras are realized. In such contexts, ONERT-S is decisive and favours a structure where all moras underlyingly associated with a vowel are integrated under a syllable node. The morphemic affix mora consequently remains unintegrated in the context of a long affix vowel and a Subtractive Suffix is not predicted to have any effect. This is apparently no misprediction. No contexts where a Subtractive Suffix precedes another affix could be found; they attach directly to the base in all examples.

Note that if the two base moras were already integrated underlyingly under a syllable node in (30-i), the effect would be the same: the affix mora and only one base mora are integrated under the last syllable node in a phonetically visible way. The only difference is that one underlying association line between the syllable and a base mora would be marked as phonetically invisible.

It is clear that such a defectively integrated morphemic mora could in principle also result in segment deletion if, for example, coda consonants are always moraic in a language. If a morphemic mora must be dominated by a base syllable that is expected to host two moras dominating a base vowel and consonant respectively, the consonantal mora could be predicted to remain phonetically unrealized in order to avoid a superheavy syllable.

(30)   *Subtractive Affixation in Mam*
   i.   *Vowel shortening*

	$PVIs_S$	$COL!_\sigma$	$PVIs_{\mu\text{-}AF}$	$*\mu...Af_S$	$*\sigma_{\mu\mu\mu}$	$PVIs_\mu$	$\mu{>}Dom_P{>}S$
a. [noːxna]			**	*!		*!	*
b. [noːːxna]			**	*!	*!		
c. [noːxna]			***!				*
d. [noːxna]			**			*!	*
☞ e. [noxna]			**			*	*

ii. *No effect for short vowels*

$\mu_○$ $\mu_•$ $\mu_•$ $\vert$ $\vert$ k'$_○$ u$_○$ b$_○$ + n$_•$ a$_•$ ṣ$_•$	PVIs$_s$	Col!$_\sigma$	PVIs$_{\mu\text{-}AF}$	*μ…Af→S	*σ$_{\mu\mu\mu}$	PVIs$_\mu$	μ>Dop^m>S
a. σ σ ($\mu_○\mu_•$)($\mu_•$) k'$_○$ u$_○$ b$_○$ n$_•$ a$_•$ ṣ$_•$ [kuːbnaṣ]		**		*!			
☞ b. σ σ ($\mu_○$)($\mu_•$)($\mu_•$) k'$_○$ u$_○$ b$_○$ n$_•$ a$_•$ ṣ$_•$ [kubnaṣ]		**					*
c. σ σ ($\mu_○$)($\mu_•$)($\mu_•$) k'$_○$ u$_○$ b$_○$ n$_•$ a$_•$ ṣ$_•$ [kbnaṣ]	*!	**				*	*

3.2.1.4 *Vowel shortening and length polarity in Anywa* Another instance of subtractive MLM that results from mora affixation can be found in Anywa, a Western Nilotic language. All bases in Anywa are monosyllabic and if they contain a long vowel, this vowel is shortened in, for example, the formation of the antipassive, as can be seen in (31).[22]

(31)   *Subtraction in Anywa*   (Reh, 1993: 222, 223; Trommer, 2011a: 104)

    Base   Antipassive

    a. *Short Base Vowel*

cam	cạm	'eat sth.'
ŋɔl	ŋɔl	'cut sth. off'
kan	kạn	'hide sth.'

    b. *Long Base Vowel*

riːw	riw	'to lay sth. crosswise'
maːṱ	maṱ	'drink sth.'
puːr	pur	'cultivate sth.'

Trommer (2011a) presents an analysis for Anywa Subtraction that is based on the assumption that a morphemic mora is affixed and only defectively integrated: it must

---

[22] In addition, the stem vowel gets [+ATR]—see Trommer (2011a) for a detailed and comprehensive analysis of the various (cooccurring) non-concatenative morphological processes in Western Nilotic languages.

be dominated by a syllable node but since the syllable dominates too many moras if it dominates the two moras of an underlyingly long vowel as well, one underlying association line between a mora and a long vowel remains phonetically unrealized. The analysis for Mam in (30) mirrors this logic. The main difference between Trommer's analysis and the present one is the assumption of a stratal optimization system in the latter where every morpheme is optimized prior to concatenation (=Egalitarian Stratal OT, see Trommer, 2011*a*; Bermúdez-Otero, in preparation). This assumption makes the representation of, for example, the mora usurping morphemes discussed in section 3.1 impossible. The analysis for Anywa in Trommer (2011*a*), however, can be reimplemented into the present framework of PDM without problems. Interestingly enough, Anywa also exhibits an additional MLM process of length polarity. The frequentative in Anywa is marked by lengthening of a short vowel (32-a) and shortening of a long vowel (32-b) (and additional gemination of the stem-final consonant). In fact, Anywa is apparently the only instance where morphological segment lengthening and shortening alternate productively in the same morphological context. Another often-cited example for length polarity is Diegueño, discussed in some more detail in 5.2.2.1.

(32) *Length Polarity in Anywa*   (Reh, 1993: 44, 244, 245; Trommer, 2011*a*: 109)

BASE	FREQUENTATIVE STEM	
a. *Short Base Vowel*		
cam	caːmː	'eat sth.'
bil	biːlː	'soak sth.'
ŋɔl	ŋɔːlː	'cut'
b. *Long Base Vowel*		
caːn	canː	'tell'
kaːt	katː	'weave basket'
kaːl	kalː	'jump over'

Trommer (2011*a*) gives an intriguing analysis for the length polarity in terms of mora affixation. The morphemic mora in the frequentative triggers shortening if the base vowel is already long since it must be integrated under the syllable node but no syllable can phonetically dominate three moras. If the base vowel is short, however, it can be fully integrated resulting in vowel lengthening. The difference between the shortening antipassive affix mora and the frequentative affix mora that results in length polarity is the fact that the former is suffixed and the latter is prefixed. Since all bases in Anywa are monosyllabic and exhibit a moraic coda consonant, a suffix mora can never be associated with a base vowel without crossing association lines; a prefix mora, however, can be fully integrated into the base structure and dominate the base vowel if it is underlyingly short. This analysis is sketched in (33) and the reader is referred to Trommer (2011*a*) for more details.

(33)   *MLM in Anywa*   (Trommer, 2011a: 106–112)

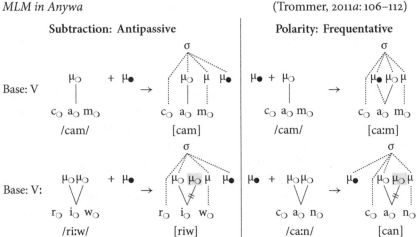

Subtraction: Antipassive | **Polarity: Frequentative**

3.2.1.5 Summary: defective mora integration   The list in (34) summarizes all the instances of subtractive MLM triggered by mora affixation discussed in the preceding section. A defectively integrated morphemic mora can either predict non-realization of a segment or shortening of a long segment.

(34)   *Subtractive MLM analysed as defective morphemic* μ

    3.2.1.1   **Mauritian Creole**   ↦ Non-realization of the final V

$$\mu_O \quad \mu_O \; \mu_\bullet$$
$$v_O \; i_O \; n_O \; i_O$$
$$[vin]$$

    3.2.1.1   **Modern Hebrew**   ↦ Non-realization of the initial V

$$\mu_\bullet \; \mu_O \quad \mu_O \quad \mu_O$$
$$t_O \; i_O \; m_O \; a_O \; l_O \; e_O$$
$$[tmale]$$

    3.2.1.2   **Canela Krahô**   ↦ Non-realization of the final C

$$\mu_O \quad \mu_O \; \mu_\bullet$$
$$k_O \; a_O \; t_O \; \mathit{ɔ}_O \; l_O$$
$$[katɔ]$$

3.2.1.2 **Mebengokre**   ↣ Non-realization of the initial C

[ur]

3.2.1.3 **Mam**   ↣ Shortening of a V

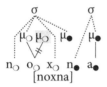

[noxna]

3.2.1.4 **Anywa**   ↣ Shortening of a V (Trommer, 2011*a*)

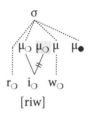

[riw]

↣ Length Polarity (Trommer, 2011*a*)

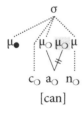 

[can]   [caːm]

That the defective integration of a morphemic mora can even result in a segmental feature-change effect is argued in D'Alessandro and van Oostendorp (2016) where the model proposed in Trommer and Zimmermann (2014) is extended to metaphony in Abruzzese. It is argued that certain morphemes usurp (or 'eat' in their terminology) the vowel element |A| in a segment representation based on elements (Harris and Lindsey, 1995).

3.2.2 *Defective syllable integration*

The mechanism of defective integration illustrated in the preceding section for morphemic moras is also predicted for morphemic syllable nodes. The surface effects that can result from defectively integrated morphemic syllable nodes overlap to some degree with the MLM effects predicted by defectively integrated morphemic moras. This follows since a morphemic syllable can only dominate a mora in a certain context—if the morphemic syllable remains uninterpreted and all elements that it dominates, the surface effect is indistinguishable from the effects predicted by defective integration of a morphemic mora. For certain languages with a pattern where a mora remains phonetically invisible in a certain morphological context, however, it is clear that they employ defective integration of a morphemic syllable, not a morphemic mora. These are languages where subtractive and additive MLM coexist. In the theoretical framework adopted here where integration of prosodic nodes is enforced via bidirectional parsing constraints, this is a straightforward prediction: full integration into the prosodic structure can be demanded for a morphemic node on tier x whereas a morphemic node on another tier y is only defectively integrated under the same constraint ranking. Such a coexistence of defective and full integration of different morphemic prosodic nodes predicts the coexistence of additive and subtractive MLM in a language—a prediction that is indeed borne out in several languages of the world. Some of the languages in the present data sample for which it is argued that a subtractive MLM follows from a defectively integrated morphemic syllable and an additive MLM from a fully integrated morphemic mora are listed in (35) together with an illustrating example for additive and subtractive MLM. Chapter 6 gives a complete overview over the languages in the present data sample and their (cooccurring) MLM patterns.

(35)   *Coexistence of additive and subtractive MLM: syllable and mora affixation*

Additive MLM	Subtractive MLM
=full integration of a morphemic μ	=defective integration of a morphemic syllable

Alabama

IMPERFECT	PLURAL
coko: → cok:o: 'sit down'	bala: → bal 'lie down'
(Hardy and Montler, 1988*a*: 400)	(Hardy and Montler, 1988*b*: 391)

Diegueño

PLURAL	PLURAL
múɬ → mú:ɬ 'gather'	sa:w → saw 'eat'
(Wolf, 2007: 54)	(Wolf, 2007: 54)

Dinka

	3.Sg				Plural	
wɛ̰c	→	wɛ̰ːc	'kick'	wǎːl	→ wàl	'plant'
(Flack, 2007*b*: 750)				(Ladd et al., 2009: 662)		

Hausa

	Verbal Noun				Proper Noun	
gudù	→	gudùː	'walk'	baːkoː	→ baːko	'stranger
(Schuh, 1989: 41)				(Schuh, 1989: 38)		(man's name)'

Lardil

	Passive				Nominative	
kupari	→	kupariː	'make, repair'	jalulu	→ jalul	'flame'
(Klokeid, 1976: 81)				(Klokeid, 1976: 46)		

Oromo

	Negative				1.Ps	
nama	→	namaːmihi	'man'	magalaː	→ magalan	'market'
(Owens, 1985: 12)				(Owens, 1985: 11)		

Tohono O'odham

	Distributive				Perfect	
bábad	→	bábːad	'frog'	gátwid	→ gátwi	'to shoot object'
(Fitzgerald, 2012: 456)				(Fitzgerald and Fountain, 1995: 5)		

This coexistence of subtractive and additive MLM and its account in PDM is shown in some more detail in section 3.2.2.1 with a discussion of Tohono O'odham. In the sections following this discussion, the typology of subtractive MLM patterns that are predicted from defective integration of a morphemic syllable are presented with several shorter case studies and analyses.

3.2.2.1 Consonant deletion in Tohono O'odham   A first MLM pattern predicted from defective syllable integration is non-realization of a consonant, absolutely parallel to the prediction from defective integration of a morphemic mora. An often-cited example for morphological consonant deletion can be found in Tohono O'odham, an Uto-Aztecan language spoken in Arizona and Mexico (Mason, 1950; Hale, 1965; Mathiot, 1973; Lombardi and McCarthy, 1991; Hill and Zepeda, 1992; Fitzgerald and Fountain, 1995; Fitzgerald, 1997; Hill and Zepeda, 1998; Horwood, 2001; Kosa, 2006; Fitzgerald, 2009, 2012). The language allows complex codas but no onset clusters and length is contrastive for vowels and consonants. Long consonants are, in contrast to long vowels, only found in morphologically derived environments. The perfective is now formed from its imperfect counterpart by subtracting the final consonant of the base as can be seen in (36). Note that this morphological deletion might also feed phonological vowel deletion since the language does not allow final sequences of coronal consonants followed by high vowels. In (36-b), exactly such a sequence is expected after consonant deletion and repaired via vowel deletion.

(36)   *Perfective in Tohono O'odham*   (Hale, 1965; Fitzgerald and Fountain, 1995)

	IMPERFECT	PERFECT		
a.	má:k	má:	'giving'	FF5
	híhim	híhi	'walking' (pl)	FF5
	gátwid	gátwi	'to shoot object'	FF6
	nákog	náko	'enduring'	FF9
	bihiwig	bihiwi	'coiling oneself'	FF9
	si:mun	si:mu	'hoeing object'	FF9
b.	míliw	míl	'arriving by running or driving'	FF7
	gigosid	gigos	'feeding'	FF7
	huḍuŋ	huḍ	'descending'	H301
	ta:pan	ta:p	'splitting'	H301

In the PDM framework, this is predicted from assuming that the perfect exponent in Tohono O'odham is a morphemic syllable that is defectively integrated. The relevant constraint ranking for Tohono O'odham is hence one where the constraint *Φ...Af...σ penalizing any integration of an affix syllable into higher prosodic structure[23] (excluding candidate (37-a)) dominates σ>Do>μ demanding that any syllable must dominate at least one mora via some kind of association line (excluding candidate (37-b)). That it is insufficient for the morphemic syllable to dominate only a mora that does not dominate anything in turn is ensured by undominated μ>Do>S, excluding (37-c). Since ONeRt-S is undominated in the language, every segment that is integrated under this defectively integrated syllable node must remain unrealized, making candidate (37-d) impossible. And since PVis_V is ranked higher than PVis_C, candidate (37-f) finally wins the competition where the final consonant remains phonetically invisible.

---

[23] Again, it is silently assumed that a direct association with a higher node, i.e. the prosodic word node in this case, is excluded from undominated constraints as well (see footnote 16).

(37)   *Morphemic syllable and consonant deletion*

$\mu_\circ\ \mu_\circ$ / $m_\circ\ a_\circ\ k_\circ$ + $\sigma_\bullet$	σ>Do>μ	μ>Do>S	*Φ...Af σ	OneRt-S	PVisv	PVisc
a. [maːk]			*!			
b. [maːk]	*!					
c. [maːk]		*!				
d. [maːk]				*!		
e. [mk]					*!	
☞ f. [maː]						*

This analysis is different from the analysis proposed in Trommer and Zimmermann (2014) (see also Trommer, 2011a) for Tohono O'odham. There, it is assumed that a defectively integrated mora triggers non-realization of the consonant. This assumption is in fact highly problematic in the light of the full MLM pattern of the language. In fact, Tohono O'odham employs mora-augmenting additive MLM as well, shown in (38). The distributive is formed by gemination of the consonant following the first vowel.[24]

(38)   *Distributive in Tohono O'odham*   (Mathiot, 1973; Fitzgerald, 2012)

SINGULAR	DISTRIBUTIVE		
bábad	báb:ad	'frog'	F456
tátamko	tát:amko	'jaw'	F456
tá:tam	tá:t:am	'tooth'	F456
nó:nha	nó:n:ha	'egg'	F456

This additive MLM is best analysed as the result of affixing a mora that is fully integrated in its base. Under the alternative analysis that Subtraction results from mora affixation as well, we are then left with a situation where a suffixed morphemic mora remains defectively integrated and triggers non-realization of a segment whereas a prefixed morphemic mora is fully integrated and results in additive MLM. It is not trivial to implement such a situation without introducing morpheme-specific constraints or rankings. The same critique applies to the analysis given in Trommer and Zimmermann (2014) for Lardil (see (35)) where additive MLM and subtractive MLM coexist as well. One pattern analysed in Trommer and Zimmermann (2014) where subtractive and additive MLM coexist in one language is Alabama. There, the asymmetry that a certain morphemic mora (=the plural exponent) is only defectively integrated and triggers Subtraction whereas another morphemic mora (=the imperfect exponent) is fully integrated resulting in gemination or vowel lengthening, is due to the fact that

---

[24] The base forms in (i-a) are apparently reduplicated. Interestingly, some words make a three-way-distinction between singular, plural, and distributive as in (i-b). For these words, it seems reasonable to assume that the plural is formed from the singular via reduplication and the distributive then via reduplication and gemination (Saba Kirchner, 2010). For the forms in (37), it is not clear whether unreduplicated stems exist or whether the distributive for these stems is marked via gemination only. For an analysis, however, it does not make a crucial difference whether gemination is an exponent on its own or only cooccurs with reduplication. In the latter case, the analysis would be absolutely parallel to the analysis proposed for Balangao in section 6.2.4.3.

(i)   *Distributive in Tohono O'odham*   (Mathiot, 1973; Fitzgerald, 2012)

SINGULAR	PLURAL	DISTRIBUTIVE		
a. *Two-way contrast*				
bábad	báb:ad		'frog'	F456
tátamko	tát:amko		'jaw'	F456
ʔoʔodham	ʔoʔ:odham		'people(s), Papago(s)'	M45
b. *Three-way contrast*				
náhagio	nánhagio	nán:hagio	'earring'	F456
kótoŋ	kóktoŋ	kók:toŋ	'shirt'	F456
kaviu	kakaviu	kak:aviu	'horse'	M45

the latter mora affix is assumed to be underlyingly associated with a high tone (that is consistently realized in the imperfect in addition to segmental lengthening). That this mora must be fully integrated then follows since the tone must be realized. This account nicely captures the coexistence of additive and subtractive MLM in Alabama but cannot be generalized to all other languages where additive and subtractive MLM can be found. As was illustrated with the list in (35), such a coexistence of additive and subtractive MLM is in fact abundant in languages employing MLM. The restriction that only moras exist as possible morphemic prosodic nodes is hence too strong and the typology of full and partial integration of other morphemic prosodic nodes needs to be taken into account as well in order to capture the whole picture of MLM.

In the PDM account, morphemic moras in Tohono O'odham are hence taken to be fully integrated into their base structure resulting in gemination (and reduplication). Morphemic syllables, on the other hand, are only defectively integrated resulting in non-realization of a consonant.[25]

3.2.2.2 Multi-segment deletion in Murle and Alabama The prediction made from assuming morphemic syllables is that other segmental portions that can constitute a syllable can remain unrealized after defective integration of such a morphemic syllable. This prediction is indeed borne out. A syllable only dominating a consonant as the structure assumed for Tohono O'odham is marked since syllables strive to have a vocalic nucleus. It is assumed that this is ensured by the constraint (39). It is different from the PARSE constraints introduced in section 2.2.2, (28)/(29) since it does not demand immediate dominance between two elements, only that one element is contained in the other.

(39) σ-DO-V   Assign a violation mark for every σ node that does not dominate a vowel.

An obvious prediction from this constraint is a language where adding a morphemic syllable can result in deletion of the initial or final vowel. An analysis along these lines is proposed for final vowel deletion in Aymara, discussed in detail in section 4.2. Non-realization of an even larger syllable-sized portion of segments is attested in Alabama and Murle. Alabama and the closely related language Koasati form a subgroup of Eastern Muskogean and the crucial generalizations about Subtraction are identical in both languages (Martin, 1988; Kimball, 1991; Broadwell, 1993). Similar facts can be also be found in Choctaw, a Western Muskogean language (Nicklas, 1974; Kimball,

---

[25] There are several reduplication patterns in Tohono O'odham, at least a prefixing light syllable and a prefixing heavy syllable reduplication pattern (Fitzgerald, 2009), see also footnote 24. The present analysis implies that these patterns cannot result from syllable affixation since morphemic syllables are always defectively integrated in the language. In contrast, it is assumed here that those result from prefixed morphemic moras as well: one mora for the light reduplicant and two moras for the heavy syllable reduplication. Whenever possible, morphemic moras are realized by gemination. If, however, the morphemic mora cannot be associated with an intervocalic consonant, reduplication becomes optimal to realize a morphemic mora. This is perfectly in line with the argumentation in Fitzgerald (2012) that codas contribute to weight in Tohono O'odham at least in the domain of prosodic morphology.

1985, 1991; Lombardi and McCarthy, 1991; Ulrich, 1993, 2003; Broadwell, 2006). The plural/repetitive is formed in Alabama via non-realization of the final syllable rhyme (40) (Lupardus, 1982; Hardy and Montler, 1988*a*, *b*; Lombardi and McCarthy, 1991; Samek-Lodovici, 1992; Broadwell, 1993; Grimes, 2002). As is discussed in section 4.3, this subtractive MLM is in fact only one of two patterns that are found in this context: other stems are lexically marked for subtracting only their final coda consonant. An account for this allomorphy is presented below in section 4.3. All stems in (40), are followed by one of the two stem classifier suffixes /−li/ or /−ka/ (Hardy and Montler, 1988*b*).[26] In (40-a), the final vowel and following final base consonant remain unrealized in the plural and in (40-b), a final long vowel is deleted in the plural form.

(40)   *Subtraction in Alabama*   (Hardy and Montler, 1988*b*; Broadwell, 1993)

	BASE		PLURAL		
a.	batatli	'hit once'	batli	'hit repeatedly'	B417
	kolof:i (kolof+li)	'cut once'	kol:i	'cut repeatedly'	B417
	haɬapka	'kick once'	halka	'kick repeatedly'	HM391
b.	misi:li	'close eyes once'	misli	'close eyes repeatedly'	HM391
	bala:ka	'lie down' (sg)	balka	'lie down' (pl)	B417
	ibacasa:li	'join together' (sg. object)	ibacasli	'join together' (pl. object)	B417

A quite similar pattern can be observed in the Kwa language Murle (Arensen, 1982; Haspelmath, 2002) where non-realization of the final consonant and the final vowel (41) is one of various strategies to form the plural of nouns.[27] Some examples are given in (41).

(41)   *Subtraction in Murle: plural formation*   (Arensen, 1982: 40–43)

BASE		PLURAL
keloc	'flea'	kel
ziza:coc	'termite'	ziza:c
cinotot	'moustache'	cinot
miniɲit	'spirit'	miniɲ
amotat	'saliva'	amot
mu:roc	'habil tree'	mu:r

---

[26] This interpretation is doubted in Grimes (2002) where it is assumed that these final segments were suffixes at an earlier stage of language development and are frozen by now. However, there are no additional explanations or empirical arguments for this claim and the generalization is apparently based on the descriptions in Lupardus (1982) and Hardy and Montler (1988*a*, *b*) where the suffixes are apparently interpreted as productive. The same conclusion that these are indeed synchronically productive affixes is reached by Bye (2006) for Koasati.

[27] This subtraction is actually only one lexical allomorph for the plural formation of nouns. Other (lexically marked) nouns form their plural by non-realization of only the final consonant. This coexistence of different subtraction patterns is discussed in more detail below in section 3.2.3.

It is now argued that subtractive MLM in these languages follows from assuming a morphemic syllable that is only defectively integrated. As in Tohono O'odham (37), this syllable results in non-realization of the mora(s) it dominates. In contrast to Tohono O'odham, however, the syllable is forced to dominate a vowel due to σ-Do-V. This is shown in tableau (42) for the Murle data. Non-realization of only a consonant in candidate (42-a) is excluded by σ-Do-V and candidate (42-b) that leaves both the final vowel and the final consonant unrealized wins the competition. That non-realization of the morphemic syllable implies non-realization of the elements it dominates follows again from ONERT-S, excluding candidate (42-c).[28] Note that in the tableau (42), any candidates that fully integrate the morphemic syllable or do not integrate it at all are excluded since they violate high-ranked σ>Do>μ and *Φ...Af...σ.[29]

(42)   *Subtraction in Murle*

	σ-Do-V	σ>Do>μ	*Φ..Af..σ	ONERT-S	COL!μ	PVISᵥ	PVISᴄ
a. [ke.lo]	*!				*		*
☞ b. [kel]						*	*
c. [ke.loc]				*!			*

That association of the morphemic syllable with the mora dominating the base-vowel in candidate (42-b) necessarily implies non-realization of the final consonant

[28] This makes no misprediction for bases where the final vowel lacks a mora underlyingly if V<DD<μ is undominated. Every vowel is hence supplied with an epenthetic mora if it lacks one underlyingly.

[29] The pattern might in fact be slightly different since there is a single example showing deletion of the final consonant and shortening of a preceding long vowel: /dazaːc/ → /daza/ '2nd durra crop' (Arensen, 1982: 43). If this is indeed the general pattern, ONERT-S must be ranked low and the Subtraction in Murle is more similar to the shortening-deletion allomorphy patterns in Hidatsa and Lomongo analysed in section 3.2.2.4. Since both patterns easily follow under the PDM account, the generalizations for Murle don't take this apparent shortening into account since the empirical base for it is so scarce.

is straightforwardly expected since consonant clusters are illicit in Murle (Arensen, 1982: 12). A language-independent reason for this collateral deletion is the avoidance of the standard linear CONTIGUITY constraint discussed in section 2.2.3, (39), repeated in (43). It penalizes morpheme-internal non-realization of a segment—a marked structure (44) that is avoided if the final consonant remains unrealized as well.

(43)   CNTPVIS   Assign a violation mark for every phonetically invisible segment $S_\bigcirc$ that is preceded and followed by segments $A_\bigcirc$ and $B_\bigcirc$ that belong to the same morpheme.

(44)   *Excluded vowel-only deletion in Murle*

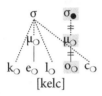

An analysis for the Alabama Subtraction pattern given so far is absolutely parallel to this analysis for Murle. We return to a complete analysis of Alabama in section 4.3.

3.2.2.3 Segment shortening in Hausa and Korean   In a language with a slightly different ranking where ONERT is ranked lower than PVISs, adding a morphemic syllable can also result only in shortening of long segments, never in non-realization. Patterns of morphological vowel shortening are widely attested in the languages of the world. Examples are Dinka, Diegueño, Hausa, Kashaya, or Hindi. Some exemplifying data from Hausa is given in (45) (Hayes, 1990; Wolff, 1993; Smirnova, 1985; Schuh, 1989; Newman, 2000; Jaggar, 2001; Crysmann, 2004; Álvarez, 2005). In Hausa, final vowel shortening applies to form a proper noun from a common noun (Schuh, 1989; Crysmann, 2004). As in Tohono O'odham and Choctaw, the language also employs an instance of additive MLM, namely final vowel lengthening to form the verbal noun (see (35), Schuh, 1989).

(45)   *Subtraction in Hausa: vowel shortening*   (Schuh, 1989: 38)

BASE		PROPER NOUN	
marka:	'height of rainy season'	marka	'name of woman born at this time'
ba:ko:	'stranger'	ba:ko	'man's name'
baki:	'black'	baki	"Blackie"
ku:matu:	'cheeks'	kuma:tu	'name of so. with fat cheeks'

An analysis for Hausa vowel shortening in terms of syllable affixation is given in tableau (46-i). The proper noun formation morpheme is taken to consist of a morphemic syllable. This morphemic syllable must dominate a mora but is not integrated into the higher prosodic structure. This excludes candidates (46-i-a) and (46-i-b). Association of a mora with the morphemic syllable, however, results in non-realization of this mora due to ONERT-μ that excludes candidate (46-i-c). Crucially now, ONERT-S is ranked low and lower than PVIS_S. From this it follows that association of the syllable with a mora does not result in non-realization of the dominated segment as in candidate (46-i-e). In the winning candidate (46-i-d), no vowel remains unrealized, only one of the two moras with which the vowel is underlyingly associated. This implies that the final vowel in (46-i-d) is dominated by two highest prosodic nodes: the phonetically invisible morphemic syllable and the prosodic word node. Since ONERT-S is ranked lower than σ>Do>μ, this marked structure is tolerated. Multiple root nodes for moras, on the other hand, are excluded by higher-ranked ONERT-μ. The morphemic syllable can hence not directly dominate a phonetically visible mora as in candidate (46-i-c). Candidate (46-i-f) illustrates yet another excluded structure where an epenthetic mora is inserted to satisfy the need for the syllable to be associated with a mora. This candidate is suboptimal since insertion of epenthetic moras is excluded by COL!_μ, ranked in the same high stratum as PVIS_S. Note that V>Do$_p^m$>μ is taken to be undominated in Hausa and insertion of epenthetic moras to license underlyingly mora-less vowels is still predicted. It is only excluded as a repair to supply the morphemic syllable with a mora. Since PVIS_S is so high-ranked, the morphemic syllable has only an effect for long vowels, never for short vowels as is shown in (46-ii). Any association of the morphemic syllable with a mora that dominates a short vowel will result in segment deletion and is excluded by PVIS_S. In this case, the morphemic syllable simply cannot be associated with any mora and a violation of σ>Do>μ is unavoidable as in the winning candidate (46-ii-a).

(46) *Morphemic syllable in Hausa*
  i. *Vowel shortening*

	COL!_μ	PVIS_S	*Φ...Af...σ	σ>Do>μ	ONERT-μ	ONERT-S
a.				*!		
b.			*!			

		CoL!_μ	PVis_S	*Φ..Af..σ	σ>Do>μ	OneRt-μ	OneRt-S
c.	[marka:]					*!	*
☞ d.	[marka]						*
e.	[mark]		*!				
f.	[marka:]	*!					

ii. No effect for short vowels

		CoL!_μ	PVis_S	*Φ..Af..σ	σ>Do>μ	OneRt-μ	OneRt-S
	m a r o k o a +						
☞ a.	[marka]				*		
b.	[mark]		*!				
c.	[marka]	*!					

This ranking also predicts a pattern of Subtraction where underlying geminates are shortened to singleton consonants. Both patterns have in common that a defectively integrated syllable triggers non-realization of a mora without causing non-realization of a segment. Such an effect of morphological degemination can be found in Korean where the effective suffix /−ɨni/ triggers shortening of a long vowel (47-a)[30] or degemination of a long consonant (47-b). No subtractive MLM is triggered for bases where neither a vowel nor a consonant is long in the syllable directly preceding the Subtractive Suffix (47-c). Since Korean does not allow closed syllables with a long vowel and hence only one segment per syllable can be long, vowel shortening and degemination are in complementary distribution. Note the well-known allophony of /ɾ/ and /l/ in Korean: the former appears in onsets, the latter elsewhere.

(47) *Subtractive Suffix and shortening allomorphy in Korean*   (Ko, 1998: 10,382)

	BASE		EFFECTIVE
a.	táːm	'to put in'	tamɨni
	áːn	'to hug'	anɨ́ni
	sáːlm	'to boil'	salmɨ́ni
b.	colː	'nag'	coɾɨni
	kəlː	'filter'	kəɾɨni
	nulː	'press'	nuɾɨni
c.	sak	'decomposed'	sakɨni
	takʔ	'wipe'	takʔɨni
	sʔip	'chew'	sʔipɨni

The same ranking that was obtained in Hausa predicts this pattern in Korean under the assumption that all geminate consonants are underlyingly moraic. The suffix /−ɨni/ is assumed to contain a morphemic syllable in its representations that is defectively integrated into the prosodic structure. It strives to dominate a mora that then becomes phonetically invisible but it cannot trigger non-realization of a segment. It can hence only dominate the second mora of a vowel (48-a) or a mora that dominates a final consonant (48-b). In case the final base syllable contains only a (non-moraic) singleton consonant and a short vowel, the morphemic syllable has no surface effect (48-c).

(48) *Subtractive Suffix in Korean*
  a. *Vowel shortening*   b. *Degemination*   c. *No effect for short segments*

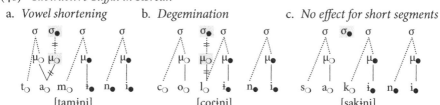

[tamɨni]   [coɾɨni]   [sakɨni]

[30] Vowel shortening is analysed by Ko (2010) as a side-effect of stress-shift. A stressed suffix makes stress on the preceding base syllable impossible and in addition induces shortening of the now unstressed vowel. However, this cannot be the general explanation since there are polysyllabic bases with initial stress where the suffix remains unstressed: /jóːŋsəha/ 'forgive' → /jóːŋsəhaɨni/ (Ko, 2010: 386). In addition, it has to be noted that the phonemic status of long vowels in Korean is not uncontroversial and some researchers argue that the contrast is not active anymore (Carando, 2009; Ko, 2010).

3.2.2.4 Shortening or deletion in Hidatsa and Lomongo   In Korean and Hausa, ranking PVis$_S$ above σ>Do>μ ensures that association of the defectively integrated morphemic syllable to a mora only results in shortening, never in segment deletion. If, however, PVis$_S$ is ranked lower than σ>Do>μ, affixation of a morphemic syllable is predicted to result in an alternation between segment shortening and segment deletion. There are at least two languages exemplifying such a pattern where subtractive MLM results in vowel shortening or deletion. The first example is imperative formation in Hidatsa (Matthews, 1873; Robinett, 1955*a*, *b*, *c*; Hardy and Montler, 1988*b*; Bowers, 1996; Boyle, 2007). As can be seen in (49), the imperative is formed by shortening of an underlying final long vowel (or monophthongization of a diphthong) (49-a) or deletion of an underlying short final vowel (49-b).[31]

(49)   *Imperative formation in Hidatsa*   (Park, 2012: 245–247)

	BASE		IMPERATIVE
a.	núdare:	'grab sth. soft (as mud)'	núdare
	báca:	'string sth. lace sth.'	báca
	habê:	'hack sth. up'	habé
	hacâ:	'cut narrow stripes of sth.'	hacá
	nágara:	'tear sth. up with teeth'	nágara
	diríá	'run'	dirí
	núcarua	'drag sth.'	núcaru
b.	ga:rí	'ask for sth.'	ga:r
	náhdabi	'attack sb. (as a dog)'	náhdab
	nagagíbi	'shave or scrape sth.'	nagagíb
	ma:ru:dí	'eat'	ma:rú:d
	náhcagi	'bite off sth. as a string'	náhcag

Another example for phonologically predictable allomorphy between morphological vowel shortening and deletion can be found in Lomongo (Hulstaert, 1938; Horwood, 2001; Kosa, 2006). In Lomongo, the vocative for personal names is apparently formed by shortening a final long vowel (50-a) and non-realization of a final CV sequence (50-b). It is, however, striking that coda consonants are generally illicit in Lomongo. The data in (50-b) can hence reasonably be interpreted as non-realization

---

[31] The pattern is in fact only a subset of a more complex ablaut pattern: words ending in a short vowel preceded by /h/ or two consonants do not undergo deletion but vowel change: /naga:hí/ 'pull sth.' → /naga:há/ (Park, 2012: 245). It is assumed that this blocking of Subtraction is due to restrictions about possible (derived) final consonant(s) (clusters). In addition, the imperative morpheme is taken to contain additional vocalic features that will always be realized on the final vocalic mora. These vocalic features are hence not realized on a phonetically visible vowel in all those contexts where Subtraction applies but only in contexts where subtractive MLM is blocked. In addition, it is apparent that all words ending in a short vowel that can undergo deletion end in /i/: 'Future research will, perhaps, uncover active stems that end with other short vowels' (Park, 2012: 244).

of a short vowel and phonologically predictable non-realization of a final coda (Horwood, 2001).

(50) *Vocative for personal names in Lomongo*   (Hulstaert, 1938: 157)

BASE	VOCATIVE
a. bokaá	boká
b. isúke	isû
ɛkɔmélá	ɛkɔmé
njoli	njó

The tableaux (51-i) and (51-ii) illustrate how a PDM ranking predicts such an alternation between vowel shortening and vowel deletion with the Hidatsa examples /núdareː/ → /núdare/ and /gaːrí/ → /gaːr/. The ranking differs from the ranking proposed for Hausa only in the position of σ>Do>μ and PVis$_S$. That the former is ranked above the latter predicts that the defectively integrated morphemic syllable must dominate a mora even if this results in segment deletion. Tableau (51-i) shows that vowel shortening is predicted for a base with a final long vowel in the imperative. The morphemic syllable dominates a mora and both these prosodic nodes remain phonetically invisible. However, the segment that is dominated by the phonetically invisible mora must not become phonetically invisible as well since ONERT-S is ranked below PVis$_S$. In tableau (51-ii), on the other hand, a short vowel precedes the morphemic syllable. In this case, non-realization of the vowel becomes optimal. COL!$_\mu$ prohibits an alternative strategy in candidate (51-ii-d) where an epenthetic mora is inserted and the segment can remain phonetically visible. Again, the high position of COL!$_\mu$ does not prohibit mora insertion to license underlyingly mora-less vowels.

(51) *Subtraction in Hidatsa*

i. *Shortening of a final long vowel*

$\sigma_\bullet$ $\mu_\circ$ $\mu_\circ$ $\mu_\circ\mu_\circ+$ n$_\circ$ u$_\circ$ d$_\circ$ a$_\circ$ r$_\circ$ e$_\circ$		σ>Do>σ	*Φ...Af. σ	COL!$_\mu$	ONERT-μ	PVis$_S$	ONERT-S
a.	σ σ σ σ$_\bullet$ μ$_\circ$ μ$_\circ$ μ$_\circ$μ$_\circ$ n$_\circ$ u$_\circ$ d$_\circ$ a$_\circ$ r$_\circ$ e$_\circ$ [nudareː]	*!					
b.	σ σ σ$_\bullet$ μ$_\circ$ μ$_\circ$ μ$_\circ$μ$_\circ$ n$_\circ$ u$_\circ$ d$_\circ$ a$_\circ$ r$_\circ$ e$_\circ$ [nudareː]		*!				

c. [nudare:]				*!		*
☞ d. [nudare]						*
e. [nudar]					*!	

ii. Deletion of a final short vowel

	σ>Doᴍμ	*Φ...Afσ	Coɪ!μ	OɴᴇRᴛ-μ	PVɪss	OɴᴇRᴛ-S
a. [ga:ri]	*!					
b. [ga:ri]		*!				
☞ c. [ga:r]					*	
d. [ga:ri]		*!				*

3.2.2.5 Summary: defective syllable integration   The list in (52) summarizes all subtractive MLM patterns that were analysed as result of a defectively integrated morphemic syllable. It illustrates how the assumption of a morphemic syllable node that remains defectively integrated can result in different subtractive MLM patterns that affect different syllable-sized portions depending on how many moraic and/or segmental items the syllable is forced to dominate.

(52)   *Subtractive MLM analysed as defective morphemic syllable*

    3.2.2.1   **Tohono O'odham** ⇢ Non-realization of the final C

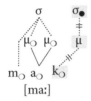

[ma:]

    3.2.2.2   **Murle I, Alabama** ⇢ Non-realization of the final V and C

[kel]

    3.2.2.3   **Hausa** ⇢ Shortening of a final V

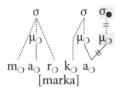

[marka]

    3.2.2.3   **Korean** ⇢ Shortening of a final C or V

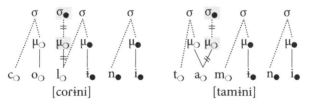

[corɨni]   [tamɨni]

    3.2.2.4   **Hidatsa, Lomongo** ⇢ Shortening or deletion of a final V

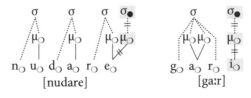

[nudare]   [ga:r]

3.2.3 *Coexistence of defective mora- and syllable-integration: Murle*

A very interesting instance of subtractive MLM is lexical allomorphy between different Subtraction patterns in one morphological context where the size of the non-realized portion varies between different stems. In Murle and Alabama, stems are lexically marked for subtracting either a vowel or a vowel and a consonant. It is argued that such a lexical difference can follow from two general mechanisms: a different underlying prosodic structure for the two types of stems or a lexical choice for one of two different morpheme representations. The latter phenomenon is discussed in this section with an account for allomorphy in Murle and the former mechanism is presented in section 4.3 with an analysis of Alabama.

Subtraction in Murle was already mentioned as an example for non-realization of the final vowel and consonant in the last section (see tableau (42)). However, this is only one plural allomorph (Arensen, 1982; Haspelmath, 2002). For some nouns, non-realization of only the final consonant forms the plural (53-b). In (53-a), the data already presented in (41) is repeated for comparison. The choice between both Subtraction strategies is lexical. Arensen (1982) even cites examples where deletion of three or four segments marks the plural. However, only very few examples undergo this plural formation and it is apparently no productive process.[32]

(53)   *Subtraction in Murle: plural formation*   (Arensen, 1982: 40–43)

	BASE		PLURAL
a.	keloc	'flea'	kel
	ziza:coc	'termite'	ziza:c
	cinotot	'moustache'	cinot
	mininjit	'spirit'	mininj
	amotat	'saliva'	amot
	mu:roc	'habil tree'	mu:r
b.	bawot	'goat'	bawo
	zo:c	'foot'	zo:
	idinj	'meat'	idi
	korton	'anthill'	korto
	onji:t	'rib'	onji:
	jɛ:lac	'dove'	jɛ:la
	koloktec	'intestines'	kolokte

This pattern follows from assuming that the noun stems in Murle are lexically marked for taking one of two allomorphs. These two exponents are taken to be a morphemic mora and a morphemic syllable. Both these morphemic prosodic nodes suffix to their

---

[32] In the 500 words specified for their plural formation in Arensen (1982), there are six examples with final CVC deletion and three examples with final VCVC deletion. For yet other nouns, the plural is formed via affixation of segmental affixes.

base and are defectively integrated, resulting in non-realization of the material they dominate. In contrast to the languages listed above in (35) where morphemic moras are fully integrated but morphemic syllables remain defectively integrated, Murle is taken to be an instance where both types of morphemic prosodic nodes remain defectively integrated.

The tableaux (54-i) and (54-ii) briefly show how these two different exponents have different MLM effects under a single ranking for Murle. The tableau (54-i) is the context already derived in (42): a morphemic syllable is added and triggers non-realization of the final vowel and consonant. The constraint σ-Do-V is crucial here demanding that every syllable needs to integrate a vowel. The base in (54-ii), on the other hand, is lexically marked for suffixing a morphemic mora in the plural. Association of this mora to the final vowel and consequently non-realization of this vowel (candidate (54-ii-c)) is dispreferred over only associating the mora with the final consonant (candidate (54-ii-b)). This simply follows since non-realization of the vowel always implies non-realization of the consonant (see the discussion of (44) above). Since the mora is satisfied with only dominating a consonant, this additional violation of $PVis_V$ can be avoided and candidate (54-ii-b) hence wins the competition. Only if σ-Do-V becomes relevant, are the additional violations of $PVis_V$ tolerated as in tableau (54-i). To make the tableaux easier to read, high-ranked μ>Do>S and σ>Do>μ ensuring that the morphemic syllable and the morphemic mora must dominate some element and $*μ...^{Af}...S$ and $*Φ...^{Af}...σ$ ensuring that the morphemic nodes cannot be dominated by a higher prosodic node are excluded.

(54) *Subtraction in Murle*
  i. *Syllable affixation*

		σ-Do-V	OneRt-S	PVis_V	PVis_C
a.	[ke.lo]	*!			*
☞ b.	[kel]			*	*

ii. *Mora affixation*

$\mu_\bigcirc$ $\mu_\bigcirc$ $\mu_\bullet$ + $b_\bigcirc$ $a_\bigcirc$ $w_\bigcirc$ $o_\bigcirc$ $t_\bigcirc$	σ-Do-V	ONeRt-S	PVis$_V$	PVis$_C$
a. $\mu_\bigcirc$ $\mu_\bigcirc$ $\mu_\bullet$ $b_\bigcirc$ $a_\bigcirc$ $w_\bigcirc$ $o_\bigcirc$ $t_\bigcirc$ [ba.wot]		*!		
☞ b. $\mu_\bigcirc$ $\mu_\bigcirc$ $\mu_\bullet$ $b_\bigcirc$ $a_\bigcirc$ $w_\bigcirc$ $o_\bigcirc$ $t_\bigcirc$ [ba.wo]				*
c. $\mu_\bigcirc$ $\mu_\bigcirc$ $\mu_\bullet$ $b_\bigcirc$ $a_\bigcirc$ $w_\bigcirc$ $o_\bigcirc$ $t_\bigcirc$ [baw]			*!	*

3.3 Learning PDM

The structures that predict subtractive MLM in the theory of PDM can rightly be classified as rather 'abstract' in the sense that they contain non-interpretable or 'invisible' phonological structure. The learner has to deduce this phonological structure simply from the observed surface effect of length alternations between morphologically related forms. The learning of MLM patterns is hence similar to the learning of zero-exponence (or ø-morphemes, see McGregor (2003); Segel (2008); Trommer (2012)). After the learner has deduced morphemes and their meaning (via, for example, simple intersection as in Pertsova (2007)), she is potentially left with morphological information without a stored form and with unexplained alternations in base forms that are not phonological. She then starts making hypotheses that these (length-)alternations are triggered by subsegmental or prosodically defective morpheme representations.

In Wolf (2009), an interesting argument is made that mutation patterns are indeed learnable under an item-based approach. The example discussed there is featural mutation in Javanese where the elative form of adjectives is marked via raising and tensing the final vowel: /alʊs/ → /alus/ 'most refined'. This morphologically derived form is otherwise illicit in the language that excludes tensed vowels in closed syllables in non-derived contexts. As in many OT-learning algorithms (Prince and Tesar, 2004; Tesar and Prince, to appear), the learner is assumed to first pass through a stage of phonotactic learning where morphological structure is ignored. At the end of this stage, the Javanese learner will end up with a grammar that ranks the faithfulness constraint MAX[+HIGH] above the markedness constraint *TENSECLOSED simply because she encountered surface forms with tensed vowels in closed syllables. In the next stage, the morphological structure is taken into account as well and the learner will make hypotheses about possible subsegmentations into morphemes. This allows her to calculate a new grammar hypothesis based on the assumption that the input is morphologically complex. In the case of Javanese /alus/, she will hence consider the possibility that floating features are present in the input and that MAXFLOAT[+HIGH] demanding preservation of underlyingly non-associated features (Wolf, 2007) outranks *TENSECLOSED, not MAX[+HIGH]. This learning hypothesis is hence consistent with the claim that learners prefer to outrank markedness constraints by more specific faithfulness constraints.

Learning of MLM under the assumption of PDM is slightly different. For one, the standard assumption that the learner starts with a ranking where all markedness constraints outrank all faithfulness constraints (Tesar and Smolensky, 2000) has obviously no effects for a containment-based system where all constraints are markedness constraint. The assumption mirroring this is a preference for ranking all constraints specified only for phonetically visible structure above all constraints sensitive to all structure. This has the same effect as the M ≫ F assumption in that the learner starts with a restricted subset grammar and allows marked structure only if there is positive evidence for it.

A second deviation from the learning proposal in Wolf (2009) is necessary since only the special case of a mutation that is not structure preserving is considered there. For a general learning mechanism of MLM, it is assumed that after completing the phonotactic learning, the learner is simply confronted with alternations that do not follow from the phonotactics she acquired. For our Gidabal example, the learner will hence at some point have the occurrences of /gida/ and /gida:/ identified as instances of the same morpheme. Only the length of the final vowel alternates in different contexts and since this alternation cannot be attributed to any phonological constraint she acquired, she will retreat to the assumption that this alternation is due to the presence of another morpheme. Taking into account the morphological contexts in which the different forms appear, she then can attribute the trigger for the length-alternation to a morpheme that is consistent throughout the alternation contexts.

For MLM, this of course crucially relies on the background assumption that the learner is able to hypothesize that length-alternations might be due to the affixation of morphemic prosodic nodes as non-segmental morphemes. Additive MLM is hence not crucially different from learning (featural) mutation. The learning of subtractive MLM patterns then only adds the additional step of assuming defective prosodic integration. The learner needs to hypothesize a defective morpheme representation (a morphemic node, for example) and needs to modify her ranking in a way that allows defective integration. Instead of ranking the parsing constraints demanding phonetically visible integration in the highest stratum, rankings are hence considered where phonetically invisible association lines are also sufficient to integrate a morphemic node. Absolutely parallel to standard learning algorithms in OT, the learner hence gradually allows and considers marked structures. The only deviation is that this gradual learning is not due to ranking faithfulness constraints above the respective markedness constraints but ranking constraints about phonetically visible structure lower than those specified for all structure.

And finally, there is luckily no reason to believe that learners are incapable of deducing highly abstract structures from their linguistic evidence. The intriguing study presented in Ettlinger (2008) is concerned with a different topic, namely the learning of rule interactions. However, it is an interesting contribution to the more general point that learners are capable of deducing abstract structures without an overt surface effect. In this artificial learning experiment, participants that were presented with evidence for two transparent rules (like AB → AA and BC → BB) were in the testing phase confronted with a context where they could apply one rule transparently (ABC → AAC) or apply both rules whereas one applies opaquely without any surface evidence for its applicance (ABC → AAB). And indeed the participants were able to learn the opaque rule interaction without problems. Similarly, the learners of a subtractive MLM pattern are assumed to deduce prosodic structure for which they only have the indirect surface evidence of other elements that are *absent*.

3.4 Summary: subtractive MLM and PDM

The focus of this chapter was the proof that subtractive MLM can indeed follow under the assumption that all morphology is additive concatenation of morphemes. It was argued that in the containment-based PDM framework pursued here, two general mechanisms can result in subtractive MLM: usurpation of prosodic nodes if the underlying base representation lacks prosodic nodes (section 3.1) and defective integration of morphemic prosodic nodes (section 3.2). It was shown that these mechanisms are restricted in what possible MLM patterns they predict. For mora usurpation, it was argued that it can only have an effect on prosodic nodes underlyingly present: It was shown in a detailed case study in Yine that this correctly excludes any subtractive effect on an adjacent morpheme that is itself a trigger for the subtractive operation. In section 3.2, the typology of possible defective integration of morphemic moras and syllables was discussed in detail. It was shown how different MLM patterns arise from these mechanisms that are all restricted in that they only affect different mora- and syllable-sized portions of their base and are all found in a fixed position that is close to or directly at the base edge. This analysis also captures the observation made, for example, by Arndt-Lappe and Alber (2012) that subtractive morphology is generally templatic in the sense that the part of a base which is deleted corresponds to an invariable prosodic shape, hence the content of a prosodic node. The containment-based PDM system straightforwardly predicts this function of prosodic nodes as 'prosodic delimiters' (as counterpart to 'prosodic targets' in truncatory deletion (Mester, 1990)). The empirical insight that subtractive morphological processes are restricted in that sense is a claim made various times before (for a typological overview see Weeda (1992)). The theory of PDM now allows us to predict it from simple affixation of prosodic elements without additional rules or constraints regulating the mapping of the segmental content of a base to a prosodic template (Weeda, 1992; McCarthy and Prince, 1986/1996; et seq.) but from simple parsing constraints that ensure realization of prosodic elements.

A point that was particularly emphasized in section 3.2.2 was the ability of the PDM framework to account for the coexistence of additive and subtractive MLM patterns in one language. Assuming morphemic prosodic nodes on all tiers of the prosodic hierarchy that are subject to different constraints demanding their integration into the overall prosodic structure predicts such patterns that are indeed well-attested in the languages of the world. This discussion is one major departure to the approach in Trommer and Zimmermann (2014) where Subtraction as result of defective mora integration was proposed first.

4

Prosodically Defective Morphemes and blocking

This chapter is devoted to lexical exceptions in the domain of MLM. Several case studies illustrate how the framework of PDM allows us to reduce apparent idiosyncratic behaviour of certain morphemes to differences in their underlying prosodic specification. Section 4.1 focusses on lexical exceptions to MLM operations: Some morphemes in some languages generally resist an expected MLM pattern. It is shown how such exceptions easily fall out in the PDM framework when taking into account the full typology of possible underlying defective morpheme representations: given that subtractive MLM is in PDM the usurpation or defective integration of prosodic elements, morphemes are expected to resist subtractive MLM if they contain 'too much' prosodic structure. In section 4.2, a detailed case study introduces the so-called 'rescuer' morpheme in Aymara that blocks an expected subtractive MLM on a neighbouring morpheme. An interesting difference to the exceptional non-undergoers discussed in 4.1 is the fact that this morpheme has no other surface effect; it only blocks an expected MLM operation. It is shown that this blocking is expected from a morphemic mora as exponent for the morpheme in question. This analysis receives intriguing support from a comparison with a closely related dialect where the corresponding morpheme has the standard lengthening effect expected from a completely integrated morphemic mora. In section 4.3, finally, a pattern of lexical allomorphy in Alabama is discussed. It is shown that the difference between Subtraction patterns that mark the same morphological category but differ in the size of the subtracted portion they affect, follows from assuming contrastive syllabification for the different stems.

The main aim of this chapter is hence to show that the framework of PDM receives independent support since another expected effect from defective morpheme representations is borne out: they can not only trigger MLM, they can also block it.

4.1 Exceptional non-undergoers

It was argued in chapter 3 that subtractive MLM can result from mora usurpation or defective integration of prosodic nodes. In both cases, phonological elements remain unrealized since they are deprived of their ability to be integrated into the prosodic structure in a phonetically visible way. On the other hand, a standard account of additive MLM is the assumption of additional morphemic prosodic nodes in the representation of morphemes. This now predicts a possible interaction between triggers for additive and subtractive MLM: if the former has additional prosodic nodes and the latter results in non-realization of prosodic nodes, the expected surface effect in the context of both is the non-application of both MLM processes. This section discusses several examples that such effects are indeed borne out.

4.1.1 *Exceptional non-lengthening in Dhaasanac*

Additive Affixation in Dhaasanac (Tosco, 2001; Nishiguchi, 2007, 2009) was already briefly discussed in section 2.2.3 where the focus was on the interesting alternation of the plural suffix /−am/: it triggers gemination of a final base consonant for monosyllabic bases (e.g. /kur−am/ → /kurːam/) but surfaces as long after polysyllabic bases where gemination is impossible (/ʔarːoŋodˈ−am/ → /ʔarːoŋodaːm/). Interestingly, there are more Additive Affixes in Dhaasanac that do not show this length alternation. An example is the plural suffix /−anu/ in (1).[1] As can be seen in (1-a), it triggers gemination for monosyllabic bases but never for polysyllabic bases (1-b). This blocking of gemination for polysyllabic bases is identical to the restriction found for alternating /−am/. In contrast to /−am/, however, the /−anu/ remains short in those contexts where gemination is impossible.

(1)   *Additive suffixes in Dhaasanac*   (Tosco, 2001: 91)

	Sg		Pl
a.	dúm	'tail end'	dumːanu
	náːb	'central meeting-points of the elders'	naːbːanu
b.	ɲemiɲ	'small white ostrich feather'	ɲemiɲanu
	faːjam	'news'	faːjamanu
	suom	'giraffe tail'	suomanu

The analysis sketched in section 2.2.3 for the pattern of alternate lengthening in the context of /−am/ was to assume a morphemic mora in the representation of the suffixes that preferably associates to a heteromorphemic segment due to ALTERNATION. In case such a heteromorphemic association is impossible, however, the mora associates to the vowel of the suffix under violation of ALTERNATION since realization of the mora is more important (2-a). The absence of intramorphemic vowel lengthening for Additive Suffixes like /−anu/ simply follows under yet another possible defective morpheme representation: The suffixes contain an underlyingly unassociated morphemic mora and a vowel that itself is not dominated by a mora. In

---

[1] Note that /−anu/ marks plurality as well: there are multiple plural suffixes in Dhaasanac. Their context is not always clear; /−am/ and /−anu/, for example, are said to be used interchangeably with the same nouns (Tosco, 2001: 91).

contexts where the morphemic mora can not associate to base segments, it associates to this underlyingly mora-less affix vowel as a last resort, sketched in (2-b).[2] This association induces a violation of ALTERNATION but is tolerated since realization of the mora is more important.

(2)   *Alternating and non-alternating suffixes in Dhaasanac*
    Monosyllabic base: **Polysyllabic base:**
    a. *Alternating suffix vowel: morphemic mora and a moraic vowel*
        i. *Gemination*   ii. *Vowel lengthening*

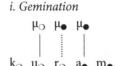   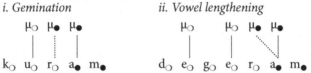

    b. *Non-alternating suffix vowel: morphemic mora and a non-moraic vowel*
        i. *Gemination*   ii. *No surface effect*

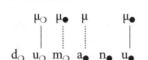   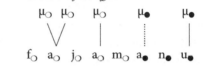

As was argued in section 3.1, exactly this representation of a mora-less vowel assumed for the suffix /−anu/ can also result in subtractive MLM if mora usurpation is predicted as optimal strategy to supply the mora-less vowel with a mora. In Dhaasanac, this is obviously not the case since the suffixes in question do not trigger any subtractive MLM. This is easily predicted if COL!$_\mu$ is low-ranked and mora epenthesis is an available repair to avoid mora-less vowels. This observation is still interesting since it illustrates the nature of PDM even further that crucially relies on OT and violable constraints: the same underlying (defective) prosodic specification for a morpheme may have different MLM effects or none at all, depending on the language-specific grammar.

4.1.2 Exceptional non-deletion in Yine

In the discussion of Subtractive Affixes in Yine in section 3.1, it was mentioned that there is an exceptional class of suffixes that never undergo vowel deletion. Its vowel is always realized even if it is followed by a Subtractive Suffix. This additional empirical fact is discussed in Kisseberth (1970) and Pater (2009) but not analysed in Lin (1997*b*)

---

[2] The Dhaasanac pattern is similar to patterns that are discussed in section 5.2.2 under the heading of 'certain-vowel-lengthening' languages. Formally, this is argued to be due to low-ranked *V$_O$ <$_O$ μ• in those languages. A vowel can hence only be dominated by a mora with a different morphological affiliation. Interestingly, the absence of lengthening in Dhaasanac non-alternating suffixes is in contrast due to the fact that an instance of intramorphemic lengthening is expected, not due to a low-ranked *V$_O$ <$_O$ μ•. The constraint *V$_O$ <$_O$ μ• is not violated if the affix vowel is only dominated by the morphemic mora simply because both elements have the same morphological affiliation. The absence of lengthening in these contexts hence tells us nothing about the ranking of *V$_O$ <$_O$ μ• in Dhaasanac.

(et seq.). There is in fact only a single example for such an affix, namely /−wa/, meaning 'yet, still'. Examples for contexts where this suffix is followed by a Subtractive Suffix are given in (3). We know from other contexts that /−lu/ is a Subtractive Suffix and consequently we would expect */hetawlu/ and */nuʃinikawlu/ in (3), which are well-formed strings with respect to all consonant cluster restrictions in Yine. However, /−wa/ resists the vowel deleting nature of all Subtractive Suffixes.

(3) *Exceptional non-undergoer*   (Pater, 2009: 6)
    h̃eta−wa−<u>lu</u>   h̃etawalu   'going to see him yet'
    n−h̃iʃinika−wa−<u>lu</u>   nuʃinikawalu   'I'm still thinking about it'

The typology Pater (2009) gives for affixes in Yine is hence the three-fold distinction in (4).

(4) *Yine affixes*
    a. those that undergo vowel deletion but do not trigger it
    b. those that undergo and trigger vowel deletion
    c. those that neither undergo nor trigger vowel deletion

In section 3.1.1, a mora usurpation analysis for the Subtractive Affixes in Yine was proposed. All the suffixes that trigger non-realization of a vowel immediately preceding them are taken to lack a mora underlyingly, usurp the underlying mora of a preceding vowel, and hence make realization of this vowel impossible. The crucial tableau (6) from 3.1.1 is repeated for convenience in (5).

(5) *Mora usurpation*

$\mu_\bigcirc \quad \mu_\bigcirc$ $\mid \qquad \mid$ $n_\bigcirc\, e_\bigcirc\, t_\bigcirc\, a_\bigcirc + l_\bullet\, u_\bullet$	PVIs_μ	$\text{V<DD}^{m}_{P}\text{<}\mu$	$*^{\mu}_{V}{}_{V}$	$*\sigma\text{-CoL}!_\mu$	PVIs_V
a. $\;\;\mu_\bigcirc \quad \mu_\bigcirc$ $\quad\mid \qquad \mid$ $\;\;n_\bigcirc\, e_\bigcirc\, t_\bigcirc\, a_\bigcirc\, l_\bullet\, u_\bullet$ [ne.ta.l°]		*!			*
b. $\;\;\mu_\bigcirc \quad \mu_\bigcirc \quad \mu$ $\quad\mid \qquad \mid \qquad \vdots$ $\;\;n_\bigcirc\, e_\bigcirc\, t_\bigcirc\, a_\bigcirc\, l_\bullet\, u_\bullet$ [ne.ta.lu]				*!	
☞ c. $\;\;\mu_\bigcirc \quad \mu_\bigcirc$ $\quad\mid \qquad \ddagger$ $\;\;n_\bigcirc\, e_\bigcirc\, t_\bigcirc\, a_\bigcirc\, l_\bullet\, u_\bullet$ [ne.tᵊ.lu]					*

The exceptional behaviour of the /−wa/ suffix is now predicted by yet another logically possible representation of vowels and their moraic specification, more concretely the assumption that the suffix /−wa/ is not only provided with a mora that dominates its affix vowel but with an additional morphemic mora as well, depicted in (6).

(6)   *Suffix /−wa/*

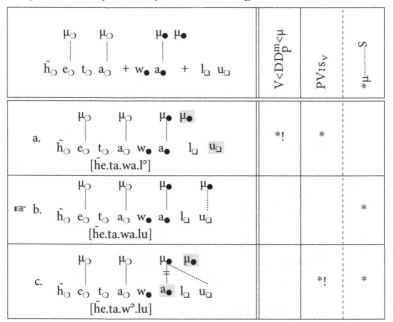

If /−wa/ is now followed by a Subtractive Suffix, the morphemic mora can be associated with the underlyingly mora-less vowel of the Subtractive Suffix. The demand that all vowels must be dominated by a mora is then satisfied without mora usurpation and the resulting vowel deletion. This is illustrated in tableau (7), where /−wa/ is followed by the Subtractive Suffix /−lu/. In candidate (7-a), the underlyingly mora-less affix vowel /u/ is not associated with a mora in the output and therefore incurs a fatal violation of $V{<}DD_p^m{<}\mu$. If the additional morphemic mora in the representation of /−wa/ is associated with the mora-less vowel as in the winning candidate (7-b), the mora is associated to a segment and the vowel is supplied with a mora without mora usurpation and hence vowel deletion (7-c).

(7)   *Exceptional /−wa/ followed by a Subtractive Suffix*

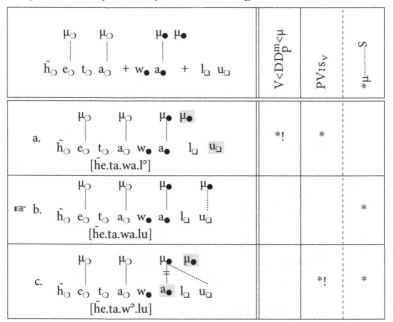

An alternative analysis for the morpheme-specific vowel deletion and the exceptional non-undergoer based on lexically indexed constraints is given in Pater (2009) (for a discussion of this alternative OT account to MLM see section 7). In the PDM account proposed here, the exceptional behaviour follows from yet another logically possible underlying prosodic representation of the morpheme in question. Apparent idiosyncratic information is hence reduced to a simple difference in the phonological representation and the regular phonology predicts the correct outcome without any explicit reference to morphological information.

A straightforward question arising from such an analysis is what happens to this additional mora in the representation of /−wa/ in contexts where no Subtractive Suffix follows. There is no surface effect in such contexts, the mora hence simply remains unassociated. But wouldn't we expect lengthening of a following vowel in order to avoid such an unassociated mora? Even more so since there is indeed a vowel lengthening process in Yine, namely compensatory lengthening after consonant deletion (see footnote 2 in section 3.1.1). However, long vowels in Yine are not only restricted to derived environments, they are also restricted to only occur in stems, never in affixes (Matteson, 1965: 31).[3] Regular compensatory vowel lengthening is hence excluded since $^*\mu...\underline{Af}...S$ penalizing epenthetic association lines between a mora and a segment for affixes is ranked above $\mu > Do_p^m > S$. Insertion of a new association line between a vowel and an affix mora is hence worse than a mora that does not dominate a vowel phonetically or morphologically. On the other hand, $^*\mu...\underline{Af}...S$ is ranked below $V < DD_p^m < \mu$ ensuring that every vowel is dominated by a mora phonetically or morphologically. The additional morphemic mora in /−wa/ consequently only associates to a vowel if it is underlyingly mora-less. The demand to 'rescue' mora-less vowels from non-realization is hence more important than avoidance of an unassociated mora.

4.1.3 *Exceptional non-deletion and non-shortening in Hungarian*

Assuming that an additional morphemic mora in the representation of a morpheme allows that it exceptionally resists mora usurpation predicts that the other possible effects of mora usurpation discussed in section 3.1.4 can also be blocked by an additional mora in an adjacent morpheme. This prediction is in fact borne out. It was argued in the analysis for Hungarian in section 3.1.4 that only certain stems show the subtractive effects triggered by class III suffixes. Those class III suffixes were analysed as Subtractive Suffixes that trigger mora usurpation. The stems that do not show a second stem form are now taken to contain an additional morphemic mora

---

[3] The generalization given in the source is inconsistent with at least one counterexample: /kawa−<u>kaka</u>−<u>ka</u>−na/ 'bathe themselves' (Matteson, 1965: 144) is realized as /kawka:kana/ with a long affix vowel. The generalization is hence not entirely understood and future empirical research is definitely necessary.

in their representation, absolutely parallel to the /−wa/ in Yine. This morphemic mora remains unassociated in most contexts given that the demand that every mora is associated with a segment is lower-ranked than the constraint against epenthetic association lines between moras and segments. The mora is hence only fully integrated if it provides otherwise mora-less vowels with a mora. This is illustrated in (8) where stems lexically marked for not having a secondary form are followed by a Subtractive Suffix and the morphemic mora of the stem is associated with the otherwise mora-less affix vowel. As in Yine above, mora usurpation is again unnecessary and causes unreasonable vowel deletion.

(8)   *Hungarian: Stems without a second form*
       a. Underlying   *b. Resulting*

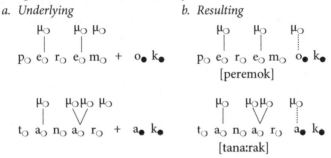

[peremok]

[tanaːrak]

The lexical contrast in Hungarian between stems that undergo subtractive MLM and those that resist it is hence analysed in the same way as the exceptional non-undergoer suffix in Yine: all those morphemes have an additional morphemic prosodic node in their representation that makes non-realization of an underlyingly associated mora unnecessary. The exceptional behaviour of a class of morphemes hence results from their underlying prosodic structure, not from an arbitrary marking in the lexicon.

4.2 The rescuer morpheme in Aymara

In this section a detailed case study of MLM in Aymara is presented, more concretely of MLM in two varieties of Aymara that differ with respect to one crucial aspect, namely the presence of phonemic vowel length. This difference makes a comparison of the two varieties highly conclusive for an analysis of their MLM. A morpheme that is realized via vowel lengthening in one variety hence has a different effect in the other variety: it only blocks a subtractive MLM.

The section starts with some morphological and phonological background facts about Aymara before the Muylaqʼ Aymara MLM pattern is presented in subsection 4.2.1. An analysis assuming PDM is then given in subsection 4.2.2. It is argued that the 'rescuer morpheme' in Muylaqʼ Aymara receives a straightforward representation as morphemic mora in an analysis based on PDM. An analysis that receives independent support in subsection 4.2.3 where the Muylaq' Aymara facts are compared with MLM in La Paz Aymara. It is shown that the 'rescuer morpheme' corresponds to a pattern of Addition in this variety of Aymara. The morpheme is hence argued to have the same underlying representation in both varieties, only its surface effect is different. Subsection 4.2.4 summarizes the case study of Aymara. Note that we return to the rescuer morpheme in section 7.2 where possible alternative accounts for the length-manipulation in Muylaq' Aymara are presented and it is concluded that all alternatives fail in deriving the existence of the rescuer morpheme.

4.2.1 MLM in Aymara

Aymara is a language of the Andes, spoken in Bolivia and Peru, roughly between Lake Titicaca and Lake Poopó. Whereas some researchers assume a 'macro-language' Aymaran (Coler, 2010), others assume that Aymara belongs to the Jaqi language stock, together with Jaqaru (Bickel and Nichols, ongoing). As Coler (2010) notes, there are not many in-depth studies for different varieties of Aymara; the best-studied is the one spoken in and around La Paz. In this chapter, the MLM in La Paz Aymara is compared with another Aymara variety, namely Muylaq' Aymara, spoken in the village of Muylaque, that is described in detail in Coler (2010). Both varieties of Aymara are independently interesting in terms of the MLM they exhibit. *First*, in Muylaq' Aymara, an interesting 'rescuer morpheme' can be found that blocks an expected segment deletion. And *second*, the MLM in La Paz Aymara is intriguing since it combines four different MLM patterns in a single language. As was already argued above (especially in section 3.2.2.1), such a coexistence of additive and subtractive MLM straightforwardly falls out inside the PDM framework and involves full integration of morphemic prosodic nodes on tier n and defective integration of morphemic prosodic nodes on another tier n±x.

Phonological and morphological background The two varieties of Aymara that are the focus of this chapter are relatively similar in many respects. If not explicitly mentioned, the Aymara facts discussed in this background section therefore hold for both varieties of Aymara and exemplifying examples are taken either from the Muylaq' variety (Coler, 2010) or the La Paz variety (England, 1971; Briggs, 1976; Landerman, 1997; Cerrón-Palomino, 2000; Hardman, 2001; Hardman et al., 2001; Adelaar and Muysken, 2004; Cerrón-Palomino, 2008). The crucial difference between the Muylaq' and the La Paz variety is emphasized in section 4.2.3.

For an analysis of the relevant MLM category, some background facts about the expected order of morphemes is necessary. Aymara is a highly agglutinative language and has no prefixes. There are three sets of suffixes: nominal suffixes, verbal suffixes, and what Briggs (1976) calls 'syntactic suffixes'. The latter type of suffixes can occur on verbs, nouns, or particles and is further divided into nonfinal (='independent') suffixes and final ones (='sentence suffixes'). For nouns, all sentence suffixes follow all noun suffixes, but for verbs, the independent suffixes stand between derivational and inflectional suffixes. The general template for affixes is summarized in (9).

(9)   *Morphological structure*

Most roots have the shape CVCV(CV), while most suffixes are CV. There are no word-final codas in the language. In roots, only intervocalic consonant clusters are possible that are restricted to sonorant+obstruent in most cases (Hardman, 2001: 28). In derived contexts, however, (especially after vowel deletion) clusters of up to six consonants are possible. An impressive example is /aka.n.k.k.t.ti/ 'I am here?' (Kim, 2003: 2). Muylaq' Aymara has the three vowels /a/, /i/, and /u/ and there is no phonemic length contrast for vowels. This is actually the crucial difference between the two Aymara varieties discussed here since vowel length is indeed contrastive in the La Paz variety of Aymara (see section 4.2.3). Stress in Aymara is phonologically predictable and occurs regularly on the penultimate vowel (Briggs, 1976; Hardman, 2001; Hardman et al., 2001; Kim, 2003).[4]

Before we turn to morphologically triggered length-manipulations, it is worth mentioning that there is also a phonologically triggered vowel deletion process. Diphthongs are not allowed in Aymara and vowel clusters are avoided via vowel deletion. An example for such a context is the suffixation of a vowel-initial suffix to a vowel-final base. There are only a few vowel-initial suffixes, most of them starting with /i/. The example in (10) is the 'actor/purposive' suffix /−iri/. If this vowel-initial suffix is added to a verbal stem ending in /u/, the stem-final vowel is preserved as in (10-a). In all other contexts, the stem-final vowel is deleted and the suffix-vowel is preserved (10-b) (Briggs, 1976; Kim, 2003). If two /i/'s are expected to be adjacent, only one short vowel surfaces (10-c).[5]

---

[4] According to Briggs (1976), 'stress may appear to fall on a final vowel if the final vowel is long' in La Paz Aymara (Briggs, 1976: 90). An example is /saraː/ 'I will go' transcribed as [sará] with a stressed final vowel. Unfortunately, there are not many stress data (stress is not marked consistently in the descriptions). For now, one could assume a trochaic right-aligned foot that is binary on the moraic or syllabic level (but actually nothing in the following hinges on that).

[5] Yet another instance of Subtraction is presumably the so-called 'three-vowel rule' that demands deletion of the final vowel of an adjectival or nominal modifier in a nominal phrase if it is longer than three syllables. That only bases with a certain length undergo vowel deletion in these contexts is apparently due to a templatic requirement about the minimal size of certain morphological categories. This highly interesting pattern is ignored in the following, mostly because the empirical generalizations in the sources are not entirely clear about this process.

(10) *Vowel hiatus avoidance*(Briggs, 1976; Kim, 2003; Adelaar and Muysken, 2004)

a.	tʰuqu	'dance'	tʰuquri	'dancer, in order to dance'	B165
	katu	'grab'	katuri	'he who grabs'	K3
	qapu	'spin'	qapuri	'spinner'	AM274
b.	tʃura	'give'	tʃuriri	'giver'	B165
	qama	'stay at home'	qamiri	'rich person'	K3
	apa	'carry'	apiri	'carrier'	AM274
c.	hitʰi	'slide'	hitʰiri	'slider'	AM274

This predominance of /u/ in phonological vowel deletion contexts, however, only holds for verbs. In nouns, a base-final /u/ is deleted as can be seen in (11).

(11) *Vowel hiatus avoidance for nouns*   (Briggs, 1976: 165)
      axanu 'face' −itu 'little' axanitu 'little face'

Although this phonological vowel deletion process is interesting enough in itself, it is ignored in the following where the focus is only on the MLM patterns.

Subtractive MLM in Aymara   It is a salient feature of Aymara that vowels might be lost in different contexts. *First*, there is the phonologically triggered vowel deletion to avoid a vowel hiatus (see above in (10)), and *second*, there are morphological contexts for vowel deletion.[6] The data in (12) gives some examples for Subtractive Suffixes, notated again as underlined. The comparison between, for example, /−ta/ and /−qa/, makes it clear that those suffixes are not distinguished by any phonological property from suffixes not triggering deletion and that it is irrelevant whether a stem (12-a) or an affix vowel (12-b) remains unrealized.

(12) *Subtractive Suffixes*   (Briggs, 1976; Hardman, 2001; Kim, 2003)

a.	mara	−patʃa			marpatʃa	
	year	all, same			'all year'	B290
	wali	−xama			walxama	
	well, good	like			'pretty good'	B293
	apa	−χata	−ɲa		apχataɲa	
	carry	ALL	INF		'to put sthg. on top'	K3
	sara	−naqa	−ɲa		sarnaqaɲa	
	go	around, aimlessly	INF		'to wander'	K3
	uma	−ta	−wa		umtawa	
	drink	2>3 S	AFF		'you drink'	H34
	q'ipi	−ta	−wa		q'iptawa	
	carry on the back	2>3 S	AFF		'you carry'	H77
b.	sara	−qa	−χa	−ɲa	saraqχaɲa	
	go	downward	COMPL	INF	'to go down/away'	K1

---

[6] In addition, there is an apparent stylistic vowel deletion at the end of words or phrases in La Paz Aymara (e.g. Hardman, 2001: 26) and in Muylaq' Aymara (Coler, 2010: 71). However, vowel deletion in this context is not systematic and ignored for now.

A very interesting investigation of the phonological and morphological factors that might govern the regularities of vowel deletion in Aymara can be found in Kim (2003). There, it is concluded that there are good reasons to believe that vowel deletion was phonological once and is in a transitional stage to get completely lexicalized at the current stage of language development. In fact, Hardman (2001) assumes that suffixes can be lexically marked for whether they must be preceded by a consonant and for whether they tend to delete their own vowel. These two subcategorization statements are notated as $/-_CCV/$ and $/-CV_C/$ respectively, hence are taken to be right- and left-hand specifications of a suffix for being adjacent to a consonant. As Kim (2003) argues convincingly, a simpler analysis is possible. *First*, it can be shown (for La Paz Aymara where long vowels are possible) that Subtractive Suffixes trigger deletion of a mora and not a vowel. They can very well be preceded by a short vowel and a left-hand specification $_C$ is empirically flawed. And, *second*, it is striking that all affixes with a right-hand specification $_C$ that tend to 'lose' their own vowel all end in the default vowel /i/ that never surfaces before another suffix but only word-final. A licit reanalysis is thus that those suffixes are underlyingly vowel-less.

In conclusion, neither the existence of a right-hand subcategorization frame nor a subcategorization for a preceding consonant seems to capture the empirical situation and an analysis assuming that certain suffixes trigger non-realization of a preceding mora is empirically more adequate.

A second morphological vowel deletion process can be found in the accusative, called the 'zero complement' in some descriptions (Briggs, 1976: 188). The final vowel of a noun stem remains unrealized to mark it as the direct object. Some examples are given in (13) where word forms based on the same root /kʰiti/ 'who' in the accusative and the nominative are contrasted. The noun is followed in both cases by the very same interrogative suffix /−sa/. Vowel deletion only applies in the accusative (13-a), not in the nominative (13-b). The accusative morpheme whose only surface effect is the deletion of a vowel is notated as /−ø/ in the following.[7]

(13)   *Subtraction in the accusative*   (Adelaar and Muysken, 2004: 273)
    a. kʰiti−ø−sa   sujpatʃa
        who-ACC-IR wait.DPST.3.S
        kʰits sujpatʃa
        'He must be waiting for someone?'

---

[7] Actually the present notation of morphemes is different from the forms Adelaar and Muysken (2004) and Coler (2010) give. Both sources notate all vowels that are lost on the surface as '(V)'—irrespective of whether this vowel deletion is triggered by a Subtractive Suffix, by Subtraction, by (stylistic) final vowel deletion, or a 'right-hand specification' of a vowel that tends to lose its own vowel. As was just argued, it is assumed together with Kim (2003) that these latter vowels are not underlyingly present. The (V) vowels are hence replaced as follows: (V) is V before a Subtractive Suffix, in the context of Subtraction, or in the context of stylistic vowel deletion; and (V) is absent in cases where it corresponds to the concept of 'right-hand specifications'. In order to minimize confusion, only underlying forms and morpheme segmentations for the relevant words are given in the following.

b. kʰiti—sa utar   sarani
   who-IR   house.ALL go.F.3.S
   kʰitis utar sarani
   'Who will go to the house?'

The vowel that is lost in the accusative is either word-final (14-a-c) or word-medial (14-d-f).[8] Given the existence of a stylistic final vowel deletion in Aymara (see fn. 6), only the latter are truly convincing examples for MLM. Medial vowel deletion arises from the simple fact that certain (independent) suffixes follow the noun base and consequently the zero complement (see the morphological overview given in (9); Adelaar and Muysken, 2004: 272). As neither of the final suffixes following the noun base triggers vowel deletion, the vowel loss must therefore be due to the fact that the noun is in the accusative. This can be seen for the completive suffix /—χa/ when comparing (14-c) where the vowel preceding it surfaces faithfully and (14-e) where the vowel preceding it is lost since it is the final vowel of a noun base in the accusative.

(14) *Subtraction in the accusative*
                    (Briggs, 1976; Hardman, 2001; Adelaar and Muysken, 2004)
       a. wawa—mpi—ø   apasma   B190
          baby-with.and-ACC
          wawamp apasma
          'You should take the baby, too'

       b. uma—ø   wajtaŋawa   B528
          water-ACC
          um wajtaŋawa
          'To bring up water is necessary'

       c. qamaqiχa   iwisa—ø   xiwajatajnaw   B619
                     sheep-ACC
          qamaqiχ iwis xiwajatajnaw
          'The fox killed the sheep'

       d. kunat   huk'ampi—ø—raki   qulʲqi—ø   munχtasti   AM272
                      more-ACC-and   money-ACC
          kunát huk'amprák qulʲq munχtásti
          'And how much money will you need?'

       e. Inklisa—ki—ø—χa—j   parlapχstχa   B299
          English-just-ACC-...
          Inklisakχaj parlapχstχa
          'We speak only English'

---

[8] Note that only for the relevant noun in the accusative, a proper segmentation into morphemes and their underlying structure is given.

f. Marija—ø—wa   H38
   Maria-ACC-AFF
   Marijwa
   'Maria'
   (possible answer to the question /Kʰitis qipiχa/ 'Who carried (something or someone) on her back?')

The examples so far were taken from the La Paz variety of Aymara. The examples in (15) are added for completeness to illustrate that both instances of subtractive MLM are attested in Muylaq' Aymara as well. In both examples in (15), final vowel deletion in the accusative can be observed for the direct objects and the effect of a Subtractive Suffix; /—t̲/ in (15-a) and /—t̲a in (15-b).

(15) *Vowel deletion in Muylaq' Aymara*   (Coler, 2010)
      a. aka—ø   muna—t—χa   165
         what-ACC   want-1SG-TOP
         ak muntχa
         'I want this'

      b. kawka—ø   sara—t̲a—sti   359
         where-ACC   go-2SG-IRR
         kawk sartast
         'Where did you go?'

The 'rescuer morpheme' in Muylaq' Aymara   In Muylaq' Aymara, there is now a third interesting phenomenon related to subtractive MLM. It can be found in verbalized contexts. The verbalizer has no surface exponent in most contexts (Coler, 2010: 60), illustrated in (16) where the expected position of the verbalizer morpheme is notated as '□'.[9]

(16) *Rescuer morpheme without a following Subtractive Suffix*   (Coler, 2010)
      a. jumanχa   jiwa—ta—□—wa—t̲ʃi—χalʲ   74
                       die-RE-VB-BFR-3.DUB-DIS
         jumanχa jiwatawt̲ʃiχalʲ
         'Yours must be dead'

      b. jiwasanakaχ   Aymar   jaqi—□—tan—wa   118
                                 people-VB-4.S-AF
         jiwasanakaχ Aymar jaqitanwa
         'We are all Aymara people'

---

[9] Note that not all of the glosses in the examples taken from Coler (2010) are given in the list of abbreviations. This is simply due to the fact that Coler (2010) gives no list for his glosses. The suffix /—wa/ is glossed as BFR, meaning 'buffer' morpheme. Coler (2010) states that it has no clear semantics but separates 'different categories of morphemes' (p. 362). In all other contexts, this morpheme varies between the shapes /—wja/jwa/wjwa/—I have nothing to say about why it is notated as /—wa/ here.

Interestingly, if a verbalized base is now followed by a Subtractive Suffix, the vowel that is expected to remain unrealized, unexpectedly surfaces. Due to this peculiar property, the verbalizer is termed the 'rescuer morpheme'. Examples are given in (17) where the position of the verbalizer morpheme at the end of the nominal base is again marked by '□'—the locus of the expected vowel deletion. That the second person singular suffix /−ta/ (17-a) and the first person singular suffix /−t/ (17-b-d) trigger deletion of a preceding vowel was illustrated in (15).

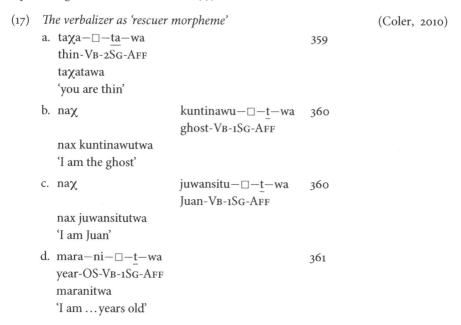

(17)   *The verbalizer as 'rescuer morpheme'*   (Coler, 2010)

  a. taχa−□−ta−wa   359
   thin-Vʙ-2Sɢ-Aғғ
   taχatawa
   'you are thin'

  b. naχ   kuntinawu−□−t−wa 360
           ghost-Vʙ-1Sɢ-Aғғ
   nax kuntinawutwa
   'I am the ghost'

  c. naχ   juwansitu−□−t−wa 360
           Juan-Vʙ-1Sɢ-Aғғ
   nax juwansitutwa
   'I am Juan'

  d. mara−ni−□−t−wa   361
   year-OS-Vʙ-1Sɢ-Aғғ
   maranitwa
   'I am ... years old'

The three relevant contexts in terms of MLM in Muylaq' Aymara are summarized in (18): Subtraction in the accusative (18-I), Subtractive Suffixation (18-II), and the verbalizer morpheme that blocks the effect of a Subtractive Suffix (18-IIb). The first two of the patterns can be found in the La Paz Aymara variety as well; only the rescuer morpheme in this form is unique to the Muylaq' variety.

(18)   *Two MLM patterns in Muylaq' Aymara*

Base	Derived	Example	
I. Subtraction			
CV#	→ C	/kawka/	→ /kawk/ (15)
IIa. Subtractive Suffix			
CV# + C(V)	→ CC(V)	/muna−t/	→ /munt/ (15)
IIb. Subtr. Suffix + Rescuer Morpheme			
CV# + □ + C(V)	→ CVC(V)	/taχa−□−ta−wa/	→ /taχatawa/ (17)

4.2.2 *An analysis based on PDM for Muylaq' Aymara*

It is argued that the two subtractive MLM patterns in Muylaq' Aymara follow from affixation of a morphemic syllable node that is defectively integrated into the overall prosodic structure, absolutely parallel to the analyses presented in section 3.2.2.

(19)   *Defective syllable integration: Subtraction*

$+ \; \sigma_\bullet$ $\mu_\bigcirc \quad\quad \mu_\bigcirc$ $k_\bigcirc \; a_\bigcirc \; w_\bigcirc \; k_\bigcirc \; a_\bigcirc$	$\sigma{>}\text{Do}{>}\mu$	$*\Phi....\text{Af}...\sigma$	ONeRT-S	COL!μ	PVIS$_s$
a. $\sigma \quad\quad \sigma \;\; \sigma_\bullet$ $\mu_\bigcirc \quad \mu_\bigcirc$ $k_\bigcirc \; a_\bigcirc \; w_\bigcirc \; k_\bigcirc \; a_\bigcirc$ [kaw.ka]	*!				
b. $\sigma \quad\quad \sigma_\bullet$ $\mu_\bigcirc \quad \mu_\bigcirc$ $k_\bigcirc \; a_\bigcirc \; w_\bigcirc \; k_\bigcirc \; a_\bigcirc$ [kaw.ka]		*!			
c. $\sigma \quad\quad \sigma \;\; \sigma_\bullet$ $\mu_\bigcirc \quad \mu_\bigcirc$ $k_\bigcirc \; a_\bigcirc \; w_\bigcirc \; k_\bigcirc \; a_\bigcirc$ [kaw.ka]			*!		
☞ d. $\sigma \quad\quad \sigma_\bullet$ $\mu_\bigcirc \quad\quad \mu_\bigcirc$ $k_\bigcirc \; a_\bigcirc \; w_\bigcirc \; k_\bigcirc \; a_\bigcirc$ [kawk]					*
e. $\sigma \quad\quad \sigma \;\; \sigma_\bullet$ $\mu_\bigcirc \quad \mu_\bigcirc \; \mu$ $k_\bigcirc \; a_\bigcirc \; w_\bigcirc \; k_\bigcirc \; a_\bigcirc$ [kaw.ka]				*!	

A tableau for subtractive MLM in Aymara is given in (19). The accusative morpheme is assumed to consist of a morphemic syllable that is suffixed to the base. In candidate (19-a), this morphemic syllable remains completely unintegrated, a structure that is excluded by undominated σ>Do>μ. In candidate (19-b), on the other hand where the morphemic syllable is fully integrated into the overall prosodic structure a fatal violation of *Φ...^{Af}...σ is invoked since the morphemic affix syllable is associated with a higher prosodic node. Candidates (19-c)–(19-e) avoid this violation since the morphemic syllable is not dominated by a higher prosodic node and hence remains phonetically uninterpreted. If, however, this morphemic syllable dominates a mora that in turn dominates a segment, a violation of ONeRT-S arises (candidate (19-c)) since the segment is now dominated by the morphemic syllable and the highest prosodic (word) node. Since ONeRT-S is only defined over phonetically visible segments, this violation is avoided if the segment remains uninterpreted as well. This is the structure in winning candidate (19-d). Since COL!$_\mu$ is high-ranked, insertion of an additional epenthetic mora to avoid segment deletion in candidate (19-e) has a worse constraint profile.

An analysis for Subtractive Suffixation is taken to be absolutely parallel, the only difference is the fact that the representation for the affix contains not only a morphemic syllable node but segments as well. This is shown in tableau (20) for the first person Subtractive Suffix /−t̲/, attaching to the base /muna/ 'want' (15). In the winning candidate (20-b), the morphemic syllable is not integrated under a higher prosodic node but dominates the rightmost base mora that in turn remains phonetically uninterpretable. Due to ONeRT-S, the vowel it dominates remains phonetically invisible as well. The affix consonant /t/, on the other hand, can very well be associated with the preceding phonetically visible syllable node in order to avoid a further violation of PVIs$_S$. Note that this structure is no problem for the N℺C𝕣 (although the depiction might suggest it), simply because the phonetically invisible morphemic syllable links to a mora and the phonetically visible syllable directly to a consonant. The two elements the syllables are linked to are hence on different tiers.

This analysis for Subtractive Suffixation is fundamentally different from the analysis proposed for Subtractive Suffixation in Yine that was based on mora usurpation. As was argued in section 3.1, a mora usurpation analysis is only possible if an affix contains at least one segment that demands integration under a mora. Subtraction patterns where no segments are present at all can hence trivially never be the result of mora usurpation. In addition, the Subtractive Suffixation patterns in Yine and Aymara are crucially different in the contexts of multiple adjacent Subtractive Suffixes (21). In contrast to the pattern in Yine, every vowel preceding a Subtractive Suffix remains unrealized and a three consonantal cluster surfaces.[10]

[10] Briggs (1976) does not give full segmentations and glosses for all morphemes in all contexts—the meaning for some single morphemes is therefore missing in some examples. Since the identity of the adjacent morphemes is undoubtedly clear, this is no apparent problem.

(20) *Defective syllable integration: Subtractive Suffixation*

$\sigma_\bullet$ $\mu_\circ \quad \mu_\circ$ $+$ $m_\circ u_\circ n_\circ a_\circ \qquad t_\bullet$	$\sigma>\text{Do}>\mu$	$*\Phi...\text{Af}..\sigma$	OneRt-S	Col'$_\mu$	PVIs$_s$
a. $\sigma \qquad \sigma_\bullet$ $\mu_\circ \quad \mu_\circ$ $m_\circ u_\circ n_\circ a_\circ t_\bullet$ [mu.nat]		*!			
☞ b. $\sigma \qquad \sigma_\bullet$ $\mu_\circ \quad \mu_\circ$ $m_\circ u_\circ n_\circ a_\circ t_\bullet$ [munt]					*

(21) *Multiple Subtractive Suffixes*   (Briggs, 1976; Hardman, 2001; Kim, 2003)

apa	−ta	−t'a	−ŋa	aptt'aŋa	
carry	up	temporary	INF	'to raise momentarily'	K3
uma	−ta	−ta	−wa	umtːawa	
drink	up	2>3.S	AFF	'you drank fast'	H35
qʰawa	−su	−ta	−ŋa	qʰawstaŋa	
snake skin	COMPL		INF	'to shed its skin'	B325
sawu	−ni	−ja	−tʰa[11] wa	sawunjtʰwa	
weave	CONT		1>3 AFF	'I'm weaving'	B366

Such a multiple vowel deletion is impossible under a mora usurpation analysis. As was emphasized in section 3.1.5, non-realization of a mora (and consequently of a segment) results from usurping an underlying mora. Since usurpation-triggering vowels lack a mora themselves, they can never be deprived of one and hence cannot be usurped by another adjacent Subtractive Suffix.

Tableau (22) illustrates how the multiple vowel deletion is predicted in Aymara in contexts with multiple morphemic syllables. The example /qʰawa−su−ta−ŋa/ from (21) contains two Subtractive Suffixes and is realized as /qʰawstaŋa/. Both Subtractive Suffixes have a morphemic syllable in their representation and both morphemic syllables must dominate a mora but cannot be integrated into the higher prosodic structure—as can be seen in the winning candidate (22-d), this results in

---

[11] The example is from the Salinas dialect where La Paz /−ta/ corresponds to /−tʰa/.

multiple vowel deletion on the surface. Again, the depiction wrongly suggests that the association of the /s/ to its syllable is an instance of line crossing. Since the NoCr is formulated over elements on identical tiers, this prosodic configuration is perfectly licit—the phonetically visible association line does not cross another association line that links a syllable to a segment.

(22) *Multiple Subtractive Suffixes in Aymara*

	σ>Do>μ	*Φ...Af..σ	OneRt-S	Col!ᵘ	PVis_s
a. [qʰa.wa.su.ta.ŋa]	*!*				
b. [qʰa.wa.su.ta.ŋa]		*!*			
c. [qʰa.wa.su.ta.ŋa]			*!*		
☞ d. [qʰaw.sta.ŋa]					**

Since the structure of the winning candidate (22-d) is rather complex, it is repeated below in (23-a) with the additional information of which syllables reflect which morphemes. It becomes clear that the structure is perfectly licit with respect to the RMO. This might become more evident if one considers an imaginable structure where the exponent order is not reflected on all tiers. This is the case for the potential structure in (23-b) where the syllables defectively integrate elements following them. In this configuration, the penultimate syllable reflects only the first● and the second suffix▢ but is preceded by a syllable that reflects the third suffix■. The exponent order that the third suffix■ follows the second suffix▢ is hence not recoverable on the morphemic tier. The analysis hence correctly predicts multiple vowel deletion of vowels preceding the affixes containing morphemic syllables.

(23) *Multiple morphemic syllables and exponent order*

Exponent order: $M_O \gg M_\bullet \gg M_\square \gg M_\blacksquare$

a. *Optimal structure (23-d)*   b. *Impossible rightward integration*

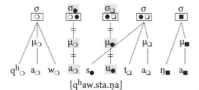

[qʰaw.sta.ŋa]

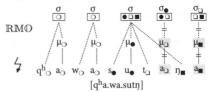

[qʰa.wa.sutŋ]

In the tableaux for Aymara above, all vowels were underlyingly equipped with moras and COL!$_\mu$ excluded insertion of moras to provide the morphemic syllable with a mora (see (19)). Given the assumption of Richness of the Base, however, we must consider a possible input where the base vowels are not underlyingly equipped with moras. It is argued that insertion of epenthetic moras becomes optimal in these contexts. This follows since V<DD<μ demanding that every vowel must be dominated by a mora is ranked higher than COL!$_\mu$. Epenthesis of moras is therefore a licit strategy to avoid mora-less vowels but it is no possible repair to avoid segment deletion in the context of morphemic syllables. The tableaux in (24) illustrate how moraic licensing is predicted for underlyingly mora-less vowels. V<DD<μ is ranked above COL!$_\mu$ and two moras are inserted to license the base vowels in (24-i).

(24) *Underlyingly mora-less vowels in Aymara*

i. *Mora epenthesis to license vowels*

k_O a_O w_O k_O a_O	V<DD<μ	σDOμ<O	*Φ...Af. σ	ONERT-S	COL!$_\mu$	PVIS$_S$
a. k_O a_O w_O k_O a_O	*!*					*****
☞ b. [kaw.ka]					**	
c. [kawk]	*!					*

ii. *Mora epenthesis to license vowels and segment deletion*

$\sigma_\bullet$ + $k_\bigcirc\ a_\bigcirc\ w_\bigcirc\ k_\bigcirc\ a_\bigcirc$	V<DD<μ	σ>Do>μ	*Φ...Af..σ	ONERT-S	COL!μ	PVIs$_s$
a. $\quad$ [kaw.ka]					***!	
☞ b. $\quad$ [kawk]					**	*

In (24-ii), a morphemic syllable is preceded by a base that underlyingly lacks any moras. The parsing constraint still demands insertion of moras for all vowels and the final mora is then dominated by the morphemic syllable and hence becomes phonetically invisible.

So far, the account of Muylaq' Aymara in fact mirrors the defective syllable integration analyses presented in section 3.2.2. The most interesting part of the analysis is now the effect of the verbalizing rescuer morpheme. Recall that this rescuer morpheme does not have any surface representation if it is followed by a 'normal' suffix. In the presence of a Subtractive Suffix, however, the vowel preceding the Subtractive Suffix surfaces unexpectedly. Given that Subtractive Suffixes result in non-realization of a mora (and all material this mora dominates), a morphemic mora in direct adjacency to such an affix is expected to block vowel deletion. The verbalizer morpheme in Muylaq' Aymara is hence taken to consist only of a morphemic mora. This is reminiscent of the analysis for the exceptional non-undergoer in Yine but crucially different since the verbalizer does not contain any additional segmental material, it only consists of the rescuing property that is taken to be a morphemic mora. This morphemic mora in the Muylaq' Aymara verbalizer is not expected to have any surface effect in contexts without an adjacent Subtractive Suffix simply because long vowels are impossible in Muylaq' Aymara and the morphemic mora can consequently not be associated with a vowel that is already associated with a mora underlyingly. The impossibility of a morphemic mora to result in vowel lengthening is shown in tableau (25). It is assumed that μ>Do$_p^m$>S demanding that every mora must dominate a segment is ranked below *$^\mu$V$^\mu$. In addition, codas are taken to be non-moraic in Aymara, ensured by undominated *C$_\mu$. If association of the morphemic mora with a vowel results in a long vowel as in (25-b), the morphemic mora hence remains unassociated as in winning candidate (25-a).

(25)   *No association of the morphemic mora in a context without a Subtractive Suffix*

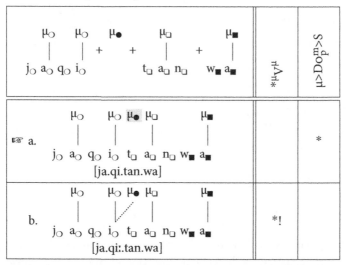

The verbalizer morpheme only has an effect in contexts where it is followed by a Subtractive Suffix. In this context, the morphemic syllable can be associated with the morphemic mora and a violation of σ>Do>μ can be avoided without segment deletion. Quite parallel to the exceptional non-undergoer in Yine, the rescuer morpheme in Aymara hence provides an additional mora that makes an association with a mora that dominates segmental material unnecessary. This is shown in tableau (26). It can be seen that an association of the morphemic syllable with the morphemic mora in candidate (26-c) has a better constraint profile than an association of the morphemic syllable with an underlying mora resulting in non-realization of a segment as in candidate (26-b). The ranking of constraints is the same as the one given in the tableaux (19) and (20); only μ>Do$_p^m$>S is added, the constraint demanding that every mora must dominate some segment. As was already shown in (25), it is quite low-ranked in Aymara since additional morphemic moras never result in segment lengthening.

(26) *Rescuer morpheme in Muylaq' Aymara*

	V<DD<μ	μ<Do<σ	*Φ.Af.σ	OneRt-S	Col!μ	PVis$_S$	μ>DO$_P^m$>S
a. [ta.χa.ta.wa]		*!					*
b. [taχ.ta.wa]						*!	*
☞ c. [ta.χa.ta.wa]							*

The analyses for the two subtractive MLM patterns and the rescuer morpheme in Muylaq' Aymara are summarized in (27).

(27) *Analyses for Muylaq' Aymara*

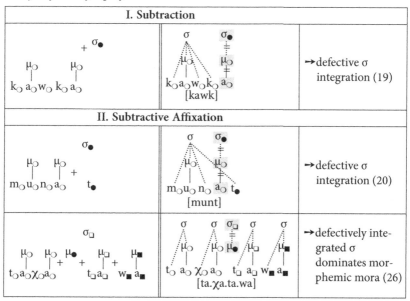

I. Subtraction		
(kₒaₒwₒkₒaₒ + σ•)	[kawk]	→defective σ integration (19)
II. Subtractive Affixation		
(mₒuₒnₒaₒ + t•)	[munt]	→defective σ integration (20)
(tₒaₒχₒaₒ + tₒaₒ + wₐaₐ)	[ta.χa.ta.wa]	→defectively integrated σ dominates morphemic mora (26)

4.2.3 *An insightful comparison: La Paz Aymara*

The relevant and most crucial difference between the Muylaq' and the La Paz variety of Aymara is the fact that vowel length is contrastive in La Paz Aymara. An example for a minimal pair is /tʃaka/ 'bridge' and /tʃaːka/ 'dry quinoa stem' (Hardman, 2001: 20). Another source for underlying long vowels is the optional suppression of the glide /j/ between two identical vowels as in (28).

(28)   *Optional glide deletion*   (Adelaar and Muysken, 2004: 270)

      maja   ~ maː   'one'

      tiji   ~ tiː   'cave'

      suju   ~ suː   'parcel of land'

Coler (2010) discusses vowel length in detail and presents phonetic evidence that length is indeed not contrastive in the Muylaq' variety. For some contexts where morphological vowel length surfaces in La Paz Aymara, segmental correspondents can be found. Two examples are given in (29) where the first person future suffix /−χa/ in Muylaq' Aymara corresponds to an Addition pattern in La Paz Aymara and the segmental suffix /−mama/ to the Additive Suffix /−ːma/.

(29)   *Long vowels in La Paz Aymara*   (Coler, 2010: 60)

Base	Future		
	La Paz	Muylaq'	
a. sara	saraː	saraχa	'I shall/will go'
b. tʃura	tʃuraːma	tʃuramama	'I will give it to you'

Interestingly enough, underlying long vowels are very rare in La Paz Aymara and Kim (2003) notes that all long vowels are (diachronically or synchronically) derived. Since the Muylaque people live relatively isolated in a valley surrounded by mountains and the traditional life (and language) survived there longer than in other areas (Coler, 2010: 27), one can conclude that the grammaticalization of vowel length is a relatively recent development in Aymara and the Muylaq' variety has simply not (yet) participated in this language change. One crucial source for long vowels in La Paz Aymara is in fact the morphology: there are morphological Addition patterns as well as Additive Affixes triggering vowel lengthening.

Two examples for Additive Suffixes are given in (30), both involving person-specific future morphemes. That this lengthening is truly bound to the presence of these morphemes is apparent since some lengthening suffixes are homophonous with suffixes that do not trigger lengthening. The second example in (30), for example, can be contrasted with the form /sarata/ where the homophonous resultant nominalizer suffix /−ta/ is suffixed and no lengthening surfaces (Hardman, 2001: 20).

(30) *Additive Suffixes*   (Hardman, 2001)

BASE		FUTURE	
alja	—ːma	aljaːma	
'sell'	'1>2.Fut'	'I will sell'	211
sara	—ːta	saraːta	
'go'	'2>3.Fut'	'you will go'	152
apa	—ːtam	apaːtam	
'bring, have'	'3>2.Fut'	'he will bring'	211

Another example for an Additive Affix is the locational suffix /—ːχa/ 'besides' as can be seen in the sentence in (31), taken from (Hardman et al., 2001: 203).

(31) japu—pa—χa—ːχa—ru   usku—ni—ma
      chacra-3.Poss-encima-al.lado.de-a poner-Approx-2>3
      japupχaːχar uskunim
      'Ponlo al lado de su chacra de él'

Addition, on the other hand, can be found in, for example, the first person future, illustrated in (32) (see also (29) above) where the only difference between the verb base and its future form is the length of the final vowel. This vowel lengthening can affect the final vowel of the verb stem (32-a) or the final vowel of an inflectional suffix like /—ni/ 1.Ps in (32-b).

(32) *Addition in the future*   (Briggs, 1976)

	BASE	FUTURE	
a.	sara	saraː	
	'go'	'(I) will go'	265+266
b.	sata	sataniː	
	'plant'	'I am going to plant'	269

Together with the Additive Suffixes (30), there are actually four future exponents that involve vowel lengthening processes as is summarized in (33) where all exponents of person-specific future morphemes are listed.[12]

(33) *Future suffixes*   (Hardman, 2001: 145)

1>2	—ːma	1>3	—ː	3>4	—istani
2>1	—itaːta	4>3	—ɲani	2>3	—ːta
3>3	—ni	3>1	—itani	3>2	—ːtam

---

[12] The actual number of Additive Affixes and Addition patterns will be different if one assumes a different subsegmentation into smaller morphemes. It is, for example, very plausible to assume only a single Additive Suffix /—ːta/ for 2<->3.Fut and a segmental suffix /—m/ for the 3>2.Fut context. Or a combination of Addition and person markers /—ma/, /—ta/, and /—tam/ in all direct (=higher on lower argument on the person hierarchy) first/second person contexts. Only the lengthening in 3>2 would remain mysterious under such a reanalysis. It is clear that either segmentation analysis hence has drawbacks in the form of homophonous marker entries. In the following, the segmentation given in the descriptive sources is adopted (see footnote 9 in section 1.1.3 for a general discussion of this subsegmentation problem).

Recall from section 4.2.1 that the two subtractive MLM patterns we found in Muylaq'
Aymara are attested in La Paz Aymara as well; Subtraction in the accusative and several
instances of Subtractive Suffixes (see the underlined suffixes in (33)). An instance of
the 'rescuer morpheme' in exactly the form it was attested in the Muylaq' variety is
unattested in La Paz Aymara. However, yet another pattern of MLM can be observed
in the morphological context where the rescuer morpheme occurs in Muylaq' Aymara:
Addition. Strikingly enough, verbalization is marked via lengthening of a final vowel
in La Paz Aymara. In (34), some nouns are contrasted with their verbalized form
and the only surface difference between both forms is the length of the final vowel
(note that the verbalized stems are followed by the infinite suffix /—ɲa/ as well). This
observation is in fact compelling evidence that the analysis presented for the rescuer
morpheme in section 4.2.2 is on the right track: it was assumed to be a morphemic
mora that is neutralized in most contexts and only shows a surface effect if it is
followed by a Subtractive Suffix. In this closely related variety, the same morpheme
is a morphemic mora with a consistent surface effect of vowel lengthening—simply
due to the fact that vowel length is phonemic in this language. In (35), some more
examples of verbalized forms in full sentence contexts are added.

(34) *Lengthening in the verbalizer*   (England, 1971; Hardman et al., 2001)[13]

BASE		VERBALIZED		
warmi	'woman'	warmi:ɲa	'to be a women'	H90
wawa	'baby'	wawa:ɲa	'to be a baby'	H89
uta	'house'	uta:ɲa	'to be a house'	E11

(35) *The Verbalizer*   (Hardman et al., 2001; Adelaar and Muysken, 2004)

    a. naja—χa   tʃura—ɲa—:—ta—wa   AM289
       1-Top   give-Inf-Vb-1.S-Aff
       najaχ tʃuraɲa:twa
       'I must give it to him/her'

    b. sara—naqa—wi—ni—:—ɲa   AM290
       go-around-Ln-having-Vb-Inf
       sarnaqawini:ɲa
       'to have culture/good behaviour'

    c. ura—:—χa—i—wa   H203
       hour-Vb-complete/already-3>3.S-Aff
       ura:χiw
       'It's time to …'

The empirically adequate generalization about Subtractive Suffixes in the La Paz
variety is that they trigger non-realization of a mora. The relevant context that proves

---

[13] Hardman et al. (2001) is written in Spanish; the glosses and translations of examples are translated
into English in the following.

this is the combination of long vowels and Subtractive Suffixation. As was already discussed, underlying long vowels are rather rare in La Paz Aymara. However, there are contexts where Addition is expected to lengthen a vowel preceding a Subtractive Suffix. Such a context is given in (36) where the deletion-inducing suffix /−t/ 1>3, SIMPLE TENSE attaches to a verbalized base and the vowel surfaces as short. In derivational terms, this can be interpreted as shortening since the long vowel lacks one of the moras it is expected to be associated with.

(36) *Addition and Subtractive Suffixation*   (Briggs, 1976; Hardman, 2001)
      warmi:ɲa   'to be a woman'   warmitwa   'I am a woman'   B171
      jatitʃiri:ɲa 'to be a teacher' jatitʃiritwa 'I am a teacher' H20

Given these empirical facts, the PDM analysis for both Aymara varieties is nearly identical in terms of the constraint ranking and involves the same representations for the relevant morphemes—only the surface effect they have is different.

Subtractive MLM in La Paz Aymara is also assumed to be the result of affixing a morphemic syllable that is only defectively integrated into its base, absolutely parallel to the analysis provided for Muylaq' Aymara in the tableaux (19) and (22). Additive MLM on the other hand, is the result of affixing a morphemic mora that is fully integrated into its base, resulting in long vowels. The crucial ranking difference between the two varieties of Aymara is hence the fact that in La Paz Aymara, $*^{\mu}V^{\mu}$ is ranked low and crucially below μ>Do_p^m>S. In Muylaq Aymara, the reverse ranking is assumed to account for the fact that morphemic moras never result in vowel lengthening (see (25)). The tableau (37) illustrates vowel lengthening after affixation of a morphemic mora in La Paz Aymara.

(37) *Addition in La Paz Aymara*

$\mu_\circ$ $\mu_\circ$ $\mu_\bullet$ + $w_\circ a_\circ w_\circ a_\circ$	σ>Do>μ	*Φ......Af..σ	OneRt-S	CoL!μ	PVis$_s$	μ>Do$_p^m$>S	*$^{\mu}V^{\mu}$
a. $\mu_\circ$ $\mu_\circ \mu_\bullet$ / $w_\circ a_\circ w_\circ a_\circ$ [wa.wa]						*!	
☞ b. $\mu_\circ$ $\mu_\circ \mu_\bullet$ / $w_\circ a_\circ w_\circ a_\circ$ [wa.wa:]							*

If such a morphemic mora, however, is adjacent to a morphemic syllable as in tableau (38), it is predicted to associate only with the morphemic syllable that remains defectively integrated. The defectively integrated syllable hence blocks the expected vowel lengthening and no surface effect is predicted to arise, absolutely parallel to the rescuer morpheme derivation in Muylaq' Aymara in tableau (26).

The morphemic syllable is forced to dominate a mora due to $\sigma{>}Do{>}\mu$ (excluding candidate (38-a)) but it cannot be integrated into the higher prosodic structure due to $*\Phi...Af...\sigma$ (excluding (38-b)). If this syllable now dominates a mora that in turn dominates a segment, either a fatal violation of ONERT-S (excluding candidate (38-c)) or of PVIS$_S$ arises (candidate (38-d)). Non-realization of a segment is unnecessary in this configuration since the morphemic syllable is happy with only dominating the morphemic mora and no segment in turn as in winning candidate (38-e).

(38)   *Addition and Subtractive Suffixation in La Paz Aymara: vowel shortening*

(input: σ, μ μ μ + + μ / u m a t a)	σ>Do>μ	*Φ...Af...σ	OneRt-S	Col.μ	PVis$_S$	μ>Dom^m>S	*μ$^\mu$
a. [u.ma:.ta]	*!						*
b. [u.ma:.ta]		*!					*
c. [u.ma.ta]			*!			*	
d. [um.ta]					*!	*	
☞ e. [u.ma.ta]						*	

The complete picture of PDM analyses for the length-manipulation in La Paz Aymara is summarized in (39). The pattern is especially interesting since it is another example where additive and subtractive MLM are attested (see the discussion in section 3.2.2.1). In PDM terms, this simply follows since defective integration of morphemic syllables and full integration of morphemic moras coexist. The existence of the constraints against epenthetic association relations between certain tiers of the prosodic hierarchy and the bidirectional parsing constraints predict exactly such a pattern of full integration on one tier but defective integration on another tier.

(39)   *Analyses for La Paz Aymara*

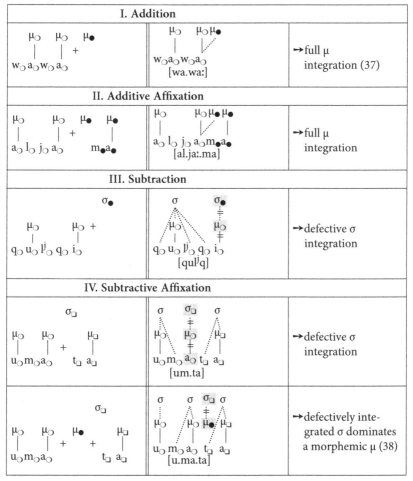

Strikingly, the structures relevant for PDM and the basic ranking in the two languages are identical although they show crucially different surface effects: only La Paz Aymara shows additive MLM and only in Muylaq' Aymara does the 'rescuer' morpheme exist.

These different surface effects are simply due to the different ranking of $*^{\mu}V^{\mu}$. The constraint is undominated in Muylaq' Aymara since the language has no phonemic contrast between long and short vowels but it is relatively low-ranked in La Paz Aymara, allowing additive MLM.

4.2.4 *Summary: the rescuer morpheme in Aymara*

In the Muylaq' variety of Aymara, the only surface effect for the verbalizer morphemes is that it blocks the morpheme-specific subtractive effect of another morpheme. As in Yine, this rescuing property follows straightforwardly in PDM if one assumes a morphemic prosodic node in the representation of the morpheme in question. This highly abstract analysis for Muylaq' Aymara received independent and interesting evidence from the comparison with the similar dialect of La Paz Aymara where the other expected surface effect for this morphemic prosodic node—full integration and vowel lengthening—is indeed attested. The underlying morpheme representations are hence taken to be identical, only their surface effect is different since the languages employ slightly different constraint rankings and only La Paz Aymara allows full integration of the mora if it results in vowel lengthening.

4.3 Lexical allomorphy in Alabama

In the analyses presented in sections 4.1 and 4.2, certain morphemes showed or triggered an exceptional non-applicance of an otherwise expected subtractive MLM process. A third interesting pattern where different underlying prosodic specifications predict an apparently idiosyncratic behaviour with respect to an MLM process is allomorphy between MLM operations that target elements of different size . Such an allomorphy can be found in Alabama, already introduced in section 3.2.2.2. In contrast to the patterns discussed above in sections 4.1 and 4.2, the lexical contrast that can be observed in Alabama is not a contrast between whether a subtractive MLM process surfaces or not but the concrete shape of the subtractive MLM operation.

In section 3.2.2.2, final rhyme deletion in Alabama plural formation was introduced as the result of morphemic syllable affixation. The pattern is in fact more complex since another class of stems shows only non-realization of the final consonant in the same morphological environment. The full pattern is given in (40) (Lupardus, 1982; Hardy and Montler, 1988a,b; Lombardi and McCarthy, 1991; Samek-Lodovici, 1992; Broadwell, 1993; Grimes, 2002). Recall that all stems are followed by one of the two stem classifier suffixes /−li/ or /−ka/ in the examples below. For the bases in (40-a), the last vowel and the final coda consonant or only the last long vowel of the base preceding these suffixes remain unrealized in the plural. For the bases in (40-b), on the other hand, only the final coda consonant remains unrealized in the plural form. Interestingly, this non-realization of the final coda consonant is accompanied by lengthening of the now final base vowel. No phonological property distinguishes these two classes of bases, as can easily be seen with the contrast between /kolof–li/ 'cut once' and /kajof–li/ 'scrub'—both bases are nearly identical in their phonological make-up but the former undergoes rhyme deletion whereas the latter only coda deletion.

(40) *Subtraction in Alabama*   (Hardy and Montler, 1988*b*; Broadwell, 1993)

BASE		PLURAL		
a. *Rhyme deletion*				
batatli	'hit once'	batli	'hit repeatedly'	B417
kolof:i (kolof+li)	'cut once'	kol:i	'cut repeatedly'	B417
haɬapka	'kick once'	halka	'kick repeatedly'	HM391
misi:li	'close eyes once'	misli	'close eyes repeatedly'	HM391
bala:ka	'lie down' (sg)	balka	'lie down' (pl)	B417
ibacasa:li	'join together' (sg. object)	ibacasli	'join together' (pl. object)	B417
b. *Coda deletion*				
salatli	'slide once'	sala:li	'slide repeatedly'	B417
ha:tanatli	'turn around once'	ha:tana:li	'turn around repeatedly'	B417
kajof:i (kajof+li)	'scrub' (sg. obj)	kajo:li	'scrub' (pl. obj)	B417
ɬopotli	'pass through' (sg)	ɬopo:li	'pass through' (pl)	HM394
noktiɬifka	'choke once'	noktiɬi:ka	'choke repeatedly'	HM394

It is now argued that the analysis presented for Alabama in section 3.2.2.2 must not be modified at all to account for this additional empirical fact, only more possible underlying representations for stems need to be taken into account. Subtraction in the plural formation in Alabama generally follows from suffixation of a morphemic syllable that is defectively integrated into the overall prosodic structure and hence predicts non-realization of the material it dominates. Crucially now, a different number of segments is expected to remain unrealized depending on the underlying prosodic structure of its base. More concretely, it is argued that non-realization of the final rhyme is only possible if the final segments are not underlyingly associated with a syllable node. The lexical difference between the two subtractive allomorphs is hence taken to be a difference in the underlying prosodic structure of the stems.

In tableau (41), the morphemic syllable attaches to a base without any underlying syllable structure. As is already familiar now, undominated $*\Phi...^{Af}...\sigma$ and $\sigma{>}Do{>}\mu$ demand that the syllable remains defectively integrated (excluding candidate (41-a)) but must dominate a mora. If the syllable only dominates a mora that in turn dominates a consonant, however, a fatal violation of σ-Do-V arises, excluding candidate (41-b). The defectively integrated syllable must hence dominate a vowel as in candidates (41-c) and (41-d). Since candidate (41-d) avoids one of the violations of PVIs$_S$ that (41-c) causes, this candidate finally wins the competition. Note that codas are taken to be moraic in Alabama, ensured by the combination of $C{<}DD^m_p{<}\mu$ and $*\mu$-ONs (both are excluded in the tableaux below), and this is discussed in more detail below.

(41)   *Subtraction in Alabama: Rhyme deletion*

$\mu_○\ \mu_○$ / $b_○\ a_○\ t_○\ a_○\ t_○$ + $\sigma_{\bullet}$	*Φ..Af..σ	σ>Do>μ	OneRt-S	*σ ⊣⊢ μ	σ-Do-V	PVis$_s$
a. [ba.tat]	*!					
b. [ba.ta]					*!	*
c. [ba]						***!
☞ d. [bat]						**

An interesting prediction from the constraints demanding realization of underlying prosodic structure arises for stems that—possible given Richness of the Base—are underlyingly equipped with prosodic structure, more concretely that contain an underlying final syllable. If this underlying prosodic integration must be preserved via high-ranked *σ ⊣⊢ μ, another subtractive pattern is predicted from defective integration of the morphemic syllable. In such a context, the morphemic syllable can only dominate a final consonant, never a vowel. This is shown in tableau (42). The expected non-realization of the final rhyme in candidate (42-a) that was optimal in (41-d) is impossible in this context since it implies that underlying association lines between syllables and moras are marked as phonetically invisible, penalized by *σ ⊣⊢ μ. In contrast, candidate (42-c) where the morphemic syllable dominates only the final base mora that in turn dominates the final consonant becomes optimal (for now). Note that the pointing hand in (42) is in parentheses since this is not yet the final structure that becomes optimal—a point that is discussed below.

(42) *Subtraction in Alabama: Coda deletion*

		$*\Phi.\text{Af}..\sigma$	$\sigma{>}\text{Do}{>}\mu$	ONERT-S	$*\mu{+}\sigma$	$\sigma\text{-Do-V}$	PVIS$_s$
a.	[sal]			*!	*!*		**
b.	[sa.lat]			*!			
(☞) c.	[sa.la]					*	*

The tableaux (41) and (42) illustrate how affixation of the very same morphemic prosodic node can result in different surface effects for bases that only differ in their underlying prosodic structure. Yet again, an apparently idiosyncratic lexical feature of certain morphemes was reduced to contrastive prosodic structure and hence a difference in the abstract phonological structure of the morphemes in question.

The only remaining part of the analysis is the compensatory vowel lengthening. A final base vowel is lengthened after coda deletion (/salatli/ → /salaːli/) whereas any lengthening is absent after rhyme deletion (/batatli/ → /batli/, */baːtli/). There are two possible interpretations of this lengthening. Either it is taken to be a compensatory lengthening process that applies after coda deletion or it is taken to be the result of a rhythmic lengthening rule that lengthens every non-final vowel in a CV syllable that is followed by a CV syllable. The former interpretation is put forward in Hardy and Montler (1988b) (see also Horwood (2001) for the same interpretation of Koasati). The latter rule of rhythmic lengthening can be found in Western Muskogean (see, for example, Munro and Ulrich, 1984) and Broadwell (1993) concludes that the rule 'yields the same output as the rules in [Eastern Muskogean, EZ] Alabama and Koasati for many examples'. Both interpretations are compatible with the present account. In the following, it is shown how compensatory vowel lengthening is predicted in the analysis for Alabama, well aware of the fact that it might also simply be due to rhythmic lengthening.

Compensatory lengthening is predicted if codas are moraic in Alabama and $\mu>Do_p>S$ is ranked high, demanding that every mora strives to dominate a segment in a phonetically visible way. In candidate (42-c), two moras violate $\mu>Do_p>S$: the epenthetic mora and the final base mora both dominate only the phonetically invisible consonant. If we integrate $\mu>Do_p>S$ in the ranking as in (43), a candidate (43-b) becomes optimal where the final base mora is associated with the last base vowel since it avoids one of the violations of this Parse constraint. Since the last base vowel is now associated with two moras in a phonetically visible way, a long vowel results. The second mora, however, has no chance to be associated with any phonetically visible segment. If it is associated with the final vowel as well, a superlong vowel would result that is excluded by an undominated markedness constraint in Alabama and an association with a segment preceding the vowel is not possible without crossing of phonetically visible association lines. In tableau (43), this derivation of compensatory lengthening is illustrated. In contrast to the tableau in (42), undominated $\sigma>Do>\mu$ and $*\Phi...^{Af}...\sigma$ are excluded for ease of exposition.

(43)   *Subtraction in Alabama and compensatory lengthening after coda deletion*

$\overset{\sigma_O \qquad \sigma_\bullet}{\underset{s_O\ a_O\ l_O\ a_O\ t_O\ +}{\mu_O\ /\mu_O\ \mu_O}}$	$*\overset{\mu}{\underset{\sigma}{+}}$	$\mu>Do_p>S$	$Col_\mu^!$	σ-Do-V	OneRt-S	PVIs$_s$
a. [sa.la]		*!*	*	*		*
☞ b. [sa.laː]		*	*	*		*

The interesting asymmetry that compensatory lengthening only applies after coda deletion, never after rhyme deletion, follows straightforwardly under the analysis presented so far. A moraic coda intervenes between the vowel that could be lengthened and the non-realized mora in contexts where a rhyme remains non-realized. Compensatory lengthening would consequently result in an illicit crossing association line (44).[14]

---

[14] The structure in (44) would obviously still be insufficient to predict CL: the additional mora dominating the vowel needs to be phonetically visible. Since the structure is excluded anyway, those additional prosodic (re)integrations are ignored.

(44) *No compensatory lengthening after rhyme deletion*

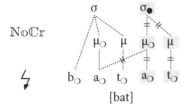

[bat]

This analysis is another interesting contribution to the claim that morpheme-specific phonology can arise from a prosodically defective representation for a morpheme: The lexical difference between the different stem types in Alabama is due to their different underlying prosodic structure. The crucial difference to the Subtraction allomorphy in Murle discussed in section 3.2.3 is the fact that in Alabama, a single representation— a morphemic syllable—predicts different Subtraction patterns whereas in Murle, different underlying representations for the same morpheme are assumed to result in different Subtraction patterns. In Trommer and Zimmermann (2014), an alternative analysis for the different Subtraction patterns in Alabama is given where it is assumed that—parallel to the account for Murle—two different representations for the allomorphs in question are stored. In their account, these two different morphemes are two mora affixes that are linearized in different positions of their base. In contrast, the PDM account only stores a single representation for the morpheme in question and thus reduces the number of lexical entries necessary for a morphological analysis of Alabama.

4.4 Factorial typology

The preceding sections have presented various PDM analyses for subtractive MLM that all rely on structures that are only possible in containment theory. For most of these analyses, the underlying logic is simply that a phonetically invisible association line is still better than no association line between two elements. It is clear that this system enriches both the inventory of constraints and of phonological structures. It is hence good to pause for a moment and consider the factorial typology and predictive power of such a system. The contexts of adding a morphemic mora (45), adding a morphemic syllable (46), and the addition of both a morphemic mora and syllable at the same base edge (47) are considered in the following . Especially that last context is particularly interesting since various case studies in the preceding chapter have argued that such interactions between different morphemic nodes might lead to a neutralization of an expected MLM effect. A variety of output structures are listed below for those inputs, including structures where the morphemic nodes are fully integrated and those where the morphemic nodes remain defectively integrated. Violations for the most relevant constraints are given for each structure. This includes the constraints demanding that segments, moras, and syllables must be realized and the parsing constraints demanding that every mora dominates a segment and every syllable dominates a mora. These latter constraints are given in all three versions specified for only phonetically visible associations, association lines that are morphological or phonetically invisible, or all associations. Furthermore, the constraints against multiple root nodes for segments and moras and the constraints penalizing epenthetic association lines between segments, moras, and syllables for affix material are given. Finally, the markedness constraint against long vowels is included. This last constraint is simply included since complete mora affixation always results in vowel lengthening in this abstract structure. These blocks of related constraints are separated by double dotted lines in the tableaux to ease the readability.

The possible grammars arising from these candidates and constraints were then calculated with the software OTHelp (Staubs et al., 2010). The three tableaux with 19 candidates in total give rise to potentially 252 languages. The software found an OT solution for 90 of them. Although this is a very impressive number at first sight, the number of predicted surface effects is much smaller. This is simply due to the fact that many of the structures in the tableaux in (45)–(47) are indistinguishable on the surface. Or put differently: the vast majority of possible defective integrations of morphemic prosodic nodes are not expected to have any surface effect for the phonetic interpretation. In fact, only one candidate in all of the tableaux below results in deletion, namely candidate f.

(45)　*Factorial typology: morphemic mora*

	PVis$_S$	PVis$_\mu$	PVis$_\sigma$	μ-Do$_p$-S	μ-Do$_p^m$-S	μ-Do-S	σ-Do$_p$-μ	σ-Do$_p^m$-μ	σ-Do-μ	ONERT-S	ONERT-μ	*Φ..Af..σ	*σ..Af..μ	*μ..Af..S	*μ^μ
a.		*		*	*	*									
b.													*	*	*
c.				*	*	*							*		
d.		*			*	*							*	*	
e.		*			*	*					*			*	
f.	*	**			**	*								*	

(46) *Factorial typology: morphemic syllable*

	$PVIs_S$	$PVIs_\mu$	$PVIs_\sigma$	$\mu\text{-}Do_P\text{-}S$	$\mu\text{-}Do_P^m\text{-}S$	$\mu\text{-}Do\text{-}S$	$\sigma\text{-}Do_P\text{-}\mu$	$\sigma\text{-}Do_P^m\text{-}\mu$	$\sigma\text{-}Do\text{-}\mu$	$OneRt\text{-}S$	$OneRt\text{-}\mu$	$*\Phi..Af..\sigma$	$*\sigma..Af..\mu$	$*\mu..Af..S$	$\mu^\wedge\mu*$
a.			*				*	*	*						
b.												*	*		
c.							*	*	*			*			
d.			*				*	*				*	*		
e.			*				*	*		*	*		*		
f.	*	*	*	*			*	*					*		

(47) *Factorial typology: morphemic mora and syllable*

	$PVIs_S$	$PVIs_\mu$	$PVIs_\sigma$	$\mu\text{-}Do_P\text{-}S$	$\mu\text{-}Do_P^m\text{-}S$	$\mu\text{-}Do\text{-}S$	$\sigma\text{-}Do_P\text{-}\mu$	$\sigma\text{-}Do_P^m\text{-}\mu$	$\sigma\text{-}Do\text{-}\mu$	$OneRt\text{-}S$	$OneRt\text{-}\mu$	$*\Phi..Af..\sigma$	$*\sigma..Af..\mu$	$*\mu..Af..S$	$\mu^\wedge\mu*$
a.		*	*	*	*	*	*	*	*						
b.			*				*	*	*				*	*	*
c.	*			*	*	*						*	*		

	Candidate																
d.	σ σ□ / μo /μo μ• / VoCoVo														*	**	*	*
e.	σ σ σ□ / μo /μo μ• / VoCoVo	*	*	*	*		*	*	*						*	*	
f.	σ σ□ / μo μo μ• / VoCoVo	*	**	*	**	*		*	*						*	*	
g.	σ σ σ□ / μo /μo μ• / VoCoVo	*	*	*	*	*	*	*						*			

Table (48) summarizes the expected surface effects arising in the 90 grammars for the three contexts. In 61 languages (=67.78% of all languages), mora affixation has no surface effect. The number given in brackets is the number of languages where candidate c. in (45) becomes optimal, hence the structure with a catalectic mora. This has no direct effect on the length of the segments but can indeed have indirect effects for, for example, stress assignment (Kager, 1999a). In 17 languages, vowel lengthening is expected. Deletion, finally, is only predicted for 12 languages. For morphemic syllables, the only expected surface effect is deletion.[15] Consequently, the distribution is even clearer: in 77 grammars (=85.56%), no surface effect is predicted, and deletion is only expected in 13 languages. Again, the number in brackets indicates the number of catalectic integrations without any direct surface effect. These findings are consistent with the typological distribution that MLM is rare (compared to normal affixes). A crucially interesting effect in the light of the preceding sections are the predicted grammars for the final context where a morphemic mora and a syllable are present. As can be seen in (48), there are many more instances of grammars with lengthening (26) compared to those with deletion (9). The somewhat surprisingly high number of grammars with lengthening compared to those without any surface effect (55) is in fact due to the simple fact that by far not all candidates that are not harmonically bound are part of the factorial typology in (47). For example, no candidates with catalectic structures are taken into account in (47) but two candidates with lengthening. These distributions of predicted surface effects are hence only relative tendencies. One interesting effect, however, is the indeed relatively low number of deletion patterns. Exactly this effect that the presence of an additional morphemic mora indeed neutralizes the effect of a morphemic syllable that is otherwise expected to trigger deletion was the

---

[15] That the addition of morphemic syllables can indeed lead to additive MLM if more constraints are considered is discussed in the following chapter 6. This factorial typology hence only takes into account one interesting subset of effects.

analysis for the rescuer morpheme in Aymara presented in section 4.2 and also the core of many other of the blocking analyses presented in this chapter.

(48) *Factorial typology: mora and syllable affixation*

	NoChange	Lengthening	Deletion
Morphemic Mora (45)	61 (19)	17	12
Morphemic Syllable (46)	77 (25)	–	13
Morphemic Mora & Syllable (47)	55	26	9
Total	193 (44)	43	34
	71.49%	15.93%	12.59%

Table (49) lists the results of the typology according to the expected surface effects in some more detail. The list gives only the predicted combinations of surface effects, abstracting away from different candidates with the same surface structure. In the line 'NoLg', the number of actual rankings predicting this surface pattern is listed. It can be seen that the 90 possible rankings only result in 26 different combinations of surface effects. The La Paz Aymara pattern discussed in 4.2.3, for example, would be one instantiation of the general pattern 15: Mora affixation results in lengthening, syllable affixation in deletion, and the combination of both results in no surface effect.

Note that the 'NoChange*' notates patterns of catalectic integration that might have indirect effects.

(49) *90 Grammars: surface effects*

	NoLg	Morphemic Mora (45)	Morphemic Syllable (46)	Morphemic Mora and Syllable (47)
1.	18	NoChange	NoChange	NoChange
2.	8	NoChange	NoChange*	NoChange
3.	8	NoChange*	NoChange	NoChange
4.	6	Lengthening	NoChange	NoChange
5.	4	NoChange	NoChange	Lengthening
6.	4	NoChange	Deletion	NoChange
7.	4	NoChange	NoChange*	Lengthening
8.	4	NoChange*	NoChange	Lengthening
9.	4	Lengthening	NoChange	Lengthening
10.	3	NoChange*	NoChange*	NoChange
11.	2	NoChange	NoChange	Deletion
12.	2	NoChange*	NoChange*	Lengthening
13.	2	NoChange*	Deletion	NoChange
14.	2	Lengthening	Deletion	Lengthening
15.	2	Lengthening	Deletion	NoChange
16.	2	Lengthening	NoChange*	Lengthening

17.	2	Deletion	NoChange	NoChange
18.	2	Deletion	NoChange	Lengthening
19.	2	Deletion	NoChange*	Lengthening
20.	2	Deletion	NoChange	Deletion
21.	2	Deletion	NoChange*	NoChange
22.	1	NoChange	NoChange*	Deletion
23.	1	NoChange	Deletion	Deletion
24.	1	Lengthening	Deletion	Deletion
25.	1	Deletion	NoChange*	Deletion
26.	1	Deletion	Deletion	Deletion

It was emphasized in section 3.2.2.1, that many languages show the coexistence of additive and subtractive MLM. The list in (49) proves that the system indeed predicts various combinations of different MLM patterns for one grammar.

This discussion is clearly only a subset of a factorial typology of PDM. Various constraints and possible defective prosodic structures in input and/or output are not part of this factorial typology. However, an important result of this small scale investigation is that although many different (prosodically defective) phonological structures are in principle possible, they don't predict too many different surface effects. And it also showed that although MLM can be predicted from affixing morphemic prosodic nodes, the expected unmarked case is neutralization to a complete prosodic structure and hence no surface effect.

4.5 General summary: PDM and blocking

This chapter illustrated several effects of blocking and/or lexical exceptions in the domain of MLM. In Dhaasanac, Hungarian, and Yine, morphemes are exceptional non-undergoers for an expected subtractive or additive MLM operation that affects all other morphemes in comparable contexts. It was shown that differences in the prosodic structure of those morphemes predict this blocking effect. Interestingly, different prosodically defective morpheme representations were relevant in the different languages simply because the MLM operations were different. In Hungarian and Yine where it was argued that mora usurpation is the mechanism that explains Subtractive Suffixation, the exceptional non-undergoers were taken to contain an additional morphemic mora. This makes mora usurpation unnecessary since the morphemic mora easily supplies the underlying mora-less vowel of the Subtractive Suffix with a mora without segment deletion. In Dhaasanac, on the other hand, an additive intramorphemic vowel lengthening process was only observed for several Additive Affixes, not for others. It was assumed that the non-undergoer morphemes simply contain mora-less vowels that hence can accommodate the additional morphemic mora without any lengthening effect.

In Muylaq' Aymara, on the other hand, a morpheme blocks an expected MLM operation and this blocking is the only surface effect ever observed for the morpheme in question. How the simple mechanism of mora affixation accounts for this pattern as well was shown in section 4.2. A comparison with a closely related dialect of Aymara provides striking evidence for such an analysis since the other straightforward effect of morphemic moras—lengthening—is attested in exactly those morphological contexts that show blocking in Muylaq' Aymara.

That the defective integration of morphemic prosodic nodes may result in subtractive MLM was discussed in section 3.2. In this chapter, a case study of Alabama showed that different underlying prosodic specifications for stems might result in different subtractive patterns from affixing a single morphemic prosodic node.

In conclusion, this chapter showed how various patterns of lexical idiosyncrasies follow from differences in the underlying prosodic specification of morphemes. The PDM approach hence allows us to rely on purely phonological contrastive information where alternative accounts rely on morpheme-specific constraints or rankings. This point is discussed in more detail in chapter 7 where alternative accounts for MLM are discussed.

5

Morpheme contiguity

In this chapter, different empirical effects in the domain of additive MLM are discussed that all follow from the different modifications of morpheme CONTIGUITY proposed in section 2.2.3. *First*, it was argued that linear morpheme CONTIGUITY also extends to elements on different tiers. And, *second*, a contiguous morpheme structure is also required for the vertical dominance relations in a prosodic tree. Elements of different morphological affiliations are hence preferably not in a dominance relation. In this chapter, the predictions of these two classes of morpheme CONTIGUITY constraints in the domain of MLM are investigated in turn. In section 5.1, the constraint CNT_M demanding linear contiguity across tiers is discussed. A high-ranked CNT_M predicts that realization of a morphemic prosodic node can result in allomorphy between different MLM operations or between realization and non-realization of the morphemic prosodic node. It is shown that both predictions are borne out in the typology of attested MLM patterns. In sections 5.2 and 5.3, the concept of vertical morpheme contiguity is investigated in more detail. In section 5.2, it is shown how a vertical morpheme CONTIGUITY restricting the dominance relation between vowels and moras makes important predictions for the typology of morphemic vowel lengthening. Languages are expected to differ in whether all vowels undergo morphological lengthening in a certain context or whether certain vowels (lexical exceptions or epenthetic vowels) are exempt from morphological vowel lengthening. Various patterns of MLM are presented that show that this typology is indeed borne out. It is argued later in section 7.4 that this typology of languages can not be predicted under an alternative parallel OT account without the concept of morph-contiguous mora projection: it is a serious opacity problem. Finally, in section 5.3, the predictions of vertical morpheme CONTIGUITY for feet is investigated for analysing MLM patterns as affixation of morphemic prosodic nodes. It is shown how various patterns of phonologically predictable allomorphy of different MLM operations are predicted if a morphemic foot is affixed that is restricted in its ability to dominate elements of a different morphological affiliation.

Morphological Length and Prosodically Defective Morphemes. First edition. Eva Zimmermann.
© Eva Zimmermann 2017. First published 2017 by Oxford University Press.

5.1 Linear contiguity across prosodic tiers

The empirical observation discussed in this section is the finding that morphemic prosodic nodes are preferably realized at the edges of other morphemes. This effect is predicted from the linear contiguity constraint Cnt_M (1) (repeated from section 2.2.3, (41) demanding that a morphemic prosodic node must dominate phonological elements at the edge of another morpheme (or at the edge of a sequence of epenthetic elements). It is hence very similar to an ALIGN constraint that demands alignment between a prosodic node and the word edge (McCarthy and Prince, 1993*a*: et seq.). Cnt_M correctly predicts attested instances of phonologically predictable allomorphy.

(1) Cnt_M Assign a violation mark for every $P_\circ$ on tier n that is associated to $x_\bullet$ on tier n–1 and $x_\bullet$ is preceded by element $w_\bullet$ and followed by element $z_\bullet$.

What are the predictions Cnt_M makes for the typology of MLM effects? The assumption of the RMO inside a containment-based theory already severely restricts the options a morphemic prosodic node has to be realized 'inside' the exponent of another morpheme. For morphemic moras, the choice is basically reduced to a binary choice between associating to a consonant or a vowel given that moras can never skip one of the moras dominating base material. And in most of those contexts, phonological markedness decides between those options. For example, in the analysis of additive MLM in La Paz Aymara in section 4.2, it was taken for granted that the morphemic mora can only associate to a vowel, never to a consonant simply because the language does not employ geminate consonants. Although markedness and the RMO are hence sufficient in most cases to determine to which base elements a morphemic prosodic node can associate, there are some interesting effects that can only be predicted by Cnt_M.

5.1.1 Blocking of vowel lengthening in Bukusu

In Bukusu, a Benue-Congo language spoken in South Africa, an instance of Additive Affixation can be observed in the first person singular (Mutonyi, 2000). A prefix /n–/ is added and a following base vowel is lengthened as can be seen in (2).

(2) *Lengthening-triggering prefix in Bukusu*   (Mutonyi, 2000)

BASE	1SG		
ixala	niːxala	'sit'	216
esa	neːsa	'hangout'	216
asama	naːsáma	'open mouth'	216
ora	noːra	'bask'	216
ekesia	neːkésja	'show'	169

Given only this data, an analysis seems possible where the prefix is /nV–/ and surfaces without its vowel in order to avoid a vowel hiatus. This is especially apparent since vowel hiatus are indeed disallowed in Bukusu and one of three repair operations applies to avoid them: glide formation for prevocalic high vowels /u/ and /i/ (3-a), coalescence for sequences of /a/+/i/ to [e] (3-b),[1] or deletion of the first vowel (3-c). Crucially enough, all these strategies are accompanied by compensatory lengthening of the remaining vowel. For a putative prefix /ne−/ or /no−/, we hence might expect phonologically predictable vowel deletion to avoid a hiatus accompanied by lengthening of the remaining vowel in (2).

(3)   *Vowel hiatus avoidance in Bukusu*   (Mutonyi, 2000: 155)

    a. ku−mu−iβa   kúmwiːβa   'sugarcane'
        ki−mi−aɲa   kímjaːɲa   'holes'

    b. ka−ma−olu   kámoːlu   'noses'
        xa−xa−eni   xaxeːni   '(small) forehead'

    c. βa−βa−ifwi   βáβeːfwi   'thieves'
        ka−ma−ici   kámeːci   'water'

However, such a phonological reanalysis of the facts becomes untenable if we consider the data in (4) where the first person singular prefix attaches to consonant-initial bases. It surfaces only as a nasal without any vowel.[2] In this preconsonantal context, however, no general phonological rule predicts vowel deletion. We hence must conclude that the lengthening accompanying the first person singular prefix in (2) is indeed an instance of MLM and hence Additive Affixation. Interestingly now, this morphological lengthening is systematically absent for consonant-initial bases in (4). The first person form for a base /lima/ is /ndima/ not */ndiːma/ as we would expect after MLM triggered by the Additive Affix. On a descriptive level, an onset consonant that intervenes between the prefix and the base vowel hence blocks the lengthening.

(4)   *Additive Affixes in Bukusu: no lengthening across an onset*   (Mutonyi, 2000)

BASE	1SG		
a. lima	ndíma	'cultivate'	216
taβula	ndáβula	'tear up'	216
kona	ngóna	'sleep'	216
βukula	mbukula	'take'	173

---

[1] There are more vowel coalescence operations to avoid a vowel hiatus. The most likely generalization for all these operations is that coalescence applies whenever one of the two vowels is high and the [±back] value of the second vowel and the [±high] value from the first vowel is preserved on the resulting vowel. However, Mutonyi (2000) emphasizes that these other coalescence operations (like /e/+/o/ to [u]) only apply at the phrase-level and there is no data showing what happens in those contexts word-internally. The more restrictive generalization is taken for granted in the following.

[2] Several general phonological processes are crucial in accounting for all the segmental alternations in (4): *first*, there is a rule of post-nasal hardening for liquids, glides, and /β/, *second*, there is a regular rule of nasal place assimilation, *third*, obstruents regularly voice after a nasal, and, *fourth*, nasals are deleted before voiceless fricatives or other nasals (Mutonyi, 2000: 172ff).

OXFORD
UNIVERSITY PRESS

Sent with Compliments of Julia Steer

Distribution Services
Kettering North Business Park
Hipwell Road
Kettering
Northants NN14 1UA
United Kingdom
www.oup.com

With compliments

b. funa funa 'break' 169
xalala xalala 'get serious' 169
saβa saβa 'beg' 169

These facts can easily be captured on a descriptive level but are an interesting challenge for any theory analysing the vowel lengthening as mora affixation. Why is the mora blocked from association with the first vowel if it is preceded by an onset consonant? On the moraic tier, nothing is expected to intervene between the affix mora and the first base vowel as is illustrated in the depictions in (5). If the initial consonant was moraic, then it would indeed be impossible for the morphemic mora to be associated with the first vowel. However, there are no geminates in the language in any position and assuming the rather marked structure of an initial moraic consonant (see for discussion, Topintzi, 2008a) is empirically completely unjustified and would wrongly predict a length contrast for initial consonants. Consequently, under no standard representation is there any independent reason why a prefixed mora should be blocked from association across an initial consonant.

(5) *Additive affixation in Bukusu*

   a. *Affixation and vowel lengthening*

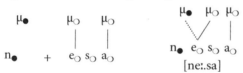

[neː.sa]

   b. *Affixation without lengthening*

[ndi.ma]

Mutonyi (2000) argues that this phenomenon in Bukusu can only be captured in a theory where skeletal elements are arrayed on the same tier as the onset and hence makes an argument for X-Slot theory (Hyman, 1982; Levin, 1985; Kaye et al., 1985). In contrast, this pattern can be predicted by the extended concept of morpheme contiguity across tiers captured by CNT_M. If it is high-ranked in Bukusu, the absence of lengthening is straightforwardly predicted for bases that do not start with a vowel. Tableaux (6-i) and (6-ii) illustrate this. The affix mora is prefixed to its base and is preferably fully integrated in its base due to PVIS_μ and $\mu > \text{Do}_p^m > S$. High-ranked CNT_M, on the other hand, ensures that the mora can only be associated with segments at the edge of the base. For a vowel-initial base as in (6-i), such an edge-association is possible without violating any other higher-ranked constraints. Only low-ranked $^{*\mu}V^\mu$ is violated in the winning candidate (6-i-b). For a consonant-initial base (6-ii), however, association of the morphemic mora with the first segment causes an additional violation of high-ranked $*C_\mu$. Association with a vowel, on the other hand, violates CNT_M.[3] The morphemic mora remains floating in the winning candidate (6-ii-a) and no segmental lengthening is predicted—exactly the blocking configuration that we find in Bukusu.

(6) *Additive affixation in Bukusu*
  i. *Vowel lengthening*

	$*C_\mu$	CNT_M	$\mu{>}\text{DoP}_{P}^{m}{>}\text{S}$	PVis_μ	$*\text{A}_\mu^\mu$
a. [ne.sa]			*!	*!	
☞ b. [neː.sa]					*

(i) *Prenasalized stop as result of coalescence*

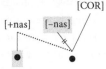

ii. *Vowel lengthening is blocked*

		$*C_\mu$	C_{NT_M}	$\mu{>}\text{D}_{\text{O}}\text{P}^{\text{m}}{>}\text{S}$	$\text{PV}_{\text{IS}_\mu}$	$*\text{H}_{\text{V}}^\mu$
☞ a.	[ndi.ma]			*	*	
b.	[ndːi.ma]	*!				
c.	[ndiː.ma]			*!		*

5.1.2 Allomorphy in Asante Twi

In Bukusu, the morphemic mora is not realized if association to a stem-initial segment is impossible. Another prediction of C_{NT_M} is an alternation between different MLM operations for bases with different segments at their edge if no markedness blocks one operation or the other. This prediction is borne out in, for example, Asante Twi, a Surmic language of the African Savannah (Christaller, 1964; Dolphyne, 1996; Adu-Amankwah, 2003; Paster, 2010). The past tense formation of verbs in Asante Twi involves segmental lengthening as can be seen in (7). The final segment of the base is lengthened, either a vowel (7-a) or a consonant (7-b).[4]

---

[4] In addition, a low tone is added to the first mora of the base. And there is a contrast between verb forms with or without an overt object. If no object follows, an additional suffix /−jɛ/ɪjɛ/ʊjɛ/ is present (e.g. /wó dànéèjὲ/ 'You turned' (Paster, 2010: 100)). It is striking that all the examples with final consonant lengthening that could be obtained end in /m/. Future research needs to disentangle what additional restrictions might be active in this pattern.

(7)   *Addition in Asante Twi*

(Dolphyne, 1996; Paster, 2010; Augustina Pokua Owusu
and Sampson Korsah, pc)

BASE			PAST (+OBJ)	
a. tɔ	'to buy'		tɔː	P80/98
dane	'to turn'		daneː	P80/99
bwa	'to help'		boaː	P80/99
kae	'to remember'		kaeː	P80/99
bisa	'to ask'		bisaː	P80/99
b. nom	'to drink'		nomː	P80/99
pam	'to sew'		pamː	D91
tim	'to remain unmoved'		timː	SK
kum	'to kill'		kumː	SK

Such a pattern is another straightforward prediction from an undominated CNT_M. The only difference to the Bukusu ranking is the fact that Asante Twi allows edge geminates. Consequently, realization of the morphemic mora at the morpheme edge is possible irrespective of whether it is affixed to a consonant- or vowel-final base. The following tableaux illustrate this. A morphemic mora is added to a vowel-final base in (8-i) and to a consonant-final base in (8-ii). High-ranked CNT_M demands that the morphemic mora can only associate to a base-final segment and since both $*C_\mu$ and $*^\mu V^\mu$ are low-ranked, alternation between vowel lengthening (8-i-b) and gemination (8-ii-b) is predicted.

(8)   *Addition in Asante Twi*
    i. *Vowel lengthening*

$\mu_\circ$ $\mu_\circ$ $\mu_\bullet$ $+$ $d_\circ$ $a_\circ$ $n_\circ$ $e_\circ$	CNT_M	$\mu{>}\text{Dop}{>}\text{S}$	PVIS_μ	$*C_\mu$	$*^\mu V^\mu$
a. $\mu_\circ$ $\mu_\circ$ $\mu_\bullet$ $d_\circ$ $a_\circ$ $n_\circ$ $e_\circ$ [da.ne]		*!	*!		
☞ b. $\mu_\circ$ $\mu_\circ$ $\mu_\bullet$ $d_\circ$ $a_\circ$ $n_\circ$ $e_\circ$ [da.neː]					*

ii. *Gemination*

$\mu_O \quad\quad \mu_\bullet$ $\mid \quad +$ $n_O \;\; o_O \; m_O$	$\textsc{Cnt}_M$	$\mu{>}\textsc{Do}_P^m{>}\textsc{s}$	$\textsc{PVis}_\mu$	$*\textsc{C}_\mu$	$*\textsc{V}_\mu$
a. $\quad$ $\mu_O \; \mu_\bullet$ $n_O \;\; o_O \; m_O$ [noːm]	*!				*
☞ b. $\quad$ $\mu_O \; \mu_\bullet$ $\mid$ $n_O \;\; o_O \; m_O$ [nomː]				*	

5.2 Vertical contiguity: vowels and moras

5.2.1 Introduction: certain- vs. all-vowel-lengthening grammars

In this subsection, we turn to vertical morpheme CONTIGUITY, extending the discussion of opaque mora licensing from section 2.2.4. The constraint $*V_O <_O \mu_\bullet$ (see section 2.2.3, (47)), repeated in (9), demands that every vowel is dominated by its own mora, i.e. a mora with the same morphological affiliation or with no affiliation at all.

(9) $*V_O <_O \mu_\bullet$ Assign a violation mark for every vowel V that does not project a morph-contiguous μ that bears the same morphological colour or no morphological colour at all.

The most interesting empirical finding discussed in this section is the existence of long epenthetic vowels that constitute strong evidence for the concept of morph-contiguous mora projection proposed here. In the context of epenthetic vowels, the opacity problem of moraic licensing discussed in section 2.2.4, is of crucial relevance since those vowels are by definition not underlyingly associated with a mora—they are not underlyingly present. In addition, it is argued in section 7.4 that this phenomenon is deeply problematic under an alternative OT-account without a concept of morph-contiguous mora projection.

As is argued in section 2.2.4, $*V_O <_O \mu_\bullet$ is able to predict that the addition of a morphemic mora results in lengthening for all vowels, even those that are not underlyingly associated with a mora and hence solves an apparently serious problem arising from Richness of the Base. On the other hand, if the constraint is low-ranked, it is predicted that only certain bases undergo morphological vowel lengthening while others resist this lengthening. This is summarized in (10) where an underlyingly mora-less vowel (=a possible representation given Richness of the Base) is adjacent to a morphemic mora that is expected to link to a vowel. In (10-i), $^{*}V_O <_O \mu_{\bullet}$ is ranked higher than COL!_{μ} and mora epenthesis is required for all vowels that are not under-lyingly dominated by a mora. This can be termed an 'all-vowel-lengthening' grammar since morphological vowel lengthening is predicted for all vowels, irrespective of their underlying moraic specification. In (10-ii), on the other hand, $^{*}V_O <_O \mu_{\bullet}$ is ranked low and COL!_{μ} prohibits additional mora epenthesis to supply every vowel with a morph-contiguous mora. If a morphemic mora becomes adjacent to a vowel that is underlyingly mora-less, this mora simply associates to the vowel. Vowel lengthening is hence not expected under such a 'certain-vowel-lengthening' grammar.

(10) $^{*}V_O <_O \mu_{\bullet}$ *and underlying vowels*

   i. *'All-vowel-lengthening' grammar: vowel lengthening*

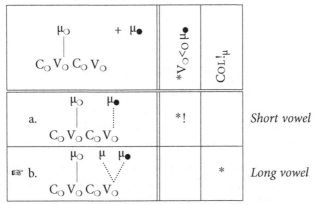

   ii. *'Certain-vowel-lengthening' grammar: no vowel lengthening*

Interestingly, no such prediction exists for consonants since no counterpart $^{*}C_O <_O \mu_{\bullet}$ exists. This is simply due to the major representational difference between long vowels and long consonants in the standard mora model adopted here: a long vowel is linked to two moras whereas a long consonant is linked to one mora (and doubly linked to two syllables for vowel-medial geminates).

Another area where $^*V_O <_O \mu_\bullet$ makes some interesting predictions is the interaction of vowel epenthesis and morphemic mora affixation. Crucially, the constraint $^*V_O <_O \mu_\bullet$ is not only violated if an underlying vowel does not project a morph-contiguous mora but also if an epenthetic vowel is only dominated by a mora with a morphological affiliation. An epenthetic vowel has no morphological affiliation and every underlying mora dominating it hence has a 'different' morphological affiliation. In the 'all-vowel-lengthening' grammar, a morphemic mora is hence predicted to lengthen even an epenthetic vowel, whereas in the 'certain-vowel-lengthening' grammar, an epenthetic vowel adjacent to a morphemic mora is predicted to be generally short. Tableaux (11-i) and (11-ii) illustrate these further predictions of $^*V_O <_O \mu_\bullet$.

(11) $^*V_O <_O \mu_\bullet$ *and epenthetic vowels*

i.   *'All-vowel-lengthening' grammar: long epenthetic vowels*

$\mu_O \quad + \mu_\bullet$ | $C_O\,V_O\,C_O$	$^*V_O<_O\mu_\bullet$	$\text{COL}\colon\mu$	
a. $\mu_O \quad \mu_\bullet$ | ⋮ $C_O\,V_O\,C_O\ V$	*!		*Short epenthetic vowel*
☞ b. $\mu_O \quad \mu \quad \mu_\bullet$ | \\/ $C_O\,V_O\,C_O\ V$		*	*Long epenthetic vowel*

ii.   *'Certain-vowel-lengthening' grammar: short epenthetic vowels*

$\mu_O \quad + \mu_\bullet$ | $C_O\,V_O\,C_O$	$\text{COL}\colon\mu$	$^*V_O<_O\mu_\bullet$	
☞ a. $\mu_O \quad \mu_\bullet$ | ⋮ $C_O\,V_O\,C_O\ V$		*	*Short epenthetic vowel*
b. $\mu_O \quad \mu \quad \mu_\bullet$ | \\/ $C_O\,V_O\,C_O\ V$	*!		*Long epenthetic vowel*

The existence of such long epenthetic vowels is surprising from a typological perspective. There is a general tendency for epenthetic elements to be unmarked and short, sometimes even shorter than the non-epenthetic vowels of a language (for discussion and literature see, for example, Vaux, 2002; Hall, 2011). Epenthetic vowels are hence rather well-known for containing very little structure and an intriguing analysis for epenthetic vowels in certain languages is to assume that they are completely mora-less (Piggott, 1995). In the following, it is shown that the other extreme—epenthetic vowels associated with two moras—is indeed attested in the languages of the world as well.

Recall that epenthesis as instance of MLM was only included in the present data set if it alternates phonologically predictably with a Long-Short-Alternation. This followed mainly from the simple fact that a non-alternating epenthesis pattern to realize a morphemic prosodic node is on the surface in principle indistinguishable from a segmental affix. All the following examples are hence instances of phonologically predictable allomorphy in contexts of Addition or Additive Affixation.

In the following, it is argued that the two types of languages introduced above are indeed attested. In section 5.2.2, examples for 'certain-vowel' languages are discussed. The two diagnostics for this language type are lexical exceptions to a morphological vowel lengthening process and short epenthetic vowels in the context of morphological lengthening. In section 5.2.3, on the other hand, languages characterized as 'all-vowel-lengthening' are presented. Those languages are predicted to lack lexical exceptions to morphological vowel lengthening and should employ long epenthetic vowels in the context of morphological vowel lengthening. Several examples for such long epenthetic vowels are discussed and special attention is paid to a detailed case study of additive MLM in Southern Sierra Miwok where long epenthetic consonants and vowels are attested.

5.2.2 *Certain-vowel-lengthening languages*

5.2.2.1 Exceptions to morphological lengthening in Diegueño An example for a 'certain-vowel-lengthening' language is Diegueño (Walker, 1970; Langdon, 1970; Miller, 1999; Wolf, 2007; de Lacy, 2012). In this Yuman language of California, various strategies to form the plural for verb and noun bases are attested. Walker (1970) lists five and Miller (1999) lists nine strategies to mark plural in Jamul Diegueño. These strategies involve affixation of segments and, most importantly, also vowel lengthening of the final vowel.[5] Vowel lengthening, illustrated in (12-a), is in fact the most frequent strategy to form the plural in Diegueño. In (12-b), the alternative strategy to mark plural via prefixation of /n−/ or /tʃ−/ is illustrated.

---

[5] In fact, Diegueño is often cited as an example for length polarity where short base vowels are lengthened (12) and long base vowels are shortened (i) to form the plural and this alternation can be predicted by the underlying representation of the base (Wolf, 2007; Topintzi, 2008*b*).

(12)　*Plural formation in Diegueño*　　　　　(Miller, 1999; Walker, 1970; Wolf, 2007)

Base	PLURAL		
a. ɬʲap	ɬʲaːp	'to burn'	Wa7
múɬ	múːɬ	'gather'	Wo54
tʃuːpúɬ	tʃuːpúːɬ	'to boil'	Wa7
ʃuːpít	ʃuːpíːt̪	'to close'	Wa7
uʔis	uʔiːs	'to sneeze'	M105
b. amp	namp	'to walk'	M104
aː	naː	'to go'	M104
uʔux	tʃuʔux	'to cough'	M103

These different plural allomorphs can even surface in combinations, as is shown in (13) where vowel lengthening cooccurs with prefixation or infixation of segmental affixes.

(13)　*Cooccurrence of plural allomorphs in Diegueño*　　　　　(Miller, 1999)

Base	PLURAL		
kaːkap	nekaːkaːp	'to go around'	M105
xtup	xuːtuːp	'to jump'	M105
akːwi	atʃkwiːp	'to ask a question'	M106

The choice between these different plural strategies is, for the most part, a lexical one.[6] With respect to the vowel lengthening plural formation, the important conclusion is hence that some stems are lexically marked for lengthening their base vowel to form the plural (12-a) and others are lexically marked for not lengthening their vowel in the plural (12-b). Obviously, the pattern is more complex and lengthening/non-lengthening stems are further differentiated since they can show any number of

(i)　*Subtraction in Diegueño*　　　　　(Walker, 1970; Wolf, 2007)

BASE	PLURAL		
saːw	saw	'to eat'	Wo54
kiːxáːr	kiːxár	'complain'	Wo54
siː	sitʃ	'to drink'	Wa7
maː	matʃ	'to eat soft things'	Wa7

This interpretation of the facts, however, is far from convincing (de Lacy, 2012). For one, lengthening is a rather frequent plural formation strategy whereas shortening is rather rare. Lengthening in the plural is listed for 72 per cent of all bases (Miller, 2001) whereas shortening is attested for only seven words. Most importantly there are various bases with a long vowel that is not shortened in the plural. It is not clear whether shortening is indeed a productive process to form the plural or whether the seven shortening stems are simply stored as suppletive forms. In any case, it is safe to say that there is no length polarity in the sense that the alternation between lengthening and shortening is a phonologically predictable allomorphy pattern to form the plural in Diegueño.

[6] Walker (1970) argues that two prefixation strategies are predictable: /tʃ−/ prefixation can be found for all bases ending in a vowel and prefixation of /n−/ for all verbs that denote a 'verb of motion'. However, these predictable allomorphs can also be accompanied by additional plural formations whose choice is again unpredictable.

additional plural formation strategies. However, at least the lexical choice between lengthening and non-lengthening bases can be attributed to a difference in the prosodic representation of these bases in the present framework: lengthening bases contain a vowel that is underlyingly dominated by mora whereas non-lengthening bases contain a vowel that is not underlyingly dominated by a mora. This reduces the complex pattern of plural formation strategies since it allows an analysis where the exponent for Addition (=a morphemic mora) is added in all contexts. The choice whether vowel lengthening surfaces or not then follows from the moraic specification of the base. Diegueño is thus assumed to be an example for a 'certain-vowel-lengthening' language, briefly shown in the tableaux below. In (14-i), the morphemic mora that is assumed to be a regular plural exponent is added to a base with an underlying moraic vowel and vowel lengthening is predicted. In (14-ii), on the other hand, the final base vowel happens to lack a mora underlyingly and the morphemic mora simply associates to this vowel: $*V_o <_o \mu_\bullet$ is ranked low and no vowel lengthening is predicted.[7]

(14)   *Addition in Diegueño*
    i. *Vowel lengthening*

μ_o $\mu_\bullet$ / $m_o u_o \l_o$ +	$\mu{>}\mathrm{Dop}^m{>}S$	$V{<}DD_p{<}\mu$	$\mathrm{Col!}_\mu$	$*A_\mu^\mu$	$*V_o{<}_o\mu_\bullet$
a. μ_o $\mu_\bullet$ / $m_o u_o \l_o$ [muł]	*!				
☞ b. μ_o $\mu_\bullet$ / $m_o u_o \l_o$ [muːł]					*

[7] Recall that the analysis only derives the contrast between lengthening and non-lengthening plural formations and is agnostic to the question whether any of the other allomorphy patterns is phonologically predictable as well. The presence or absence of the segmental prefix is hence simply taken as being dependent on some lexical marking.

ii. *Lexical exception to lengthening*

μ_O $\mu_\bullet$ | u_O $?_O$ u_O x_O +	$\mu{>}Do^m_P{>}S$	$V{<}DD_P{<}\mu$	$CoL!_\mu$	$*\mu_\mu V^\mu$	$*V_O{<}o\ \mu_\bullet$

a. μ_O $\mu_\bullet$
     |
   u_O $?_O$ u_O x_O
     [u?x]
	*!	*!			

☞ b. μ_O $\mu_\bullet$
    | ⋮
   u_O $?_O$ u_O x_O
    [u?ux]
					*

c. μ_O μ $\mu_\bullet$
    | ∨
   u_O $?_O$ u_O x_O
    [u?u:x]
				*!	*!

5.2.2.2 *Short epenthetic vowels in Arbizu Basque*   Another prediction of a low-ranked $*V_O <o\ \mu_\bullet$ is that epenthetic vowels are expected to be short in the context of a morphemic mora. An instance of such a pattern can be found in Arbizu Basque (Hualde, 1990, 1991; van de Weijer, 1992; Artiagoitia, 1993; Hualde and Ortiz de Urbina, 2003; Hualde, 2012). Most Basque dialects do not have phonemic length for vowels but some have grammaticalized it, including the Arbizu dialect (Hualde, 1990). The genitive indefinite and the superlative are marked in Arbizu Basque by suffixing /−n/ and lengthening of the preceding vowel (15a). For consonant-final stems, insertion of /e/ before /−n/ takes place (15b). This epenthesis is now independently motivated since a nasal can never be the second part of a coda cluster. Only fricatives followed by /t/ or sonorants followed by /t/, /k/, a fricative or an affricate are possible coda clusters in Basque (see, for example, Hualde and Ortiz de Urbina, 2003: for Basque in general).

(15)   *Additive suffixes in Arbizu Basque*   (Hualde, 1990: 283)

     BASE   GEN.INDEF

   a. *V-final stems*

alaba	alaba:n	'daughter'
pa:te	pa:te:n	'wall'
asto	asto:n	'donkey'
mendi	mendi:n	'mountain'
esku	esku:n	'hand'

b. *C-final stems*

txakurː	txakurːen	'dog'
gizon	gizonen	'man'

The representation for the Additive Affixes in the genitive indefinite (and the superlative) is taken to be the standard representation for Additive Affixes in PDM that contains a morphemic mora.[8] In case this suffix is attached to a vowel-final base as in (16-i), the morphemic mora is associated with the final vowel of the base, resulting in vowel lengthening. Full integration of the morphemic mora under a syllable is predicted by high-ranked $\mu > Do_p^m > S$ and $PVIS_\mu$, that are not included in the tableaux in (16). In cases where the base ends in a consonant (16-ii), however, vowel epenthesis is independently predicted between the base-final consonant and the affix consonant to avoid an illicit coda cluster. In (16), this is ensured by $*CN]_\sigma$ ('Assign a violation mark for every phonetically visible coda cluster of a consonant followed by a sonorant.') that excludes candidates (16-ii-a) and (16-ii-b). This epenthetic vowel is then predicted to be dominated by the morphemic mora in the winning candidate (16-ii-c). Additional insertion of an epenthetic mora that dominates the epenthetic vowel (16-ii-d) is excluded by $COL!_\mu$. We can hence conclude that $*V_O <_O \mu_\bullet$ is ranked lower than $COL!_\mu$ in Arbizu Basque. The vowel epenthesis hence receives a double motivation in Arbizu Basque since it avoids an illicit consonant cluster and realizes a morphemic mora at the same time.

---

[8] Note that an apparent alternative analysis assuming that the affix is simply /−en/ and vowel deletion followed by subsequent compensatory vowel lengthening applies to avoid an illicit vowel cluster is deeply problematic given the regular phonology of the language. Regular vowel-initial suffixes show a different behaviour if attached to a vowel-final base as can be seen in (i) where the paradigms for the absolute singular and genitive plural are given—the latter is in fact indeed assumed to be /−en/ in Hualde (1990).

(i)   *V-initial suffixes in Arbizu Basque: /−a/ and /−en/*   (Hualde, 1990: 281, 283)

Base	Abs.Sg	Gen.Pl	
V-final stems			
alaba	alaba	alaben	'daughter'
paːte	paːtia	paːtien	'wall'
mendi	mendija	mendijen	'mountain'
esku	eskuba	eskuben	'hand'

(16)   *Additive affixation in Arbizu Basque*
  i. *Vowel lengthening*

	μ_o μ_o $\mu_\bullet$ a$_o$ s$_o$ t$_o$ o$_o$ + n$_\bullet$	*CN]$_\sigma$	μ>Do$_p^m$>S	Col!S	*$^\mu$A$_\mu$	Col!$_\mu$	*V$_o$<o$_\mu$
a.	μ_o μ_o $\mu_\bullet$ a$_o$ s$_o$ t$_o$ o$_o$ n$_\bullet$ [as.ton]		*!				
☞ b.	μ_o μ_o $\mu_\bullet$ a$_o$ s$_o$ t$_o$ o$_o$ n$_\bullet$ [as.toːn]				*		

  ii. *Epenthesis*

	μ_o μ_o $\mu_\bullet$ g$_o$ i$_o$ z$_o$ o$_o$ n$_o$ +n$_\bullet$	*CN]$_\sigma$	μ>Do$_p^m$>S	Col!S	*$^\mu$A$_\mu$	Col!$_\mu$	*V$_o$<o$_\mu$
a.	μ_o μ_o $\mu_\bullet$ g$_o$ i$_o$ z$_o$ o$_o$ n$_o$ n$_\bullet$ [gi.zonn]	*!	*!				
b.	μ_o μ_o $\mu_\bullet$ g$_o$ i$_o$ z$_o$ o$_o$ n$_o$ n$_\bullet$ [gi.zoːnn]	*!			*		
☞ c.	μ_o μ_o $\mu_\bullet$ g$_o$ i$_o$ z$_o$ o$_o$ n$_o$ e n$_\bullet$ [gi.zo.nen]			*			*
d.	μ_o μ_o μ $\mu_\bullet$ g$_o$ i$_o$ z$_o$ o$_o$ n$_o$ e n$_\bullet$ [gi.zo.neːn]			*	*!	*!	

5.2.2.3 Short epenthetic/underlying vowels in Lardil   Another apparent instance of a a short inserted vowel in the context of a morphemic mora can be found in Lardil (Hale, 1973; Klokeid, 1976; Wilkinson, 1988; McCarthy and Prince, 1993b; Horwood, 2001; Bye, 2006; Round, 2011). The passive in Lardil is formed via lengthening of the

final vowel for polysyllabic roots (17-a) and insertion of /−ji/ for monosyllabic roots
(17-b).[9] Crucially, this inserted /−ji/ has a short vowel, despite the morphological
vowel lengthening process observed in (17-a).

(17)   *Passive/Reflexive in Lardil*   (Klokeid, 1976: 81)

	ACTIVE		PASSIVE
a.	warnawu	'burn, cook'	warnawu:
	kupari	'make, repair'	kupari:
	mirntilnja	'crush'	mirntilnja:
	padki	'chop'	padki:
	terlte	'break'	terlte:
b.	ma-tha	'get'	maji
	ne-tha	'hit, kill'	neji
	pe-tha	'bite'	peji
	ra-tha	'spear'	raji

Whereas the status of /j/ as epenthetic in Lardil is uncontroversial (Klokeid, 1976), the
status of the /i/ is less clear. The epenthetic vowel to avoid subminimal monomoraic
words in Lardil that Round (2011) describes is /a/. However, a possible analysis that the
passive/reflexive morpheme is /−i/ and vowel coalescence applies in case it is added to
vowel-final stems is implausible given the fact that vowel hiatus is normally resolved
via deletion, not via coalescence (/kela−ur−u/ → /kelaru/ 'beach' FEM.ACC (Klokeid,
1976: 83)). However, since $^{*}V_O <_O \mu_\bullet$ does not differentiate between epenthetic and
underlying vowels, the morphological status of the vowel is in fact irrelevant for the
predictions of the present constraint system. A low-ranked $^{*}V_O <_O \mu_\bullet$ predicts that the
vowel surfaces as short if it is not associated to a mora in the input—either because it
is epenthetic or because it is underlyingly mora-less.

5.2.2.4 *Double lengthening in La Paz Aymara*

An indirect ranking argument for the
position of $^{*}V_O <_O \mu_\bullet$ can be found in La Paz Aymara, discussed in detail in 4.2.
Since multiple patterns of Addition and Additive Affixes coexist in the language, the
situation can arise that double-lengthening is expected for a vowel. Since superlong
vowels are illicit in the language, an alternative strategy to realize both moras can be
found in those contexts, namely insertion of /−ja/. In (18-a, b), examples are given
where the verbalizer is followed by the suffix for 1>3 future, hence a context where
two Addition morphemes are adjacent. The surface form leaves the final stem vowel
unchanged but adds /ja:/. In (18-c), the verbalizer suffix is followed by the suffix /−ta/
that requires a long preceding vowel: once again, /−ja/ is inserted instead of a double-
lengthening of an underlying vowel.

---

[9] The base forms for monosyllabic stems contain an additional augment /a/ to make the form bisyllabic
and the suffix /th/ that is present for all verbs prior to the adding of tense of negation markers (Klokeid,
1976: 84, 85).

(18) *Allomorphy between : and ja:*   (Beesley, 2000)
a. warmi—:—:
    women-VB-1>3.FUT
    'I will be a woman'
    warmija: *warmi::

b. jatitʃa—iri—:—:—wa
    teach-actor/purposive-VB-1>3.FUT-FS
    'I will be a teacher'
    jatitʃirija:wa   *jatitʃiri::wa

c. qulʲqi—ni—:—:ta
    money-possessor-VB-1>3.FUT
    'You will have money'
    qulʲqinija:ta   *qulʲqini::ta

The fact that the inserted /—ja/ is long is straightforwardly expected since two mor-phemic moras are present in such a context given the analysis of Additive Affixes and Addition as morphemic moras, depicted in (19). However, it is clear that the inserted vowel is dominated by two moras that have a different morphemic affiliation in (19-a). This structure that derives the correct surface effect hence violates $^*V_O <_O \mu_\bullet$. It is predicted to be optimal in a ranking where COL!_μ dominates $^*V_O <_O \mu_\bullet$. A possible alternative candidate that avoids a violation of $^*V_O <_O \mu_\bullet$ is shown in (19-b): the first morphemic mora associates to the final stem vowel and only the second morphemic mora dominates the inserted /a/. In addition, an epenthetic mora is inserted to ensure morph-contiguous mora projection for the /a/. The ranking $\text{COL!}_\mu \gg {}^*V_O <_O \mu_\bullet$ excludes this alternative candidate.

(19) *Insertion in La Paz Aymara*

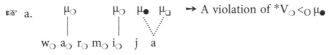

☞ a. μ_O μ_O $\mu_\bullet$ $\mu_\square$ → A violation of $^*V_O <_O \mu_\bullet$

        w_O a_O r_O m_O i_O j a

 * b. μ_O $\mu_O \mu_\bullet$ μ $\mu_\square$ → Morph-contiguous licensing for all vowels

        w_O a_O r_O m_O i_O j a

5.2.3 All-vowel-lengthening languages

In all the analyses above, $^*V_O <_O \mu_\bullet$ was assumed to be ranked below COL!_μ and insertion of a mora to ensure morph-contiguous mora licensing was hence excluded. Under the reverse ranking, all vowels are expected to be lengthened in the context of a morphemic mora. This includes underlying vowels with an underlying mora, underlying vowels without a mora, and epenthetic vowels. In this section, several examples for languages that are of this 'all-vowel-lengthening' type are presented. The discussion starts with a detailed case study of Southern Sierra Miwok.

5.2.3.1 Long epenthetic vowels in Southern Sierra Miwok   Southern Sierra Miwok (=SSM) is one of five moderately diverse Miwok languages that belong to the Yokuts-Utian language stock. SSM has only a few semispeakers or passive speakers today (Hinton, 1994; Golla, 2011).[10] The third person singular morpheme in SSM is an instance of Addition whose surface effect is final vowel lengthening as can be seen in (20-a). In addition, there are Additive Affixes that trigger either lengthening of a preceding vowel (20-b) or gemination of a preceding consonant (20-c). This complementary distribution that certain Additive Affixes only trigger gemination and others only vowel lengthening is predicted by the general phonology of the language since SSM does not allow complex syllable margins or superheavy syllables. The latter excludes CVːC syllables in all non-final positions. They are possible word-finally since the last consonant is taken to be extrametrical, an assumption that also receives support from the observation that final CVC syllables count as light for stress assignment whereas closed syllables elsewhere in the word count as heavy (Freeland, 1951: 6). The impossibility of complex consonant clusters predicts that consonant-initial suffixes can never trigger gemination of a preceding consonant since an illicit *VCːCV structure is expected. And that vowel-initial suffixes never trigger lengthening of a preceding vowel follows since vowel clusters are impossible in SSM and a vowel-initial suffix is necessarily always preceded by a (possibly epenthetic) consonant. As is argued below, it is taken for granted that the default strategy to realize a morphemic mora in SSM is gemination and hence an Additive Suffix preceded by a consonant will trigger gemination if possible.[11]

(20)   *Additive MLM in SSM*   (Broadbent, 1964)
　　a. *Addition*

wɨn−si−na−ː	wɨnsinaː	'he just now came'	B84
ʔamːu−k−a−ː	ʔamːukaː	'he got hurt just now'	B82
jɨHŋ−akː−a−ː	jɨːŋakːaː	'he got drunk just now'	B83
teːp−a−ː	teːpaː	'he cut it'	B48
joːh−k−a−ː	joːhukaː	'he got killed'	B82

　　b. *Additive Affixation: vowel lengthening*

lit−h−a−ːmeʔ	lithaːmeʔ	'it's risen on us'	63
kelːa−na−ːmeʔ	kelːanaːmeʔ	'it snowed on us'	63

---

[10] The following data for SSM are mainly from Broadbent's (1964) grammar that is also the base for the theoretical work in Sloan (1991). Another source that was consulted is Freeland (1951) (written in 1936) who focusses on Central Southern Miwok but gives information on Northern and Southern Sierra Miwok as well.

[11] The notational conventions used in Broadbent (1964) are adopted where 'Y' represents an /u/ if the following syllable contains an /u/ or an /o/ and an /ɨ/ elsewhere. It is the epenthetic default vowel of the language that exists underlyingly as well. The symbol 'H' marks either a preceding long segment, i.e. stands for ː, if it is not followed by another consonant and a juncture or followed/preceded by a C-cluster (except VH+CH).

c. *Additive Affixation: gemination*

ʔenup−:e−niːte−ʔ	ʔenupːeniːteʔ	'I chased you'	B48
halik− :e−te−ʔ	halikːeteʔ	'I hunted'	B106
joːh−:a−ci−ʔ−hY:	johːaciʔhɨː	'it was killed'	B119
joːh−k−:a−koː	joːhukːakoː	'they were killed'	B82

It has to be emphasized that these instances of vowel lengthening are indeed morpheme-specific since the language employs an additional phonological process of iambic vowel lengthening. Main stress in SSM is always on the first heavy syllable and must be on the first or second syllable; since only CVː or non-final CVC syllables count as heavy, vowel lengthening may arise (Broadbent, 1964; Callaghan, 1987; Hayes, 1995; Buckley, 1998). However, the vowel lengthening instances in (20) cannot be instances of this iambic lengthening process. Certain vowels are lengthened although the initial syllable is already heavy (e.g. in /lit.haː.meʔ/, (20-b)) and/or there are instances of vowel lengthening in syllables which are neither the first nor the second (e.g. in /wɨn.si.naː/ (20-a)). And gemination as in (20-c) must be taken to be morphologically triggered—there is no phonologically motivated gemination process. All these instances of additive MLM could easily be predicted by affixing a morphemic mora.

Two phonological processes now interact in a crucial way with these instances of additive MLM. *First*, a vowel hiatus is avoided by epenthesis of /ʔ/. And, *second*, complex syllable edges or superheavy syllables are avoided via insertion of an epenthetic vowel. This is illustrated with the examples in (21). The epenthetic vowel is realized as /o/ if an /o/ is in the preceding syllable, as /u/ if /u/ is in the preceding syllable, and as /ɨ/ elsewhere.

(21) *Phonological vowel epenthesis in SSM*   (Broadbent, 1964: 20)

UNDERLYING	SURFACE		
heːl−maː	heːlɨmaː	'I am fighting'	
hikaHh−j	hikahɨj	'deer' (Acc)	

Vowel epenthesis now interacts in a very interesting way with additive MLM. First, if a consonant-initial Additive Suffix follows a sequence of a long vowel and a consonant (22-a), vowel epenthesis applies and interestingly enough, this epenthetic vowel is long. Similarly, if a vowel-initial Additive Suffix follows a vowel-final base (22-b), a /ʔ/ is inserted between the vowels and the glottal stop surfaces as a geminate. Phonologically predictable epenthetic segments are hence lengthened if they precede a suffix that triggers lengthening.

(22) *Additive Suffixes in SSM: long epenthesis*   (Sloan, 1991)

	UNDERLYING	SURFACE		
a.	ʔumuːc−:meʔ	ʔumuːcɨːmeʔ	'it's raining on us'	B63
	ʔopaː−t−:meʔ	ʔopaːtiːmeʔ	'it's clouding up on us'	B63
b.	leːleː−nY−:a	leːleːniʔːa	'school'	S29
	ʔeseːl−NHe−:a−ci−ʔ−hY:	ʔeseːlŋːeʔːaciʔhyɨ:	'his birth'	B119

And finally, long epenthetic vowels can also be found in Addition contexts. In (23), the word is expected to end in a final consonant cluster and vowel epenthesis hence breaks up this cluster. This epenthetic vowel also surfaces as long.

(23)   *Addition in SSM: long epenthesis*   (Broadbent, 1964: 82)
       haːja—ŋk—ː   haːjaŋkɨː
       daylight—Vʙ—3.Sɢ   'it is daylight'

In the following, it is shown how long epenthesis is straightforwardly predicted in an OT-system with $*V_O <_O \mu_\bullet$. It is assumed that a morphemic mora is part of the representation for all Additive Affixes and Addition morphemes in SSM. That the realization of the morphemic mora results in vowel lengthening in some contexts and in gemination in other contexts, follows if gemination is the preferred strategy to realize an additional mora but regular syllable structure restrictions prohibit it in many contexts. The markedness constraints $*\overset{*}{\mu}\mu\mu$ and $*CC$ are taken to be undominated and exclude three-moraic syllables and complex syllable margins. The ranking $*\mu...^{Af}...C \gg *\mu...^{Af}...S$, on the other hand, implements the preference for gemination over vowel lengthening in SSM. In (24-i) where the Additive Suffix precedes a vowel-final base, the morphemic mora has no chance to be associated with a consonant simply because it is suffixed to its base and must hence follow all moras dominating base material. In (24-ii), on the other hand, where the morphemic mora precedes a consonant-final base, it can be associated with either the final base vowel (24-ii-a) or with the final base consonant (24-ii-b) and the choice is made in favour of the latter. Given that moraic onsets are impossible in SSM, a moraic intervocalic consonant results in a doubly linked consonant, that is a geminate.

(24)   *Additive Affixes in SSM*
       i. *Vowel lengthening*

μ>Dop->S	*CC	$*\overset{\sigma}{\mu\mu\mu}$	$*\mu...^{Af}...V$	$*\mu...^{Af}...S$
*!				
			*	*

ii. *Gemination*

$\mu{\triangleright}\mathrm{Dom}^m_P{>}S$	*CC	*σμμμ	*μ⌣⌣Af V	*μ⌣⌣Af S

Input: $\mu_\bigcirc$ $e_\bigcirc$ $n_\bigcirc$ $u_\bigcirc$ $p_\bigcirc$ $\mu_\bullet$ $+$ $a_\bullet$
$?_\bigcirc$ $e_\bigcirc$ $n_\bigcirc$ $u_\bigcirc$ $p_\bigcirc$ $+$ $a_\bullet$

	$\mu{\triangleright}\mathrm{Dom}^m_P{>}S$	*CC	*σμμμ	*μ⌣⌣Af V	*μ⌣⌣Af S
a. $?_\bigcirc$ $e_\bigcirc$ $n_\bigcirc$ $u_\bigcirc$ $p_\bigcirc$ $a_\bullet$ [ʔe.nuː.pa]				*!	*
☞ b. $?_\bigcirc$ $e_\bigcirc$ $n_\bigcirc$ $u_\bigcirc$ $p_\bigcirc$ $a_\bullet$ [ʔe.nupːa]					*

Now we can turn to the lengthening of epenthetic segments. The geminated epenthetic consonant is in fact straightforwardly predicted by the constraints assumed so far: a morphemic mora must be fully integrated into the base structure and association with a consonant is preferred over association with a vowel. The insertion of epenthetic consonants is taken to be due to ONSET!, shown in tableau (25-i) (*CC is excluded for reasons of space since it is not relevant in the optimization below). The morphemic mora is then predicted to dominate this epenthetic consonant in winning candidate (25-i-d).

(25) *Additive Affixes in SSM*

    i. *Gemination of an epenthetic consonant*

Input: $l_\bigcirc$ $e_\bigcirc$ $l_\bigcirc$ $e_\bigcirc$ $+$ $n_\bullet$ $i_\bullet$ $+$ $a_\square$

	$\mu{\triangleright}\mathrm{Dom}^m_P{>}S$	*V${<}$Oμ⌣	ONS!	*σμμμ	*μ⌣⌣Af V	COL⌣S	COL⌣μ	*μ⌣⌣Af S
a. $l_\bigcirc$ $e_\bigcirc$ $l_\bigcirc$ $e_\bigcirc$ $n_\bullet$ $i_\bullet$ $a_\square$ [leː.leː.ni.a]	*!		*!					
b. $l_\bigcirc$ $e_\bigcirc$ $l_\bigcirc$ $e_\bigcirc$ $n_\bullet$ $i_\bullet$ $?$ $a_\square$ [leː.leː.ni.ʔa]	*!						*	
c. $l_\bigcirc$ $e_\bigcirc$ $l_\bigcirc$ $e_\bigcirc$ $n_\bullet$ $i_\bullet$ $?$ $a_\square$ [leː.leː.niː.ʔa]					*!	*		*
☞ d. $l_\bigcirc$ $e_\bigcirc$ $l_\bigcirc$ $e_\bigcirc$ $n_\bullet$ $i_\bullet$ $?$ $a_\square$ [leː.leː.niʔːa]						*		*

ii. *Vowel lengthening of an epenthetic vowel*

	μ<Dop>S	*V$_O$ <$_O$ μ•	ONS!	*μμμ	*μ...Af..V	COL!S	COL!μ	*μ...Af..S
a. [ʔo.paːt.meʔ]	*!				*!		*	
b. [ʔo.paː.tɨ.meʔ]	*!				*	*	*	
c. [ʔo.paː.tɨ.meʔ]		*!			*	*		*
☞ d. [ʔo.paː.tiː.meʔ]					*	*	*	*

Tableau (25-ii), on the other hand, derives an instance of long vowel epenthesis. The Additive Suffix /−meʔ/ is added to a base ending in a heavy syllable. Vowel epenthesis is consequently predicted by the constraint against superheavy syllables. In contrast to the Arbizu Basque constraint ranking, *V$_O$ <$_O$ μ• is ranked above COL!$_μ$ and *all* vowels (including epenthetic ones) must project their own mora in addition to a potential morphemic mora. This excludes the short epenthesis candidate in (25-ii-c) where only the morphemic mora is associated with the epenthetic vowel. The winning candidate (25-ii-d) is hence one where the epenthetic vowel is associated with an epenthetic mora and the morphemic mora. High-ranking of *V$_O$ <$_O$ μ• also predicts that all underlying vowels will always become long in the scope of the morphemic mora. Even if the underlying vowel /a/ that precedes the Additive Affix in (25-i), for example, were underlyingly mora-less, a long vowel would become optimal since *V$_O$ <$_O$ μ• demands an epenthetic mora-licensing for this underlying vowel.

A possible alternative analysis for the long epenthetic vowels in SSM that must be discussed is the complete rejection of any morphemic moras and the relatively simple assumption that the Additive Affixes contain an additional long initial segment that remains unrealized in certain contexts and is realized in others. Such an analysis is shown in (26). The vowel-lengthening suffix /−meʔ/ is assumed to contain an additional long vowel /ɨː/ (26-a). If this vowel is preceded by another vowel, it cannot be realized since an illicit vowel cluster would arise, but its length is rescued on the base segment (=compensatory lengthening). If the long vowel is preceded by a consonant, it can be realized. Something similar could be assumed for the geminating suffixes that are assumed to contain an additional long consonant (26-b).

(26) *An alternative: underlying long segments instead of segmental lengthening*
    a. litha   −iːme?   lithiːme?
          umuːc   −iːme?   umuːciːme?

    b. joːh   −?ːa   joːhːa
          leːleːnɨ −?ːa   leːleːni?ːa

This analysis is deeply problematic if we consider the regular phonology of the language: illicit vowel or consonant clusters are avoided by epenthesis, never by non-realization of a segment. Apparently, morpheme- or construction-specific phonology would need to account for this exceptional repair.

Another alternative analysis is the assumption of two morphemic moras in the representation of some Additive Affixes and Addition morphemes. Such an analysis is sketched in (27) for an underlying (27-i) and an epenthetic vowel (27-ii). Two affix moras strive to be fully integrated into the prosodic structure of their base and in case a preceding vowel is mora-less (=epenthetic), both affix moras find a host. This analysis apparently captures the empirical templatic nature of the facts: the base must end in a long vowel. Note that this analysis apparently implies that vowel-initial Additive Suffixes only contain a single floating mora: they only trigger gemination of a preceding consonant and hence only a single mora is ever able to associate to a preceding base segment.

(27) *An alternative: two morphemic moras*
    i. *Vowel lengthening*

		μ>Dom>S	*σμμμ	PVIs_{μ-AF}	*μ..Af..S
	μ₀ μ□ μ■ μ■ μ■ l₀ i₀ t₀ + h● + a□ + m■ e■ ?■				
a.	μ₀ μ μ□ μ■ μ■ μ■ l₀ i₀ t₀ h● a□ m■ e■ ?■ [lit.ha.me?]		*!*	**	
☞ b.	μ₀ μ μ□ μ■ μ■ μ■ l₀ i₀ t₀ h● a□ m■ e■ ?■ [lit.haː.me?]				**

ii. *Vowel lengthening of an epenthetic vowel*

$\mu_{\bigcirc}$ $\mu_{\bigcirc}\mu_{\bigcirc}$ $\mu_{\square}\mu_{\square}\mu_{\square}$ ʔ$_{\bigcirc}$ o$_{\bigcirc}$ p$_{\bigcirc}$ a$_{\bigcirc}$ + t$_{\bullet}$ + m$_{\square}$ e$_{\square}$ ʔ$_{\square}$		$\mu>\mathrm{Do}^{m}_{p}>S$	$*\sigma\mu\mu\mu$	$\mathrm{PVis}_{\mu}\text{-}\mathrm{AF}$	$*\mu...\mathrm{Af}...S$
$\mu_{\bigcirc}$ $\mu_{\bigcirc}\mu_{\bigcirc}\mu$ $\mu_{\square}\mu_{\square}\mu_{\square}$ ʔ$_{\bigcirc}$ o$_{\bigcirc}$ p$_{\bigcirc}$ a$_{\bigcirc}$ t$_{\bullet}$ m$_{\square}$ e$_{\square}$ ʔ$_{\square}$ [ʔo.paːt.meʔ]	a.	*!*	*!	**	
$\mu_{\bigcirc}$ $\mu_{\bigcirc}\mu_{\bigcirc}$ $\mu_{\square}\mu_{\square}$ $\mu_{\square}$ ʔ$_{\bigcirc}$ o$_{\bigcirc}$ p$_{\bigcirc}$ a$_{\bigcirc}$ t$_{\bullet}$ i m$_{\square}$ e$_{\square}$ ʔ$_{\square}$ [ʔo.paː.tiː.meʔ]	☞ b.				**

However, such a standard mora affixation account without $*V_O <_O \mu_{\bullet}$ becomes empirically problematic if we consider examples like /joːh−k−ːa−koː/ that surfaces as /joːhukːakoː/. The affixed mora hence associates to the preceding consonant although vowel epenthesis applies directly before this consonant and hence necessitates the insertion of an epenthetic mora. An alternative structure */joːhukakoː/ where the affixed mora associates to the epenthetic vowel and not to the preceding consonant should hence always harmonically bind the correct gemination structure since it avoids a violation of DEP-μ and associates the affix mora. Assuming that the gemination-triggering affixes contain two floating moras as well (parallel to (27)) would solve this problem since a mora for the epenthetic vowel and for the following consonant would be present. However, such a move creates new problems since we then expect double segmental lengthening in structures such as /ʔenup−ːe−niːte−ʔ/. The presence of two floating moras in the Additive Affix is expected to result in illicit */ʔenːupːeniːteʔ/, not in single gemination as in empirically correct /ʔenupːeniːteʔ/. A theory about the possible landing sites of morphemic moras (similar to the one presented here in section 2.2.6) can potentially solve this problem but it is clear that a standard mora affixation account along the lines sketched in section 2.1.1 is insufficient for this pattern.

We can hence conclude that an alternative mora affixation analysis without $*V_O <_O \mu_{\bullet}$ is problematic and requires some additional restrictions about linear ordering and possible landing sites for morphemic moras. In contrast, the constraint $*V_O <_O \mu_{\bullet}$ that received independent support from the fact that it solves the opaque mora assignment problem of standard parallel OT, easily predicts long epenthesis in SSM with the simple analysis that all Additive Affixes and Addition morphemes simply contain one morphemic mora. As is shown in detail in section 7.4, this long epenthesis is unaccounted for in alternative OT analyses for MLM that do not rely on mora affixation.

5.2.3.2 Long epenthetic vowels in Czech   Another instance of long epenthetic vowels can be found in Czech (Scheer, 2001; Caha and Scheer, 2008; Ziková, 2013). There are several apparently templatic length-manipulating processes in Czech (see, for example, Caha and Scheer, 2008; Scheer, 2001); the relevant non-templatic morphological lengthening process is an instance of Additive Affixation, illustrated in (28). The diminutive suffix /−ek/ triggers lengthening of a preceding base vowel. If now the suffix is expected after a base ending in a cluster of a consonant and a liquid, a long epenthetic vowel surfaces as can be seen in (28-b).

(28) *Additive Suffix in Czech*   (Ziková, 2013: 3, 4), (Scheer, 2004: 754)

	BASE		DIMINUTIVE	
a.	vlak	'train'	vlaːt͡ʃek	S
	xlap	'man'	xlaːpek	Z
	kluk	'boy'	klout͡ʃek	Z
b.	cukr	'sugar'	cukiːrek	Z
	svetr	'sweater'	svetiːrek	Z
	maxr	'boffin'	maxiːrek	Z

5.2.3.3 Long epenthetic/underlying vowels in Guajiro   In the Arawakan language Guajiro (Goulet and Jusayú, 1978; Adelaar and Muysken, 2004; Álvarez, 2005; Álvarez and Dorado, 2005), the infinitive is marked by lengthening of the final vowel (29-a) if the final syllable is light and realization of /−waː/ if the base is heavy (29-b) to avoid superheavy syllables. Closed syllables in Guajiro are heavy as can be concluded from the stress system (Adelaar and Muysken, 2004: 118).

(29) *Addition in Guajiro: Infinitives*   (Álvarez, 2005)

	BASE	INFINITIVE	
a.	kaʔwajuːse	kaʔwajuːse	'have spouse'
	kapiʃi	kapiʃiː	'have maternal family'
	aʃakata	aʃakataː	'descend'
b.	kamaneː	kamaneːwaː	'be kind'
	japïi	japïiwaː	'be shy'
	kat͡ʃon	kat͡ʃonwaː	'have children'

Although insertion of /w/ can productively be found in Guajiro to avoid adjacent long vowels (Vaux, 2002: 12) and the sound can hence reasonably be analysed as being epenthetic, the status of /a/ as epenthetic is less clear. As in Lardil, however, the concrete nature of the sound as underlying or epenthetic is not crucial for the prediction of the theory. Whereas the inserted vowel in Lardil is always short, it is always long in Guajiro: exactly predicted from ranking $*V_O <_O \mu_\bullet$ above (Guajiro) or below COL!$_\mu$ (Lardil).

5.2.3.4 Long epenthetic vowels in Huallaga Quechua   In Huallaga Quechua (Weber, 1947, 1996; Adelaar, 1984; Adelaar and Muysken, 2004), the first person (either on verbs or as possessor on nouns) is expressed via lengthening of the final vowel of the base. If the base ends in a consonant, however, a long /−ni:/ surfaces (30-b). Lengthening of the base vowel is impossible in such a context since the language does not allow long vowels in closed syllables.[12]

(30) *Addition in Huallaga Quechua: first person*   (Weber, 1996; Adelaar, 1984)

	BASE		1.SG		
a.	wata	'tie'	wata:	'I tie'	A189
	wata-ra	'tied'	watara:	'I tied'	A219
	ajwa	'walk'	ajwa:	'I walk'	W96:246
	ka	'be'	ka:	'I am'	W96:246
	waska	'rope'	waska:	'my rope'	A189
	uma	'head'	uma:	'my head'	W96:97
b.	majur	'(the) older'	majurni:	'my older (brother)'	W96:97
	hatun	'big'	hatun:i:	'my big one'	W47:465

As in Lardil and Guajiro, the (morphological) status of the inserted segments in this context is not entirely clear. Cerrón-Palomino (2008) explicitly states that /ni/ is a vacuous default morpheme (p. 87) and Adelaar (1984) glosses the /ni/ as 'connective element'. And in fact one can find contexts where it is inserted for phonological reasons. An example is given in (31). Since the language allows no consonant clusters and no long vowels closed by a coda, /ni/ is inserted at some morpheme boundaries to avoid an illicit syllable structure.

(31) *Insertion of /ni/*   (Weber, 1947: 465)

UNDERLYING	SURFACE	
maqa−ma−q−ntsi:	maqamaqnintsi:	'the one who hit us (incl)'
ñatin−jnaq	ñatin:ijnaq	'not having a liver'
papa:−n	papa:nin	'his father'

5.2.4 Long epenthetic vowels as a severe opacity problem

Given a standard parallel model of OT, these instances of long epenthetic vowels are problematic. In fact, they extend the opacity problem of mora licensing discussed in section 2.2.4. The long epenthetic vowels that can be observed in, for example, SSM

---

[12] The grammar by Weber (1996) is written in Spanish; the glosses and translations of examples are translated into English in the following.

are taken to be dominated by their 'own' epenthetic mora in addition to the affix mora. In a standard parallel OT model where the morphemic mora is present in the input, however, mora epenthesis is unnecessary without a concept of morph-contiguous mora projection and is always expected to be harmonically bounded. This opacity is illustrated in (32) with a rule-based analysis for SSM. A long epenthetic vowel only arises since rule ii. that associates every mora-less vowel with an epenthetic mora applies before rule iii. that associates underlyingly unassociated moras. This rule interaction is an instance of counter-bleeding (Kiparsky, 1973; see also the discussion in section 2.2.4).

(32) *A rule-based analysis for long epenthetic vowels*
       Underlying:

$$\mu_\circ \quad \mu_\circ\,\mu_\circ \qquad \mu_\square \quad \mu_\square$$

?$_\circ$ o$_\circ$ p$_\circ$ a$_\circ$ + t$_\bullet$ + m$_\square$ e$_\square$?$_\square$

   i. Insert an epenthetic V to avoid illicit CVCC-σ's:

$$\mu_\circ \quad \mu_\circ\,\mu_\circ \qquad \mu_\square \quad \mu_\square$$

?$_\circ$ o$_\circ$ p$_\circ$ a$_\circ$ t$_\bullet$ ɨ m$_\square$ e$_\square$?$_\square$

   ii. Associate every μ-less vowel with an epenthetic μ:

$$\mu_\circ \quad \mu_\circ\,\mu_\circ \quad \mu \quad \mu_\square \quad \mu_\square$$

?$_\circ$ o$_\circ$ p$_\circ$ a$_\circ$ t$_\bullet$ ɨ m$_\square$ e$_\square$?$_\square$

   iii. Associate unassociated μ's with a segmental host:

$$\mu_\circ \quad \mu_\circ\,\mu_\circ \quad \mu \quad \mu_\square \qquad \mu_\square$$

?$_\circ$ o$_\circ$ p$_\circ$ a$_\circ$ t$_\bullet$ ɨ m$_\square$ e$_\square$?$_\square$

In OT, Col!$_\mu$ is expected to harmonically bind a candidate where a mora is inserted *and* this mora is associated with the affix mora. This opacity problem is far more serious than the general problem of opaque mora licensing in OT in general. A vowel that was not underlyingly present must be dominated by 'its own' mora and that vowel is not motivated in a derivational step before the morphemic mora is present. The constraint *V$_\circ$ <$_\circ$ μ$_\bullet$, on the other hand, easily predicts long epenthetic vowels in the context of morphological vowel lengthening.

5.2.5 *Summary: vertical contiguity for vowels and moras*

In this section, the predictions made by the different rankings of *V$_\circ$ <$_\circ$ μ$_\bullet$ with respect to Col!$_\mu$ were discussed. Either it is more important that an epenthetic vowel is dominated by a morph-contiguous mora or it is more important to avoid epenthetic moras. Under the former ranking, all vowels are predicted to be long if they are adjacent to a morphemic mora and vowel lengthening is the licit strategy to realize a morphemic mora in this context. This includes epenthetic vowels as well. Under the latter ranking, only certain vowels are lengthened by a morphemic mora; underlyingly mora-less and epenthetic vowels are expected to surface as short. It is argued that both types of languages are indeed borne out in the typology of attested MLM patterns. All the languages discussed are summarized in (33).

(33)   *Morph-contiguous mora licensing and morphemic moras: the predictions*

Languages	Evidence
I. Certain-vowel-lengthening	
Dieguéño (5.2.2.1)	lexical exceptions to lengthening
Arbizu Basque (5.2.2.2)	short epenthetic V
Lardil (5.2.2.3)	short epenthetic V
La Paz Aymara (5.2.2.4)	double lengthening
II. All-vowel-lengthening	
Southern Sierra Miwok (5.2.3.1)	long epenthetic V
Czech (5.2.3.2)	long epenthetic V
Guajiro (5.2.3.3)	long epenthetic V
Huallaga Quechua (5.2.3.4)	long epenthetic V

An interesting prediction now apparently arises from the existence of colour indices in the theory of PDM. After index fusion, an originally epenthetic mora could be expected to have the same lengthening effect as a morphemic mora in a language where $^{*}V_{\bigcirc} <_{\bigcirc} \mu_{\bullet}$ is high-ranked. In (34), a morphemic mora followed by a colour index is suffixed to its base that has underlyingly no moras. If this is a language with high-ranked $^{*}V_{\bigcirc} <_{\bigcirc} \mu_{\bullet}$ that allows long vowels and prefers them over gemination, consonant epenthesis, and copying, we expect lengthening of the penultimate vowel. Interestingly now, the final base vowel dominated by the originally epenthetic mora that now bears the colour index of the affix, also induces a violation of $^{*}V_{\bigcirc} <_{\bigcirc} \mu_{\bullet}$. Insertion of another epenthetic mora and lengthening of the final vowel in (34-b) avoids the violation of $^{*}V_{\bigcirc} <_{\bigcirc} \mu_{\bullet}$ and one apparently predicts collateral lengthening: the presence of one morphemic infixing mora results in lengthening of two vowels. As can be seen in (34-i-b), this is in fact an impossible structure given the RMO. The epenthetic mora ensuring morph-contiguous licensing for the final base vowel would reflect only the stem $_{\bigcirc}$ but would follow a mora that also reflects the Additive Suffix $_{\bullet}$. The exponent order that the suffix$_{\bullet}$ follows the stem$_{\bigcirc}$ would hence not be reflected on the moraic tier. For epenthetic or copied segments, on the other hand, such a collateral lengthening could indeed be predicted since no problem for the RMO would arise (34-ii-b).

(34)   *Collateral lengthening after index fusion?*

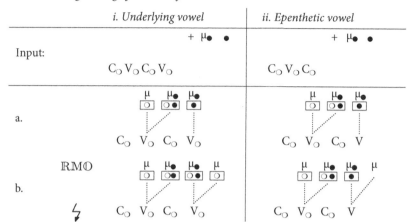

Collateral lengthening is no misprediction since such multiple MLM effects at a base edge are indeed attested. An example is Balangao that is analysed in 6.2.4.3 as an instance of multiple morphemic prosodic nodes. On the surface, the effect for $^*V_O <_O \mu_\bullet$ on epenthetic moras is hence not distinguishable from the MLM predicted from affixing multiple morphemic moras.

5.3 Vertical contiguity: feet and segments

In the last section, the predictions of $^*V_O <_O \mu_\bullet$ were discussed in detail, a constraint demanding a weak type of vertical morpheme contiguity: segments strive not to be dominated only by a mora that is affiliated with another morpheme. In this section, effects of another vertical morpheme CONTIGUITY constraint are discussed, namely the preference for prosodic nodes to not dominate elements with a different morphemic affiliation. The constraint $^*\Phi_O < S_\bullet$ (35) demands that a foot with a prosodic affiliation preferably does not dominate segments with a different morphological affiliation (repeated from section 2.2.3, (43-b)).

(35) $^*\Phi_O < S_\bullet$ Assign a violation mark for every Φ_O that phonetically dominates a segment with another morphological colour $_\bullet$.

Its effect is briefly illustrated in tableau (36). A morphemic foot is added to a base and must be realized, hence must minimally dominate a syllable and segmental material due to $\Phi > Do_p^m > \sigma$, excluding candidate (36-a). Integrating the whole base under the morphemic foot as in (36-c) induces four violations of $^*\Phi_O < S_\bullet$ since four segments with a different morphological affiliation are dominated by the morphemic foot. Under the current ranking, candidate (36-b) will hence become optimal that only integrates one syllable and two base segments under the morphemic foot. As is discussed in section 5.3.1, several other repair operations can become optimal to avoid violations of $^*\Phi_O < S_\bullet$ in such a configuration—repair operations that will result in MLM in some cases.

(36)   *Vertical morpheme contiguity for feet:* $^*\Phi_O < S_\bullet$

$\Phi_\bullet$ + σ_O σ_O p_O a_O t_O a_O	$\Phi > Dop_P^m > \sigma$	$^*\Phi_O < S_\bullet$
a. ω $\Phi_\bullet$ Φ σ_O σ_O p_O a_O t_O a_O	*!	
☞ b. ω $\Phi_\bullet$ σ_O σ_O p_O a_O t_O a_O		**
c. ω $\Phi_\bullet$ σ_O σ_O p_O a_O t_O a_O		***!*

As is shown in detail below, this constraint makes relevant predictions for the analyses of MLM if one takes into account a type of morphemic prosodic node that was absent in the preceding analyses of MLM patterns, namely morphemic feet. In principle, the affixation of a morphemic foot does not straightforwardly predict any phonological operation that manipulates the segmental content of the base. Rather, a potentially new stress pattern is predicted. Such an analysis where affixation of a morphemic foot results in a fixed stress pattern that is the only marking for a morphological category is proposed in van Oostendorp (2012) for the tense formation in Modern Greek (see section 2.1.2). In this section, it is shown how the vertical morpheme contiguity constraint $^*\Phi_O < S_\bullet$ predicts segmental length-manipulating operations resulting from affixing a morphemic foot. Several instances of phonologically predictable allomorphy are argued to follow from exactly this mechanism.

Note that in contrast to $^*V_O <_O \mu_\bullet$ that restricts the morphological affiliation of the prosodic nodes dominating an element X, this type of vertical morpheme CONTIGUITY restricts the morphological affiliation of elements that are dominated by an element X. A second difference to $^*V_O <_O \mu_\bullet$ is the fact that the $^*\Phi_O < S_\bullet$ is specified for a foot with a morphological affiliation. $^*V_O <_O \mu_\bullet$, on the other hand, is specified for any vowel and penalizes certain configurations with respect to the moras dominating it. Whether the vowel has a morphological affiliation or not, is irrelevant for $^*V_O <_O \mu_\bullet$ (a point that was crucial in the discussion of long epenthetic vowels above in 5.2.3).

Interestingly, the constraint system proposed here already indirectly predicts another vertical morpheme contiguity effect. More concretely, the assumption discussed in section 2.2.3 that the constraints penalizing inserted association lines can be sensitive to the status of being an affix or a stem predicts that a morphemic prosodic node prefers to dominate as few elements as possible. This effect is briefly illustrated in the abstract tableau (37) for the affixation of a morphemic foot node. Integrating the whole base under the morphemic foot in candidate (37-c) violates $^*\Phi...{}^{Af}...\sigma$ twice whereas candidate (37-b) only violates the constraint once: only a single epenthetic association line is inserted between an affix foot and a syllable.

(37) *Indirect vertical morpheme contiguity for feet:* $^*\Phi...{}^{Af}...\sigma$

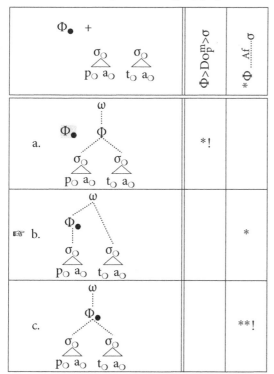

$\Phi_\bullet$ + $\sigma_O \quad \sigma_O$ $P_O\,a_O \quad t_O\,a_O$	$\Phi > DoP^m > \sigma$	$^*\Phi...{}^{Af}...\sigma$
a.	*!	
☞ b.		*
c.		**!

In the following case studies, it is shown that the vertical morpheme CONTIGUITY effects predicted by two different theoretical mechanisms are indeed borne out. Two instances of morphemic foot nodes are discussed that all result in a surface allomorphy of different phonological operations. Section 5.3.1 presents a detailed analysis for non-concatenative allomorphy in Upriver Halkomelem and sections 5.3.2 and 5.3.3 add shorter discussions of Rotuman and Choctaw respectively. This section hence also adds evidence for another type of morphemic prosodic node that has been absent from the preceding discussions: affixation of a morphemic foot.

5.3.1 *Non-concatenative allomorphy in Upriver Halkomelem*

Upriver Halkomelem is one of three dialects of Halkomelem, a Central Salishan language spoken in the South-Eastern end of Vancouver island and in British Columbia that had no more than two speakers in 2004 (Brown, 2004: 1). The language employs an interesting instance of non-concatenative allomorphy where different non-concatenative strategies can be observed to realize one morpheme. For the context of the present discussion, it is most crucial that some of these non-concatenative strategies are length-manipulating operations. As can be seen in (38), the continuative form is derived from its non-continuative counterpart by either stress shift (38-a), reduplication (38-b), vowel lengthening (38-c), or insertion of /hɛ/ (38-d).

(38)   *Verbal aspect in Upriver Halkomelem*   (Galloway, 1993)

	NON-CONTINUATIVE		CONTINUATIVE		
a.	*Stress shift*				
	ts'ɛtéːm	'crawl'	ts'ɛ́təm	'crawling'	56
	ɬelqí	'soak'	ɬélqi	'soaking'	56
	ɬəxʷɔ́ɬtsɛ	'spit'	ɬɔ́xʷəɬtsɛ	'spitting'	56
	càːlɔ́χʷəm	'bleed'	cáːl(ə)χʷəm	'bleeding'	56
b.	*Reduplication*				
	q'ísət	'tie sth.'	q'íq'əsət	'tying sth.'	68
	p'étΘ'	'sew'	p'ɛ́p'ətΘ'	'sewing'	266
	t'éjəq'	'get angry'	t'ɛ́t'əjəq'	'getting angry'	136
	jíq	'fall (of snow)'	jíjəq	'falling (of snow)'	135
	ɬéw	'run away, escape'	ɬéɬəw	'running away'	135
	mát'əs	'point, aim'	mámət'əs	'pointing'	135
c.	*Vowel lengthening*				
	ʔíməç	'walk'	ʔíːməç	'walking'	66
	ʔíχət	'scrape sth./so.'	ʔíːχət	'scraping sth./so.'	67
	ʔálmətsəl	'wait'	ʔáːlmətsəl	'waiting'	270
	hílt	'roll sth. over'	híːlt	'roll sth. over'	67
	hákʷəç	'use sth.'	háːkʷəç	'using sth.'	270
	hékʷələs	'remember sth.'	héːkʷələs	'remembering sth.'	270

d. *Epenthesis*

məq'ət	'swallow sth.'	həmq'ət	'swallowing sth.'	60
wə́q'ʷ	'drown, drift downstream'	háwq'ʷ	'drowning'	273
jə́q'ʷ	'burn'	hə́jq'ʷ	'burning'	60
jə́q'əs	'file'	hə́jq'əs	'filing'	61
lə́p'əç	'eat'	hə́lp'əç	'eating'	61
lə́qəm	'dive'	hə́lqəm	'diving'	61

The choice for one or the other of these four allomorphs to mark the continuative is completely predictable given the phonological shape of the base (Urbanczyk, 1998; Kurisu, 2001). If (main) stress is on a non-initial syllable in the non-continuative form, the continuative is marked by shifting the stress to the initial syllable as illustrated in (38-a). This often results in weakening the now unstressed base vowel to /ə/, a predictable vowel reduction process in the language. Whenever the non-continuative form is stressed on the initial syllable, one of the following three allomorphs marks the continuative. Non-continuative forms that start with a non-glottal consonant and have a full vowel (=not /ə/) in their first syllable reduplicate the initial CV sequence to form the continuative (38-b). The first vowel of the continuative is stressed and again the second vowel is often reduced to /ə/. Whenever a full vowel is preceded by a glottal onset /h/ or /ʔ/ in the first syllable of the non-continuative, vowel lengthening marks the continuative as in the examples in (38-c). And finally, when the stressed first vowel of the non-continuative base is a /ə/ rather than a full vowel, insertion of epenthetic /hɛ/[13] can be found in the continuative (38-d). The underlying /ə/ that constitutes the nucleus of the first base syllable is always lost in the continuative form. Note that the inserted vowel is realized on the surface as either /ə/ or /ɛ/. This alternation is predictable: /ə/ occurs before labial /m/ and /w/ and /ɛ/ elsewhere (Urbanczyk, 1998: 659; Galloway, 1993: 60).

Three of the four allomorphs involve length-manipulation, one is a Long-Short-Alternation and two are Segment-Zero-Alternations (see the terminology introduced in section 1.1.3, (10)). Since the choice between the four allomorphs is completely predictable from the phonological structure of the base, an analysis is desirable that assumes one underlying representation for the continuative morpheme that is realized differently in different contexts. This makes the Upriver Halkomelem pattern so interesting from a theoretical perspective: Is it possible that these different strategies result from adding a single (abstract) morpheme representation? Given the PDM background discussed so far, the vowel lengthening allomorph as well as the copying and epenthesis allomorph could be the result of realizing a morphemic mora. However, it is not clear how the stress shifting allomorph would fall out under such an analysis.

---

[13] The assumption that /hə/ is epenthetic follows the analysis in Urbanczyk (1998) but is not uncontroversial. See Zimmermann (2013a) for a more detailed discussion.

There are at least two existing theoretical OT accounts for this pattern, namely the REALIZEMORPHEME based account in Kurisu (2001) and the account in Urbanczyk (1998) that is based on the assumption that the continuative is in fact the reduplicative-triggering morpheme RED and a constraint MORPHOLOGICAL EXPRESSION forces additional operations in case reduplication is blocked. The core of this analysis is thus similar to the REALIZEMORPHEME-based approach in that a constraint explicitly forces paradigmatic distinctness for morphologically related forms. The REALIZEMORPHEME based approach is critically reviewed in chapter 7.

In the following, it is argued that the continuative morpheme in Upriver Halkomelem consists of a morphemic foot.[14] This morphemic foot is completely integrated into the base and overwrites all underlying prosodic structure resulting in a fixed stress pattern in the continuative. That the morphemic foot is preferably filled with segmental material that is not affiliated with the base is demanded by high-ranked $*\Phi_O < S_{\bullet}$: as is shown in detail below, vowel lengthening, epenthesis, and copying are predicted.

5.3.1.1 Stress overwriting   Since the continuative formation crucially interacts with the stress assignment, some background facts about stress in Upriver Halkomelem are necessary. Stems and affixes are taken to be underlyingly marked for being stressed or unstressed in the language (Elmendorf and Suttles, 1986; Brown, 2004) and the location of stress in morphologically complex forms is predictable given the stress patterns of stems and affixes. Unstressed[15] affixes simply attach to their stem without triggering any change in the stress pattern of their stem. Stressed affixes, however, make any stress on the stem impossible (Galloway, 1993: 52), a mechanism termed 'stress overwriting' in the following. The mechanism of stress overwriting is highly relevant for an analysis of the continuative allomorphy since the latter involves a change in the stress pattern as well. Some examples of stress overwriting are given in (39) where several stressed affixes attach to a stressed base that consequently becomes systematically unstressed.

(39)   *Main stressed affix overwrites stress pattern of the stem*   (Galloway, 1993)

cákʷ	−á:ləs	cakʷá:ləs	
'be distant'	'in the eye'	'goatsbeard plant'	240
		(=blooms can be seen from far away)	
qá:	−á:ləs	qəʔá:ləs	
'water'	'in the eye'	'tear'	240

---

[14] A claim that was first put forth in the analysis in Zimmermann (2013a). However, the analysis presented there is implemented in correspondence-theoretic OT and different in many respects from the present proposal.

[15] In Galloway's terminology: or mid-stressed affixes. These are taken as unstressed long or stressed short.

Θέːt	−íːl	Θətíːl	
'darkness'	'go, come'	'go dark, get dark'	242
kʷə́m−ət[16]	−láːmət	kʷəmláːmət	
'raise so.'	reflexive, 'oneself'	'raise oneself'	257

Two of the examples in (39) illustrate that there are some additional implications between length, stress, and vowel quality in the language. *First*, long vowels are always stressed in Upriver Halkomelem and *second*, unstressed vowels are often reduced to /ə/ (see, for example, Czaykowska-Higgins and Kinkade, 1998: 15). If a long vowel becomes unstressed by stress overwriting, it is often reduced to a short one or to /ə/; sometimes it even remains unrealized.

In the following, it is assumed that lexical stress is represented as underlying foot structure (Inkelas, 1999; Revithiadou, 1999). Default stress assignment in the absence of any lexical stress, on the other hand, is assumed to follow from assigning a left-aligned trochee.[17] This assumption allows a straightforward representation of light initial stressed syllables that exist in Upriver Halkomelem. An alternative iambic analysis would need to assume the rather marked foot structure #(L) for those; in contrast to the claim that only (LH) and (LL) are possible iambic feet (see, for example, Prince, 1990; Hayes, 1995).

The constraint RʜT:T demanding initial prominence for a foot (Kager, 1999*b*) is hence assumed to be ranked above RʜT:I in Upriver Halkomelem. Default foot assignment in case no underlying foot is present is assumed to be left-aligned, ensured by Aʟʟ-Fᴛ-Lᴇғᴛ (McCarthy and Prince, 1993*a*; Kager, 1999*b*). In addition, codas are assumed to be moraic.

Finally, the overwriting of the stem with affix prosody is motivated by end rule constraints given in (40) penalizing multiple feet in a word (McCarthy, 2003*a*: 37).

(40) a. Eʀ-R   Assign a violation mark for every phonetically visible Φ that is preceded by a phonetically visible Φ in the same prosodic word.

   b. Eʀ-L   Assign a violation mark for every phonetically visible Φ that is followed by a phonetically visible Φ in the same prosodic word.

That the stress on the affix surfaces and the stress on the stem is impossible to realize follows in OT from ranking the PVɪs-Φ$_{AF}$ constraint demanding phonetically visible integration of an affix foot (41-a) above the corresponding constraint demanding integration of stem prosody (41-b).

---

[16] The verb stem is followed by a so-called control suffix. Transitive verbs are obligatorily followed by one of six control suffixes in Upriver Halkomelem; examples are /−(ə)t/ 'do purposely to so.' or /−(ə)m/ 'intransitive' (Galloway, 1993: 244).

[17] See Zimmermann (2013*a*) for a more detailed discussion and empirical motivation for this claim.

(41) a. $\dfrac{\text{PVis}}{\Phi_{\text{AF}}}$ Assign a violation mark for every phonetically invisible affix Φ.

  b. $\dfrac{\text{PVis}}{\Phi_{\text{ST}}}$ Assign a violation mark for every phonetically invisible stem Φ.

Tableau (42) now illustrates stress overwriting in the context of a stressed suffix /−á:ləs/ that is attached to a stressed stem /cákʷ/.

(42) *Stress Overwriting*

/cákʷ + á:ləs/	Er-L	Er-R	PVis-Φ_{AF}	PVis$_{\text{V}}$	PVis-Φ_{ST}	*Φ≠σ
a. [cá.kʷá:.ləs]	*!	*!				
b. [cákʷ]			*!	*!		**
c. [á:.ləs]				*!	*	*
☞ d. [ca.kʷá:.ləs]					*	*
e. [cá.kʷa:.ləs]					*	**!

Since both morphemes are underlyingly stressed, both have an underlying foot structure in their representation. Given high-ranked ER-L and ER-R, it is now impossible to realize both these feet, excluding candidate (42-a). The candidates (42-b) and (42-c) avoid this marked structure of multiple phonetically visible feet under a single prosodic word node and only integrate either the stem (42-b) or affix (42-c) foot under the prosodic word node. Candidate (42-c) has a better constraint profile than (42-b) since it realizes the affix foot instead of the stem foot—the ranking of PVIS-Φ_{AF} over PVIS-Φ_{ST} ensures that the former is more important than the latter. However, this is not the optimal candidate since the stem segments remain completely unintegrated and hence are phonetically invisible. The violation of PVIS$_V$ demanding phonetic realization for every full vowel [18] can easily be avoided by integrating the remaining syllables directly under the prosodic word node as is done in candidates (42-d) and (42-e). The winning candidate is (42-d) where the underlying affix foot and the stem syllables are associated with the prosodic word node. It has a better constraint profile than candidate (42-e) that integrates the first syllable into the foot since the latter induces an additional violation of $*\Phi$ -⊩- σ. This additional violation arises since trisyllabic feet are assumed to be impossible and integration of the first syllable implies that the final syllable is associated directly with the prosodic word node, thus its association to the foot is marked as phonetically invisible.

5.3.1.2 Foot affixation in the continuative It is now argued that this very same mechanism applies in the formation of the continuative as well: a morphemic affix foot is added and the high-ranked constraints ER-R and ER-L ensure that it overwrites the prosodic structure of the base. The crucial difference is that the morphemic foot does not dominate any segmental material of its own. The only additional mechanism that is relevant in the context of the morphemic foot are constraints ensuring that the morphemic prosodic node is integrated into the prosodic structure of its base in the first place. This follows from the interaction of PVIS-Φ_{AF} (41-a) and $\Phi > Do_p^m > \sigma$ (43).

(43) $\Phi > Do_p^m > \sigma$ Assign a violation mark for every Φ that does not phonetically or morphologically dominate a σ.

Given that the continuative foot is prefixed to its base and must be realized, we hence expect that it overwrites all potential underlying feet in the input.[19] This predicts initial stress for all continuative forms. This already predicts the fixed stress pattern in the continuative but does not yet explain the additional vowel lengthening, epenthesis,

---

[18] PVIS$_C$ is ranked in the same high stratum ensuring that as many consonants as possible are realized. The general PVIS$_S$, however, is ranked lower in Upriver Halkomelem. As is discussed in detail below, this is due to the fact that PVIS$_V$ and PVIS$_\partial$ are ranked differently and non-realization of /ə/ is a licit repair operation in the language.

[19] Given that the constraint (43) demands a phonetically visible *or* a morphological association line, non-realization of an association line to an underlying affix foot does not induce an additional violation of the constraint. Although PVIS$_\Phi$ does not distinguish between affix feet that are underlyingly associated to segmental material and those that don't, $\Phi > Do_p^m > \sigma$ always favours realization of the morphemic affix foot.

or copying for some base. These operations are assumed to be repairs avoiding that the morphemic foot dominates more segments with a different morphemic affiliation than absolutely necessary. This effect is predicted by $^*\Phi_O < S_\bullet$ (recall (35) and (36)).

Every base segment that is integrated under the morphemic foot induces an additional violation of $^*\Phi_O < S_\bullet$ since the base segments and the affix foot are necessarily affiliated with different morphemes. Given that the parsing constraints in Upriver Halkomelem demand a full integration of the foot into the prosodic structure, it must nevertheless be filled with segmental material—preferably with epenthetic or copied segments since this avoids violations of $^*\Phi_O < S_\bullet$. However, it is impossible in Upriver Halkomelem to completely avoid violations of $^*\Phi_O < S_\bullet$ since higher-ranked ΦOVRL (44) demands a minimal overlap between an underlying foot and a phonetically realized foot. The constraint unifies effects from, *first*, faithfulness constraints demanding that an underlying stress pattern should be preserved and, *second*, faithfulness constraints demanding that a prosodic constituent should be faithful to its form and content in the output. The first class of faithfulness constraints can be found in numerous versions in the literature, including, for example, MAX-ACCENT (Alderete, 2001b: 9), MAX-STRESS, or MAX-PROM (Alderete, 1999, 2001b; Smith, 2002; Gouskova and Roon, 2008).

(44) ΦOVRL   Assign a violation mark for every Φ_O if there is no segment integrated under Φ_O that is phonetically associated with a phonetically visible Φ.

The picture emerging from ranking these constraints is that a morphemic foot in Upriver Halkomelem preferably does not dominate any base segments but must at least dominate one segment that was underlyingly integrated into a foot. However, the prefixed continuative foot must also be 'big enough' to form a good binary foot, due to the standard markedness constraint FTBIN (Prince and Smolensky, 1993/2002). Given that codas are assumed to be moraic in Upriver Halkomelem, either two syllables or a heavy syllable (CV: or CVC) must hence be integrated under the morphemic foot. The strategies of inserting epenthetic /hɛ/, copying base segments, or vowel lengthening are then predicted in a quite straightforward way. On the one hand, epenthesis and copying introduce segmental material that has no morphological colour and therefore material that can be integrated under the continuative foot without any violations of $^*\Phi_O < S_\bullet$. Vowel lengthening, on the other hand, can make an underlying light base syllable heavy. This heavy syllable is then alone sufficient to fill the morphemic foot and additional violations of $^*\Phi_O < S_\bullet$ are again avoided.

The four continuative allomorphs, their prosodic structure, and their violations of the constraint $^*\Phi_O < S_\bullet$ that are crucial in the derivation of the continuative are given in (45). In all the structures below, an underlying foot structure is present that remains phonetically unrealized since it is more important to realize the affix foot. ΦOVRL is hence ranked above $^*\Phi_O < S_\bullet$ in Upriver Halkomelem. From this it follows that all optimal structures in (45) violate $^*\Phi_O < S_\bullet$ at least once: since at least one base segment that is morphologically associated with a foot must be integrated under the phonetically visible foot in order to ensure a minimal overlap between feet. In (45-I), ΦOVRL ensures that all five base segments are integrated under the morphemic affix foot. Since the segments and the foot are affiliated with different morphemes, five violations of $*\Phi_\circ < S_\bullet$ arise. Note that in (45-II), the copied portion is prefixed to the base and the now unstressed base vowel is reduced to /ə/.

(45)   *The continuative allomorphs*

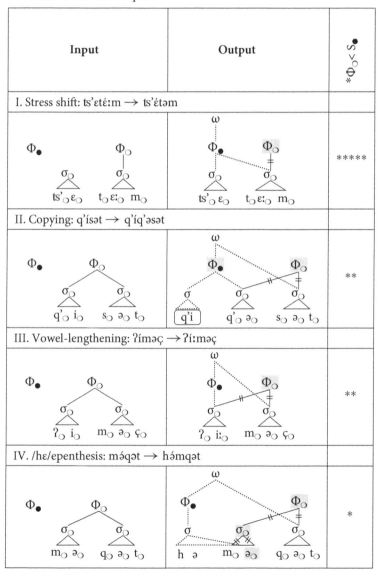

Input	Output	$*\Phi_\circ < S_\bullet$
I. Stress shift: tsʼɛtéːm → tsʼétəm		*****
II. Copying: qʼísət → qʼíqʼəsət		**
III. Vowel-lengthening: ʔíməç → ʔíːməç		**
IV. /hɛ/epenthesis: máqət → həmqət		*

Given the constraint violations of $^*\Phi_O < S_\bullet$ in (45), epenthesis (45-IV) should always be predicted as the optimal output for a continuative form since it integrates fewest base segments under the continuative foot. In the example (45-IV), it is only the morphologically coloured segment /m/ that is dominated by the morphemic foot, whereas in (45-II) and (45-III), two base segments are integrated under the affix foot. The avoidance of one additional violation of $^*\Phi_O < S_\bullet$ is possible in (45-IV) since the first base vowel is deleted and resyllabification results. Stress shift (45-I) on the other side is an apparently very bad strategy to realize the continuative foot since it invokes many violations of $^*\Phi_O < S_\bullet$. As becomes apparent below, it nevertheless becomes optimal since it is a candidate that avoids a violation of ΦOVRL.

That the dispreferred strategies (45-II)–(45-III) nevertheless apply to bases with certain phonological forms follows since other constraints are relevant in the derivation of the continuative foot as well. *First*, copying, creates marked phonotactic structures for bases starting with a glottal segment. This follows since the initial base vowel that becomes unstressed after adding the copied portion is reduced to /ə/ and together with the glottal onset, a placeless syllable results where no segment is specified for place. That these syllables are indeed dispreferred in Upriver Halkomelem is empirically supported by a statistical examination about stem shapes discussed in Urbanczyk (1998) which led to the conclusion that placeless syllables are truly rare in the language. This marked structure is penalized by the constraint *Ɂə (Kurisu, 2001; Urbanczyk, 1998), defined in (46). As is discussed in more detail below, epenthesis also has the potential to result in such marked placeless syllables for certain bases.

(46) *Ɂə   Assign a violation mark for every σ that phonetically only integrates segments without a phonetically visible place feature specification.

Second, copying in Upriver Halkomelem is restricted to contexts where the original segment and its copied counterpart end up in different syllables. Copying is hence only licit for a structure like /qʼí.qʼə.sət/ where the the copied consonant and vowel form a syllable on their own; it is impossible in a structure */mə́m.qət/ where the base vowel remains unrealized and the copied consonant hence ends up in the onset position of a syllable that contains the copied base segment in its coda. This is ensured by an OCP constraint banning identical segments inside one syllable, given in (47). That OCP effects are indeed weaker if the elements in question are in different syllables (or morphemes) is argued in, for example, Berkley (2000) or Walter (2007).[20]

(47)   OCP$_\sigma$ Assign a violation mark for every pair of phonetically visible identical segments that are phonetically visible associated to the same syllable node.

---

[20] In correspondence-theory, the same effect for Upriver Halkomelem is predicted by IDENT[σ-ROLE] in, for example, McCarthy and Prince (1994a); Rose and Walker (2004); Kenstowicz (2005), or Bye and Svenonius (2012), demanding that corresponding segments should be in the same syllable position. A copy structure /C$_1$VC$_1$/ hence violates IDENT[σ-ROLE] specified for BR-relations whereas /C$_1$V.C$_1$V/ does not.

These two constraints are only violated if a base with a certain shape undergoes one of the four strategies to form the continuative. There are, however, also general constraints that are inherently violated if copying, epenthesis, or vowel lengthening applies. Vowel lengthening induces an additional violation of $*^{\mu}V^{\mu}$, copying violates Col!ₛ, and /hɛ/ epenthesis violates Col!ₛ and Lic!ₛ.

The ranking of these three constraints in Upriver Halkomelem is taken to be the one in (48) which predicts that copying is the least marked strategy to provide colourless material. Epenthesis of /hɛ/ violates Lic!ₛ in addition to Col!ₛ and is therefore a less preferred option. Vowel lengthening violates higher-ranked $*^{\mu}V^{\mu}$ and should only surface if the other strategies are impossible.

(48)   *Preference hierarchy to realize the continuative*
     $*^{\mu}V^{\mu} \gg \{\text{Lic!}_S, \text{Col!}_S\}$

5.3.1.3 The choice for one of the four allomorphs   In the following tableaux it is illustrated how the constraint system chooses the optimal strategy to realize the continuative foot for different bases. Competing candidates that do not integrate the continuative foot into the prosodic structure or that integrate more than one foot into the prosodic word node in a phonetically visible way are not included in the tableaux since it was already shown that those are excluded by the undominated constraints $\Phi > \text{Do}_p^m > \sigma$, Er-L, Er-R, and PVis-$\Phi_{AF}$ (see the general tableau on overwriting in (42)).

We begin the discussion with the stress shifting allomorph. Recall from (45) that it is the allomorph with the worst constraint profile with respect to $*\Phi_O < S_\bullet$. Nevertheless, stress shifting becomes optimal for non-continuative forms with stress on a non-initial syllable. An example is /tsʼɛtéːm/ 'crawl' that is realized as /tsʼétəm/ in the continuative. That the non-continuative base is stressed on the second syllable follows if only this second syllable is parsed into a foot with initial prominence underlyingly. This can be seen in tableau (49). If the base foot remains phonetically invisible, hence 'overwritten' by the morphemic foot, the constraint ΦOvrl demands that at least one of the segments of the syllable /tɛːm/ must be integrated into the phonetically visible foot. Integration of only the first base syllable into the morphemic foot (49-a), copying in candidate (49-c), vowel lengthening in candidate (49-d) and epenthesis in candidate (49-e) are all excluded by ΦOvrl since they parse neither /t/, /ɛ/, nor /m/ into the continuative foot.[21] The crucial ranking in the context of a stress shifting allomorph is therefore the ranking of ΦOvrl over $*\Phi_O < S_\bullet$ which predicts that all base segments are integrated into the foot as in the winning candidate (49-b). Other constraints that are included in the ranking in (49) will become relevant for the optimization of other allomorphs below: FtBin, and the constraints against non-realization of segments PVisᵥ and PVisₔ.

---

[21] Given that three-syllabic feet are impossible and a candidate like */(hə́tsɛtɛm)/ is generally excluded.

(49) *Stress Shift*

	*ʔə	PVIs$_V$	ΦOVRL	*Φ$_O$ < S$_•$	PVIs$_ə$	FtBin	*$^μγ^μ$	Lic!s	Col!s
a. [ts'ɛ́.təm]			*!	**		*			
☞ b. [ts'ɛ́.təm]				*****					
c. [ts'ɛ́.tsə.tɛm]			*!	**					**
d. [ts'ɛ́:.təm]			*!	**		*			
e. [hɑ́ts'.təm]	*!		*!	*				**	**

In contrast, it is possible to avoid more violations of *Φ$_O$ < S$_•$ if stress is on the first syllable in the non-continuative form. Only the first base segment must be integrated under the morphemic foot in order to satisfy ΦOVRL. To ensure that the foot is binary, additional syllabic weight is required: epenthetic or copied segments are inserted or a vowel is lengthened to increase the moraic count of the material dominated by the morphemic foot. The choice between these strategies is optimized in the following tableaux. The order of candidates is always the same: the continuative foot is filled with the first base syllable (candidates a.), a CV sequence is copied and prefixed (candidates b.), the first base syllable is parsed into the foot and its vowel is lengthened (candidates c.), or epenthetic /hɛ/ is inserted and the first base vowel is deleted (candidates d.). The closely related logically possible candidate that inserts epenthetic /hɛ/ but realizes all underlying vowels as in */hɛ́tsɛtɛm/ is suboptimal under the current ranking since it does not integrate fewer base segments under the affix foot than a competing copying candidate but additionally violates COL!ₛ.

Recall from (48) that copying, which violates only lowest-ranked COL!ₛ, is taken to be the default strategy for providing non-base segments. This preference for copying is crucial in tableau (50) where the continuative for the base /q'ísət/ is optimized and the copying candidate (50-b) wins the competition. That the initial consonant is copied as well although a vowel alone would be sufficient to fill the initial syllable with segmental material follows from the general onset requirement active in Upriver Halkomelem. In the present OT analysis, an undominated ONSET constraint is simply assumed that is omitted in all following tableaux. Note that candidate (50-d) fares best with respect to $^*\Phi_O < S_\bullet$ since it integrates only one base segment under the morphemic foot. Avoidance of one violation of $^*\Phi_O < S_\bullet$ is possible since resyllabification after non-realization of the base vowel results in a structure where only the first base segment is integrated under the morphemic foot (as coda consonant of the first syllable). However, this vowel deletion is excluded by high-ranked PVISᵥ penalizing non-realization of vowels with a place specification ($\neq$/ə/). In sum, tableau (50) illustrates the ranking argument of PVISᵥ above $^*\Phi_O < S_\bullet$ and of $^{*\mu}V^\mu$ over COL!ₛ in Upriver Halkomelem.

For monosyllabic bases like /jíq/ 'fall (of snow)' with the continuative form /jíjəq/ 'falling (of snow)' (see 38b), however, it is clear that the continuative form with copying does not minimize the number of $^*\Phi_O < S_\bullet$ violations. The same three base segments are integrated under the continuative foot as are dominated by the foot in an alternative continuative form */jíq/ without any additional phonological operation. The constraint $^*\Phi_O < S_\bullet$ is therefore not the trigger for providing non-base segments in such a context. However, given the assumption that final codas are not moraic in Upriver Halkomelem, every word consisting only of a CVC string violates FTBIN. Copying and subsequent insertion of an additional mora avoids this marked structure. The fact that copying only applies in the continuative and monosyllabic words of the shape CVC are perfectly fine in other morphological contexts is an Emergence of the Unmarked effect: phonological repair operations to create an unmarked bisyllabic foot are predicted inside a newly created affix foot but not inside an underlying stem foot. It follows since FTBIN is lower-ranked than the constraint against the integration of epenthetic syllables into stem prosody but higher-ranked than the constraint against epenthetic integration of syllables into affix prosody ($*\Phi...^{St}...\sigma \gg \text{FtBin} \gg *\Phi...^{Af}...\sigma$). Copying as a strategy to avoid a subminimal foot is only possible under an affix foot, never under a stem foot or for stem syllables.

(50) *Copying*

$\Phi_\bullet + \Phi_\circ$ (base diagram) $q'_\circ i_\circ \; s_\circ \partial_\circ t_\circ$	*ʔə	PVISᵥ	ΦOVRL	*Φₒ<Sₒ	PVISₐ	FtBin	*ᵘVᵘ	Lıc!s	Coʟ!s
a. [qí.sət]				**		*!			
☞ b. [qí.qə.sət]				**					**
c. [qíːsət]				**			*!		
d. [həq.sət]	*!		*					*	*

Copying as a strategy to fill the continuative foot with non-base segments is excluded for bases starting with a glottal consonant. This is due to the constraint already introduced in (46), the markedness constraint against placeless syllables. As can be seen in (51), copying (51-b) and /hɛ/ insertion (51-d) result in a placeless syllable whenever the non-continuative base starts with a glottal consonant. The optimal output for such a non-continuative form is therefore the vowel lengthening candidate (51-c) where the first base vowel is associated with an additional epenthetic mora under violation of $*^{\mu}V^{\mu}$. This mora is necessary since FtBin demands that every foot is bimoraic and excludes candidate (51-a) that only integrates the first syllable without vowel lengthening.

(51) *Vowel lengthening*

		*ʔə	PVis_V	ΦOVRL	*ΦO<S•	PVis_ə	FtBin	*Vμμ	Lic!S	Col!S
a.	[ʔí.məç]				**		*!			
b.	[ʔí.ʔə.məç]	*!			**					**
☞ c.	[ʔíː.məç]				**			*		
d.	[hə́ʔ.məç]	*!	*!		*				**	**

The tableau (51) shows that the markedness constraint against placeless syllables *ʔə is ranked high in Upriver Halkomelem and at least in the same high stratum as ΦOVRL and PVis_V. As in the contexts of monosyllabic bases that undergo copying in the continuative, *ΦO < S• cannot be the trigger for the additional vowel lengthening in monosyllabic contexts: the continuative form /hí:lt/ includes as many base segments that are underlyingly associated with a foot under the affix foot as the form */hílt/. Again, it is FtBin that ensures the extension of the syllable into a bimoraic structure. That epenthesis and not copying applies to make the base bisyllabic follows from the same constraint ranking that is relevant for the choice of continuative allomorphs: copying would create a violation of *ʔə.

(52)   *Epenthesis*

	OCP$_\sigma$	*ʔə	PVIS$_v$	ΦOVRL	*Φ$_o$>S$_\bullet$	PVIS$_\partial$	FtBin	*$^{\mu\mu}$V$^\mu$	LIC!s	COL!s
a. [mə́.qət]					**!		*			
b. [mə́.mə.qət]					**!					**
c. [mə́:.qət]					**!		*			
☞ d. [hə́m.qət]					*	*			**	**
e. [mə́m.qət]	*!				*	*				**

In all the preceding derivations, candidate e. that only integrates a single base segment under the morphemic foot and thus violates $^*\Phi_O < S_\bullet$ only once was excluded by high-ranked PVis$_V$ since it involves non-realization of the full first base vowel. Non-realization of a placeless /ə/, however, only violates lower-ranked PVis$_ə$. Integration of only one base segment is therefore possible for bases with /ə/ as their first vowel. This is illustrated in tableau (52) for the non-continuative base /mə́qət/. The first base vowel /ə/ can remain unrealized without a violation of PVis$_V$ given that the constraint only penalizes the non-realization of 'full' vowels with a place feature specification. Resulting resyllabification of the first base consonant /m/ as coda of the new preceding syllable hence allows us to integrate only a single base segment under the continuative foot. As was argued above, the violations of L$_{IC!S}$ and C$_{OL!S}$ favour copying as a strategy to insert non-base segments and we hence expect candidate (52-e) to win. However, this default strategy is excluded in a resyllabification context since two identical segments surface in one syllable under violation of OCP$_\sigma$ (47). Copying is therefore impossible and insertion of epenthetic material as the second-best strategy to provide non-base material results as optimal output (52-d). This winning candidate violates $^*\Phi_O < S_\bullet$ only once. All other candidates (no phonological operation as in (52-a), copying in (52-b), or vowel lengthening in (52-c)) incur two violations of $^*\Phi_O < S_\bullet$ since two base segments /mə/ are integrated into the continuative foot.

As in the copying contexts above, undominated O$_{NSET}$ requires insertion of two additional segments, excluding a candidate */ə́mqət/. Evidence for this assumption are facts from reduplicated continuative forms with the stative prefix /s−/. If this consonantal prefix precedes the continuative form, copying of the consonant is unnecessary to provide the word with an onset. The additional violations of L$_{IC!S}$ and C$_{OL!S}$ violations in ungrammatical */shəltsət/ are avoided in the surface form /səltsət/ 'fill it/filled' (Urbanczyk, 1998: 662).

5.3.1.4 Stems without underlying stress In all derivations above, the stem was underlyingly marked for stress, i.e. the stem segments were underlyingly integrated under a foot structure. This underlying foot structure is crucial since ΦO$_{VRL}$ ensures that the continuative foot cannot be filled with epenthetic or copied segmental material only and that there must be a minimal overlap between underlying and surface foot structure. This straightforwardly leads to the question of what the proposed system predicts for non-continuative bases without an underlying stress, perfectly possible and predictable given the assumption of Richness of the Base. Since ΦO$_{VRL}$ is vacuously satisfied, we would expect that $^*\Phi_O < S_\bullet$ demands abundant copying as in the hypothetical forms in (53) where the morphemic foot is only filled with copied segments. Note that for bases starting with a glottal segment as in our example /ʔíməç/, vowel lengthening is predicted in the continuative irrespective of whether underlying foot structure is present or not. Double copying /ʔíʔəʔəməç/ and epenthesis /həhəʔíməç/ avoid a violation of $^*\Phi_O < S_\bullet$ but both structures contain syllables with only placeless segments, excluded by high-ranked *ʔə. And finally, stress shift as realization of the continuative morpheme is only possible for bases with an underlying foot structure for trivial reasons: only those bases are underlyingly stressed.

(53)   *Bases without underlying foot structure*

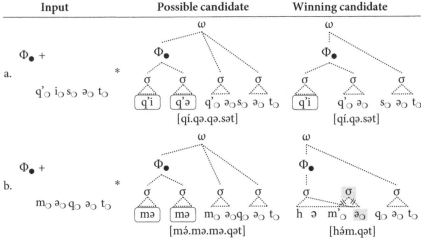

Input	Possible candidate	Winning candidate

These structures are marked since the foot is only and exclusively filled with colour-less segmental material. The relevant constraint (54) excluding such a structure is another member of the constraints ensuring morph-contiguous prosodic structures introduced in 2.2.3.

(54)   *Φ-CoL!S   Assign a violation mark for every Φ node that only dominates colourless segments phonetically or morphologically.

This constraint is violated in structures as in (53) and has actually the same effect ΦOVRL had for bases with initial underlying stress: it demands that at least the first base segment must be integrated under the morphemic foot.

5.3.1.5 Summary: non-concatenative allomorphy in Upriver Halkomelem   This ana-lysis of Upriver Halkomelem showed how another mechanism expected under the framework of PDM is able to predict a complex pattern of non-concatenative allo-morphy: foot affixation can result in phonologically predictable non-concatenative allomorphy where only some of the allomorphs are instances of MLM. The analysis for the continuative allomorphy in Upriver Halkomelem is based on two main mecha-nisms: *First,* the interaction of *Φ₀ < S•, ΦOVRL, and FtBin demands that the prefixed morphemic foot is fully integrated (=a fixed stress pattern arises) and filled with as much non-base material as possible without completely ignoring the underlying foot structure (=a preference for non-base material at the left edge). *Second,* the ranking of constraints that are violated whenever copying, epenthesis, or vowel lengthening applies (*$^\mu$V$^\mu$, LiC!S, CoL!S) predicts a preference order for phonological operations to supply the foot with additional non-base material (see (48)). The interaction with constraints that are only violated if bases of a certain shape undergo one of these phonological strategies restricts these phonological operations to certain contexts. For example, *ʔə is only violated when epenthesis or copying applies to bases starting with a glottal sound.

5.3.2 *Non-concatenative allomorphy in Rotuman*

Another pattern of non-concatenative allomorphy that straightforwardly follows from a foot affixation analysis is the formation of the incomplete phase in Rotuman (Churchward, 1940; Vamarasi, 2002). The Rotuman pattern has received considerable theoretic interest; theoretical discussions include Cairns (1976); Besnier (1987); Odden (1988); Blevins (1994); McCarthy (1996), or McCarthy (2000c). The incomplete phase is one of two morphological 'phases' that are distinguished for every major-class word in Rotuman indicating indefiniteness and non-emphasis. The crucial generalization about the incomplete phase is that all forms end in a bimoraic foot. This structure is derived via four different allomorphs: *first*, 'metathesis' of the final vowel with the preceding consonant when the final vowel is lower than the penultimate vowel (55-a), *second*, non-realization of the final vowel and umlaut if a back vowel in the penultimate syllable precedes a front vowel in the final syllable (55-b), *third*, non-realization of the final vowel for all remaining VCV# contexts (55-c), and, *fourth*, diphthongization for bases ending in two adjacent vowels (55-d). If the final vowel is already long, no change applies (55-e). Interestingly, the final syllable in the incomplete is an exception to the general syllable structure (C)V in the language.

(55)   *Phase difference in Rotuman*   (McCarthy, 2000c; Vamarasi, 2002)

	COMPLETE	INCOMPLETE		
a.	iʔa	iaʔ	'fish'	M2
	seseva	seseav	'erroneous'	M2
	fupa	fwap	'to distribute'	V3
b.	tafi	taf	'to sweep'	M2
	mose	møs	'to sleep'	V3
	futi	fyt	'to pull'	V3
c.	tokiri	tokir	'to roll'	M2
	sulu	sul	'coconut-spathe'	M2
	asa	as	'name'	V3
d.	pupui	pupu͡i	'floor'	M2
	lelei	lele͡i	'good'	M2
	keu	ke͡u	'to push'	M2
e.	riː	riː	'house'	M2
	reː	reː	'to do'	M2
	sikaː	sikaː	'cigar'	M2

The crucial insight is that the incomplete phase ends in a foot that contains only one heavy syllable. For this generalization it is important to distinguish two types of diphthongs in Rotuman: light monomoraic ones as in (55-a) and heavy bimoraic ones as in (55-d). Inside the PDM framework, it is assumed that a morphemic foot is suffixed in the incomplete and must be fully integrated into the prosodic structure of its base. Similar to the pattern in Upriver Halkomelem, a morph-contiguous prosodic structure is preferred and the foot strives to avoid dominating too much structure affiliated with another morpheme. In contrast to Upriver Halkomelem, this avoidance of base structure dominated by the morphemic foot is not ensured by $*\Phi_{\circ} < S_{\bullet}$ but by $*\Phi...\text{Af}...\sigma$. This constraint penalizes every inserted association line between a syllable and a foot if one or both elements are affiliated with an affix. Since the affix foot must dominate some material due to high-ranked $\Phi > Do_p^m > \sigma$, one violation of $*\Phi...\text{Af}...\sigma$ is unavoidable. It is, however, avoided to integrate another syllable under the morphemic affix foot. Since the foot must nevertheless be big enough to form an unmarked bimoraic foot, different phonological operations adjust final CV syllables.

In (56), the structures assumed in the present containment-based framework for the different allomorphs are given. All incomplete forms have in common that a suffixed affix foot is completely integrated into the structure but integrates only a single syllable in order to minimize the $*\Phi...\text{Af}...\sigma$ violations. Only in (56-e), can the existing base structure be integrated under the affix foot without further modification since it already contains a heavy final syllable. In all other contexts, some additional operation is necessary to ensure that the foot is bimoraic. In (56-e), for example, the final vowel remains unrealized in order to ensure that a heavy syllable can be integrated under the morphemic foot.

Since the choice of the different allomorphs to realize this one heavy syllable has been discussed extensively elsewhere, these existing analyses are not repeated and the reader is referred to, for example, the thorough analysis in McCarthy (2000c).

Only for the 'metathesis' strategy (56-a), is some special comment necessary. Recall that in containment, any 'reordering' and hence 'metathesis' is impossible. The surface impression of metathesis arises from the combination of insertion and non-realization as in (56-a). The final vowel remains unrealized and an epenthetic vowel is inserted after the penultimate vowel that then fully harmonizes with the non-realized vowel. It is assumed that this feature association is due to the pressure to realize as many vocalic features from the unrealized final vowel as possible. In case an attested light diphthong would result, the vocalic features hence associate to the epenthetic vowel. Such a repair is impossible in (56-b) since no light diphthong would result.

Note finally that in the structure (56-a), the mora that was underlyingly associated with the final vowel now dominates the final consonant—nothing hinges on that assumption and the mora dominating the consonant could also be assumed to be epenthetic. The association lines in (56-c) and (56-d) that apparently end in nothing indicate association with the prosodic word node (or another foot, nothing hinges on that).

(56) *The incomplete phase: five allomorphs*

	INPUT	INCOMPLETE FORM	$\Phi > \text{Dop}^m > \sigma$	FtBin	$*\Phi...^{Af}...\sigma$
a.					*
b.					*
c.					*
d.					*
e.					*

Recall that Rotuman syllables are restricted to (C)V in all other contexts. It is assumed that the syllable markedness constraints are hence ranked below $*\Phi...^{Af}...\sigma$: It is more important to avoid integration of multiple syllables under the affix foot than avoiding coda consonants. The Rotuman pattern is hence in an interesting way similar to the allomorphy in Upriver Halkomelem: a morphemic foot is affixed and results in, *first*, a fixed stress pattern at a certain edge of the base and, *second*, phonological (length-manipulating) operations ensuring that only the minimally necessary amount of base structure is integrated under the affix foot. In Upriver Halkomelem, as few base segments as possible are integrated under the affix foot and in Rotuman, as few syllables dominating base segments are integrated under the foot. And in both languages, the foot must still be unmarked and thus be bimoraic. Note that Rotuman is in fact not an instance of MLM in the strict sense defined above in section 1.1. In containment theory, the 'metathesis' is in fact epenthesis and hence an instance of a Segment-Zero-Alternation. However, no allomorph is an instance of a Long-Short-Alternation. Rotuman is therefore not part of the present data sample but it was nevertheless discussed since it employs a straightforward instance of foot affixation and an indirect vertical morpheme contiguity effect.

5.3.3 *The lengthening grade(s) in Choctaw*

Given the central claim in PDM that all nodes of the prosodic hierarchy are possible morphemic prosodic nodes, we also expect vertical morpheme contiguity effects for morphemic syllables. That such effects are indeed borne out is shown in this section with a case study of the challenging and interesting pattern of additive MLM in Choctaw, a Western Muskogean language (Nicklas, 1974; Kimball, 1985, 1991; Lombardi and McCarthy, 1991; Ulrich, 1993, 2003; Broadwell, 2006). All Muskogean languages employ various 'grades' that apply to verb and adjective stems adding aspectual meaning. The relevant grade in Choctaw is the so-called intensive grade. As in Alabama (see section 3.2.2.2), the words in (57) are all assumed to be morphologically complex, followed by the suffixes /−li/ 'active', /−a/ 'medio-passive', and /−tʃi/ 'causative'. As in Alabama, assimilation masks the /−li/ in some cases; the segmentations into stem and affix are hence given for clarification as well. Given this segmentation, the intensive is formed via geminating the final onset consonant (57-a) and lengthening of the final stem vowel (57-b) if the penultimate syllable of the resulting word would otherwise be light.

(57)   *Intensive formation in Choctaw I*   (Nicklas, 1974: 92–95)

	BASE			INTENSIVE
a.	talaktʃi	(talak−tʃi)	'to be tied'	tálːaktʃi
	atobːi	(atob−li)	'to pay'	átːobːi
	kobafːi	(kobaf−li)	'to break'	kóbːafːi
b.	falama	(falam−a)	'to return'	fálːaːma
	binili	(bini−li)	'to sit'	bínːiːli
	tokwikili	(tokwiki−li)	'to shine'	tokwíkːiːli

Crucially, there are other formations for the intensive grade, given in (58). In those forms, an additional sequence /jːV/ surfaces after the final stem vowel, the V being a copy of the preceding stem vowel. This /jː/-insertion might trigger shortening of a preceding vowel since CVːC syllables are impossible medially in Choctaw. If the penultimate syllable of the word is expected to be light, additional vowel lengthening of the copied vowel surfaces (58-b).

(58)　*The intensive formation in Choctaw II*　　　　　(Nicklas, 1974: 92–95)

Base			Intensive
a. taktʃi	(tak–tʃi)	'to tie'	tájːaktʃi
oktabli	(oktab–li)	'to dam up'	oktájːabli
b. pisa	(pis–a)	'to see'	píjːiːsa
ona	(on–a)	'to arrive there'	ójːoːna
toksali	(toksa–li)	'to work'	toksájːaːli
ʃaːli	(ʃaː–i)	'to carry'	ʃájːaːli

Some analyses summarize both patterns in (57) and (58) as the /j/-grade formation in Choctaw. A unified account for both sets of data is given in Lombardi and McCarthy (1991). With the background of prosodic circumscription theory, it is argued there that the base is mapped onto a canonical LH iambic foot after the final syllable became extrametrical (no segmentation into classifier suffixes is assumed for the intensive formation) and that a mora is suffixed to the first base mora in a second step, modifying the resulting form to a HH foot. The mora always triggers gemination of the penultimate onset consonant; either of an underlying consonant as in (57-a, b) or of the inserted epenthetic /j/ as in (58-a, b). That the iambic foot has the unmarked structure LH, on the other hand, is ensured by insertion of a long vowel (as in (58-b)) or lengthening of the penultimate vowel (as in (57-b)).

However, this interpretation of the facts as one /j/-grade is not unchallenged. Ulrich (2003), for example, argues for a distinction into a /g/-grade triggering gemination (57) and a /j/-grade triggering insertion (58). The striking argument for this claim is that many verbs can appear in both grades without a semantic difference. An example is /wakajah/ 'he stood up' that can surface as /wákːaːjah/ or /wakájːajah/ 'he finally stood up' (Ulrich, 2003: 175).[22]

In the following, a PDM analysis for the Choctaw additive MLM under this latter interpretation is given. Two different underlying representations for the intensive morpheme are assumed to be stored as two lexical allomorphs. The /g/-grade in (57) follows from an analysis that is similar in some respects to the one presented for Rotuman. The intensive morpheme is taken to consist of a morphemic foot and a morphemic mora that are both suffixed to their base, sketched in (59). Due

---

[22] The lack of expected vowel lengthening in the example is discussed below.

to final extrametricality, this foot can not dominate the final syllable and due to $*\Phi...\text{Af}...\sigma$, it strives to dominate only a single syllable. Since it must be bimoraic due to FtBin, some additional operation must supply syllable weight in case the penultimate syllable is light. Gemination is the default strategy that is preferred over vowel lengthening due the ranking of $*^{\mu}V^{\mu}$ above $*C_{\mu}$. In addition, the suffixed mora strives to be fully integrated as well. Crucially, integration of this mora never results in gemination simply because $*\mu...\text{Af}...C$ is taken to be high-ranked in Choctaw. Although gemination is in principle the default strategy to realize additional syllable weight, it is hence never employed if the mora in question is an affix mora. Gemination in the penultimate syllable in (59) only involves association between an epenthetic mora and stem consonants and is hence not affected by $*\mu...\text{Af}...C$ Given that non-final CV:C syllables are illicit in Choctaw, vowel lengthening is impossible for final vowels that are followed by a coda consonant (59-b). In such contexts, the morphemic mora remains unassociated (given that it cannot associate to a consonant and make mora epenthesis unnecessary).

(59) *The /g/- or gemination-grade in Choctaw: suffixation of a foot and a mora*

	Input	Intensive
a.	$\Phi_{\bullet}$ + $\mu_{\circ}$ $\mu_{\circ}$ $\mu_{\bullet}$ / $b_{\circ}$ $i_{\circ}$ $n_{\circ}$ $i_{\circ}$	$\Phi_{\bullet}$ / σ σ / $\mu_{\circ}$ μ $\mu_{\circ}$ $\mu_{\bullet}$ / $b_{\circ}$ $i_{\circ}$ $n_{\circ}$ $i_{\circ}$
b.	$\Phi_{\bullet}$ + $\mu_{\circ}$ $\mu_{\circ}$ $\mu_{\bullet}$ / $t_{\circ}$ $a_{\circ}$ $l_{\circ}$ $a_{\circ}$ $k_{\circ}$	$\Phi_{\bullet}$ / σ σ / $\mu_{\circ}$ μ $\mu_{\circ}$ μ $\mu_{\bullet}$ / $t_{\circ}$ $a_{\circ}$ $l_{\circ}$ $a_{\circ}$ $k_{\circ}$

The /j/-grade or insertion grade is taken to follow from a slightly different representation, namely the additional suffixation of a morphemic syllable. Absolutely parallel to the analysis for Upriver Halkomelem where $*\Phi_{\circ} < S_{\bullet}$ triggers epenthesis and copying, $*\sigma_{\circ} < S_{\bullet}$ now ensures that this morphemic syllable dominates as few base segments as possible. And insertion of /j/ and copying of the vowel are strategies to ensure that no base segment is dominated by the morphemic syllable, shown in (60). That the inserted /j/ is geminated and the copied vowel lengthened is straightforwardly predicted if this allomorph contains a morphemic foot and a mora as well (see (59)).

The insertion grade formation in (58) hence follows from a morpheme representation that is a superset of the representation assumed for the g-grade: *first*, realization of the mora triggers final vowel lengthening, *second*, affixation of the morphemic foot requires that the penultimate syllable is heavy, ensured by gemination, and, *third*, affixation of the morphemic syllable results in insertion to avoid a morphemic syllable that dominates too many segments with a different morphological affiliation. This latter mechanism yet again strengthens the claim for constraints ensuring vertical morph-contiguous representations.

(60)   *The /j/- or insertion-grade in Choctaw: suffixation of a foot, a syllable, and a mora*

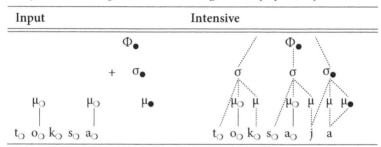

That the three additive processes of vowel lengthening, gemination, and insertion are in principle independent from each other and triggered by different parts of the representation of the morpheme in question receives striking support from the fact that Ulrich (2003) reports that final vowel lengthening is in fact absent for his consultants in the insertion-grade data (58). Recall the example given above where /wakajah/ 'he stood up' surfaces as /wakáj:ajah/ 'he finally stood up' (Ulrich, 2003: 175). This empirical fact is straightforwardly predicted if the morphemic mora is not part of the morpheme representation (anymore) for this one of the two intensive allomorphs. And the absence of lengthening for only those /j/-grade forms (58) but not the /g/-grade forms (57) is in fact an additional strong argument to analyse the two grades as two separate morphological processes.

5.4 General summary: morpheme contiguity

The focus of this chapter was specific phenomena of additive MLM that show morpheme CONTIGUITY effects of various types. The first section 5.1 drew attention to additive MLM patterns that fall out under a standard mora affixation account that acknowledges a preference for morphemic prosodic nodes to be realized at morpheme edges. This complements the discussion of possible linearization sites in chapter 6 with adding a violable CONTIGUITY constraint that restricts the possible landing sites for a morphemic prosodic node. Sections 5.2 and 5.3 then argued for extending the traditional morpheme CONTIGUITY to vertical relations inside prosodic structures.

The main empirical contribution of section 5.2 is the argument for long epenthesis in the domain of morphological segment lengthening. It was argued that such patterns are not only unexpected given general arguments about the nature of epenthetic segments but are also strikingly challenging under alternative accounts without the concept of vertical morpheme CONTIGUITY. Section 7.4 will add some more discussion on this latter point. This discussion directly continues the investigation of opacity problems for mora affixation accounts inside standard parallel OT from section 2.2.4. Section 5.3 was particularly concerned with additive MLM that results from foot affixation. A detailed case study of Upriver Halkomelem showed how the affixation of a morphemic foot together with the constraint for morph-contiguous foot projection straightforwardly predicts the complex pattern of non-concatenative allomorphy in the language. This argument for morphemic feet is particularly crucial for the general claim of PDM that is based on exactly this assumption that all nodes of the prosodic hierarchy can exist as (part(s) of) morpheme representations and goes beyond existing claims for mora affixes.

6

The complete empirical picture
of MLM and the linearization
# of morphemes

In the preceding chapters, various analyses for additive and subtractive MLM patterns inside the theory of PDM were presented. The aim of this chapter is to test this theoretical framework and its predictions against the typological generalizations of (un)attested MLM patterns. The representative data set of MLM that served as the basis for the theoretical argumentation in this book is presented and it is shown that the present system indeed predicts all the MLM patterns that are attested and excludes patterns that are generally unattested. Special focus is paid to the linearization of MLM patterns. As is argued in chapter 7, the lack of restrictions on base positions that can be affected by an MLM operation is one argument against alternative accounts.

In section 6.1, some background facts about the data set are given and the complete list of included MLM patterns is presented. Sections 6.1.2 and 6.1.3 then discuss the empirical generalizations with respect to base positions that are affected by MLM for additive and subtractive MLM respectively. The argumentation that all these attested MLM instances indeed fall out in the PDM framework follows in section 6.2. It consists of two basic points: that PDM predicts all attested MLM patterns and that it systematically excludes non-attested patterns. In section 6.2.1 to 6.2.4, the assumed PDM analyses for all the MLM patterns that are part of the data sample are presented according to three categories that are relevant for the question of linearization of exponents: MLM at the edge of its base, infixing MLM, and multiple MLM operations in one base. Finally, putative MLM patterns are discussed that are generally impossible in the framework of PDM and are indeed systematically absent in the sample (section 6.2.5).

6.1 (Un)attested patterns of MLM

6.1.1 A representative data sample for MLM

The definition of MLM pattern that underlies the theoretical argumentation in this book was introduced in section 1.1.3 and is repeated again in (1) for convenience.

Morphological Length and Prosodically Defective Morphemes. First edition. Eva Zimmermann.
© Eva Zimmermann 2017. First published 2017 by Oxford University Press.

Based on this definition, a data sample was conducted that arguably contains a representative list of MLM patterns attested in the languages of the world. It contains MLM patterns that are discussed in the theoretical literature on non-concatenative morphology and morpheme-specific phonology and adds various patterns that were found in an empirical search for the phenomena in descriptive grammars.

(1) *MLM pattern (see section 1.1.3, (14))*
    A set M_x of MLM operations M_1–M_n constitutes a pattern of MLM iff
    a. the choice between the operations in M_x is predictable given the phonological structure of the base, and
    b. one MLM operation in M_x is a Long-Short-Alternation (10-b-i), and
    c. no prosodic restriction on the number of syllables or segments holds for all bases that results from the application of M_1 to M_x.
    (If no such restriction holds in the rest of the language.)

In order to ensure that the sample is genetically and areally balanced, the criteria in (2) were applied that exclude languages with identical MLM patterns from the same language stock.

(2) *Language stock balance*
    A set of MLM pattern M_1 in language L_1 is only included in the sample iff there is no language L_2 in the sample such that:
    a. L_1 and L_2 are in the same language stock,
    and
    b. the set of MLM pattern M_2 in L_2 is identical to M_1 in L_1.

For illustration of this criterion recall the data from Gidabal introduced in section 1.1.1 where the final vowel of the base is lengthened to form the imperative. An identical instance of final vowel lengthening can be found in Martuthunira (Dench, 1995; Paster, 2006) where the final vowel is lengthened to mark the accusative, illustrated in (3). Both languages are from the Pama-Nyungan language stock; hence only one of the patterns (=Gidabal) is included in the sample. Note that the fact that both MLM patterns are associated with different morphological contexts is not relevant for this exclusion: as soon as the number and type(s) of MLM patterns are identical, only one language is taken into account.

(3) *Accusative in Martuthunira*   (Dench, 1995: 39)

BASE		ACC
muji	'dog'	muji:
pawulu	'child'	pawulu:
tharnta	'euro'	tharnta:

On the other hand, MLM patterns are part of the sample if they are from languages in the same language stock but the set of MLM patterns in the languages is different.

An example are the Subtraction patterns in Mebengokre (Salanova, 2004, 2007, 2011) and Canela Krahô (see section 3.2.1.2). Both languages are Macro-Ge languages spoken in North-East South America and in both languages, an instance of Subtraction can be found. Recall that in Canela Krahô, the final consonant of a verb base is subtracted to form the finite form for a verb (4-a). In Mebengokre, on the other hand, the third person is marked via non-realization of the initial consonant of the base (4-b). Although both MLM patterns are very similar and are found in the same language stock, both are included since the Subtraction instances are different in affecting different edges of their base.

(4) *Subtraction in Macro-Ge*
   a. *Finite verbs in Canela Krahô*   (Popjes and Popjes, 2010: 192, 193)

INFINITE		FINITE
ihkulan	'(so.) kills it'	ihkula
tɔn	'(so.) makes it'	tɔ
ihkahːɯl	'(so.) whips it'	ihkahːɯ
katɔl	'he arrives'	katɔ

   b. *Third person in Mebengokre*   (Salanova, 2004: 15, 16)

BASE		3.Ps	1.Ps
jamak	'ear'	amak	ijamak
ʤur	'pus'	ur	iʤur
ɲikra	'hand'	ikra	iɲikra
pɯtʌ	'to adopt'	utʌ	ipɯtʌ

The data sample conducted according to these criteria contains 100 different patterns of MLM in 62 languages. The languages represented in the sample are listed in (5), classified into language stocks, areas, and continents based on the classification in the AUTOTYP project (Bickel and Nichols, ongoing). In brackets, the ISO 639.3 code for every language is given in order to avoid confusion in cases where multiple language names exist. Especially for this latter information, the Ethnologue (Lewis et al., 2014) was consulted as well for some languages. The languages are sorted according to, *first*, their distribution on continents, *second*, their affiliation into stocks, and, *third*, alphabetically inside groups of languages belonging to the same stock spoken on the same continent. The data set contains MLM patterns from all the 7 'continents' (=continent-sized 'macro-areas' (Nichols et al., 2013)) differentiated in the AUTOTYP database and the 62 languages are distributed over 33 different language stocks. The biggest group of languages employing different patterns of MLM can be found in Africa, the smallest in New Guinea and Oceania. At this point, it should again be emphasized that the data set only contains languages with *different* MLM patterns from one stock.

(5)   *Languages with MLM in the data sample*

Language	Stock	Area	Continent
Bukusu (bxk)	Benue-Congo	S Africa	Africa
Leggbo (agb)	Benue-Congo	African Savannah	Africa
Lomongo (lol)	Benue-Congo	S Africa	Africa
Luganda (lug)	Benue-Congo	S Africa	Africa
Anywa (anu)	Nilotic	Greater Abyssinia	Africa
Dinka (din)	Nilotic	African Savannah	Africa
Lango (laj)	Nilotic	S Africa	Africa
Pulaar (fuc)	Atlantic	African Savannah	Africa
Wolof (wol)	Atlantic	African Savannah	Africa
Dhaasanac (dsh)	Cushitic	Greater Abyssinia	Africa
Oromo (hae)	Cushitic	S Africa	Africa
Mauritian Creole (mfe)	Mauritian Creole	S Africa	Africa
Asante Twi (aka)	Surmic	African Savannah	Africa
Hausa (hau)	Chadic	African Savannah	Africa
Murle (mur)	Kwa	African Savannah	Africa
Alabama (akz)	Muskogean	E North America	EN America
Choctaw (cho)	Muskogean	E North America	EN America
Creek (mus)	Muskogean	E North America	EN America
Hidatsa (hid)	Siouan	Basin and Plains	EN America
Tohono O'odham (ood)	Uto-Aztecan	Basin and Plains	EN America
Zuni (zun)	Zuni	Basin and Plains	EN America
Ojibwa (ojg)	Algic	E North America	EN America
West Greenlandic (kal)	Eskimo-Aleut	E North America	EN America
Guajiro (guc)	Arawakan	NE South America	S America
Nanti (cox)	Arawakan	Andean	S America
Yine (pie)	Arawakan	NE South America	S America
Canela Krahô (xra/ram)	Macro-Ge	NE South America	S America
Mebengokre (xra/ram)	Macro-Ge	NE South America	S America
La Paz Aymara (ayr)	Jaqui	Andean	S America
Muylaq' Aymara (ayr)	Jaqui	Andean	S America
Huallaga Quechua (qub)	Quechuan	Andean	S America
Czech (ces)	Indo-European	Europe	W & SW Eurasia
Eastern Franconian (deu)	Indo-European	Europe	W & SW Eurasia
Hessian (deu)	Indo-European	Europe	W & SW Eurasia
Kalam Kohistani (gwc)	Indo-European	Europe	W & SW Eurasia
Slovak (slk)	Indo-European	Europe	W & SW Eurasia
Arbizu Basque (eus)	Basque	Europe	W & SW Eurasia
Hungarian (hun)	Uralic	Europe	W & SW Eurasia
Modern Hebrew (heb)	Semitic	Greater Mesopotamia	W & SW Eurasia
Kwak'wala (kwk)	Wakashan	Alaska-Oregon	WN America
Nuuchahnulth (noo)	Wakashan	Alaska-Oregon	WN America
Kashaya (kju)	Pomo	California	WN America
Upriver Halkomelem (hur)	Salishan	Alaska-Oregon	WN America
Southern Sierra Miwok (skd)	Yokuts-Utian	California	WN America
Shoshone (shh)	Uto-Aztecan	Basin and Plains	WN America
Tarahumara (tar)	Uto-Aztecan	Mesoamerica	C America
Hiaki (yaq)	Uto-Aztecan	Mesoamerica	C America
Mam (mam)	Mayan	Mesoamerica	C America
Diegueño (dih)	Yuman	California	C America

Shizuoka Japanese (jpn)	Japanese	N Coast Asia	N-C Asia
Standard Japanese (jpn)	Japanese	N Coast Asia	N-C Asia
Korean (kor)	Korean	N Coast Asia	N-C Asia
North Saami (sme)	Uralic	Inner Asia	N-C Asia
Gidabal (bdy)	Pama-Nyungan	S Australia	Australia
Guugu Yimidhirr (kky)	Pama-Nyungan	N Australia	Australia
Yidiñ (yii)	Pama-Nyungan	N Australia	Australia
Lardil (lbz)	Tangkic	N Australia	Australia
Balangao (blw)	Austronesian	Oceania	S/SE Asia
Keley-i (ifb)	Austronesian	Oceania	S/SE Asia
Hindi (hin)	Indo-European	Indic	S/SE Asia
Tawala (two)	Austronesian	S New Guinea	NG and Oceania
Marshallese (mah)	Austronesian	Oceania	NG and Oceania

A first interesting empirical fact about the data set is the attested instances of different MLM patterns in a single language. In section 3.2.2 (especially 3.2.2.1), it was argued that such a coexistence of MLM is a strong argument for the present PDM approach and shows that the analyses for subtractive MLM in Trommer and Zimmermann (2014) only capture a subset of the attested patterns. Table (6) lists all languages together with the information about which of the general MLM patterns of Addition (=A), Subtraction (=S), Additive Affixation (=AA), and Subtractive Affixation (=SA) they employ. Length polarity in Anywa (see section 3.2.1.4) receives a special marking with a '*' for Subtraction and Addition, even though, this pattern does not perfectly fit into this classification. A superscript '2' marks instances where two different MLM patterns of this type exist in the language (either lexical allomorphs or different morphemes). An example is Keley-i where one Addition pattern results in gemination of the initial consonant and another Addition pattern marking another morphological category results in gemination of the consonant after the first vowel. In 38 languages, only one MLM type is attested and in 24, more than one could be found.

(6) *Coexistence of different MLM patterns*

Language	A	AA	S	SA	Stock	Area
Luganda (lug)	✓				Benue-Congo	Africa
Asante Twi (aka)	✓				Surmic	Africa
Creek (mus)	✓				Muskogean	EN America
Ojibwa (ojg)	✓				Algic	EN America
Shoshone (shh)	✓				Uto-Aztecan	WN America
Upriver Halkomelem (hur)	✓				Salishan	WN America
Shizuoka Japanese (jpn)	✓				Japanese	N-C Asia
North Saami (sme)	✓				Uralic	N-C Asia
Tawala (two)	✓				Austronesian	NG and Oceania
Marshallese (mah)	✓²				Austronesian	NG and Oceania
Guajiro (guc)	✓				Arawakan	S America
Kalam Kohistani (gwc)	✓				Indo-European	W & SW Eurasia
Hiaki (yaq)	✓				Uto-Aztecan	C America
Keley-i (ifb)	✓²				Austronesian	S/SE Asia

Continued

Language						Genus	Area
Bukusu (bxk)		✓				Benue-Congo	Africa
Leggbo (agb)		✓				Benue-Congo	Africa
Pulaar (fuc)		✓				Atlantic	Africa
West Greenlandic (kal)		✓				Eskimo-Aleut	EN America
Czech (ces)		✓				Indo-European	W & SW Eurasia
Kwak'wala (kwk)		✓				Wakashan	WN America
Tarahumara (tar)		✓				Uto-Aztecan	C America
Standard Japanese (jpn)		✓				Japanese	N-C Asia
Yidiñ (yii)		✓				Pama-Nyungan	Australia
Balangao (blw)		✓				Austronesian	S/SE Asia
Lomongo (lol)			✓			Benue-Congo	Africa
Mauritian Creole (mfe)			✓			Mauritian Creole	Africa
Murle (mur)			✓²			Kwa	Africa
Nanti (cox)			✓			Arawakan	S America
Canela Krahô (xra/ram)			✓			Macro-Ge	S America
Mebengokre (xra/ram)			✓			Macro-Ge	S America
Eastern Franconian (deu)			✓			Indo-European	W and SW Eurasia
Hessian (deu)			✓			Indo-European	W and SW Eurasia
Modern Hebrew (heb)			✓			Semitic	W and SW Eurasia
Hidatsa (hid)			✓			Siouan	EN America
Hindi (hin)			✓			Indo-European	S/SE Asia
Yine (pie)				✓		Arawakan	S America
Hungarian (hun)					✓	Uralic	W and SW Eurasia
Mam (mam)					✓	Mayan	C America
Lango (laj)	✓	✓				Nilotic	Africa
Dhaasanac (dsh)	✓	✓				Cushitic	Africa
Zuni (zun)	✓	✓				Zuni	EN America
Arbizu Basque (eus)	✓	✓				Basque	W and SW Eurasia
Southern Sierra Miwok (skd)	✓	✓				Yokuts-Utian	WN America
Gidabal (bdy)	✓	✓				Pama-Nyungan	Australia
Alabama (akz)	✓			✓²		Muskogean	EN America
Choctaw (cho)	✓²		✓			Muskogean	EN America
Tohono O'odham (ood)	✓		✓			Uto-Aztecan	EN America
Dinka (din)	✓		✓			Nilotic	Africa
Diegueño (dih)	✓		✓			Yuman	C America
Lardil (lbz)	✓		✓			Tangkic	Australia
Korean (kor)	✓				✓	Korean	N-C Asia
Wolof (wol)		✓			✓	Atlantic	Africa
Muylaq' Aymara (ayr)				✓	✓	Jaqui	S America
Kashaya (kju)				✓	✓	Pomo	WN America
Oromo (hae)	✓²	✓			✓	Cushitic	Africa
Hausa (hau)	✓	✓	✓			Chadic	Africa
Anywa (anu)		*	✓*			Nilotic	Africa
Huallaga Quechua (qub)	✓	✓			✓	Quechuan	S America
Slovak (slk)	✓	✓			✓	Indo-European	W and SW Eurasia
Nuuchahnulth (noo)	✓	✓			✓	Wakashan	WN America
Guugu Yimidhirr (kky)	✓	✓			✓	Pama-Nyungan	Australia
La Paz Aymara (ayr)	✓	✓		✓	✓	Jaqui	S America

How the 100 MLM patterns are distributed over the four empirical categories: Addition, Subtraction, Additive Affixes, and Subtractive Affixes is listed in more detail in (7). The only pattern that cannot be classified according to this four-fold typology is length polarity in Anywa, discussed in section 3.2.1.4. In this representative sample, additive MLM is hence far more frequent than subtractive MLM. This simple fact is not entirely surprising given the fact that subtractive MLM is the one challenge to the insight that morphology is always additive in the sense that it adds surface material or structure. Inside the PDM account, subtractive MLM indeed follows from affixation of phonological elements that results in a marked defective prosodic integration. As is briefly discussed in section 3.3, these structures are hence more abstract and more complex to learn.

(7) *Number of MLM patterns*

	Addition	Subtraction	
	38	24	
	+ Polarity: 1		
	Additive Affixes	Subtractive Affixes	
	24	13	
Total:	62 (+1)	37	100

6.1.2 Additive MLM patterns: empirical generalizations

The table in (8) gives a first overview over the languages with additive MLM in the data set. They are sorted according to the different MLM operations of lengthening or insertion for consonants or vowels. In total, there are 62 patterns of additive MLM: 38 instances of Addition and 24 instances of Additive Affixation. These patterns are distributed over 45 different languages. Four languages in the sample employ different additive MLM patterns, namely Keley-i, Marshallese, Choctaw, and Oromo.

(8) *Additive MLM patterns*

	A	AA			
I. Long-Short-Alternation: Vowels					
Creek (mus)	✓		Muskogean	E North America	EN America
Ojibwa (ojg)	✓		Algic	E North America	EN America
Hiaki (yaq)	✓		Uto-Aztecan	Mesoamerica	C America
Diegueño (dih)	✓		Yuman	California	C America
Dinka (din)	✓		Nilotic	African Savannah	Africa
Kalam Kohistani (gwc)	✓		Indo-European	Europe	W & SW Eurasia
Gidabal (bdy)	✓	✓	Pama-Nyungan	S Australia	Australia
Guugu Yimidhirr (kky)	✓	✓	Pama-Nyungan	N Australia	Australia
Hausa (hau)	✓	✓	Chadic	African Savannah	Africa

	A	AA			
I. Long-Short-Alternation: Vowels					
Zuni (zun)	✓	✓	Zuni	Basin and Plains	EN America
La Paz Aymara (ayr)	✓	✓	Jaqui	Andean	S America
Slovak (slk)	✓	✓	Indo-European	Europe	W & SW Eurasia
Nuuchahnulth (noo)	✓	✓	Wakashan	Alaska-Oregon	WN America
Bukusu (bxk)		✓	Benue-Congo	S Africa	Africa
Tarahumara (tar)		✓	Uto-Aztecan	Mesoamerica	C America
Yidiñ (yii)		✓	Pama-Nyungan	N Australia	Australia
II. Long-Short-Alternation: Consonants					
North Saami (sme)	✓		Uralic	Inner Asia	N-C Asia
Korean (kor)	✓		Korean	N Coast Asia	N-C Asia
Tohono O'odham (ood)	✓		Uto-Aztecan	Basin and Plains	EN America
Shoshone (shh)	✓		Uto-Aztecan	Basin and Plains	WN America
Keley-i (ifb)	✓^{2}		Austronesian	Oceania	S/SE Asia
Marshallese (mah)	✓^{2}		Austronesian	Oceania	NG and Oceania
Dhaasanac (dsh)	✓	✓	Cushitic	Greater Abyssinia	Africa
Leggbo (agb)		✓	Benue-Congo	African Savannah	Africa
Pulaar (fuc)		✓	Atlantic	African Savannah	Africa
Wolof (wol)		✓	Atlantic	African Savannah	Africa
West Greenlandic (kal)		✓	Eskimo-Aleut	E North America	EN America
III. Long-Short-Alternations: Vowels & Consonants					
Asante Twi (aka)	✓		Surmic	African Savannah	Africa
Alabama (akz)	✓		Muskogean	E North America	EN America
IV. Long-Short-Alternation & Segment-Zero-Alternation					
Luganda (lug)	✓		Benue-Congo	S Africa	Africa
U. Halkomelem (hur)	✓		Salishan	Alaska-Oregon	WN America
Choctaw (cho)	✓^{2}		Muskogean	E North America	EN America
Guajiro (guc)	✓		Arawakan	NE South America	S America
Shizuoka Japanese (jpn)	✓		Japanese	N Coast Asia	N-C Asia
Lardil (lbz)	✓		Tangkic	N Australia	Australia
Tawala (two)	✓		Austronesian	S New Guinea	NG and Oceania
Lango (laj)	✓	✓	Nilotic	S Africa	Africa
Oromo (hae)	✓^{2}	✓	Cushitic	S Africa	Africa
S. Sierra Miwok (skd)	✓	✓	Yokuts-Utian	California	WN America
H. Quechua (qub)	✓	✓	Quechuan	Andean	S America
Arbizu Basque (eus)	✓	✓	Basque	Europe	W & SW Eurasia
Czech (ces)		✓	Indo-European	Europe	W & SW Eurasia
Kwak'wala (kwk)		✓	Wakashan	Alaska-Oregon	WN America
Standard Japanese (jpn)		✓	Japanese	N Coast Asia	N-C Asia
Balangao (blw)		✓	Austronesian	Oceania	S/SE Asia

The empirical generalizations that are of particular interest in the present discussion are the base positions affected by MLM operations. Or put differently: the question of how (non)local MLM patterns are. The table (9) summarizes all Addition patterns in the sample according to the base position they affect. In the headline, the possible base positions affected by MLM operations are given in form of abstract C and V segmental positions. A ⟦ː⟧ in a line of the table symbolizes segmental lengthening of the respective sound in this column whereas a ⟦x⟧ indicates that epenthetic or reduplicated segments are inserted. Symbols that are connected with a line indicate instances where multiple MLM operations apply in one context. An example is Balangao where initial reduplication and gemination cooccur (see section 6.2.4.3). Symbols in the same line that are not connected are thus instances of phonologically predictable allomorphy that are in complementary distribution. A superscript [All] denotes that additional phonologically predictable allomorphs that are not length-manipulating exist for this morpheme. This is only the case for Upriver Halkomelem that was analysed in section 5.3.1.[1] The 'A' simply indicates that this summarizes the Addition patterns in order to avoid confusion with the following tables. Roman numbers indicate different MLM morphemes/lexical allomorphs in one language.

(9) *Affected base position: Addition*

Language	#C	V	C	...	V	C	V	C#
Oromo AI	⟦CV⟧⎯⎯	⟦ː⟧						
Luganda A	⟦ı̄⟧	⟦ː⟧						
Tawala A	⟦CV(CV)/VC⟧	⟦ː⟧						
U. Halk.[All] A	⟦hɛ/CV⟧	⟦ː⟧						
Korean A		⟦ː⟧						
Marshallese AI		⟦ː⟧						
Keley-i AI		⟦ː⟧						
Marshallese AII		⟦ː⟧⎯⎯⎯⎯⎯⎯⎯⎯⎯⎯⎯⎯⎯⎯⎯						⟦CVC⟧
Ojibwa A		⟦ː⟧						
Sh. Japanese A		⟦ː⟧	⟦N⟧	⟦ː⟧				
Hiaki A		⟦ː⟧	⟦ː⟧					
Keley-i AII			⟦ː⟧					
T. O'odham A			⟦ː⟧					
Alabama A					⟦ː⟧	⟦ː⟧		
Dhaasanac A						⟦ː⟧		
North Saami A						⟦ː⟧		

---

[1] And probably for North Saami where consonant gradation results in gemination for consonants but also, for example, preaspiration. See Bals Baal et al. (2012) for an insightful analysis of this complex pattern and that it indeed can follow from associating a consonant with an additional mora.

Language						
Choctaw AI			◌——◌			
Choctaw AII			vjː—◌			
Oromo AII			◌			
Creek A			◌			
G. Yimidhirr A			◌			
Ar. Basque A			◌			
Kalam Kohistani A			◌			
Gidabal A			◌			
Zuni A			◌			
Hausa A			◌			
Diegueño A			◌			
Slovak A			◌			
Asante Twi A			◌	◌		
Lango A			◌	◌	j	
LP Aymara A			◌		jaː	
Guajiro A			◌		waː	
H. Quechua A			◌		niː	
SSM A			◌		iː	
Lardil A			◌		ji	
Dinka A	VL for monosyllables					
Nuuchahnulth A	VL for monosyllables					
Shoshone A	Gem. of intervocalic C in bisyllabic words					

In the following table (10), all instances of Additive Affixation (=AA) are summarized in the same way. The only additional symbols are → and ← marking the position of the segmental part of the Additive Affix.

(10)   *Affected base position: Additive Affixes*

Language	#(C)	V	C	...	C	V	(C)#
Balangao AA	CV——————◌						←
Bukusu AA	→	◌					
Nuuchahnulth AA		◌					←
W. Greenl. AA			◌				←
Yidiñ AA						◌	←
Tarahumara AA						◌	←
Guugu Yimidhirr AA						◌	←
Gidabal AA						◌	←
Zuni AA						◌	←

H. Quechua AA			□		←
Slovak AA			□		←
LP Aymara AA			□		←
Hausa AA			□		←
Oromo AA			□	□	←
Lango AA			□	□	←
SSM AA			□	□	[iː] ←
Czech AA			□		[iː] ←
Ar. Basque AA			□		[e] ←
Kwak'wala AA			□		[CV] ←
Wolof AA				□	←
Dhaasanac AA				□	←
Pulaar AA				□	←
Leggbo AA	monosyllabic: Gem. of initial and final C				←
St. Japanese AA	bisyllabic: Gem. of intervocalic C/[ŋ] after first V				←

Nuuchahnulth is the only example of an Additive Affix where realization of the segmental affix and the MLM effect are found on different base edges. In the PDM account, this is analysed as a straightforward instance of circumfixation: the segmental portion is an exponent that is suffixed to its base and the morphemic prosodic node (=mora) triggering initial vowel lengthening is an exponent that is prefixed. A first generalization that can be drawn from the tables in (9) and (10) is that additive MLM affects the right edge of the base far more frequently than the left edge, 12 Addition patterns affecting the left edge of the base are part of the sample and 22 that affect the right edge. For Additive Affixation, the picture is even more clear since only 3 patterns affect the left edge but 19 the right edge. Four Addition and two Additive Affixation patterns cannot be unambiguously classified as affecting the right or left base edge since the affected base position is either equi-distant from both base edges or because both edges are affected (in Marshallese Addition). These tendencies are summarized in the table in (11).

(11) *Right vs. left edge of the base: additive MLM*

	Affected base edge:			
	Left	Right	ambiguous/both	Total
Addition:	12	22	4	38
Additive Affixation:	3	19	2	24

If we take it for granted that all MLM is the result of affixation, this preference is straightforwardly expected given the general prevalence of segmental suffixes over segmental prefixes (Greenberg, 1963; Hawkins and Gilligan, 1988). This predominance of MLM affecting the right edge of their base is hence a straightforward consequence from maintaining the concatenativist hypothesis that all morphology is additive. Under the alternative accounts discussed in chapter 7, this preference for the right edge remains a mere coincidence. With respect to the linearization of MLM effects, the first rough generalization is a strong edge bias: no MLM at the left edge of its base targets a position further inside its base than the first coda position and no MLM effect at the right edge affects a position further inside its base than the penultimate vowel. In the vast majority of cases, the first or last vowel is affected by an additive MLM operation. A second important observation is that the different allomorphs in patterns of phonologically predictable allomorphy involving MLM always affect adjacent positions in their base. In (10), for example, the phonologically predictable allomorphy in Oromo and Lango Additive Affixation affects either the final vowel or the final consonant. And allomorphy triggered by Additive Affixes in Czech, Arbizu Basque, Kwak'wala affects either the final vowel or the position after all base segments.

6.1.3 Subtractive MLM patterns: empirical generalizations

There are significantly fewer instances of subtractive MLM in the data set than additive MLM. In total, 37 different patterns of subtractive MLM were included, 24 of these patterns are instances of Subtraction and 13 are instances of Subtractive Affixation. These subtractive MLM patterns are distributed over 32 languages. A brief overview of all subtractive MLM patterns in the sample is again given in (12) where they are sorted according to whether they are instances of deletion (12-I), shortening (12-II), or an alternation between the two (12-III).

(12)   *Subtractive MLM patterns*

	S	SS			
I. Segment Deletion					
Choctaw (cho)	✓		Muskogean	E North America	EN America
Alabama (akz)	✓²		Muskogean	E North America	EN America
Tohono O'odham (ood)	✓		Uto-Aztecan	Basin and Plains	EN America
Mebengokre S (xra/ram)	✓		Macro-Ge	NE South America	S America
Canela Krahô (xra/ram)	✓		Macro-Ge	NE South America	S America
Nanti (cox)	✓		Arawakan	Andean	S America
Mauritian Creole (mfe)	✓		Mauritian Creole	S Africa	Africa
Murle (mur)	✓²		Kwa	African Savannah	Africa
Modern Hebrew (heb)	✓		Semitic	Greater Mesopotamia	W & S Eurasia
Hessian (deu)	✓		Indo-European	Europe	W & S Eurasia
Lardil (lbz)	✓		Tangkic	N Australia	Australia
Muylaq' Aymara (ayr)	✓	✓	Jaqui	Andean	S America
Yine (pie)		✓	Arawakan	NE South America	S America

II. Segment Shortening

Hausa (hau)	✓	Chadic	African Savannah	Africa
Dinka (din)	✓	Nilotic	African Savannah	Africa
Anywa (anu)	✓	Nilotic	Greater Abyssinia	Africa
E. Franconian (deu)	✓	Indo-European	Europe	W & SW Eurasia
Dieguéño (dih)	✓	Yuman	California	C America
Hindi (hin)	✓	Indo-European	Indic	S/SE Asia
Kashaya (kju)	✓ ✓	Pomo	California	WN America
Oromo (hae)	✓	Cushitic	S Africa	Africa
Wolof (wol)	✓	Atlantic	African Savannah	Africa
H. Quechua (qub)	✓	Quechuan	Andean	S America
Slovak (slk)	✓	Indo-European	Europe	W & SW Eurasia
Nuuchahnulth (noo)	✓	Wakashan	Alaska-Oregon	WN America
Guugu Yimidhirr (kky)	✓	Pama-Nyungan	N Australia	Australia
Mam (mam)	✓	Mayan	Mesoamerica	C America
Korean (kor)	✓	Korean	N Coast Asia	N-C Asia

III. Alternation between segment shortening and deletion

Lomongo (lol)	✓	Benue-Congo	S Africa	Africa
Hidatsa (hid)	✓	Siouan	Basin and Plains	EN America
La Paz Aymara (ayr)	✓ ✓	Jaqui	Andean	S America
Hungarian (hun)	✓	Uralic	Europe	W & SW Eurasia

Many of these patterns were discussed and analysed in detail above. That these analyses were indeed representative for the attested base positions affected by MLM can be seen in (13). Parallel to (9) and (10), all subtractive MLM patterns are summarized with respect to the affected base position: ● marks deletion of (a) segment(s) and ⋮ shortening of a segment. Since fewer subtractive MLM patterns are attested, all instances are summarized into a single table. Subtractive Affixation (=SA) can easily be distinguished from Subtraction (=S) below since the former has a ⟵ symbol marking the position of the segmental part of the Subtractive Affix. Interestingly enough, I have not encountered a convincing instance of Subtractive Prefixation.

(13) *Affected base position: Subtraction and Subtractive Affixation*

language	#(C)	V	C	...	C	V	(C)#
Mebengokre S	●						
Modern Hebrew S		●					
Nanti S		●					
Hindi S						⋮	
Dieguéño S						⋮	

Hausa S		ⅰ		
Kashaya S		ⅰ		
Kashaya SA		ⅰ		←
Slovak SA		ⅰ		←
Guugu Yimidhirr SA		ⅰ		←
Oromo SA		ⅰ		←
H. Quechua SA		ⅰ		←
Mauritian Creole S		●		
Lardil S		●		
M Aymara S		●		
M Aymara SA		●		←
Yine SA		●		←
LP Aymara S		●		
LP Aymara SA		● ⅰ		←
Lomongo S		● ⅰ		
Hidatsa S		● ⅰ		
Hungarian SA		● ⅰ		←
Korean SA		ⅰ	ⅰ	←
Alabama SI		●		
Choctaw S		●		
Murle SII		● :	●	
Wolof SA			ⅰ	←
Murle SI			●	
Canela Krahô S			●	
Hessian S			●	
Alabama SII			●	
Tohono O'odham S			●	
Dinka S	monosyllables: V ⅰ			
Anywa S	monosyllables: V ⅰ			
Eastern Franconian S	monosyllables: V ⅰ			
Nuuchahnulth SA	monosyllables: V ⅰ			←
Mam SA	monosyllables: V ⅰ			←

That MLM pattern affecting the right edge of the base are more frequent than those affecting the left base edge is even more apparent than it was for additive MLM in (9) and (10). Only 3 patterns unambiguously affect the left edge whereas 29 affect the right edge. In 5 subtractive MLM patterns, the affected base is always monosyllabic or bisyllabic and the locus of the MLM is equi-distant to both base edges. These numbers are summarized in table (14).

(14)   *Right vs. left edge of the base: subtractive MLM*

	Affected base edge:			
	Left	**Right**	ambiguous/both	Total
Subtraction:	3	18	3	24
Subtractive Affixation:	–	11	2	13

And the bias for affecting edge segments is stronger for subtractive MLM as well: no segment further inside its base than the first or last vowel is ever affected by a subtractive MLM pattern.

6.2 Linearization of affixes: possible patterns of MLM

In sections 6.1.2 and 6.1.3, it was shown that the empirical patterns of MLM are restricted in that there are far more patterns affecting the right than the left edge and that there is a strong bias for affecting edge positions of the base. The first generalization trivially follows from assuming that all MLM is the result of affixation: then this strong tendency simply conforms to the general prevalence of suffixes over prefixes. That the second generalization falls out in the present framework of PDM is intuitively clear as well: in section 2.2.6, a severely restricted theory of morpheme linearization was assumed. This, together with the assumption of containment where reordering is impossible, restricts the phonological effect of affixes necessarily to only a limited set of possible base positions. That these restricted positions are indeed sufficient to predict all attested MLM patterns is shown in this section. It basically summarizes all the analyses assumed inside PDM for the various MLM instances.

6.2.1 Additive MLM at the base edge

By far the most common MLM pattern in the data set is final vowel lengthening. As long as a putative final consonant is not moraic in a language, association of a morphemic mora to a final base vowel will never result in a configuration that is problematic for the RMO since the morphemic mora never precedes another mora that reflects the morphemic affiliation of its base. And in the majority of morphological vowel lengthening, this final vowel is indeed the absolute final segment of its base and not followed by a consonant. In cases where the final vowel can be followed by a consonant, those consonants are never moraic (e.g. in Slovak or Guugu Yimidhirr).

The straightforward mirror image to final vowel lengthening is lengthening of an initial base vowel. In the absence of an initial moraic (geminate) consonant, the initial base vowel is a position that can also easily be targeted by a morphemic mora without a colour index. (15) lists all the MLM patterns that are analysed as those straightforward instances where a morphemic mora associates to the edgemost vowel, potentially across a non-moraic consonant.[2] In all the summarizing abstract depictions below, the morphemic colours reflected by the relevant prosodic nodes are given as well in order to prove yet again that they are all in conformity with the ℝ𝕄𝕆.

(15)   *Morphemic moras without a colour index: vowel lengthening*

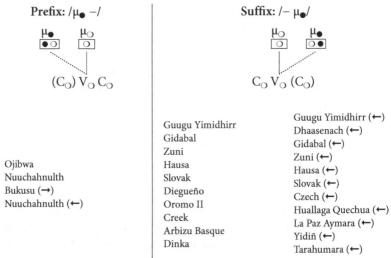

	Guugu Yimidhirr	Guugu Yimidhirr (←)
	Gidabal	Dhaasenach (←)
	Zuni	Gidabal (←)
Ojibwa	Hausa	Zuni (←)
Nuuchahnulth	Slovak	Hausa (←)
Bukusu (→)	Diegueño	Slovak (←)
Nuuchahnulth (←)	Oromo II	Czech (←)
	Creek	Huallaga Quechua (←)
	Arbizu Basque	La Paz Aymara (←)
	Dinka	Yidiñ (←)
		Tarahumara (←)

Another straightforwardly expected pattern is morphemic moras that associate to the initial or final consonant of its base resulting in gemination (16). Since those moras are associated to the edgemost segment of their base, they trivially conform to the ℝ𝕄𝕆.

(16)   *Morphemic moras without a colour index: gemination*

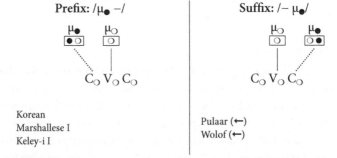

Korean	
Marshallese I	Pulaar (←)
Keley-i I	Wolof (←)

A combination of these two patterns is attested as well: a suffixed mora associates to either the final consonant or a final vowel in Asante Two, Oromo, and Lango (17). Both

---

[2] In the following depictions, all underlying vowels are equipped with moras. It was extensively discussed in section 5.2 that the PDM framework developed here can predict 'all-vowel-lengthening' languages where even underlyingly mora-less vowels become long in the context of a morphemic mora.

of these phonologically predictable strategies are summarized in one depiction in (17) but it should be clear that they are in complementary distribution.

(17)   *Morphemic moras without a colour index: vowel lengthening or gemination*

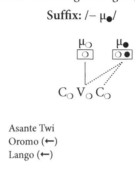

Asante Twi
Oromo (←)
Lango (←)

Another quite common pattern of additive MLM is an alternation between vowel lengthening and realization of (a) copied or epenthetic segment(s) preceding or following all base material. In terms of affix ordering, these patterns are not different from the simple vowel lengthening since the additional segmental material bears no morphological affiliation of its own.

(18)   *Morphemic moras without a colour index: vowel lengthening or insertion*

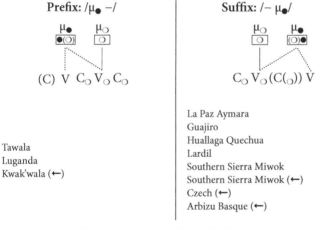

Tawala
Luganda
Kwak'wala (←)

La Paz Aymara
Guajiro
Huallaga Quechua
Lardil
Southern Sierra Miwok
Southern Sierra Miwok (←)
Czech (←)
Arbizu Basque (←)

Addition in Lango, finally, is taken to combine all these patterns: vowel lengthening, gemination, and insertion alternate predictably (19).

(19) *Morphemic moras without a colour index: vowel lengthening, gemination, or insertion*

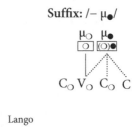

Lango

Another instance of a morphemic prosodic node without a colour index was the morphemic foot in the analysis for Upriver Halkomelem (section 5.3.1, similarly for Rotuman in section 5.3.2).

6.2.2 *Subtractive MLM at the base edge*

Inside the PDM framework, there are two basic mechanisms predicting subtractive MLM: mora usurpation and defective integration of morphemic prosodic nodes. For mora usurpation, it was already argued in section 3.1 that the possible MLM effects predicted by this mechanism are strictly adjacent to the base edge to which the Subtractive Affix attaches. Only the final mora dominating base material can be usurped (20). All other mora usurpation patterns are excluded either by the NₒCr or RMO. This point is taken up again in section 6.2.5 below. Note that in Hungarian, vowel shortening and deletion alternate predictably (see section 3.1.4) and the language is hence mentioned in two columns.

(20) *Lack of underlying moras: mora usurpation*

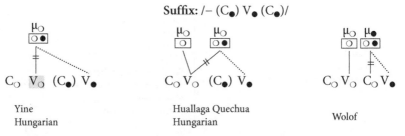

For the rest of the subtractive MLM patterns in (13), it is argued that they all result from affixing a morphemic mora or syllable that is defectively integrated. The following tables summarize the landing sites for morphemic moras and syllables that result in all remaining attested subtractive MLM patterns. The first and somewhat special case is morphemic moras that do not dominate base material but are only integrated under a syllable. It was argued in section 3.2.1.3 that this can result in shortening.

(21) *Morphemic moras without a colour index: vowel shortening*

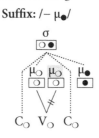

Eastern Franconian
Anywa
Mam (←)

Note that the length polarity in Anywa is absent from this list since it is neither additive nor subtractive MLM in the strict sense. The intriguing analysis given in Trommer (2011a) for Anywa in terms of mora -affixation was sketched in section 3.2.1.4.

For instances where a defectively integrated morphemic mora associates to a base segment but lacks an integration into a higher prosodic node, the options that were discussed in section 6.2.1 for additive MLM are in fact mirrored here: the mora can associate either to the absolute base-final or -initial consonant (22) or to the first or final vowel (23). The only difference is that the dominated segment is not lengthened but deleted. Tables (22) and (23) summarize this.

(22) *Morphemic moras without a colour index: consonant deletion*

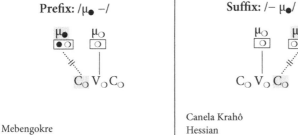

Mebengokre

Canela Krahô
Hessian
Murle I

(23) *Morphemic moras without a colour index: vowel deletion*

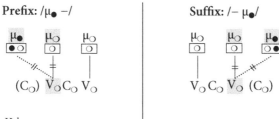

Modern Hebrew
Nanti

Mauritian Creole

All remaining subtractive MLM patterns are taken to result from the defective integration of morphemic syllables without a colour index. The crucial restriction in terms of linearization is that such morphemic syllables can never associate to elements across other elements that are dominated by another syllable node. This excludes, for example, deletion of a final vowel if a moraic coda consonant follows. Only association to a base-final consonantal mora ((25) and (27)) or to a vocalic mora across a non-moraic consonant ((24) to (27)) is possible. How this accounts for the different subtractive operations of shortening and deletion is summarized in the following tables (24) to (27), summarizing the detailed discussion in section 3.2.2. Note that the majority of instances below are suffixed morphemic syllables.

(24) *Morphemic syllables without a colour index: vowel shortening*

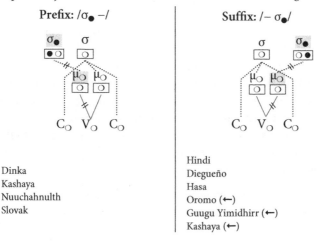

Prefix: /σ• −/   Suffix: /− σ•/

Dinka
Kashaya
Nuuchahnulth
Slovak

Hindi
Diegueño
Hasa
Oromo (←)
Guugu Yimidhirr (←)
Kashaya (←)

(25) *Morphemic syllables without a colour index: deletion*

Suffix: /− σ•/

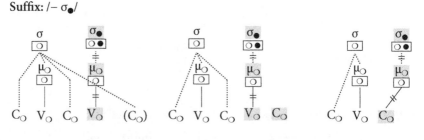

Lardil
Muylaq' Aymara
Muylaq' Aymara (←)

Choctaw
Alabama I
Tohono O'odham

Alabama II
Tohono O'odham

(26) *Morphemic syllables without a colour index: vowel shortening or deletion*

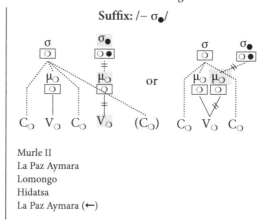

Murle II
La Paz Aymara
Lomongo
Hidatsa
La Paz Aymara (←)

(27) *Morphemic syllables without a colour index: vowel or consonant shortening*

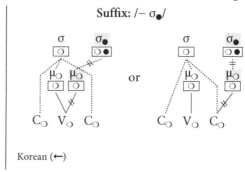

Korean (←)

This concludes the summary of PDM analyses for subtractive MLM: all patterns follow from affixation of morphemic prosodic nodes or underlyingly prosodically defective segmental affixes without a colour index.

6.2.3 'Infixing' additive MLM patterns

Only a few additive MLM patterns remain that do not follow from adding morphemic prosodic nodes without a colour index. The existence of a colour index in a morpheme representation effectively implements infixation MLM patterns. Only 11 patterns of additive MLM that are part of the data set are of this type. The relative rarity of infixation in comparison to suffixation and prefixation MLM is absolutely parallel to the relative rarity of segmental infixation (Yu, 2007). Under the present account, this asymmetry is straightforwardly explained by the relative representational complexity: 'infixing' morphemic prosodic nodes contain an additional colour index.

The depictions in (28) show an infixing morphemic mora that results in gemination of the second or final onset consonant of its base. The additional colour index that follows a suffixing morphemic mora and precedes a prefixing morphemic mora is fused with an underlying mora at the base edge in these structures.

(28)   *Morphemic syllables with a colour index: gemination*

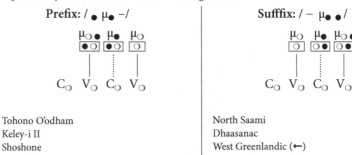

Tohono O'odham	North Saami
Keley-i II	Dhaasanac
Shoshone	West Greenlandic (←)

The table (29) summarizes four patterns of phonologically predictable alternation between different MLM patterns that result from affixing a morphemic mora with a colour index. This 'infixed' mora can associate to either the second or penultimate vowel, the first coda or last onset consonant, or trigger insertion of segments between these positions. The table summarizes these allomorphy patterns although not all of the languages listed below employ all these strategies: in Hiaki, vowel lengthening and insertion alternate; in Shizuoka Japanese, vowel lengthening, gemination, and insertion; in Standard Japanese, gemination and insertion; and in Asante Twi, gemination and vowel lengthening.

(29)   *Morphemic syllables with a colour index: gemination, vowel lengthening, or insertion*

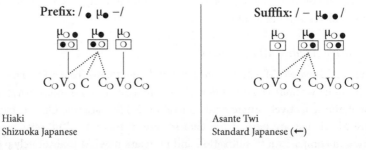

| Hiaki | Asante Twi |
| Shizuoka Japanese | Standard Japanese (←) |

A pattern that deserves special attention when discussing non-edge MLM effects is Addition in Alabama (see the discussion of Subtraction in Alabama in sections 3.2.2.2 and 4.3). The imperfect is formed by gemination of the penultimate onset consonant if the antepenult syllable is open (30-a) or by lengthening of the penultimate vowel if the antepenult syllable is closed or the word is bisyllabic (30-b).

(30) *Addition in Alabama*   (Hardy and Montler, 1988a: 400ff)

Base	Imperfect	

a. *Gemination*

balaːka	bálːaːka	'lie down'
cokoːli	cókːoːli	'sit down'
ilkowatli	ilkówːatli	'move'
atakaːli	atakːaːli	'hang one object'
afinapli	afinːapli	'lock up'

b. *Vowel lengthening*

hofna	hóːfna	'smell'
isko	íːsko	'drink'
isi	íːsi	'take, catch'
coba	cóːba	'big'
ibakpila	ibakpíːla	'turn upside down'

There are several theoretical accounts claiming that this gemination is due to mora affixation (Samek-Lodovici, 1992; Lombardi and McCarthy, 1991; Grimes, 2002) and indeed such an analysis is pursued here, too. The interesting fact about the Addition in Alabama is its apparent non-local nature. It affects the penultimate vowel that is potentially followed by two moras dominating base material and the penult onset consonant that can be followed by up to three moras dominating base material. How this pattern is predicted under the assumption of a single morphemic mora followed by a colour index is shown in the depictions in (31). The morphemic mora with a colour index is realized before the final mora dominating base material. The unmarked strategy to realize this mora is association to a consonant and hence gemination. Gemination, however, is taken to be impossible for the final onset since the final syllable is extrametrical (Samek-Lodovici, 1992; Lombardi and McCarthy, 1991) and vowel lengthening hence surfaces in (31-a). And if the segment the morphemic mora associates to already is associated to the maximal amount of moras, reassociation of a mora to a preceding segment might become optimal. In (31-b), one mora of an underlyingly long vowel is reassociated to a preceding consonant and in (31-c), the mora that dominates a coda consonant.[3] And in (31-d), finally, the preference for realizing additional syllabic weight as geminate, not as long vowel is the sole trigger for the reassociation of a mora.

---

[3] Note that this mora dominating the vowel must not be underlyingly present—in the present containment-based system where parsing constraints refer to invisible structure as well, the demand for morph-contiguous mora projection for every vowel ensures that the vowel cannot only be dominated by the morphemic mora.

(31)   *Addition in Alabama*
a. *V-lengthening* b. *V-lengthening* c. *Gemination*   d. *Gemination*

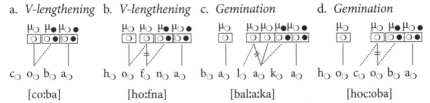

Crucially, none of these configurations is not excluded by the NKK (see section 2.2.2, (31)) given that the consonant to which the underlying vocalic mora (re)associates is a different element than the vowel. Kicking is only excluded between the same elements on a tier. This implies that the phonology makes a crucial difference between vowels and consonant—something that was already implicit in many preceding constraint types like, for example , PVis$_V$ and PVis$_C$.

6.2.4 *Multiple morphemic prosodic nodes*

The definitions of exponent and morpheme given in section 2.2.6, repeated in (32), allows that a morpheme may contain more than one morphemic prosodic node: either they are different exponents being specified for different edges of their base (one is a prefix, the other a suffix), or one prefixing or suffixing exponent contains more than one morphemic prosodic node. In the former case, the morphemic nodes have different morphological colours (see (32-b)). That MLM patterns predicted from all these different possibilities are indeed attested is discussed in this section with four case studies.

(32)   a. *Morpheme*
        A meaning paired with a set S of n exponents where different members of
        S are either
        (i)   marked for different lexical classes
        or
        (ii)   marked for different base edges (prefix or suffix).
    b. *Exponent*
        A set S of phonological elements p$_a$, p$_b$,...,p$_x$ that all share the same
        morphological colour and where all pairs p$_a$ and p$_b$ (in S) on the same tier
        are ordered to each other.

The analysis for additive MLM in Choctaw presented in section 5.3.3 was already an example for morphemes consisting of more than one morphemic node. The intensive morpheme was assumed to consist of two lexical allomorphs: one consisting of a suffixed morphemic mora and a morphemic foot, the other of a suffixed morphemic mora, a morphemic syllable, and a morphemic foot. This section adds a discussion of Leggbo 6.2.4.1, Oromo 6.2.4.2, Balangao 6.2.4.3, and Marshallese 6.2.4.4 to show that different patterns expected from the existence of multiple morphemic prosodic nodes are indeed attested in the languages of the world.

6.2.4.1 Double lengthening in Leggbo The first instance of an MLM pattern that results from assuming multiple morphemic nodes as representation for a morpheme comes from Leggbo, a minority language of the Upper Cross subgroup, spoken in the Cross River State of Nigeria by about 60,000 people (Udoh, 2004; Hyman, 2009). The language exhibits length contrasts for vowels and consonants and initial geminates. Verb bases in Leggbo are all monosyllabic and there are two strategies to form progressive verbs. The more common one, found for 80 per cent of all verbs is the affixation of /−i/ and gemination of the base consonant(s). This gemination is also termed 'fortification' since for voiced obstruents, this process apparently equals the change into a voiceless sound: Hyman (2009) describes /f/ and /s/ as fortis counterparts of /v/ and /z/, whereas Udoh (2004) notes long /ff/ and /ss/ instead. The basic pattern for the Additive Affix /−i/ is given in (33). In bases of the shape CVC and CV, all base consonants are geminated (33-a, b) and if any or both of these consonants are already long, only the remaining short consonant is geminated (33-c).

(33) *Progressive in Leggbo*   (Hyman, 2009: 15, 16)

	BASE		PROGRESSIVE
a.	bal	'to remove oil/palmnut'	bːalːi
	dum	'to bite'	dːumːi
	kum	'to pierce, stab'	kːumːi
	vɔŋ	'to want, look for'	fɔŋːi
b.	du	'to beat, pound, crush'	dːui
	ke	'to put'	kːei
	la	'to entangle'	lːai
	za	'to reject'	sai
c.	sɛŋ	'go'	sɛŋːi
	k͡pen	'stay long time'	k͡penːi
	gːu	'to blow'	gːui
	fɔ	'to return, come back'	fɔi

A PDM analysis assumes two morphemic moras in the representation for the progressive morpheme, one prefixing to the initial mora of the base, the other suffixing to the final mora of the base. The morpheme is hence assumed to be a circumfix with two exponents that are affixed to different edges of their base and consequently bear different morphological colours. The tableaux in (34) show how these two exponents are realized for a CV and a CVC base. $\mu > Do_p^m > S$ and $PVis_\mu$ demand that the two morphemic moras are fully integrated into their base. High-ranked $*\mu...^{Af}...V$ ensures that those morphemic moras are only realized via gemination, never via vowel lengthening.[4] If the two moras are added to a base with an initial and a final consonant (34-i), both moras have a chance to be associated: the first mora with the initial consonant and the second mora with the second base consonant. If the base contains no final consonant as in (34-ii), only the prefixed morphemic mora can be associated while the suffixed morphemic mora remains unassociated. Association to a vowel as a last resort strategy to realize the morphemic mora is excluded by $*\mu...\text{Af}...V$ that is higher-ranked than $\mu > \text{Do}_p^m > S$.

(34)   *Multiple morphemic moras in Leggbo*
    i.   *Double gemination*

	$*\mu...\text{Af}...V$	$\mu > \text{Do}_p^m > S$	PVis_μ	$*C_\mu$
a. [ba.li]		*!*	*!*	
b. [baːlːi]	*!			*
☞ c. [bːaːlːi]				**

---

[4] As was already discussed extensively in chapter 3, this makes no misprediction for underlyingly mora-less segments: $V < \text{DD}_p^m < \mu$ is ranked above $*\mu...\text{Af}...V$ and ensures that every vowel is supplied with a mora even if it is an affix segment and hence implies a violation of $*\mu...\text{Af}...V$.

ii. *Single gemination*

$\mu_\blacksquare$ + $\mu_\bigcirc$ + $\mu_\bullet \mu_\bullet$ | | $d_\bigcirc u_\bigcirc$ $i_\bullet$	$*\mu......\text{Af\_V}$	$\mu > \text{Do}_\text{p}^\text{m} > S$	PVIs_μ	$*C_\mu$
a. $\mu_\blacksquare$ $\mu_\bigcirc \mu_\bullet \mu_\bullet$ | | | $d_\bigcirc u_\bigcirc i_\bullet$ [dui]		**!	**!	
b. $\mu_\blacksquare$ $\mu_\bigcirc \mu_\bullet \mu_\bullet$ | | $d_\bigcirc u_\bigcirc i_\bullet$ [duːi]	*!			*
☞ c. $\mu_\blacksquare$ $\mu_\bigcirc \mu_\bullet \mu_\bullet$ | | $d_\bigcirc u_\bigcirc i_\bullet$ [dːui]		*	*	*

An additional empirical fact about the double gemination in Leggbo is that it is expected to result in a marked syllable structure in case the base vowel is underlyingly long since the language does not allow initial geminates followed by a long vowel. In such contexts, vowel shortening applies as is shown in (35).

(35)   *Double gemination and vowel shortening*   (Hyman, 2009: 16)
   Base   Progressive

   bɔːl   'to slander'   bːɔlːi
   ceːŋ   'to groan'   cːeŋːi
   maːn   'to give birth' manːi

On a descriptive level, this vowel shortening is surprising since the additional association of a mora triggers deassociation of another mora and one could expect that association of the affix mora should be blocked in the first place. In containment theory where constraints demanding integration of prosodic structure are sensitive to different types of association relations, however, such a situation is expected, shown in tableau (36). If one of the underlying association lines between a vowel and its mora is marked as phonetically invisible as in candidate (36-c) in order to avoid a superheavy syllable, excluded by $*\overset{\sigma}{\mu\mu\mu\mu}$, no additional violation of $\mu > \text{Do}_\text{p}^\text{m} > S$ is invoked since the constraint is satisfied if a phonetically visible *or* morphological association line links every mora with a vowel. The underlying association line to the vowel is hence sufficient to ensure proper prosodic integration for every mora. As for the mechanism of usurpation that was discussed in chapter 3, it is crucial that a containment-based theory is able to distinguish between a non-existent association relation and an association relation that is only marked as phonetically invisible.

(36)   *Leggbo double gemination and vowel shortening*

		$*\sigma_{\mu\mu\mu\mu}$	$*\mu...Af...V$	$\mu{>}Dop_p^m{>}S$	$PVIs_\mu$	$*C_\mu$
a.	[b:ɔːlːi]	*!				**
b.	[bɔːlːi]			*!	*	*
☞ c.	[b:ɔlːi]				*	**

In addition, there are some stems that only geminate their final consonant (e.g /ceme/ → /cemːi/ 'to divide, share' (Hyman, 2009: 16)). An analysis perfectly along the lines proposed for Dhaasanac in section 4.1.1 can account for this additional fact: these stems are taken to contain an underlyingly mora-less vowel. Given that V<DD$_p^m$<μ is higher-ranked than *μ...^{Af}...V (see footnote 4), the affix mora exceptionally associates to a vowel to avoid mora epenthesis for those stems.

6.2.4.2 *Lengthening and copying in Oromo*   The effect of another instance of multiple morphemic prosodic nodes can be found in Oromo, an Eastern Cushitic language (Heine, 1981; Owens, 1985; Stroomer, 1987; Ali and Zaborski, 1990; Lloret, 1991). The data presented here is based mainly on Owens (1985) and Ali and Zaborski (1990) where the Harar Oromo variety is described. Vowel and consonant length is contrastive in Oromo. One piece of evidence for the former comes from a rule of vowel shortening that avoids two subsequent heavy syllables. Lloret (1991) argues that for this rule, CV and CVC syllables count as light and CV:C and CV: syllables as heavy. Complex onsets or codas are illicit in Oromo and geminates are only possible intervocalically.

An interesting pattern of MLM can now be found in the frequentative (37-a, b) and intensive (37-c). Their formation involves reduplication of the initial CV sequence of the base and gemination of the initial base consonant. That the reduplicant is prefixed is a far more plausible analysis than the possible alternative that it is infixed, simply because in bases with a long initial vowel, this length is preserved on the second vowel of the derived form as can be seen in (37-b). If one assumes that the copied portions neutralize the marked structure that is preserved in the base, then this is an instance of 'Emergence of the Unmarked' (McCarthy and Prince, 1994a; Becker and Flack, 2011).

(37) *Gemination and reduplication in Oromo*   (Tola, 1981; Ali and Zaborski, 1990)

BASE		FREQUENTATIVE		
a. rukute	'I or he hit'	ruːukute	'I or he hit repeatedly'	T68
dubːaddh	'speak'	dudːubːaddh	'speak again and again'	A78
fatʃʼːaːs	'scatter'	fafːatʃʼːaːs	'scatter widely'	A78
b. reːbne	'we spanked'	rerːeːbne	'we spanked repeatedly'	T68
diːmaː	'red'	didːiːmaː	'red ones'	T68
deːbiʔ	'return'	dedːeːbiʔ	'go back and forth'	A78

BASE		INTENSIVE		
c. balʔis	'widen'	babːalʔis	'make much wider'	A77
bareːtʃː	'beautify'	babːareːtʃː	'make more beautiful'	A77
fageːs	'make far'	fafːageːs	'make much more spaces'	A77

Such an instance of MLM is predicted if an exponent consisting of two morphemic moras is prefixed to a base and C_{NT_M} demands that morphemic moras can only be associated with a segment at the base edge. The constraint hence has the interesting effect that it forces two morphemic moras in the same language to be realized via different strategies: reduplication and gemination. Tableau (38) illustrates this for the derivation of the Oromo intensive. Both prefixed moras must be realized and candidate (38-a) is hence excluded. C_{NT_M} (see section 5.1), on the other hand, demands that the morphemic moras must dominate a segment at the edge of their base and excludes candidate (38-b) where the second morphemic mora is associated with the first base vowel.[5] This predicts that only the second affix mora can dominate base material and the initial mora must dominate epenthetic or reduplicated material. That the second affix mora results in gemination and not in vowel lengthening of the copied vowel as in candidate (38-e) is predicted since $*^{\mu}V^{\mu}$ is ranked above $*C_{\mu}$. Since reduplication is preferred over epenthesis as in candidate (38-c) candidate (38-d) finally wins.

---

[5] Note that if the initial morphemic mora associates to the initial consonant, the violation of C_{NT_M} could be avoided. There are, however, no initial geminates in Oromo.

(38)   *Addition in Oromo: Reduplication and gemination*

μ• μ• + μ○ μ○ μ○ f○ a○ g○ e○ s○	μ>Domᵖ>S	CNT_M	LIC!s	COL!s	*μ_V^μ	*C_μ
a. μ• μ• μ○ μ○ μ○ f○ a○ g○ e○ s○ [fa.geːs]	*!*				*	
b. μ• μ•μ○μ○ μ○ f○ a○ g○ e○ s○ [faː.geːs]	*!	*!			**	
c. μ• μ• μ○ μ○ μ○ ʔ ə f○ a○ g○ e○ s○ [ʔə.fːa.geːs]			*!*	**	*	*
☞ d. μ• μ• μ○ μ○ μ○ (f a) f○ a○ g○ e○ s○ [fa.fːa.geːs]				**	*	*
e. μ• μ• μ○ μ○ μ○ (f a) f○ a○ g○ e○ s○ [faː.fa.geːs]				**	**!	

Oromo exhibits other instances of additive MLM as well. There are Additive Suffixes like the negative suffix /−mihi/ that trigger lengthening of a preceding base-final vowel (/nama−mihi/ → /namaːmihi/ 'not a man', (Owens, 1985: 12)), Additive Suffixes like the verbalizer /−i/ that trigger gemination of a preceding consonant (/bad−i/ → /badːi/ 'destruction', (Lloret, 1991: 159)), and instances of Addition where the final vowel is lengthened (/tana/ → /tanaː/ 'this' (emphatic) (Lloret, 1991: 159)). These MLM patterns straightforwardly fall out from the ranking presented in (38) if those morphemes contain a single morphemic mora that is suffixed to the base. Although a preference for gemination over vowel lengthening was assumed in (38), vowel lengthening becomes optimal if the base ends in a vowel (39-b, c).

(39)   *Simple additive MLM in Oromo: vowel lengthening*

   a. *Additive Suffix: gemination*   b. *Addition: vowel lengthening*

c. *Additive Suffix: vowel lengthening*

$$
\begin{array}{cccccc}
\mu_{\bigcirc} & \mu_{\bigcirc} & \mu_{\bullet}\ \mu_{\bullet} & & \mu_{\bullet} \\
| & | & |\,\cdots\ | & & | \\
n_{\bigcirc}\ a_{\bigcirc} & m_{\bigcirc}\ a_{\bigcirc} & m_{\bullet}\ i_{\bullet} & h_{\bullet} & i_{\bullet}
\end{array}
$$

[na.maː.mi.hi]

6.2.4.3 Lengthening and copying in Balangao   A very similar pattern of reduplication accompanied by additional segmental lengthening can be found in the Austronesian language Balangao (Shetler, 1976; Lombardi and McCarthy, 1991; McCarthy, 1993). In a nominalizing context translated as 'place of…', prefixing CV reduplication, gemination of the consonant after the first vowel, and suffixation of /−an/ coocur.[6] In Balangao, onsets are obligatory and complex syllable edges are excluded (Shetler, 1976). If gemination results in an illicit consonant cluster as, for example, */sosobːblak/, it is therefore blocked as can be seen in (40-b).

(40) *Additive Affixation: reduplication and gemination in Balangao*

(Shetler, 1976: 118)

	BASE		NOMINALIZED	
a.	gadaŋ	'cross'	gagadːaŋan	'place of crossing'
	ʔitij	'die'	ʔiʔitːijan	'place of dying'
	basol	'sin'	babasːolan	'place of sinning'
	ʔuma	'make kaingin'	ʔuʔumːaːn	'place of making kaingin'
b.	soblak	'wash clothes'	sosoblakan	'place of washing clothes'
	ʔamhan	'bathe'	ʔaʔamhan	'bathing place'
	hablot	'hang up'	hahablotan	'place of hanging up'

This pattern of reduplication and gemination is predicted by a morpheme that consists of two exponents. The first is the suffix /−an/, the other is prefixed and contains a morphemic syllable and a morphemic mora, the latter preceded by a colour index. How copying and gemination follow from such a representation is shown in tableau (41). Crucially, both the morphemic syllable and mora must be fully integrated into their base but the former must not dominate the latter due to ALTERNATION (see section 2.2.3). High-ranked $*\sigma_{\bigcirc} < S_{\bullet}$ demands that the affix syllable is preferably not filled with base material (absolutely parallel to the morphemic foot in Upriver Halkomelem and Rotuman (see 5.3.1 and 5.3.2) and the morphemic syllable in Choctaw (see 5.3.3)) and copying is preferred over epenthesis to provide such non-base material. The morphemic mora, on the other hand, associates to a consonant due to the ranking of $*^{\mu}V^{\mu}$ over $*C_{\mu}$.

---

[6] A similar pattern can be found in, for example, the continuous aspect or the diminutive formation where the gemination accompanying reduplication is optional.

(41)   *Balangao reduplication and gemination*

	$\mu{>}\text{Dom}_P^m{>}S$	$\sigma{>}\text{Dom}_P^m{>}\mu$	ALT	$*\mu_V^\mu$	LIC!$_S$	COL!$_S$	$*C_\mu$
a. [baː.so.lan]			*!*	*!			
b. [ʔə.basːo.lan]					*!*	**	*
☞ c. [ba.basːo.lan]						**	*
d. [ba.ba.so.lan]			*!			**	

This analysis is highly interesting with respect to the question where in their base the morphemic prosodic nodes are realized. That the prefixed affix syllable precedes all other syllables dominating base material follows naturally since it lacks a colour index on the syllable tier. The morphemic mora, on the other hand is realized after the first mora dominating base material and that mora undergoes index fusion. Another possible structure that is not excluded by the RMO is one where the morphemic mora is realized after the first mora dominating inserted material as in candidate (41-d). However, this is suboptimal since it violates high-ranked ALTERNATION since this first mora bears the same morphological colour as the morphemic syllable after index fusion. This is hence an instance where an epenthetic mora is in fact treated like an underlying affix mora after index fusion.

The core of this analysis for the Balangao pattern is similar to the analysis that is proposed in Lombardi and McCarthy (1991) for Balangao. In the prosodic circumscription analysis presented there, gemination follows from making the first base mora extraprosodic and affixing a mora, and reduplication from prefixing a light syllable to the base. The crucial difference is that the (re)analysis presented here is couched into a framework with a strict restriction about possible landing sites for morphemes. In contrast, Prosodic Circumscription theory in principle allows an unrestricted set of possible affixation linearization sites since the circumscription operation can apply recursively.

6.2.4.4 Copying and lengthening at different edges in Marshallese   Austronesian languages are well-known for their reduplication patterns. A pattern that is highly interesting for the present discussion can be found in Marshallese where reduplication cooccurs with gemination (Bender, 1968, 1974; Abo et al., 1976; Zewen, 1977; Pagotto, 1992; Byrd, 1993; Hendricks, 1999; Hale, 2000; Kennedy, 2002; Willson, 2003; Topintzi, 2010). Geminates in Marshallese are possible medially and stem-initially but are impossible word-initially. As can be seen in (42), epenthesis of /j/ applies if a geminate is expected in word-initial position. The vowel following the /j/ is a copy of the following base vowel (except this vowel is /a/ in which case the vowel following /j/ is /e/). These generalizations only hold for the Ralik dialect of Marshallese that is the empirical base for the present discussion (Willson, 2003).

(42)   *Epenthesis to avoid initial geminates in Marshallese*   (Willson, 2002: 2)

UNDERLYING	SURFACE	
dːek	jedːek	'to grow'
tʲːed	jetʲːed	'to look up'
pːej	jepːej	'sandbank'

With this background, the relevant additive MLM can be considered. Many distributive verbs are formed from their base via copying the final syllable and geminating the initial consonant of the base (43). This gemination in turn triggers epenthesis to avoid an initial geminate. This pattern is hence an instance where two MLM effects are found at different edges of their base.

(43)   *Distributive reduplication and gemination*   (Hendricks, 1999: 105)

BASE	DISTRIBUTIVE	
biqen	jibːiqenqen	'chunk'
betah	jebːetahtah	'butter'
dijlah	jidːijlahlah	'nail'
det	jedːetdet	'sunshine'
tʲekapen	jetʲːekapenpen	'less than half full'

This pattern follows inside PDM from assuming that the distributive consists of two exponents: a prefixed mora and a suffixed syllable that both must be completely integrated into the prosodic structure of their base. The two interesting asymmetries in realizing these morphemic nodes are that, *first*, the morphemic mora is realized via gemination and not via copying, and that, *second*, the morphemic syllable is realized via copying although epenthesis applies in the same structure for phonological reasons at the left edge of the base. The first asymmetry is predicted from assuming that $*\mu...^{\text{Af}}...V$ is ranked high in Marshallese. The affix mora hence strives to avoid association to a vowel that would be necessary if initial copying applied to realize the mora. On the other hand, copying is assumed to be in principle the preferred default strategy to supply additional segmental material but is blocked in the initial position due to the positional version of $*\Box$ (see section 2.2.5, (62-c)) given in (44-a).[7] This correctly predicts the two-fold nature of the repair operations that avoid initial geminates in Marshallese: the additional consonant is epenthetic, the additional vowel following it, however, is copied. The analysis is sketched in tableau (45). The optimal strategy to realize the prefixed morphemic mora is association to a consonant, excluding (45-a). This, however, makes additional phonological operations necessary since initial geminates are illicit in the language, ensured by (44-b) that excludes candidate (45-b). Epenthesis of an initial consonant and copying of a following vowel in the winning candidate (45-d) becomes the optimal strategy to supply the additional material that avoids this initial geminate.

(44) a. $*\#\Box$ Assign a violation mark for every pair of segments x and y that are associated via a phonetically invisible association line where x or y is word-initial.

    b. $*\mu$-Ons   Assign a violation mark for every vowel that is the leftmost phonetically visible segment in a prosodic word and phonetically visibly associated to a μ.

---

[7] For a discussion of positional asymmetries in terms of markedness and faithfulness, see, for example, Smith (2008).

(45)   *Gemination and copying in Marshallese*

$\mu_\blacksquare + \mu_\bigcirc\ \mu_\bigcirc + $ ... $b_\bigcirc\ i_\bigcirc\ q_\bigcirc\ e_\bigcirc\ n_\bigcirc$	$\sigma{>}\mathrm{Do}_p^m{>}\mu$	$\mu{>}\mathrm{Do}_p^m{>}S$	$*\#\square$	$*\mu\text{-Ons}$	$*\mu.\mathrm{Af.V}$	Lıc!s	Col!s	$*C_\mu$
a. [biː.qen]	*!				*!			
b. [bːi.qen.qen]				*!			***	*
c. [jibːi.qen.ji]						***!**	*****	*
☞ d. [jibːi.qen.qen]						*	*****	*
e. [bibːi.qen.qen]				*!			*****	*

6.2.4.5 Summary: multiple morphemic prosodic nodes

In this subsection, four analyses were presented where multiple morphemic prosodic nodes are affixed and completely integrated into their base. The table in (46) summarizes these four analyses. The existence of such patterns is straightforwardly predicted in the theory of PDM since there are no restrictions about the possible numbers of morphemic prosodic nodes. The insertion grade in Choctaw was in fact argued to result from affixing three different morphemic prosodic nodes on different tiers: a mora, a syllable, and a foot (see section 5.3.3). Interestingly, the present constraint system also predicts the coexistence of different strategies to realize different morphemic prosodic nodes in one language. We saw examples where morphemic prosodic nodes in different base positions are realized differently (e.g. in Balangao, section 6.2.4.3) and examples where morphemic prosodic nodes on different tiers are realized differently (e.g. in Marshallese, section 6.2.4.4).

(46) *Multiple prosodic nodes: summary*

	Prefix	Suffix	Base	Derived	MLM
Choctaw I		Φ• — μ•	bini	binːiː	Gemination & vowel lengthening
Choctaw II		Φ• — σ• μ•	toksa	toksajːaː	Gemination, vowel lengthening, & insertion
Leggbo	μ■ —	— μ• μ• ┊ i•	bal	bːalːi	2x Gemination
Oromo	μ■ μ■ —		rukute	rurːukute	Gemination & copying
Balangao	σ■ ■ μ■ —	— μ• ┊ a• n•	basol	babasːolan	Gemination & copying
Marshallese	σ• μ■ —	—	biqen	yibːiqenqen	Gemination, copying, & insertion

6.2.5 *Excluded non-local MLM patterns*

The claim that all the attested instances of MLM can be derived inside PDM is only the first part of an argument that this framework is on the right track. In addition, it needs to be shown that imaginable structures resulting in generally unattested MLM patterns are indeed excluded. This discussion is highly relevant for the point that is made in chapter 7 where the predictions of alternative accounts are summarized and it is argued that most suffer from an overgeneration problem since they lack any locality restriction about possible realization sites for MLM.

The structures in (47) abstractly summarize the possible landing sites for morphemic prosodic nodes in PDM, recapitulating the discussion in section 6.1.

(47) *Possible landing sites for morphemic prosodic nodes*
  a. Morphemic moras

Prefix	Base: $\mu_\circ \, \mu_\circ \, \mu_\circ \, \mu_\circ$	Suffix:
$/\mu_\blacksquare-/$	$\mu_\blacksquare \, \mu_\circ \, \mu_\circ \, \mu_\circ \, \mu_\circ \, \mu_\bullet$	$/-\mu_\bullet/$
$/_\blacksquare \, \mu_\blacksquare-/$	$\mu_{\blacksquare\circ} \, \mu_\blacksquare \, \mu_\circ \, \mu_\circ \, \mu_\bullet \, \mu_{\bullet\circ}$	$/-\mu_{\bullet} \, {}_\bullet/$

  b. Morphemic syllables

Prefix	Base: $\sigma_\circ \, \sigma_\circ \, \sigma_\circ \, \sigma_\circ$	Suffix:
$/\sigma_\blacksquare-/$	$\sigma_\blacksquare \, \sigma_\circ \, \sigma_\circ \, \sigma_\circ \, \sigma_\circ \, \sigma_\bullet$	$/-\sigma_\bullet/$
$/_\blacksquare \, \sigma_\blacksquare-/$	$\sigma_{\blacksquare\circ} \, \sigma_\blacksquare \, \sigma_\circ \, \sigma_\circ \, \sigma_\bullet \, \sigma_{\bullet\circ}$	$/-\sigma_{\bullet} \, {}_\bullet/$

  c. Morphemic feet

Prefix	Base: $\Phi_\circ \, \Phi_\circ \, \Phi_\circ \, \Phi_\circ$	Suffix:
$/\Phi_\blacksquare-/$	$\Phi_\blacksquare \, \Phi_\circ \, \Phi_\circ \, \Phi_\circ \, \Phi_\circ \, \Phi_\bullet$	$/-\Phi_\bullet/$
$/_\blacksquare \, \Phi_\blacksquare-/$	$\Phi_{\blacksquare\circ} \, \Phi_\blacksquare \, \Phi_\circ \, \Phi_\circ \, \Phi_\bullet \, \Phi_{\bullet\circ}$	$/-\Phi_{\bullet} \, {}_\bullet/$

What are now imaginable MLM patterns that can not be predicted in PDM? A first concrete example is the pattern in (48). Either the penultimate onset is geminated or the antepenultimate vowel is lengthened to mark a certain morpho-syntactic feature. The alternation between gemination and vowel lengthening is predictable: the latter applies in case the former is impossible since the preceding syllable is closed (modifying the Asante Twi pattern from section 5.1.2).

(48) **Asante Twi'₁: non-local additive MLM I*

	BASE	DERIVED FORM
a.	nodaneka	nodanːeka
	bisatɔ	bisːatɔ
b.	nodalneka	nodaːlneka
	kanomtɔpeː	kanoːmtɔpeː

The structures in (49) show how this pattern apparently follows in a PDM analysis. It is clear that this configuration is a fatal problem for the RMO. In (49), it is assumed that a morphemic mora is suffixed to its base. The exponent order that the suffix● follows the stem○ is not properly reflected on the moraic tier if the morphemic mora is realized between the penultimate and antepenultimate mora dominating base material. A colour index in the morpheme representation can only predict a realization between the final and penultimate mora, never between the penultimate and antepenultimate. And analysing it as a prefix does not change anything either: it could maximally reach the position between the last and penultimate mora dominating base material.

(49) *Non-local full integration of a μ*

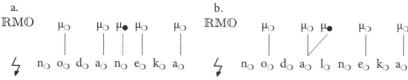

The effect that comes closest to this non-local lengthening is Addition in Alabama (see section 6.2.3). There, a 'kicking' structure was possible where a mora underlyingly associated to a vowel associates to a neighbouring consonant in order to free 'space' on the preceding vowel for a morphemic mora. However, such a configuration is impossible for the *Asante Twi'₁ pattern since this involves deassociation and new association from and to a vowel (50) and hence two elements of the same type. This is excluded by the NKK (see section 2.2.2, (31)).

(50)   *Kicking configuration*

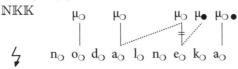

It is clear that the mirror image pattern of *Asante Twi'₁ at the left edge is impossible for exactly the same reasons. This *Asante Twi'₂ pattern would involve gemination of the third onset consonant or vowel lengthening of the third vowel as in (51).

(51)   **Asante Twi'₂: non-local additive MLM I*

	BASE	DERIVED FORM
a.	nodaneka	nodanːeka
	bisatɔ	bisatːɔ
b.	nodalneka	nodalneːka
	kanomtɔpeː	kanomtɔːpeː

The typological overview in section 6.1.2 reveals that there is no such non-local Addition pattern. The impossible non-local additive MLM patterns in *Asante Twi'₁ and *Asante Twi'₂ involve alternations between gemination and vowel lengthening for convenience: this simply shows which base segment cannot be targeted by a morphemic mora. Of course, this implies that both patterns in isolation are as unattested as the combination of them.

Now let's turn to some imaginable subtractive MLM patterns. In (52), the antepenultimate vowel of every base is shortened in case it is long in this hypothetical *Hausa'₁ pattern.

(52)   **Hausa'₁: non-local subtractive MLM I*

BASE	DERIVED FORM
moːliːkaba	moːlikaba
tolikubaːkima	tolikubakima
maːkoːba	makoːba
likuːmaːtu	likumaːtu
liːnuːkiːbami	liːnuːkibami

As for *Asante Twi*, the mirror image pattern at the left edge of its base is equally imaginable. In the case of *Hausa'*₁, this corresponding pattern would involve short-ening of the third vowel of its base. The empirical overview in section 6.1.3 showed that such subtractive MLM patterns are systematically absent in the representative data set. What would a PDM analysis for such a pattern look like? In (53), two structures are given that would predict this pattern from affixation of a morphemic syllable. This morphemic syllable remains defectively integrated and hence phonet-ically uninterpreted but dominates one of the moras the antepenultimate vowel is associated with. This structure is excluded by either the NoCr or the RMO. In the depiction in (53-a), the morphemic syllable associates to a mora that is followed by two other moras that are dominated by two syllables preceding the morphemic syllable; two crossing association lines result. And in an imaginable structure where the two epenthetic syllables dominating the final and penultimate mora are inserted after the morphemic syllable, the RMO would be violated as is shown in (53-b). There is hence no licit structure where a suffixed (or prefixed, for that matter) morphemic syllable can ever trigger non-realization of an antepenultimate vowel in PDM. The same holds for a morphemic mora: it could maximally be expected in the position preceding the final mora of its base and can hence not have a subtractive effect on the antepenultimate vowel.

(53)   *Non-local defective syllable integration*
    a. *Crossing association lines*   b. *Morpheme order not recoverable*

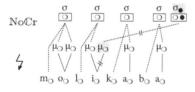   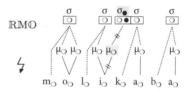

Interestingly enough, subtractive MLM targeting the penultimate vowel or final onset consonant is not attested in the representative sample of MLM. However, affixation of a morphemic syllable with a colour index can in principle predict exactly such a pattern inside the theory of PDM. The absence of such a subtractive MLM is taken to be an accidental gap that follows from the general dispreference of sub-tractive MLM. The predictions of the PDM theory are not flawed simply because the effects of morphemic prosodic nodes in this exact position are in principle attested. Multiple instances of morphemic moras with a colour index that are fully integrated into their base and hence result in 'infixing' additive MLM were discussed in section 6.2.3.

    Similarly to (53), non-local mora usurpation is also excluded in the PDM account. In (54), a very similar non-local MLM pattern is given where a Subtractive Suffix triggers shortening of a long antepenultimate vowel.

(54)   *Hausa'₂: non-local subtractive MLM II*

Base	Derived form
moːliːkaba —to	moːlikabatoto
tolikubaːkima —to	tolikubakimato
maːkoːba —to	makoːbato
likuːmaːtu —to	likumaːtuto
liːnuːkiːbami —to	liːnuːkibamito

In (55), an imaginable mora usurpation for this pattern is sketched. The vowel of a Subtractive Suffix usurps the mora of the antepenultimate base vowel. This structure, however, is excluded by both the NoCr and the RMO.

(55)   *Non-local mora usurpation: crossing association lines*

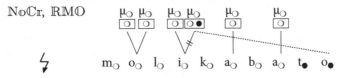

*Asante Twi'₁/₂ and *Hausa'₁/₂ represent basic examples of imaginable non-local MLM patterns that were argued to be impossible in PDM. Most importantly, patterns along those lines are systematically unattested according to the representative data set discussed in 6.1. In section 7.5.1, several additional unattested MLM patterns are discussed that are predicted by the alternative accounts that are critically reviewed in the next chapter. Again, it is shown that they can not follow under the PDM account. In some cases, this is simply due to the fact that they are modifications of the non-local patterns illustrated with *Asante Twi'₁/₂ and *Hausa'₁/₂.

7

A critical review of alternative accounts

The main claim in this book is that the framework of PDM, based on a containment-based OT theory, is able to predict all and only attested instances of MLM. It is argued that the framework is superior compared to alternative accounts both in terms of theoretical economy and empirical coverage. In this chapter, some important alternative theoretical OT accounts of MLM are discussed. This includes theoretical frameworks for which it has been claimed that they are able to account for non-concatenative morphology and/or morpheme-specific phonology in general and/or length-manipulation specifically. Crucially, none of these theories aims to derive (only and/or exclusively) the empirical range of phenomena discussed in this book. Especially undergeneration arguments against some of the alternatives are hence vacuous to a certain degree. Still, since they are in principle able to account for a very similar set of phenomena, they are the most plausible OT-contenders to PDM.

At least two types of OT-approaches to non-concatenative morphology crucially rely on a concept of 'paradigmatic distinctness'. One is the theory of Transderivational Antifaithfulness (=TAF, Alderete, 2001b, a), introduced in section 7.1.1, and the other one is based on a version of REALIZEMORPHEME (=RM, Kurisu, 2001), introduced in section 7.1.2. In both these approaches, morphologically complex forms can be forced to undergo some phonological operation in order to differentiate them from their morphologically less complex base. Two other OT approaches can be roughly summarized as theories where different constraint(-ranking)s can be active for different morphological environments: Cophonology Theory (=CT, Inkelas and Zoll, 2007), introduced in section 7.1.3, and lexically indexed constraints (=LIC, Pater, 2009), introduced in section 7.1.4. The discussion starts with a brief outline of the four alternatives in section 7.1. It is shown how they account for different MLM patterns and/or how they have difficulties to account for one or the other type of MLM. The predictions of the theories are then put to the test and it is discussed whether they successfully derive the existence of the rescuer morpheme in Aymara (section 7.2), non-concatenative allomorphy in Upriver Halkomelem (section 7.3), and long epenthetic vowels in SSM (section 7.4). For all these interesting MLM patterns,

Morphological Length and Prosodically Defective Morphemes. First edition. Eva Zimmermann.
© Eva Zimmermann 2017. First published 2017 by Oxford University Press.

a detailed analysis in terms of PDM was presented in sections 4.2, 5.2.3.1, and 5.3.1 respectively. In section 7.5, the problem of unrestrictiveness is addressed and several possible overgeneration problems for one or the other account in the domain of MLM are discussed. Section 7.6 summarizes the discussion of alternative accounts and concludes that only the account of PDM is able to predict all and only the attested typology of MLM patterns without introducing complex morpheme-specific mechanisms.

7.1 Alternative accounts to MLM

7.1.1 *Transderivational Antifaithfulness Theory*

The assumption of Transderivational Antifaithfulness (TAF) (Alderete, 2001*b, a*; Horwood, 2001) combines two theoretical ingredients: transderivational faithfulness relations in the sense of Benua (1997) and the concept of antifaithfulness constraints. The latter is simply the assumption that every standard faithfulness constraint demanding preservation for a specific phonological dimension exists in a negative version demanding *un*faithfulness. An independent proposal of such 'anticorrespondence' constraints was made by Hayes (1999) to account for Yidiñ phonology. In Alderete (2001*b*), antifaithfulness constraints were then proposed to account for affix- and/or root-controlled accent phenomena and for an interesting instance of non-concatenative morphology, namely voicing polarity in Luo. The second crucial assumption in TAF theory is the existence of transderivational correspondence relations that allow us to compare output forms. Antifaithfulness constraints, it is assumed, can only hold for morphologically related words, i.e. are impossible for IO-relations. They hence demand unfaithfulness with respect to a certain phonological dimension that distinguishes two morphologically related words—non-concatenative operations are predicted. Morphemes explicitly select or subcategorize for different OO-correspondence relations 'and since the set of transderivational (anti-)faithfulness constraints is re-rankable', different non-concatenative exponents can surface. The theory thus explicitly assumes morpheme-specific[1] constraint rankings or 'recursive hierarchies' (Alderete, 2001*b*: 119). Still, the theory is non-derivational in the sense that the input into an optimization is always the underlying representation for morphemes, never an output form.

To illustrate the TAF account, derivations for the four illustrating MLM patterns introduced in section 1.1.1 and 1.1.2 are given below. Subtraction in Canela Krahô

---

[1] It is made clear that 'there are no morpheme-specific faithfulness constraints' in TAF and '[a]ffix classes are instead defined by correspondence relations specified in the lexicon' (Alderete, 2001*a*: 209). Given that a class of affixes can only contain one member, this implies indeed the existence of what is here understood as 'morpheme-specific' constraint.

is predicted from a negated Max constraint demanding that certain segments must remain unrealized, given in (1-a). This antifaithfulness constraint now compares two output forms: if the non-finite form contains all the segments that were present in the morphologically related finite form, it is violated (2). For degemination triggered by Subtractive Affixes in Wolof, on the other hand, an antifaithfulness constraint (1-b) is assumed to be high-ranked that demands that at least one mora that is present in the output of the morphological base must remain without correspondent in the derived form (3). It is clear that this account of Subtractive Affixation is not fundamentally different from an account of Subtraction: the crucial mechanism is only that the respective antifaithfulness constraint becomes relevant in the morphological category under consideration.

(1)   a.   ¬Max-S   Assign a violation mark for every output form in which every input segment has an output correspondent.

   b.   ¬Max-μ   Assign a violation mark for every output form in which every input μ has an output correspondent.

(2)   *Subtraction in TAF: Canela Krahô*   (3)   *Subtractive Affixation in TAF: Wolof*

/tɔn/ + Non-Fin	¬Max-S [tɔn]	Max-S
a. tɔn	*!	
☞ b. tɔ		*

/segː/ + /al/Caus	Max-S	¬Max-μ [segː]	Max-μ
a. segːal		*!	
b. seal	*!		*
☞ c. segal			*

Additive length-manipulation, on the other hand, requires a version of ¬Dep demanding that additional phonological material is present in the output that was not part of the morphological base. For the analyses of vowel lengthening in Gidabal and suffix-triggered gemination in Wolof, the constraint (4) is relevant demanding the insertion of a mora that was not present in the input.

(4)   ¬Dep-μ   Assign a violation mark for every output form in which every output μ has a correspondent in the input.

Lengthening of an underlyingly short vowel (5-b) and gemination of an underlyingly short consonant (6-b) involves realization of an additional mora and satisfies this antifaithfulness constraint under violation of the corresponding faithfulness constraint Dep-μ. Again, the Additive Affixation (6) is not crucially different from the analysis for Addition in (5).

(5)   *Addition in TAF: Gidabal*

/gida/ + IMP	*GEM	¬DEP-μ [gida]	DEP-μ
a. gida		*!	
☞ b. gida:			*
c. gid:a	*!		*

(6)   *Additive Affixation in TAF: Wolof*

/ub/ + /i/REV	*V:	¬DEP-μ [ub]	DEP-μ
a. ubi		*!	
☞ b. ub:i			*
c. ubi:	*!		*

Something that is not determined in the tableaux above is the locus of the antifaithful operations, i.e. the question which segment is deleted, shortened, or lengthened. This needs to be determined by independent mechanisms and does not follow from anything in the TAF relations. According to Horwood (2001), there are two general strategies to determine the locus of the antifaithfulness effect: constraint conjunction or the ranking of positional faithfulness constraints (Beckman, 1998). If one follows the second line of reasoning, high-ranked MAX-S$_{\#\sigma}$ preserving all segments in the initial syllable together with CONTIGUITY (Landman, 2002) penalizing deletion inside a morpheme ensures that it is the final consonant that gets deleted in Canela Krahô (7). Similarly, DEP-μ$_{\#\sigma}$ together with a CONTIGUITY penalizing insertion of a mora inside a morpheme[2] ensures that the final vowel in Gidabal is lengthened.

(7)   *TAF: The locus of the deletion in Canela Krahô*

/tɔn/ + Non-Fin	MAX-S$_{\#\sigma}$	CONTIG	¬MAX-S [tɔn]	MAX-S
a. tɔn			*!	
☞ b. tɔ				*
c. ɔn	*!			*
d. tn		*!		*

For Subtractive and Additive Affixation, determining the locus of the MLM crucially relies on the principle of 'Strict Base Mutation' (Alderete, 2001b). Only the base can

---

[2] A similar opacity problem arises that was discussed for mora affixation approaches in general in section 2.2.4: If a base happens to lack any moras dominating its vowels, it is not clear how CONTIGUITY can have any effect.

be affected by the OO-relation to which an antifaithfulness constraint is specified for. Without this inherent property of the account, the antifaithfulness constraints ¬DEP-μ and ¬MAX-μ in the analysis for Subtractive and Additive Affixation in Wolof would also be satisfied if segments in the Subtractive/Additive Suffix itself are lengthened or shortened.

The TAF account is hence in principle able to predict the four different types of MLM: Addition, Subtraction, Additive Affixation, and Subtractive Affixation.

7.1.2 *Realize Morpheme*

A second OT-approach to non-concatenative morphology relying on the concept of paradigmatic distinctness is based on a version of the constraint REALIZEMORPHEME (=RM). There are various versions and implementations of such a constraint in the literature. The original definition (8) given in Samek-Lodovici (1992) demands the mapping of each morpheme to some recoverable phonological element in the output (Samek-Lodovici, 1992: 275).

(8) | AFFIX REALIZATION | Affix Realization (Afx): realize the two specifications of the affix in a syllabically overt and detectable manner. One violation for each specification which is left unrealized.

Wolf (2005) distinguishes three different types of REALIZEMORPHEME definitions in the literature: *first*, 'Preserve something' (Akinlabi, 1996), *second*, 'Preserve something distinctive' (Gnanadesikan, 1997), and *third*, 'Make something different' (Kurisu, 2001). Other examples for accounts relying on some concept of RM can be found in Rose (1997), Walker (1998, 2000*b*), Kennard (2004), van Oostendorp (2005), or Trommer (2011*a*).

The main argument for the RM definition proposed in Kurisu (2001) is that other versions of the constraint are insufficient to account for certain types of non-concatenative morphology, especially for subtractive MLM since in those cases, no overt phonological information is present in the output that can be mapped to an input morpheme. He hence argues for a less restrictive version of the constraint that only demands that a morphological category in the input must be realized in the output, i.e. there must be some phonological expression for every morpheme (9) (Kurisu, 2001: 39). The following discussion is based on this RM definition argued for in Kurisu (2001). This proposal is one of the most complete discussions of various types of non-concatenative morphological phenomena analysed with a version of RM.

(9) | REALIZE MORPHEME (RM) | Let α be a morphological form, β be a morpho-syntactic category, and $F(\alpha)$ be the phonological form from which $F(\alpha+\beta)$ is derived to express a morpho-syntactic category β. Then RM is satisfied with respect to β iff $F(\alpha+\beta) \neq F(\alpha+\beta)$ phonologically.

Similar to TAF constraints, RM is evaluated by comparing two output forms and determining whether they differ in their phonological structure. This means that a derived form stands in relation to an existing output form that is either a simple stem or an already derived morphologically complex form and RM is violated if both are identical. Although never explicitly discussed in Kurisu (2001), it follows from the architecture of the account that only the addition of one morpheme at a time is optimized, it is hence a cyclic system. Unlike TAF and standard OO-FAITH constraints in general, RM violations might also be calculated based on a relation to a form that is not an existing output form. This is the case for forms which are derived from a bare stem that is not a possible surface form in a language. In such cases, a 'possible output' is optimized by the general phonology of the language (Kurisu, 2001: 42ff). The analysis explicitly assumes that 'a faithfulness constraint is subdivided into several indexed components' (Kurisu, 2001: 58) and that in principle every faithfulness constraint is assumed to exist in an indexed version for every morpheme of a language. This assumption is necessary since different non-concatenative patterns can coexist in a language and one output form can serve as morphological base for more than one derivation. Given the formulation of RM in (9), a morpheme can be realized by any conceivable phonological operation if segmental material is absent or if the realization of available segmental material results in a phonologically marked structure. The specific phonological instantiation of a non-concatenative strategy to realize a morpheme is determined by the ranking of faithfulness constraints with respect to RM: those operations penalized by faithfulness constraints that are ranked below RM can in principle emerge as a non-concatenative exponent. Kurisu (2001) gives the list in (10) where possible non-concatenative operations and the faithfulness constraints penalizing the application of these operations are set out.

(10)   *Non-concatenative allomorphs and their constraint violations, following Kurisu (2001)*

Metathesis	* LINEARITY
Subtraction	* MAX
Reduplication	* INTEG[3]
Insertion (of epenthetic material)	* DEP
Vowel lengthening	* IDENT-LENGTH

A Subtraction pattern like the consonant deletion in Canela Krahô is then derived from ranking RM above MAX-S. Vowel lengthening as a possible alternative strategy that would satisfy RM is excluded by high-ranked DEP-μ. Quite parallel, Addition as in the vowel lengthening pattern in Gidabal follows from ranking RM above DEP-μ.

---

[3] Note that reduplication violates INTEGRITY and is therefore understood as fission of segments into multiple instances of themselves. Nevertheless (and maybe strangely), reduplication does not violate LINEARITY in Kurisu's system.

A faithful realization of the base as in (11-a) and (12-a) is excluded by high-ranked RM since a morphologically more complex form (=the output) is phonologically not different from its morphologically simpler base form (=the input). A phonological operation that only violates faithfulness constraints ranked lower than RM hence becomes optimal: segment deletion in (11-b) and vowel lengthening in (12-c).

(11)   *Subtraction in RM: Canela Krahô*

/tɔn/ + Non-Fin	Dep-µNFin	RM	Max-SNFin
a. tɔn		*!	
☞ b. tɔ			*
c. tɔːn	*!		

(12)   *Addition in RM: Gidabal*

/gida/ + IMP	Max-SIMP	RM	Dep-µIMP
a. gida		*!	
b. gid	*!		
☞ c. gidaː			*

As in the TAF approach, some additional mechanism must ensure the locus of the unfaithful operation. The introduction of positional faithfulness constraints is again one option to predict that the correct segments are deleted/lengthened.

Instances of Additive and Subtractive Affixes are unexpected in an RM-based framework in the first place. Given the nature of RM, either the addition of affix segments or the application of a non-concatenative operation is sufficient to satisfy RM and the cooccurrence of both to realize a single morpheme is expected to be harmonically bounded since it induces additional faithfulness violations.[4] The same holds for instances of multiple MLM operations in a morphological context. Example for such patterns discussed in section 6.2.4 are, for example, cooccurrence of reduplication and gemination in Balangao and double gemination in Leggbo.[5] It is argued in Kurisu (2001), that these instances termed 'double morphemic exponence' (Kurisu, 2001: §5) are correctly predicted if one introduces Sympathy Theory (McCarthy, 1999; Ito and Mester, 1998; McCarthy, 2003b), an extension of parallel standard OT that allows us to derive instances of phonological opacity. In Sympathy Theory, reference to non-optimal candidates is possible via faithfulness constraints. More formally, the most harmonic candidate among all the candidates that satisfy a designated IO-faithfulness 'selector' constraint (marked with ★) is the 'sympathetic' candidate (marked with ❀). OO-Faithfulness 'sympathy' constraints then demand faithfulness to phonological

---

[4] For a more detailed discussion of this and similar problems that Kurisu's account faces, see, for example, Ussishkin (2000): §4.3.2.4 or Wolf (2007): §3.

[5] Absolutely parallel to instances of multiple (segmental) feature mutation discussed as a problem for the RM approach in Wolf (2007).

properties of this candidate. This allows us to mirror derivational accounts since a suboptimal but sympathetic candidate can correlate to intermediate derivational steps in serial theories and inherit several of its properties to the optimal structure. The crucial part of a sympathy-theoretic account for Additive and Subtractive Affixation inside RM is a selector constraint like ★St=PrWd that penalizes every form where an affix is added to the stem. For all candidates that satisfy this selector constraint, RM forces the application of some phonological operation to make it different from its base. And a faithfulness constraint demanding inter-candidate correspondence then ensures that this non-concatenative change must be preserved faithfully in the optimal candidate that realizes the input affix material as well due to high-ranked IO faithfulness. This is illustrated in (13) for the Additive Suffixation in Wolof. High-ranked Max ensures that the segmental part of the suffix /i/ must be realized as in candidates (13-b, d). The selector constraint ★St=PrWd, on the other hand, demands that no affix may follow the base. The candidate that satisfies this constraint and has the best constraint profile is (13-c), the sympathetic candidate. Since it contains no segmental portion of the reversive morpheme, RM enforces some phonological change to realize the morpheme. The fact that Dep-μ_Rev is ranked below RM predicts that this non-concatenative operation is vowel lengthening. This length-manipulation is now preserved in the winning candidate (13-d) due to Max-μ ⊛O violated when a structure contains fewer moras than the sympathetic candidate. And since Max-S is undominated, the winning candidate also realizes all affix segments faithfully. This logic can easily be applied to Subtractive Suffixation as well, as is shown in (14) for Wolof. The relevant OO-Faith constraint preserving the non-concatenative change is Dep-μ ⊛O ensuring that the consonant that was degeminated in the sympathetic candidate (14-c) to satisfy RM remains short in the winning candidate (14-d).

(13) *Additive Affixation in RM: Wolof*

/ub/ + /i/_REV	RM	MAX-μ ⊛O	MAX-S	DEP-μ_REV	★ST=PRWD
a. ub	*!	*!	*!		
b. ubi		*!			*
🏵 c. ub:			*!	*	
☞ d. ub:i				*	*

(14) *Subtr. Affixation in RM: Wolof*

/seg:/ + /al/_Caus	RM	MAX-S	DEP-μ ⊛O	MAX-H_Caus	★ST=PRWD
a. seg:	*!	*!*	*	*	
b. seg:al			**!		*
🏵 c. seg		*!*		**	
☞ d. segal			*	*	*

The RM approach in Kurisu (2001) hence easily accounts for all MLM patterns of Addition and Subtraction. Additive and Subtractive Affixes, on the other hand, require the introduction of an additional powerful theoretical mechanism, namely Sympathy Theory.

7.1.3 Cophonology Theory

Cophonology Theory (=CT) assumes that distinct phonological systems can coexist in a single language, indexed to, for example, morphological constructions[6] (Orgun, 1996; Anttila, 2002; Inkelas et al., 2004; Inkelas and Zoll, 2005, 2007). Although morphologically indexed constraints are explicitly rejected, the framework crucially relies on the assumption of different rankings in one and the same language that might be active in different morphological contexts. As Caballero (2011) puts it, CT assumes 'morphologically blind phonological sub-grammars' (p. 763). All subrankings in one grammar are restricted by the demand to conform to a 'master ranking', a partial ranking of constraints with which every cophonology of a language is compatible. Certain constraints in the master ranking are hence not ordered with respect to each other. The hierarchical structure of morphologically complex words is crucial in this approach where it is assumed that the sub-phonology of a certain morphological category will only affect the base/stem of this construction. For the abstract morphological structure in (15), this means that a cophonology indexed to morphological category 1 has only scope over the root and suffix 1 and a cophonology 2 has scope over the stem 2 and suffix 2.

(15)   *Binary branching hierarchical structure of a morphologically complex word*

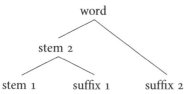

One major advantage of this theory is the fact that it predicts non-concatenative morphology as well as morphologically conditioned phonology with the same mechanism. An analysis for non-concatenative morphology based on CT implies that the resulting morphologically derived form is predicted from its base form from the ranking of regular markedness and faithfulness constraints. This is actually not completely trivial for all cases of MLM as is discussed below.

The most unproblematic case is Subtraction as in Canela Krahô, simply because deletion of a final consonant is an independently motivated phonological process in the languages of the world (for discussion and literature see, for example, Harris, 2011). In the morphological context of finiteness, a ranking as in (17-ii) is then assumed to be active that triggers deletion of the final coda. In the cophonology associated with non-finite contexts, the ranking of MAX-C and NoCODA would then simply be

---

[6] Other components of the language that can be associated with a cophonology are register or lexical class (Inkelas and Zoll, 2007).

reversed (17-i).[7] In the master ranking, the two constraints NoCoda and Max-C are consequently not ordered to each other as can be seen in (16).

(16)   *Subtraction in CT: morphological structure*

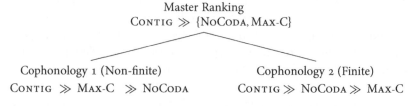

Master Ranking
Contig ≫ {NoCoda, Max-C}

Cophonology 1 (Non-finite)   Cophonology 2 (Finite)
Contig ≫ Max-C ≫ NoCoda   Contig ≫ NoCoda ≫ Max-C

(17)   *Subtraction in CT: Canela Krahô*
       i. *C-final bases in the non-finite*   ii. *Subtraction to form the finite*

/tɔn/ + Non-Fin	Max-C	NoCoda
☞ a. tɔn		*
b. tɔ	*!	

/tɔn/ + Fin	NoCoda	Max-C
a. tɔn	*!	
☞ b. tɔ		*

Similarly to the TAF approach, it is in principle irrelevant whether a morpheme only triggers the application of a non-concatenative operation or whether it also contains segmental material in its representation. The only relevant fact is that the morphological feature is indexed with a cophonology that makes the (non-concatenative or morpheme-specific) operation necessary. The analysis for Subtractive Suffixation in Wolof would hence look like in (18). The well-motivated general markedness constraint *C: is taken to be high-ranked in the cophonology indexed to, for example, the causative (18) and triggers degemination.

(18)   *Subtractive Affixation in CT: morphological structure*
       Master Ranking
       Max-V ≫ {*C:, Max-μ}

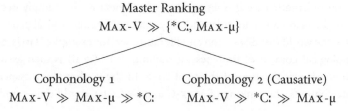

Cophonology 1   Cophonology 2 (Causative)
Max-V ≫ Max-μ ≫ *C: Max-V ≫ *C: ≫ Max-μ

---

[7] Since verb bases in Canela Krahô can be polysyllabic as well, it is assumed that some additional Contiguity constraint (Landman, 2002) ensures that only consonants at the edge of the word can be deleted. An alternative would be a constraint like NoCoda/Word (Flack, 2007a), but nothing hinges on that.

(19) *Subtractive Affixation in CT: Wolof*

i. *Preservation of a geminate*

/seːgː/	Max-V	Max-μ	*Cː
☞ a. segː			*
b. seg		*!	

ii. *Degemination in the causative*

/seːgː/+ /al/_Caus	Max-V	*Cː	Max-μ
a. segːal		*!	
☞ b. segal			*

However, for other subtractive MLM patterns, it is less clear which general markedness favours them over a faithful realization of the base. An example is non-realization of a final mora as in La Paz Aymara (see section 4.2.3): A short vowel is deleted preceding a Subtractive Suffix and a long vowel is shortened. Final vowel deletion creates a coda that is cross-linguistically more marked than the open syllable that would surface without deletion and no standard markedness constraint would hence favour the result of deletion. A possibility is apparently an ALIGN constraint demanding that the edge of the word must be aligned with a consonant ALIGN(WD,R;C,R). Such a type of constraint is adopted in the analysis for Subtractive Suffixation in Yine presented in Pater (2009). However, this solution is untenable for La Paz Aymara where non-realization of a vowel and vowel shortening alternate. The Subtractive Suffix in La Paz Aymara is on the surface adjacent to either a consonant (20-a) or a short vowel (20-b) and no ALIGN constraint demanding that the suffix must be aligned with a specific segment or syllable type can predict this alternation. This is shown in (20) where the relevant segments preceding the subtractive suffix are marked in boldface.

(20) *Aymara Subtractive Suffixes and* ALIGN

The Subtractive Suffix is aligned with . . .		*Without MLM
a. . . . a consonant	umtawa	*umatawa
b. . . . a short vowel	warmitwa	*warmiːtwa

However, for at least one language it has been argued that final mora deletion is an existing phonological process. In Trukese, an Austronesian language spoken in the Truk state of Micronesia, final vowels of morphemes only surface faithfully if the morpheme is followed by another morpheme as can be seen in (21). In isolation, short final vowels are deleted (21-a) and long final vowels are shortened (21-b) (Dyen, 1965; Hart, 1991; Davis and Torretta, 1998; Muller, 1999).[8]

---

[8] The Trukese pattern is more complex since final mora 'deletion' apparently interacts with processes of vowel lengthening and gemination that compensate for final mora delinking if the base violates word-minimality after mora deletion. These details are ignored for now.

(21)   *Final mora deletion in Trukese*   (Hart, 1991: 108)

	BASE	UNSUFFIXED FORM		SUFFIXED FORM (1.SG)
a.	omosu	omos	'turban shell'	omosuy
	fːéni	fːén	'love'	fːéniy
	mékúre	mékúr	'head'	mékúrey
	nemeneme	nemenem	'authority'	nemenemey
b.	pecheː	peche	'foot'	pecheːy
	tikːaː	tikːa	'coconut oil'	tikːaːy
	etiruː	etiru	'coconut matting'	etiruːy
	chuːchuː	chuːchu	'urine'	chuːchuːy

The OT-analysis for Trukese mora deletion in Davis and Torretta (1998) is based on the constraint FREE-µ, defined in (22).

(22)   FREE-µ   A word-final µ must not be parsed in the output.

One might argue that this constraint is rather specific and apparently an antifaithfulness constraint rather than a general markedness constraint. However, if the mora deletion in Trukese can receive no independent explanation, it is clear that *some* phonological demand must account for final mora deletion since the process is part of the general phonology of the language. CT is then able to predict the full range of MLM in Aymara given that there is some constraint favoring final non-realization of a mora.

Now we turn to additive MLM patterns. The imperative morpheme in Gidabal must be indexed to a constraint ranking that predicts a final long vowel for the base. Such a ranking is shown with its master ranking in (23) and its effect is illustrated in tableaux (24). A constraint like HAVEFINALLONGVOWEL, however, is highly problematic since it lacks any general motivation in terms of markedness. Phonological vowel lengthening is a well-motivated process in terms of stress assignment but the context for MLM is by definition not describable by such a phonological context alone. In our concrete example from Gidabal, for instance, stress falls roughly on the first syllable and all syllables with a long vowel (Geytenbeek and Geytenbeek, 1971: 2)—not necessarily and exclusively on the final vowel, not even in the imperative. This already points to a general problem of CT: Only morphological processes are possible that have an independent motivation as general phonological process. An alternative is yet again the assumption of ALIGN constraints. A constraint ALIGN(R,BASE;R,Vː) could then demand that the right edge of the base must coincide with a long vowel, abbreviated as Vː#!. In the Gidabal imperative, cophonology 2 is then assumed to be active that ranks this markedness constraint above DEP-µ, penalizing insertion of an epenthetic mora. Morphological contexts without vowel lengthening, are indexed with cophonology 1 where the faithfulness constraint is ranked higher and vowel lengthening is blocked.

(23) *Addition in CT: morphological structure*

Master Ranking
Max-μ ≫ {Dep-μ, V:#!}

Cophonology 1   Cophonology 2 (imperative)
Max-μ ≫ Dep-μ ≫ V:#!   Max-μ ≫ V:#! ≫ Dep-μ

(24) *Addition in CT: Gidabal*
  i. *Non-imperative: short final V*   ii. *Imperative: long final V*

/gida/	Dep-μ	V:#!
☞ a. gida		*
b. gida:	*!	

/gida/ + Imp	V:#!	Dep-μ
a. gida	*!	
☞ b. gida:		*

An analysis of Additive Affixation in Wolof faces a similar problem: geminates are cross-linguistically more marked than singleton consonants and the only strategy to derive the Additive Affixation in Wolof is apparently a constraint Align(Sfx,L;C:,R) demanding that every suffix must be preceded by a geminate consonant. The relevant tableaux are given in (26) and the master ranking for Wolof in (25). Such a constraint of course implies that the morphological boundaries between stems and affixes are still accessible by the phonology.

(25) *Additive Affixation in CT: morphological structure*

Master Ranking
Max-μ ≫ {Dep-μ, Align(Sfx;C:)}

Cophonology 1   Cophonology 2 (reversive)
Max-μ ≫ Dep-μ ≫ Align(Sfx;C:)   Max-μ ≫ Align(Sfx;C:) ≫ Dep-μ

(26) *Additive Affixation in CT: Wolof*
  i. *Non-reversive*   ii. *Reversive: Gemination*

/ub/	Dep-μ	Align (Sfx;C:)
☞ a. ub		*
b. ub:	*!	

/ub/ + /i/ Rev	Align (Sfx;C:)	Dep-μ
a. ubi	*!	
☞ b. ub:i		*

As with the RM and TAF approach, the locus of the MLM is determined by independent constraints in this approach. Positional faithfulness and CONTIGUITY would again be one strategy to ensure that, for example, only the final vowel is lengthened in Gidabal and the final consonant deleted in Canela Krahô. Note that for Additive and Subtractive Affixation, it is potentially more problematic to ensure that the length-manipulation affects the end of the base to which the affix attaches. A simple CONTIGUITY constraint penalizing changes inside a word is not sufficient because the edge of the base is not word-final in those configurations. The CONTIGUITY constraint must hence preserve the contiguous realization of all segments inside the (potentially morphologically complex) base to which the Subtractive Suffix attaches. In a non-stratal model, it is not clear which status this morphological complex could possibly have. This problem of restricting the locus of the MLM operation in CT is discussed in some more detail in section 7.5.

In general, we can conclude that the CT approach predicts the general patterns of Addition, Subtraction, Additive Affixation, and Subtractive Affixation. How it fares with respect to some more complex MLM patterns is discussed in sections 7.2 to 7.4.

7.1.4 Morpheme-specific constraints

An approach that is apparently very similar to CT is the assumption of lexically indexed faithfulness and markedness constraints (=LIC; see for example Ito and Mester, 1990; Golston and Wiese, 1996; Fukazawa, 1999; Pater, 2000; Pater and Coetzee, 2005; Pater, 2006; Flack, 2007*b*; Pater, 2009). One analysis proposed inside LIC for Subtractive Affixation is the analysis for Yine in Pater (2009) (see also Pater, 2006). In this LIC account, morphemes that trigger a process that is phonologically not predictable are indexed for specific markedness constraints and morphemes that fail to undergo a certain process are indexed for specific faithfulness constraints.

As in the CT approach, this approach gets potentially complicated given that not every MLM process can be triggered by a reasonable general markedness constraint. Since the argumentation is the same as in section 7.1.3, illustrating tableaux for the four MLM patterns are given below with lexically indexed versions of the constraints that were already assumed for CT above. For Subtraction in Canela Krahô, for example, we would simply assume that the general markedness constraint against final codas is indexed to the class of morphemes to which FINITE belongs. The tableaux in (27) shows how final consonant deletion is then predicted in the finite verb form. The tableaux (28)–(30) show the LIC-based accounts for degemination, vowel lengthening, and gemination that are all completely parallel to the accounts presented in (19), (24), and (26), respectively.

(27) *Subtraction in LIC: Canela Krahô*

/tɔn/ + Fin	NoCodaFin	Max-V	NoCoda
a. tɔn	*!		*
☞ b. tɔ		*	

(28) *Subtr. Affixation in LIC: Wolof*

/segː/ + /al/Caus	*Cːᴄᴀᴜꜱ	Max-μ	*Cː
a. segːal	*!		*
☞ b. segal		*	

(29) *Addition in LIC: Gidabal*

/gida/ + Imp	Align (Wd;Vː)ᴵᴹᴾ	Dep-μ	Align (Wd;Vː)
a. gida	*!		*
☞ b. gidaː		*	

(30) *Additive Affixation in LIC: Wolof*

/ub/ + /i/Rev	Align (Sfx;Cː)ᴿᴱⱽ	Dep-μ	Align (Sfx;Cː)
a. ubi	*!		*
☞ b. ubːi		*	

Given only these tableaux, LIC seems like a notational variant that makes the same predictions as CT. However, in contrast to CT, Pater (2009) assumes a locality restriction. A morphologically indexed constraint is only sensitive to contexts that contain at least some material affiliated with the morpheme it is indexed to. The abstract schema (31) for a morpheme-specific markedness constraint states that.

(31) $^*X_L$ Assign a violation mark to any instance of X that contains a phonological exponent of a morpheme specified as L.

(Pater, 2009: 10)

This assumption makes the account more restrictive than CT and solves the potential locality problem mentioned for the CT account in section 7.1.3. On the other hand, if this restriction indeed generally holds, cases of Subtraction and Addition cannot be predicted by LIC, simply because there is no phonological material indexed with the morpheme in question in Addition and Subtraction contexts. This account hence excludes a substantial amount of MLM patterns.

In addition, there are some Additive Suffixes where the MLM is found at the left edge of its base: the triggering affix and the MLM are therefore at opposite edges.[9]

---

[9] One example is Balangao, discussed in section 6.2.4.3.

The correct empirical generalization one wants to capture is hence not that MLM only affects segments adjacent to a triggering segmental affix, but that MLM is generally restricted to an edge position of its base.

In the following, two versions of LIC theories are discussed: the one assuming (31) is abbreviated as LIC^{+loc} and a possible LIC theory without any locality restriction is abbreviated as LIC^{-loc}.

7.2 Alternative accounts and the Aymara rescuer morpheme

I am not aware of existing analyses for the MLM patterns in either one of the Aymara dialects, despite the general mentioning that '[c]ophonologies...enable us to model languages like Aymara where suffixes can have differing, lexically specified morphophonological patterns' (p. 10) in Kim (2003). In this section, possible accounts of the rescuer morpheme found in Muylaq' Aymara are discussed. It is shown that most of these accounts are unable to predict the existence of such a rescuer morpheme that blocks an expected subtractive MLM. An analysis for the rescuer morpheme in Muylaq' Aymara in the PDM framework was presented in section 4.2 where it was shown that its existence is straightforwardly expected if one takes into account the full range of possible morphemic prosodic nodes. The main empirical facts about the MLM in Muylaq' Aymara are repeated in (32) below. There is Subtraction in Muylaq' Aymara that triggers non-realization of a final vowel (32-I) and Subtractive Suffixes that trigger non-realization of the vowel preceding this affix (32-IIa). In verbalizing contexts, however, any vowel that is expected to remain unrealized unexpectedly surfaces (32-IIb). The verbalizer has no surface effect in case no Subtractive Suffix follows the verbalized base; its only surface effect is 'rescuing' a vowel.

(32) *Two MLM patterns in Muylaq' Aymara*

	Base	Derived	Example	
I.	Subtraction			
	CV#	→ C	/kawka/	→ /kawk/
IIa.	Subtractive Suffix			
	CV# + C(V)	→ CC(V)	/muna−t/	→ /munt/
IIb.	Subtr. Suffix + Rescuer Morpheme			
	CV# + □ + C(V)	→ CVC(V)	/taχa−□−ta−wa/	→ /taχatawa/

7.2.1 Realize Morpheme

Interestingly, predicting the Subtractive Suffixation in Muylaq' Aymara is not completely trivial in RM. It is clear that the assumption of Sympathy Theory is crucial since segmental affixation is accompanied by the application of MLM. However, the general logic of the Subtractive Suffixation account for Wolof given in (14) in section 7.1.2 cannot be adopted for Muylaq' Aymara without problems. This follows since a crucial part of the Sympathy account for Subtractive Affixation is the high position of MAX-S ensuring that all the segmental affix material is realized in the output. However, in Muylaq' Aymara, Subtractive Affixation results in segment deletion, a high-ranked MAX-S hence predicts the fully faithful candidate realizing all input segments to be optimal. To predict faithful realization of all affix segments while still inheriting final deletion of base material from the sympathetic candidate hence requires the assumption of a constraint like MAX-S$_{AF}$ that only demands preservation of affix segments. How the Subtractive Suffixation in Muylaq' Aymara then falls out in Sympathy Theory is shown in (33).

(33) *The Subtractive Suffix in Muylaq' Aymara: RM*

/taχa/ + /ta/1>3.Npst	RM	MAX-S$_{AF}$	DEP-V ⊛O	MAX-S 1>3.NPST	★ST=PWD
a. taχa	*!	*!*	*	**	
b. taχata			**!		*
❀ c. tax		*!*		***	
☞ d. taχta			*	*	*

Given that morpheme-specific faithfulness constraints are a crucial part of the RM theory, an account of the rescuer morpheme seems apparently simple. A higher-ranked MAX-V that is specified for the morpho-syntactic features of the verbalizer should in principle be able to block any vowel deletion as soon as the verbalizer morpheme is part of the structure. If this constraint is high-ranked, the non-deletion candidate (34-b) is indeed predicted to become optimal. Note that the addition of this constraint has severe consequences for the whole analysis since now a different candidate is the sympathetic one. The constraint DEP-V ⊛O becomes irrelevant since the optimization is already decided by MAX-V$_{VB}$.

(34) *Subtractive Suffix and rescuer morpheme in Muylaq' Aymara: RM*

/taχa/ + Vb + /ta/1>3.Npst	MAX-V$_{VB}$	RM	MAX-S$_{AF}$	DEP-V ⊛O	MAX-S 1>3.NPST	★ST=PWD
❀ a. taχa	*!	*	**		**	
☞ b. taχata				*		*
c. tax	*!*		**		***	
d. taχta	*!			*	*	*

However, this analysis is highly problematic from a conceptual and empirical perspective. Conceptually, it implies that the verbalizer morpheme that lacks any further segmental content /−ø/ is still recognizable by the phonological constraints, hence that the morphological structure is still accessible. Given that the theory only evaluates realization of one morpheme at a time and that it is in principle based on OO-relations that compare existing *surface* forms, this is a problematic assumption since morphological bracketing and identity of morphemes should be inaccessible in surface word forms. And even if embedded morphological structure remains visible for the phonology, a serious empirical misprediction arises. If MAX-V$_{VB}$ is violated whenever a vowel is deleted in a word containing the verbalizer, *every* potential vowel deletion is blocked for those bases. This prediction is empirically flawed. It is very well possible that a Subtractive Suffix that not directly follows the verbalizer triggers deletion of a vowel in a morphologically more complex form. An example can be seen in (35). If MAX-V$_{VB}$ is active as soon as the verbalizer morpheme is present in a word, then vowel deletion before /−ʧi/ is expected to be blocked as well. Such a theory is hence incapable of restricting the effect of the verbalizer to its immediate locus in the word.

(35)   *Cooccurrence of a rescuer morpheme and vowel deletion in a complex form*

(Coler, 2010: 74)

jjumanχa   jiwa−ta−□−wa−ʧi−χal^j
you.GEN.TOP   die-RE-VB-BFR-3.DUB-DIS
jumanχa jiwatawʧiχal^j
'Yours must be dead'

That the RM-account is unable to predict the existence of the Aymara rescuer morpheme follows from the cyclic nature of this approach and the fact that the morpho-syntactic features of a previously added morpheme should not be relevant anymore.

7.2.2 *Transderivational Antifaithfulness*

For the TAF account, the conceptual problem discussed for RM is the same since the system also evaluates bases recursively with reference to the morphologically less complex base. This is what is termed 'base priority' in Alderete (2001a): 'Recursive constraint hierarchies simultaneously evaluate a word and its immediate morphological derivative, giving priority to the former, the base' (Alderete, 2001a: 209). The surface form of the verbalized word hence serves as base for the derivation of the more complex form to which a Subtractive Suffix might be added. A putative transderivational *faith*fulness constraint demanding preservation of the verbalized output form can hence not be active anymore and potentially outrank the effect of the antifaithfulness constraint active for the Subtractive Suffix: the verbalizer is not the morphological form derived at this point.

7.2.3 Cophonology Theory

In principle, it is not difficult to think about a cophonology that would prevent vowel deletion and could be indexed to the verbalizer rescue morpheme. One only needs to assume that the constraint triggering final vowel deletion (ALIGN(SFX;C), see the discussion in section 7.1.3) is dominated by MAX-μ in the cophonology indexed to the verbalizer in Muylaq' Aymara. However, it is impossible to hierarchically order this cophonology with respect to the mora deleting cophonology in a way that would predict the blocking of mora deletion. The rescuer cophonology will apply too early (36) or too late (37) to have the attested surface effect. For illustration purposes, ALIGN(SFX;C) is taken as the constraint triggering vowel deletion in Muylaq' Aymara.[10] In the morphological structure in (36), the verbalizer is directly adjacent to the stem whereas the Subtractive Suffix /–ta/ is affixed to the complex verbalized base. The 'rescuer' cophonology indexed with the verbalizer morpheme prohibits any deletion of stem material at the point where the verbalizer is added. If the Subtractive Suffix /–ta/, however, is added, this cophonology is not active anymore. Instead, the cophonology triggering deletion of base-final vowels associated with the subtractive suffix is predicted to be active at this point. The rescuer morpheme comes too early to have any blocking effect for the more outwards suffix that triggers deletion.

(36)   *Structural paradox I: vowel-preserving phonology applies too early*

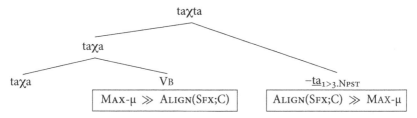

Although the morphological analysis of Muylaq' Aymara suggests that this is the right order of morphemes, let's consider for a moment a different morphological structure, namely the one in (37). This reanalysis is in principle possible since we have no other evidence for the position of the verbalizer simply because it has no other surface effect than 'rescuing' a vowel in Muylaq' Aymara. Under this alternative analysis, the verbalizer attaches after the Subtractive Suffix and hence the cophonology indexed for the verbalizer is active at a later point in the derivation. However, the rescuer phonology can only prohibit a vowel deletion that is about to happen at this point in the derivation—it is too late to prevent the vowel deletion triggered by the Subtractive Suffix that was added earlier.

---

[10] The problem discussed for La Paz Aymara in (20) is irrelevant for the Muylaq' variety that has no long vowels; the subtractive MLM effect is hence always deletion.

(37)   *Structural paradox II: vowel-preserving phonology applies too late*

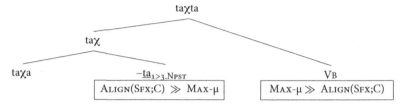

Both imaginable morphological structures of the verbalizer and a Subtractive Suffix in Aymara in (36) and (37) are hence incapable of predicting the rescuing property of the verbalizer: vowel deletion is expected to apply under both accounts.

Yet another imaginable analysis is that the rescuer morpheme in fact reverses the MLM effect of the Subtractive Suffix and simply inserts an additional vowel. This could be predicted by a cophonology penalizing coda consonants.[11] However, such an assumption makes the severe mispredictions that vowels are inserted in all verbalizer contexts; a prediction that is obviously not borne out in contexts without a Subtractive Suffix where the verbalizer simply has no surface effect. Another obvious problem is the unpredictability of the vowel quality of the inserted vowel.

7.2.4 *Morpheme-specific constraints*

For LIC, there exists in fact an analysis for a rescuer morpheme, namely for the exceptional non-undergoer /−wa/ suffix in Yine in the analysis presented in Pater (2009). It is argued that lexically indexed faithfulness constraints are able to predict the existence of morphemes that fail to undergo a certain process. A lexically indexed MAX-S_{Vb} constraint that is ranked higher than the lexically indexed markedness constraint triggering vowel deletion (e.g. ALIGN(SFX;C)) thus blocks vowel deletion. However, there is a fundamental problem with the reimplementation of this analysis for Muylaq' Aymara: the verbalizer morpheme does not have any surface exponent. Recall from section 7.1.4 that Pater (2009) argues for a strictly local theory of lexically indexed constraints where a phonological operation triggered by a lexically indexed constraint can only 'apply if and only if the locus of violation contains some portion of the indexed morpheme' (Pater, 2009: 10).

Since there is no phonological content indexed to the verbalizer ever realized in the output, a putative MAX-V constraint lexically indexed to the verbalizer is never violated in a LIC^{+loc} account of Muylaq' Aymara, shown in (38). Consequently, it is predicted that candidate (38-b) that perfectly fulfils morpheme-specific ALIGN becomes optimal. The empirically correct (38-a) is suboptimal since it violates the ALIGN constraint. The constraints in (38) are the ones introduced in Pater (2009) for

---

[11] The complication remains to ensure that only the coda directly preceding the Subtractive Suffix is avoided.

an account of Yine, but for ease of exposition the indices for lexical classes (L, L1, L2) are replaced with the morphological features in question. Given that a lexical class can only contain a single morpheme, this is no deviation from Pater's original system.

(38) *The Aymara rescuer morpheme: LIC^{+loc}*

/taχa/+Vb+/ta/₁>₃.Npst	Max-V$_{VB}$	Align (Sfx;C)₁>₃	Max-V	Align (Sfx;C)
☞ a. taχata		*!		*
☞ b. taχta			*	

If we abandon the locality restriction and take it for granted that a lexically indexed constraint can be violated as soon as the morpheme it is indexed to is (morphologically) present in a structure, the rescuing property of the verbalizer in Aymara can indeed be predicted. In the derived verbalized form, lexically indexed Max-V is violated whenever a vowel is deleted, irrespective of whether this vowel is part of the underlying representation of the verbalizer. Candidate (38-a) would hence be correctly predicted to be optimal where the verbalizer blocks vowel deletion and hence 'rescues' the vowel preceding the Subtractive Suffix. However, in a LIC^{-loc} theory that abandons any locality restriction between the locus of the violation and the relevant morpheme category, a new severe problem arises. For Aymara, the ranking in (38) then predicts that *any* vowel deletion in a verbalized form is impossible. This is the same severe empirical misprediction that was already identified for the RM-account of the rescuer morpheme in section 7.2.1.

And in fact this version of LIC^{-loc} without any locality restriction is not even adopted in Flack (2007*b*) where Pater's locality restriction is in principle abandoned. There, it is assumed that only lexically indexed markedness constraints are 'generally understood to apply to entire outputs in which the indexing morpheme occurs' (Flack, 2007*b*: 754), lexically indexed faithfulness constraints are assumed to be restricted to phonological elements underlyingly associated with the morpheme the faithfulness constraint is indexed to. We can therefore conclude that the $^{+loc}$ account that Pater (2009) assumes is inherently incapable of predicting rescuer morphemes that have no additional segmental representation. A LIC^{-loc} theory without any locality restriction on faithfulness and markedness constraints was shown to be able to account for the rescuer effect in principle, but to make severe mispredictions in morphologically more complex forms.

Note that the incapability of Pater's system to predict rescuer morphemes without a segmental representation is obviously bound to its general incapability to account for non-concatenative morphology in general (see the discussion in 7.1.4). It has to be emphasized that the latter is not the aim of the theory and hence can hardly count as a licit argument against it. However, an account like PDM that can predict both phenomena whose typology is so strikingly similar is generally to be preferred over a theory that can only predict a subset of the phenomena.

7.2.5 *Summary: alternative accounts of Aymara*

Table (39) summarizes the preceding discussion and lists how the present approach of PDM and the four alternative OT accounts fare in predicting the MLM pattern of Muylaq' Aymara that includes Subtraction, Subtractive Suffixes, and the rescuer morpheme. RM, TAF, and CT are very well able to correctly predict the existence of Subtraction and Subtractive Suffixation but are inherently incapable of deriving the existence of the rescuer morpheme in Aymara. This is mainly due to a look-ahead problem: in these accounts, it is impossible to preserve the rescuing property of a morpheme into a morphologically more complex form where the vowel deletion is expected. A LIC^{+loc} account is also unable to account for the rescuer morpheme in Muylaq' Aymara. As was already discussed in 7.1.4, the latter is also unable to predict the existence of Addition and Subtraction to begin with.

A theory based on LIC^{-loc} that abandons the assumption of locality can in principle predict the existence of the rescuer morpheme in Muylaq' Aymara. However, this account makes the empirical misprediction that *all* vowel deletion should be blocked in a verbalized form, not only vowel deletion adjacent to the verbalizer morpheme. It is hence marked with '×' in the table below since it incorrectly predicts an overapplication of the rescuing property for the whole form as soon as the rescuer morpheme is present in the structure.

(39)   *MLM in Aymara: an evaluation of theoretical accounts*

		TAF	RM	CT	LIC^{+loc}	LIC^{-loc}	PDM
i.	Subtraction	✓	✓	✓	×	✓	✓
ii.	Subtractive Suffix	✓	✓	✓	✓	✓	✓
iii.	The rescuer morpheme	×	×	×	×	×	✓

7.3 Allomorphy in Upriver Halkomelem

In this section, it is discussed whether the four alternative accounts are able to correctly predict instances of phonologically predictable non-concatenative allomorphy. Those patterns are taken as a strong argument for accounts in line with the PDM assumption (see the discussion in section 2.1.1). As an example, the non-continuative allomorphy in Upriver Halkomelem is discussed. Recall that the continuative formation in the language involves either stress shift (40-a), reduplication (40-b), vowel lengthening (40-c), or insertion of /hɛ/ (40-d). It was argued in section 5.3.1 that the pattern is predicted in the PDM account from affixation of a morphemic foot.

(40) *Verbal aspect in Upriver Halkomelem* (Galloway, 1993)

	NON-CONTINUATIVE		CONTINUATIVE		
a.	ts'ɛtéːm	'crawl'	ts'étəm	'crawling'	56
b.	q'ísət	'tie sth.'	q'íq'əsət	'tying sth.'	68
c.	ʔíməç	'walk'	ʔíːməç	'walking'	66
d.	máq'ət	'swallow sth.'	hámq'ət	'swallowing sth.'	60

7.3.1 Realize Morpheme

Instances of non-concatenative allomorphy such as the one in the Upriver Halkomelem continuative are actually taken as one strong argument for the RM-based approach in Kurisu (2001). If phonological markedness prohibits a certain preferred non-concatenative strategy to realize a morpheme, high-ranked RM can then demand that the non-concatenative operation penalized by a lower-ranked faithfulness constraint applies: allomorphy between non-concatenative operations arises. In fact, an analysis for the non-concatenative allomorphy in Upriver Halkomelem is presented in Kurisu (2001) that is briefly summarized below.

The ranking of lexically indexed faithfulness constraints that predicts the Upriver Halkomelem allomorphy is the one in (41). The continuative morpheme has no underlying phonological representation and strives to be realized by /hɛ/ epenthesis (=violating only lowest-ranked DEP), and only if this allomorph is blocked by phonological demands, reduplication violating INTEGRITY (=INTEG), and vowel lengthening violating IDENT-LENGTH can become optimal.

(41) *Preference order for satisfying RM in Upriver Halkomelem* (Kurisu, 2001: 150)
RM ≫ IDENT-LENGTH ≫ INTEG ≫ DEP

The relevant markedness constraints that prohibit reduplication and /hɛ/ epenthesis for bases with a certain phonological form are *STRESS[ə] ('Assign a violation mark for every /ə/') and *ʔə ('Assign a violation for every placeless σ').

The stress shifting allomorph is particularly interesting since it receives a double motivation in Kurisu's analysis. To account for the fact that all continuative forms have initial stress but lexical non-initial stress patterns surface in non-continuative contexts, it is assumed in Kurisu (2001) that the general markedness ALIGN(Hdσ,L;PRWD,L) demanding initial prominence is ranked below the lexically indexed faithfulness constraint PROSFAITH$_{\text{NonCont}}$[12] but above PROSFAITH$_{\text{Cont}}$. Underlying lexical stress is hence preserved in non-continuative contexts but a fixed stress pattern can be found in the continuative. Non-continuative bases with a non-initial stress pattern are therefore forced to shift the stress to the initial syllable due to ALIGN-L(HEADσ,PRWD)—a phonological operation that at the same time satisfies

---

[12] Note that PROSFAITH is not defined or explicitly discussed in Kurisu (2001). Given the logic of the account, the constraint is apparently satisfied as soon as the stress is on a syllable in the same position as in the input, irrespective of whether this is the *same* syllable that was underlyingly stressed or another (=epenthetic or reduplicated) syllable.

RM and makes any additional phonological operation unnecessary. The tableaux in (42) illustrate the basic logic of his account with a slightly modified and condensed version of the tableaux given in Kurisu (2001) on pp. 146–149.[13]

(42)   *The non-continuative allomorphy in Upriver Halkomelem:* RM

	*ʔə	ALIGN	RM	PrFthC	IdLGTH	*STRESS(ə)	INTEG	DEP
/ɬɛlqí/ + Cont	i. Stress shift							
a. ɬɛlqí		*!	*!					
☞ b. ɬɛ́lqi				*				
c. hə́ɬqi				*		*!		**
d. ɬɛ́ləlqi				*			*!*	
e. ɬɛ́:lqi				*	*!			
/məqət/ + Cont	ii. /hɛ/ epenthesis							
a. mə́qət			*!			*		
☞ b. hə́mqət						*		**
c. mə́məqət						*	*!*	
d. mə́:qət					*!	*		
/wíqəs/ + Cont	iii. Reduplication							
a. wíqəs			*!					
b. hə́wqəs						*!		**
☞ c. wíwəqəs							**	
d. wí:qəs					*!			
/ʔíməx/ + Cont	iv. Vowel lengthening							
a. ʔíməx			*!					
b. hə́ʔməx	*!					*		**
c. ʔíʔəməx	*!						**	
☞ d. ʔí:məx					*			

[13] The constraints given there are abbreviated as: ALIGN(Hdσ,L;PrWD,L) =ALIGN, ProsFaithCont=PrFthC, IdentLength=IdLgth.

Non-concatenative allomorphy as in the Upriver Halkomelem formation hence straightforwardly falls out in the RM framework and is in fact one major argument for the account.

7.3.2 *TAF, CT, and LIC*

The existence of phonologically predictable non-concatenative allomorphy is inherently difficult to implement in a TAF account. This point is also discussed by Kurisu who summarizes the problem as the fact that all non-concatenative operations demanded by lexically indexed antifaithfulness constraints that are ranked above their faithful counterpart are predicted 'irrespective of the presence or absence of markedness constraints, indicating that their distributional complementarity cannot be captured' (Kurisu, 2001: 150). This problem can be illustrated if one thinks about what an implementation of the Upriver Halkomelem pattern would look like. *First*, the antifaithfulness constraints ¬DEP$_{Cont}$, ¬INTEG$_{Cont}$, ¬IDLGTH$_{Cont}$, and ¬PRFTH$_{Cont}$ must all be ranked above their faithfulness counterpart in order to trigger the four non-concatenative operations of epenthesis, reduplication, lengthening, and stress shift. And, *second*, phonological markedness constraints must block certain of these strategies in certain contexts. ALIGN(HDσ,L;PRWD,L) blocks stress shift for all bases where it would result in non-initial stress (43-ii-iv), *ʔə blocks reduplication for bases with a glottal initial onset (43-ii), and *ə́ blocks epenthesis for bases with a full first vowel (43-iii). The tableaux (43-i) to (43-iv) illustrate this TAF analysis. Note that PRFTH is interpreted in the same sense as in Kurisu (2001), hence it is violated as soon as the stress is on a syllable in another position. ¬PRFTH is consequently violated as soon as a syllable in the same position (±first syllable) is stressed.

However, there is a fatal problem with this account (already implied in (43) since many pointing fingers are in brackets). Markedness constraints must block all the three non-surfacing alternative non-concatenative operations in all contexts, otherwise multiple non-concatenative exponence arises. In the RM-based and the PDM proposal, there is a preference order for realizing the continuative and certain allomorphs do not surface in certain contexts simply because a more preferred strategy is not blocked and already satisfies RM/realizes the prosodic foot. In the TAF approach, the default strategy to realize the morpheme are all operations satisfying the antifaithfulness constraints ranked above their faithfulness counterpart. For the Upriver Halkomelem ranking in (43), this problem becomes apparent if we take into account the full range of candidates. For bases with non-initial stress, for example, candidate (44-i-g) where stress shift, reduplication, vowel lengthening, and epenthesis cooccur, is predicted to be optimal. The same holds for all other base types where the cooccurrence of all operations is the expected default.

(43) *Non-concatenative allomorphy under TAF*

	ALIGN	*STRESS(ə)	*ʔə	¬PRFTH	¬DEP	¬INTEG	¬IDLGTH
/ɬɛlqí/ + Cont	**i. Stress shift**						
a. ɬɛlqí	*!			*	*	*	*
(☞) b. ɬɛ́lqi					*	*	*
/ʔíməx/ + Cont	**ii. Vowel lengthening**						
a. ʔíməx				*	*	*	*!
b. ʔimə́x	*!	*!			*	*	*
c. ʔíʔəməx			*!	*	*		*
d. hə́ʔməx		*!	*!	*		*	*
☞ e. ʔíːməx				*	*	*	
/wíqəs/ + Cont	**iii. Reduplication**						
a. wíqəs				*	*	*!	*
(☞) b. wíwəqəs				*	*		*
c. hə́wqəs		*!		*		*	*
d. wíːqəs				*	*	*!	
/mə́qət/ + Cont	**iv. /hɛ/ epenthesis**						
a. mə́qət		*		*	*!	*	*
b. mə́məqət		*		*	*!		*
(☞) c. hə́mqət		*		*		*	*
d. mə́ːqət		*		*	*!	*	

Undoubtedly, some of these structures are reasonably excluded by additional markedness constraints since they, for example, result in superheavy syllables, but the general problem remains that the operations are not in complementary distribution. It is, for example, impossible to exclude overapplication of vowel lengthening in (44-i), (44-iii), and (44-iv) given that long vowels in the initial syllable are indeed created for the base (44-ii). For CT and LIC theory, exactly the same misprediction arises. Although the general mechanism in these theories is rather different, the general ranking argumentation is the same: At least four different (markedness) constraints must demand the four non-concatenative operations. That only one surfaces in every context might be derivable for certain contexts but is a mere coincidence that follows from nothing principled in the theories.

(44) *Allomorphy ~ multiple non-concatenative operations*

	ALIGN	*STRESS(ə)	*ʔə	¬PRFTH	¬DEP	¬INTEG	¬IDLGTH
/ɬɛlqí/ + Cont	i. Stress shift'						
☛ b. ɬə́lqi					*!	*	*
c. ɬə́ɬəlqi					*!		*
d. hə́ɬɛɬəlqi		*!	*!			*	*
e. ɬɛ́ːlqi					*!	*	
f. ɬɛ́ːɬɛlqi					*!		
☞ g. ɬɛ́ːʔɬɛlqi							
/ʔíməx/ + Cont	ii. Vowel lengthening						
☛ e. ʔíːməx				*	*!	*	
☞ f. ʔíːʔməx				*		*	
/wíqəs/ + Cont	iii. Reduplication'						
☛ b. wíwəqəs				*	*!		*
e. hə́wəwəqəs		*!		*			*
f. wíːwəqəs				*	*!		
☞ g. wíːʔwəqəs				*			
/mə́qət/ + Cont	iv. /hɛ/ epenthesis						
☛ c. hə́mqət		*		*		*!	*
e. hə́ːmqət		*		*		*!	
☞ f. hə́ːmməməqət		*		*			

A severe additional complication is the question which independently motivated constraints demand the non-concatenative operation. It was already discussed in 7.1.3 and 7.1.4 that this is apparently non-trivial for instances of final vowel lengthening or final vowel deletion. For epenthesis and reduplication, the problem is even bigger: which independently motivated phonological markedness constraint favours /wíwəqəs/ over /wíqəs/ or /hə́mqət/ over /méqət/? Exactly such a constraint is necessary to predict the reduplication and epenthesis allomorph. It is then taken to be high-ranked in the cophonology associated with the continuative in a CT approach and lexically indexed to the continuative in an LIC based approach respectively. It is not clear which independently motivated markedness constraint triggers such an insertion that is not optimizing in terms of general phonotactic or prosodic structure and does not serve the higher purpose to ensure that the resulting base conforms to a certain templatic requirement.

7.3.3 *Summary: allomorphy in Upriver Halkomelem*

It was argued that TAF, LIC, and CT accounts have inherent problems in predicting the non-concatenative allomorphy in Upriver Halkomelem since phonologically predictable allomorphy is in such accounts in fact an instance of extended exponence and the cooccurrence of all allomorphs is expected in the default case. In addition, reduplication and epenthesis remain mysterious non-concatenative strategies under an LIC or CT approach. The summary in (45) hence distinguishes between predicting the different allomorphs to realize the continuative and predicting their complementary distribution.

(45)   *MLM in Upriver Halkomelem: an evaluation of theoretical accounts*

	TAF	RM	CT	LIC^{+loc}	LIC^{-loc}	PDM
i. Four Addition allomorphs	✓	✓	×	×	×	✓
ii. Phonologically predictable allomorphy	×	✓	×	×	×	✓

7.4 Long epenthetic vowels as an opacity problem

The focus in this section is the phenomenon discussed in section 5.2.3 under the heading of 'long epenthesis'. An instance of long epenthesis that was discussed and analysed in detail in section 5.2.3.1 is Southern Sierra Miwok that will serve as our test case in this section. In principle, however, the following argumentation holds for all the 'all-vowel-lengthening' languages discussed in section 5.2.3. Some crucial examples for long epenthesis in SSM are repeated in (46). Addition and Additive Suffixes not only trigger lengthening of an underlying base vowel (46-a, b) but also lengthening of an epenthetic vowel (46-c, d). Recall that this lengthening is also attested for long (epenthetic) consonants in SSM. It was argued above that a simple mora affixation account is possible for this phenomenon if the concept of morph-contiguous prosodic projection is assumed and if $^*V_O <_O \mu_\bullet$ is taken to be high-ranked in SSM.

(46)   *Additive MLM in Southern Sierra Miwok*   (Broadbent, 1964)

a. lit—h—a—ːmeʔ   lithaːmeʔ   'it's risen on us'   63
b. teːp—a—ː   teːpaː   'he cut it'   48
c. ʔopaː—t—ːmeʔ   ʔopaːtɨmeʔ   'it's clouding up on us'   63
d. haːja—ŋk—ː   haːjaŋkɨ   'it is daylight'   82

In this subsection, it is now discussed how the four alternative accounts fare in predicting this instance of MLM. As becomes clear below, TAF and RM accounts are unable to predict long epenthesis in the context of morphological lengthening whereas CT and LIC can derive this pattern.

7.4.1 TAF, CT, LIC, and RM

In the RM-based OT-alternative, the existence of long epenthetic vowels as the result of MLM remains mysterious. Insertion of an epenthetic vowel (under violation of DEP-V) already satisfies RM and additional insertion of a second mora (under violation of DEP-μ) is harmonically bounded as is shown in (47) for the Addition context. In (47-i), final vowel lengthening to express the third person singular is correctly derived for a vowel-final base. In (47-ii) with a consonant-final base, vowel epenthesis is necessary to avoid a superheavy syllable. Empirically correct (47-ii-d) where the epenthetic vowel is lengthened is harmonically bounded by (47-ii-c). This same problem remains in contexts of Additive Affixation where the additional assumption of Sympathy Theory must be employed (see section 7.1.2).

(47) *Addition in SSM: RM*

	$*\sigma_{\mu\mu\mu}$	RM	DEP-$S_{3.SG}$	DEP-$\mu_{3.SG}$
/teːpa/ + $_{3.SG}$	i. Vowel lengthening			
a. teːpa		*!		
b. teːpaʔ			*!	
☞ c. teːpaː				*
/haːjaŋk/ + $_{3.SG}$	ii. Epenthesis			
a. haːjaŋk		*!		
b. haːjaːŋk	*!			*
☞ c. haːjaŋkɨ			*	*
☛ d. haːjaːŋkɨː			*	**!

A similar problem holds for a TAF account: a lexically indexed antifaithfulness constraint could demand that a mora must be inserted and this mora insertion can result in epenthesis if vowel lengthening is impossible. The additional insertion of a second mora that results in vowel lengthening, however, is completely unmotivated and should always be harmonically bounded by the short epenthesis candidate that avoids another violation of DEP-μ and the general markedness constraint against long vowels, shown in (48).

(48) *Addition in SSM: TAF*

	*σ μμμ	¬DEP-μ [...]	DEP-S	DEP-μ
/teːpa/ + 3.SG	i. Vowel lengthening			
a. teːpa		*!		
☞ b. teːpaː				*
c. teːpaʔ		*!	*	
d. teːpaʔɨ		*!*	*	
/haːjaŋk/ + 3.SG	ii. Epenthesis			
a. haːjaŋk		*!		
b. haːjaːŋk	*!			*
☞ c. haːjaŋkɨ			*	*
☛ d. haːjaːŋkɨː			*	**!

LIC and CT, on the other hand, are in principle able to predict the existence of long epenthesis in the context of additive MLM. The only prerequisite is the existence of a constraint demanding that a base must end in a long vowel. As was already argued in 7.1.3 and 7.1.4, such a constraint is potentially problematic in terms of general markedness but independently required in LIC and CT to account for numerous other instances of additive MLM. In the LIC tableaux (49), ALIGN is again used demanding that a suffix must precede a long vowel or consonant. It has to be noted that the Additive Affixes are consequently indexed for different constraints: all vowel-initial Additive Suffixes for ALIGN(SFX,L;Cː,R) and all consonant-initial ones for ALIGN(SFX,L;Vː,R). In (49), it is shown how such a constraint predicts either lengthening of a final vowel (49-i) or vowel epenthesis and lengthening in (49-ii) in a LIC based account. The same holds for a CT account where different cophonologies would rank ALIGN(SFX,L;Cː,R) above or below DEP-μ.

For the Addition context, the constraint ALIGN(STEM,R;Vː,R) would ensure that every stem ends in a long vowel in the morphological categories the constraint is indexed to (3SG1P, for example).

(49) *Additive Affixation in SSM: LIC*

		$*\sigma_{\mu\mu\mu}$	ALIGN $(\text{Sfx},\text{V:})_{\text{3S1P}}$	DEP-μ
/litha/ + /me?/$_{\text{3S1P}}$	i. Vowel lengthening			
a. lithame?			*!	
☞ b. litha:me?				*
/?opa:t/ + /me?/$_{\text{3S1P}}$	ii. Epenthesis			
a. ?opa:tme?		*!	*	
b. ?opa:tɨme?			*!	*
☞ c. ?opa:tɨ:me?				**

The general inability of the strictly local LIC$^{+\text{loc}}$ account to predict instances of Addition and Subtraction, however, is the reason why the complete picture of long epenthesis in SSM is underivable in this account: long epenthetic vowels also surface in Addition contexts.

7.4.2 Summary: long epenthetic vowels as an opacity problem

The table (50) summarizes the preceding discussion whether the alternative accounts are able to predict long epenthesis in SSM. Only CT and a LIC$^{-\text{loc}}$ theory without a locality restriction can correctly account for long epenthetic vowels in the context of morphological vowel lengthening. In RM and TAF theory, the additional insertion of an epenthetic mora is always expected to be harmonically bounded.

(50) *Long epenthetic vowels in SSM: an evaluation of theoretical accounts*

	TAF	RM	CT	LIC$^{+\text{loc}}$	LIC$^{-\text{loc}}$	PDM
i. Long epenthesis: Add.Aff	×	×	✓	✓	✓	✓
ii. Long epenthesis: Addition	×	×	✓	×	✓	✓

7.5 Overgeneration problems

In this section, several overgeneration problems for the alternative OT accounts introduced in section 7.1 are discussed. It is actually a non-trivial task to argue that a certain theory overgenerates since no researcher has found a concrete instance of the predicted pattern in the languages of the world. For one, a pattern can be blocked for independent reasons or it could simply be a coincidence that no language shows this pattern although it would be perfectly possible in human language. And secondly, we obviously can be quite sure that we do not know all patterns. However, it is argued that the alternatives often fail to predict overall generalizations that hold for all the patterns in the data set that is argued to be representative for MLM. Most of the unattested patterns are illustrated with hypothetical languages based on existing MLM patterns discussed in the preceding sections.

7.5.1 Non-local MLM

In section 6.2.5, two basic non-local MLM patterns were discussed: non-local additive MLM in *Asante Twi'$_{1/2}$ and non-local subtractive MLM in *Hausa'$_{1/2}$. It was argued that these patterns are impossible to predict in PDM and are systematically absent from the representative data set of MLM. How do the four alternatives fare in predicting these two non-local patterns? Very generally, all four alternatives are able to predict non-local MLM effects. As was already emphasized at several points in section 7.1, there is no inherent locality restriction in the theories of TAF, RM, LIC^{-loc}, and CT and the localization of a non-concatenative operation follows from independent principles like positional faithfulness constraints.

This is very briefly exemplified for the RM-approach in (51) and the non-local *Asante Twi'$_2$ pattern. A positional faithfulness constraint DEP-$\mu_{\#\sigma}$ protects the initial syllable and since gemination is the preferred strategy to realize the morpheme in question (abbreviated M), non-local gemination follows. From the discussion in 7.1, it should be clear that TAF, CT, and LIC^{-loc} can predict the exact same pattern.

(51)   *Asante Twi'$_2$ in an RM-based account

/nodaneka/ + M	DEP-$\mu_{\#\sigma}$	RM	DEP-μM	*V:	*C:
a. nodaneka		*!			
b. noːdaneka	*!		*	*	
c. nodːaneka	*!		*		*
d. nodaːneka			*	*!	
☞ e. nodanːeka			*		*

It is clear, however, that this is not the full account yet: what prevents gemination from applying to the final onset in (51), resulting in /nodanekːa/? This in fact only illustrates the point even further, that the lack of some principled restriction on where a non-concatenative operation can apply in its base is severely problematic.

In the following, some additional MLM patterns that straightforwardly fall out in one or several alternatives are discussed that are also generally unattested.

In CT and LIC^{-loc}, a certain ranking/lexically indexed constraint is active in a certain morphological environment. This implies that in principle the whole base is subject to this ranking/constraint and no principled reason determines the locus of operations enforced by this ranking. This predicts unattested patterns of global MLM effects. For illustration, recall the Subtraction pattern in Hausa where shortening of a final vowel was the exponent of the proper noun formation (e.g. /markaː/ → /marka/ 'height of rainy season' (Schuh, 1989: 38)). In CT and LIC^{-loc}, such a pattern follows from *Vː that is either lexically marked for the proper noun formation or from a morpheme-specific ranking where this constraint is high-ranked. A positional faithfulness constraint preserving the initial syllable in combination with CONTIGUITY would then ensure that this vowel shortening applies only in the final base vowel. A prediction is now that a grammar should also exist where these faithfulness demands are low-ranked. In such a grammar, all long vowels (or geminates, if *GEM is relevant) are predicted to be shortened in the relevant morphological category, illustrated in (52). The tableaux in (53) show how such a pattern follows in LIC^{-loc}—it is clear that CT can predict the same pattern.

(52) *Hausa'$_3$: global shortening

BASE	DERIVED FORM
markabaː	markaba
baːkimaː	bakima
likoːbaː	likoba
kuːmaːtuː	kumatu

(53) *Mispredictions of LIC^{-loc}: Derivation of global MLM in* *Hausa'$_3$*

	*Vː$_x$	MAX-μ
i. /markabaː/ +$_x$		
a.　markabaː	*!	
☞ b.　markaba		*
ii. /kuːmaːtuː/ +$_x$		
a.　kuːmaːtuː	*!**	
b.　kuːmaːtu	*!*	*
☞ c.　kumatu		*!**

Such or a similar instance of MLM is apparently unattested. Crucially, it cannot be interpreted as a templatic MLM pattern[14] since the resulting bases do not confirm to a general prosodic shape. They simply have in common that a marked structure is generally absent.

A similar unattested pattern that is predicted by TAF and RM-based accounts can be termed 'wandering' MLM. Recall that in accounts based on TAF and RM, there is again nothing that inherently restricts the effect of the constraint in terms of the base position where it surfaces. If the faithfulness constraints restricting the non-concatenative operation to a certain base position are low-ranked, the preferred phonological operation to realize the morpheme/satisfy the antifaithfulness constraint is predicted to apply once, irrespective of the position in the base where it is able to apply. In terms of our exemplifying Hausa ranking, we predict a 'wandering' Subtraction pattern where one long vowel is shortened for every base. In (54), it is always the rightmost long vowel of the base. Such a pattern is similar but not identical to the global shortening pattern in (52) and is illustrated in (54) with *Hausa'₄.

(54)   *Hausa'₄: wandering Subtraction

BASE	DERIVED FORM
markabaː	markaba
bakiːmaː	bakiːma
likoːba	likoba
kuːmaːtu	kuːmatu
liːmakoni	limakoni

(55)   *Mispredictions of TAF: Derivation of wandering Subtraction in *Hausa'₄*

	Max-S	¬Max-μ [...]	Max-μ
i. /markabaː/ + ₓ			
a. markabaː		*!	
☞ b. markaba			*
c. markab	*!		**
ii. /kuːmaːtu/ + ₓ			
a. kuːmaːtu		*!	
☞ b. kuːmatu			*
c. kuːmaːt	*!		*

---

[14] Which are not part of the present data sample, see the discussion in section 1.1.3.

The tableau (55) shows how a high-ranked ¬MAX$_\mu$ predicts such a language if positional faithfulness demands are lower-ranked. It is clear that RM is able to predict the very same pattern if RM is ranked above MAX-μ and no further (positional) faithfulness constraint is ranked above RM.

These global and 'wandering' MLM patterns are impossible to predict in the PDM approach simply because both involve non-local MLM in the sense excluded in section 6.2.5 for PDM. They both involve at least one MLM that is of the same type as the Addition in *Hausa'$_{1/2}$ and it was shown that this cannot be predicted in PDM.

Interestingly, there is one example of morpheme-specific phonology that looks exactly like this wandering Subtraction pattern, namely the famous pattern of labialization and palatalization in Chaha (McCarthy, 1983*a*; Rose, 2007; Banksira, 2013). In some morphological constructions like the impersonal, the rightmost labializable segment becomes labialized (and absolutely parallel for palatalization in some contexts). If labialization and palatalization are the result of affixing a featural affix, the restrictive theory of morpheme linearization adopted here makes it impossible that the features are realized in these different positions. One reanalysis would rely on local spreading and hence the assumption that the feature is indeed associated to all intervening segments where it is not realized due to cooccurrence restrictions (for a discussion on this issue in the domain of consonant harmony see, for example, Rose and Walker, 2004). This of course necessitates a detailed phonological analysis of the facts. However, the RMO is only formulated for the segmental and the prosodic tiers, not for featural tiers (see 2.2.6). Since this book only presents a unified account of MLM patterns and it is beyond the scope of the present discussion to give a full account of Chaha, future research needs to answer this question.

7.5.2 *Different edge allomorphy*

As was argued in section 7.3.1, the existence of phonologically predictable non-concatenative allomorphy follows straightforwardly under an RM account and looks like a genuine argument for such an approach. However, as is briefly argued in this section, the RM account of non-concatenative allomorphy suffers from a severe lack of restrictiveness and makes some predictions about unattested non-concatenative allomorphy patterns.

The following examples are derived by slightly modifying the Upriver Halkomelem ranking given in (41). In this hypothetical language, reduplication is in principle the preferred means to satisfy RM. The positional faithfulness constraint INTEG(#σ) prohibits fission of segments in the first syllable and CONTIGUITY penalizes an infixing reduplicant; reduplication is hence predicted to be suffixing (56-a). For bases with a glottal consonant as final onset, reduplication is assumed to be blocked due to *[ʔ penalizing glottal onsets (underlying glottal onsets are preserved by higher-ranked MAX in this hypothetical language). For those bases, vowel lengthening to realize the morpheme becomes optimal (56-b). If we take it for granted that final long vowels are impossible in the language, vowel lengthening for a base like (56-b) will affect the initial vowel. How this pattern where two non-concatenative strategies to realize a morpheme alternate predictably and affect opposite edges of their bases falls out in a RM-based account is shown in the tableaux in (57).

(56) *Halkomelem'ₗ: Wandering allomorphy I*

BASE	MORPHOLOGICALLY DERIVED
a. mɛqətal	mɛqətaltal
wawəqi	wawəqiqi
b. timəʔɛt	tiːməʔɛt
lɛməʔat	lɛːməʔat

(57) *Prediction of wandering allomorphy in RM*

	RM	*[ʔ	*V:#	INTEG#σ	CONTIG	*V:	INTEG
/məqətal/ + Cont	i. Suffixing Reduplication						
a. məqətal	*!						
b. məməqətal				*!*			**
☞ c. məqətaltal							***
d. məqəqətal					*!		**
e. məːqətal						*!	
f. məqətaːl			*!			*	
/timəʔɛt/ + Cont	ii. Lengthening of the initial vowel						
a. timəʔɛt	*!	*					
b. titiməʔɛt		*		*!*			**
c. timəʔɛtʔɛt		**!					***
d. timəʔɛːt		*	*!			*	
☞ e. tiːməʔɛt		*				*	

A similar problematic prediction arises from the fact that the RM-based approach allows that non-concatenative operations can receive a double motivation, one being a standard markedness constraint whose effect is blocked in other contexts of the language. This was the case with stress shift in Upriver Halkomelem under the analysis in Kurisu (2001): it is required by ALIGN(L,HEADσ;L,PRWD) but blocked in all non-continuative contexts due to lexically indexed PRFTH. In continuative contexts, however, stress shift is possible since PRFTH is ranked lower than morpheme-specific ALIGN. Crucially, this operation now satisfies RM and no further non-concatenative operation is required to realize the continuative. Generally speaking, if a high-ranked markedness constraint ensures that a requirement about all forms in a certain morphological category (=the fixed stress in Upriver Halkomelem) holds, then RM only forces additional non-concatenative operations if this property is already given in the underlying base form. This logic easily predicts other non-local allomorphy patterns. In the hypothetical language (58), stress shift to the initial syllable marks a certain morphological category (58-a). If the stress is already on the first syllable underlyingly (58-b), non-realization of the final consonant arises. Such a pattern easily follows assuming that ALIGN(L,HEADσ;L,PRWD) specified for the morphological category in question is ranked above RM and MAX is ranked below RM—if stress shift does not satisfy RM, segment deletion will.

(58)   *Halkomelem'$_2$: Wandering allomorphy II

	BASE	DERIVED FORM
a.	ʔimáç	ʔímaç
	jaqʷétlip	jáqʷɛtlip
	hakwíçq'ət	hákwiçq'ət
b.	málq'ətjɛt	málq'ətjɛ
	wíq'ʷatstəm	wíq'ʷatstə
	líp'açwɛməl	líp'açwɛmə

Both these 'wandering' allomorphy patterns have hence in common that different strategies to realize a certain morpheme apply at different edges of their base.

The alternative accounts of TAF, LIC, and CT do not predict these different edge allomorph patterns—due to the far more severe problem that those accounts cannot predict the existence of phonologically predictable non-concatenative allomorphy in the first place.

It is argued that such patterns are generally unattested and the RM-based approach severely overgenerates. As was shown in chapter 6, the attested patterns of MLM involving allomorphy always affect adjacent base positions. Under the PDM account, non-concatenative allomorphy like that follows from affixation of a morphemic prosodic node that is either suffixed or prefixed: the phonological operations predicted from (defectively) integrating the morphemic prosodic node into the structure are hence always predicted to occur at one edge of the base. A pattern *Halkomelem'$_2$ requires at least two morphemic nodes under a PDM account: a prefixed morphemic foot predicting the fixed stress pattern and a suffixed morphemic mora or syllable that results in non-realization of the consonant. Under such an analysis, the complementary distribution of both operations that is characteristic of allomorphy is impossible to implement.

7.6 Summary and discussion

There are three main arguments against the four alternative OT accounts to MLM and in favour of an account based on PDM that are briefly summarized below: *First*, it was shown that the alternative theories suffer from different undergeneration problems and can not predict the full range of (combined) MLM patterns (see sections 7.2 to 7.4). *Second*, the theories overgenerate and predict MLM patterns that are systematically unattested (section 7.5). *Third*, all alternative accounts need to rely on additional assumptions about morpheme-specific constraints or rankings and hence enrich the phonological grammar with powerful additional theoretical tools. These three arguments are summarized below.

The undergeneration argument   Section 7.1 already focussed on the question whether and how the four alternative OT accounts can in principle account for the full range of MLM operations attested in the languages of the world. Except for a LIC^{+loc} account that is unable to predict the existence of Addition and Subtraction, all accounts can generally predict the basic existence of MLM. It has to be noted, however, that the RM approach crucially relies on the additional assumption of Sympathy Theory in order to predict Additive and Subtractive Affixation. In sections 7.2, 7.3, and 7.4, the alternatives were then put to the test and it was discussed whether they are able to predict more complex MLM patterns. In section 7.2, it was illustrated that none of the four alternative accounts can correctly predict the existence of the rescuer morpheme in Aymara. That all alternatives except RM are inherently unable to allow the existence of phonologically predictable non-concatenative allomorphy was discussed in section 7.3. And in 7.4, it was finally argued that long epenthesis in the context of additive MLM is deeply problematic to predict under an approach assuming RM, TAF, or LIC^{+loc}. These findings are summarized in table (59).

(59)   *Alternative accounts*

	Muylaq' Aymara (7.2)		Upriver Halkomelem (7.3)		S. Sierra Miwok (7.4)
	Four patterns of MLM	Rescuer morpheme	Four non-concatenative exponents	Allomorphy between them	Long epenthetic vowels
RM	✓	✗	✓	✓	✗
TAF	✓	✗	✓	✗	✗
LIC^{+loc}	✗	✗	✗	✗	✗
LIC^{-loc}	✓	✗	✓	✗	✓
CT	✓	✗	✓	✗	✓
PDM	✓	✓	✓	✓	✓

The overgeneration argument   Some concrete overgeneration problems for the alternative accounts were discussed in section 7.5 while emphasizing that such over-generation arguments have to be considered with some caution. The crucial problem that underlies most of the concrete mispredictions discussed is the fact that none of the accounts imposes a locality restriction on the MLM operations. With the exception of the LIC account in Pater (2009), in none of the alternative accounts is the locus of the operation determined by any inherent principle but must be accounted for by additional (positional) faithfulness constraints. Wolf (2007) already discusses this problem and concludes that in an autosegmental view of non-concatenative morphology, the locality problem can be tackled by a more principled mechanism: because it 'is simply the realization of particular pieces of *structure* in the output, the location of those structures can be regulated by the same kinds of alignment constraints that regulate the location of segmental affixes' (Wolf, 2007: 373). Although the assumption of alignment constraint for the linearization of affixes is rejected here, the insight that the locality of non-concatenative processes boils down to the assumption about possible linear ordering of (prosodically defective) morphemes is exactly the line of reasoning followed here (see the discussion and assumptions in section 2.2.6).

From this lack of locality restrictions, it follows that the non-local MLM patterns discussed in section 6.2.5 are predicted by all the alternative accounts.[15] The global and 'wandering' MLM patterns discussed above are predicted by some of the alternative accounts. All these patterns exemplify MLM types that are arguably unattested and contradict the empirical generalizations found for MLM patterns (see section 6). Table (60) summarizes the unattested patterns discussed above. That RM suffers from a severe overgeneration problem for phonologically predictable non-concatenative allomorphy (*Halkomelem'$_1$ and *Halkomelem'$_2$) is particularly interesting. Non-concatenative allomorphy was inherently impossible to predict in the alternative accounts of CT, TAF, and LIC since there was no way to implement an inherent complementary distribution of the different exponents in these accounts. RM can in principle predict the general logic of non-concatenative allomorphy but severely overgenerates in that the different non-concatenative exponents are not bound to one edge of the base. In contrast, PDM naturally predicts non-concatenative allomorphy at one edge of the base: a morphemic prosodic node is affixed and different phonological strategies are predicted to realize/integrate this prosodic node for bases with different phonological shapes. Phonologically predictable non-concatenative allomorphy is hence a prima facie argument for PDM and against alternative accounts.

---

[15] For LIC, this only holds for the version without any locality restriction. LIC^{+loc} excludes all those patterns since the MLM operation does not apply in a position adjacent to a triggering morpheme.

(60)   *Unattested patterns of MLM*

*Hypothetical Languages	TAF	RM	CT	LIC^{+loc}	LIC^{-loc}	PDM
*Asante Twi'$_{1/2}$ Non-local MLM (48)/(51) in 6.2.5	✓	✓	✓	×	✓	×
*Hausa'$_{1/2}$ Non-local MLM (52)/(54) in 6.2.5	✓	✓	✓	×	✓	×
*Hausa'$_3$ Global MLM (52) in 7.5.1	×	×	✓	×	✓	×
*Hausa'$_4$ Wandering Subtraction (54) in 7.5.1	✓	✓	×	×	×	×
*Halkomelem'$_1$ Wandering allomorphy I (56) in 7.5.2	×	✓	×	×	×	×
*Halkomelem'$_2$ Wandering allomorphy II (58) in 7.5.2	×	✓	×	×	×	×

The economy argument   An additional and more general argument against the alternative accounts is based on theoretical economy. Although it is obviously hard to weigh up the complexity of theories against each other, it is clear that all four alternatives invoke additional mechanisms that allow a direct reference to morphological information in the phonology. Theories allowing direct access to morphological information in the phonology are generally assumed to suffer from 'a severe lack of empirical content and heuristic power' (Bermúdez-Otero, 2012: 79) and an analysis is preferable that restricts the ability of the phonology to refer to morpho-syntactic information. This does not only hold for theories where explicit morphologically triggered rules manipulate the phonological structure as in, for example, the account proposed in Martin (1988) for Subtraction, but also for all the OT-alternatives discussed here. In Kurisu's RM-based system, the indexation of all faithfulness constraints to (potentially) all morphemes in a language is crucial. This is definitely a non-trivial extension of the correspondence-theoretic constraint system. It introduces a powerful mechanism into the phonological component of a language that crucially refers to morphological information. Something similar holds for LIC where faithfulness and markedness constraints are lexically indexed. And in TAF, the antifaithfulness constraints are inherently morpheme-specific. In CT, constraints remain general, but morpheme-specific different rankings are possible in a grammar. Specific morphological information is therefore visible in the phonology to choose the relevant ranking.

In contrast, the framework of PDM is based on the independently motivated inventory of phonological primitives. The additional assumptions made are rather assumptions that restrict the possibility of GEN. Complexity is only added at the representational level: phonetically invisible structure mirroring the original underlying structure is always present in the output structure. Many lexical idiosyncrasies like morphemes that unexpectedly do not undergo a length-manipulating operation or undergo a different length-manipulating operation are expected from taking into account the full range of possible underlying prosodic structures. Examples for such patterns include the exceptional rescuer morpheme in Muylaq' Aymara (see section 4.2).

The main argument is hence that the introduction of these powerful new mechanisms adopted in alternative accounts are unnecessary at least in the domain of MLM: the independently motivated primitives of the prosodic organization together with the assumption that prosodically defective structures exist and might have crucial consequences for the surface interpretation for segments allows us to predict all attested patterns. And if two theories are in principle able to predict the same range of phenomena and generalizations, the account is to be preferred that introduces less additional machinery and assumptions.

8

Conclusion

The theoretical proposal of PDM can be understood as a rather conservative one: the idea that all morphology is additive and results from affixation of (possibly non-segmental) morphemes has been defended various times for various phenomena (Lieber, 1992; Stonham, 1994; Bermúdez-Otero, 2012; Bye and Svenonius, 2012). The most controversial empirical area where PDM offers a new insight is subtractive length-manipulation: the prosodically defective integration of morpheme representations might result in non-realization of underlying phonological elements. Prosodic nodes either collaterally cause non-realization since they remain unrealized but need to dominate some amount of base material or elements can 'usurp' a prosodic node from their base that they lack underlyingly.

It was shown that these mechanisms suffice to predict the wide variety of attested subtractive MLM patterns. The PDM account in a sense hence complements the claims that affixation of prosodic nodes might result in templatic truncation (for an overview and literature see, for example, Arndt-Lappe and Alber, 2012). Not only the portion of a base that is *not* integrated under a morphemic prosodic node can be forced to remain unrealized, but also only and exclusively the portion of base material that *is* integrated under a morphemic prosodic node. The PDM account is hence a novel way to theoretically implement the well-motivated insight that prosodic nodes are an important element in the (non-concatenative) morphological component that received special attention for the domain of truncatory deletion and reduplication (Weeda, 1992; McCarthy and Prince, 1986/1996; et seq.). The focus of subtractive MLM in this book complements this discussion.

Crucially, the PDM account can also be understood as a superset account that predicts subtractive MLM but incorporates all the insightful claims that affixation of prosodic nodes can result in different patterns of additive MLM as well. The PDM claim thus not only reduces subtractive MLM to an epiphenomenon of simple morpheme concatenation, it also claims that additive and subtractive MLM are based on the same basic mechanism. That the concatenation of morphemic prosodic nodes can result in either additive or subtractive MLM makes some interesting predictions about their interaction and coexistence. For one, if one morphemic prosodic node results in subtractive MLM, there can't easily be a parallel additive MLM operation in

Morphological Length and Prosodically Defective Morphemes. First edition. Eva Zimmermann.

the same language that results from affixing a morphemic prosodic node on the same tier. This follows since the phonology which is blind to specific morpho-syntactic features alone determines whether a morphemic prosodic node on a tier is defectively or completely integrated into the overall prosodic structure: prosodic nodes on the same tier are hence expected to behave absolutely parallel throughout a language. It was shown that such a natural restriction about different MLM operations in one grammar is borne out. All the attested instances of coexisting additive and subtractive MLM in one language follow in the PDM account from different morphemic prosodic nodes on different tiers. One standard situation is, for example, that a morphemic mora in a language is fully integrated into its base resulting in mora-sized additive MLM whereas a morphemic syllable is only defectively integrated resulting in syllable-sized subtractive MLM. On the other hand, this unified account for subtractive and additive MLM predicts interactions between both. In a language of the type just sketched where a morphemic syllable is defectively integrated and a morphemic mora is fully integrated, the two prosodic nodes can cancel each other's surface effects if they are both present in a structure. The morphemic syllable would only dominate the morphemic mora and hence block any lengthening whereas the morphemic mora would block the subtractive effect the morphemic syllable would otherwise have. Such interactions are indeed borne out, a case in hand discussed in some detail was the MLM in Aymara: What is additive MLM in one context, is blocking of subtractive MLM in another context.

That morphemic prosodic nodes on different tiers can be expected to interact in such ways and neutralize each other's MLM effect, already points to the fact that PDM naturally predicts various types of exceptions to MLM. Either the same basic MLM operation can have different lexical allomorphs or certain morphemes can be lexically marked non-undergoers for an MLM operation. There are various instantiations of both these types of exceptions that receive a representational explanation in the PDM framework: exceptional or morpheme-specific behaviour in this area follows from different underlying prosodic structures for certain morphemes. This point is hence a general claim that many instances of allomorphy and exceptions are in fact simple epiphenomena resulting from different underlying phonological structures of certain morphemes. Morpheme-specific phonology, non-concatenative morphology, lexical exceptions, or lexical allomorphies in the domain of length-manipulation—all these processes and phenomena are hence predicted from simple differences in the prosodic make-up of morphemes.

The main theoretical ingredient which is absolutely crucial for those mechanisms and structures is containment. A potential worry arising from this assumption are the additional layers of complexity: phonological structure is enriched with 'invisible' structure that remains uninterpreted for the phonetics and the constraint system is multiplied since constraints exist in different versions, specified for being sensitive to only phonetically visible or other structure as well. On the other side, this potentially heavy burden of enriched structures and constraints is one that is now taken away from the morphology. What crucially differentiates this theoretical proposal from OT alternatives is the lack of any morpheme-specific constraints or rankings: the phonology only sees phonological structure. Morphological affiliation is only visible for the phonology to the degree that it can tell whether two elements belong to the same, some different, or to no morpheme at all.

One theoretical claim made in this book is the existence of constraints demanding contiguous morpheme structures across prosodic tiers. An example is the constraint $^*V_O <_O \mu_\bullet$ that demands 'morph-contiguous licensing' for a vowel that implies that a vowel is not only dominated by a mora of a different morphological affiliation. This constraint demanding morpheme contiguity across tiers make several interesting predictions. For one, a notorious opacity problem that standard OT accounts of mora affixation face is solved. In contrast to systems where a restriction on GEN or a pre-optimization in a stratal OT system ensures that all vowels are dominated by at least one mora, the constraint $^*V_O <_O \mu_\bullet$ ensures that a morphemic mora can result in lengthening for all vowels, even underlyingly mora-less ones. A prediction from this system is typologically highly interesting, namely the existence of long epenthetic vowels in the context of morphological lengthening. It was argued that such patterns that straightforwardly fall out in PDM indeed exist and are a serious problem to alternative accounts of MLM. On the other hand, $^*V_O <_O \mu_\bullet$ is a violable constraint and it is predicted that grammars should exist where only an underlyingly moraic vowel is morphologically lengthened whereas an underlyingly mora-less vowel remains short in a context of morphological lengthening. It was argued that this is a correct and desirable prediction. In fact, exactly this is the account proposed in PDM for exceptional non-undergoers of a morphological lengthening process: their only difference to regular undergoers is their prosodic structure. It is hence desirable that the solution to the opacity problem of mora projection is not hardwired into the grammar.

The theoretical argumentation for the theory of PDM in this book is based on a thorough empirical study and a representative data set for attested MLM patterns in the languages of the world. Only such a broadened perspective allows us to compare the predictions of theories and question their restrictiveness.

One main insight from this typological survey of MLM patterns is its close parallelism to segmental affixation. Both in terms of its distributional frequency to appear at the left or right edge of its base and also in its dispreference to 'infix' and to be realized inside its base. Neither of these findings is particularly surprising, especially not from a diachronic perspective. What is surprising might only be the fact that no account ever aimed to predict these findings and to give a unified theoretical implementation for morphological length-manipulations.

Since the theory of PDM is based on the assumption of containment, the options where in a structure an MLM operation is possible are already severely restricted by the non-existence of true metathesis or reordering of elements in containment theory. In addition, the ℝecoverableMorphemeOrderCondition (=ℝMO) was proposed that restricts possible orderings to those that 'reflect' the underlying order of exponents. In essence, this restricts the ability of morphemic prosodic nodes to infix and hence to be realized inside their base. The ℝMO correctly predicts two important generalizations about the representative data set: MLM only targets elements close to the edge of a morpheme and if several MLM strategies are phonologically predictable allomorphs for one morpheme, these strategies can always be found in the same position of their base. This was the major overgeneration argument discussed for the most prominent alternatives to PDM: transderivational antifaithfulness theory (Alderete, 2001*b*, *a*), lexically indexed constraints (Pater, 2009), REALIZEMORPHEME (Kurisu, 2001), and cophonologies (Inkelas and Zoll, 2007). It was argued that all these alternatives predict generally unattested non-local patterns of MLM.

Since the aim of this book is only a thorough theoretical and empirical discussion of MLM, the ℝMO was assumed to only hold for the segmental and prosodic tiers. Whether featural affixes are restricted by the same severe linearity requirement is hence an open question that was not addressed. Palatalization and labialization in Chaha was discussed as one possible non-local realization of a non-segmental affix that is inherently impossible if the ℝMO also holds on the segmental tier. It would be a really interesting asymmetry if featural affixes are indeed crucially different from prosodic affixes in this respect. Future research needs to shed light on this matter.

Another interesting question that is left for future research is the relative rarity of 'outwards' MLM, hence patterns where a morphemic prosodic node has an effect on phonological structure that belongs to a morpheme that is morphologically more outwards. In contrast to the 'strict base mutation' principle (Alderete, 2001*b*), such effects are not excluded and straightforwardly expected under the PDM framework. And in some of the analyses presented above, it was indeed crucial that, for example, a suffixed morphemic prosodic node showed a surface effect on following suffixed elements. In most of these patterns, however, the 'outwards'-associating morphemic prosodic nodes rather block an expected MLM pattern than cause one. It is an interesting question whether an independent principle in, for example, learning theory generally disprefers these outwards-associating structures. The crucial result from the theoretical account given in this book is that such configurations are not in principle excluded and are necessary to account for the whole range of attested MLM phenomena.

References

Abo, Takaji, Byron W. Bender, Alfred Capelle, and Tony DeBrum (1976), *Marshallese-English Dictionary*, University of Hawaii Press, Honolulu, HI.

Abrusan, Marta (2005), Underspecified precedence relations and vowel-zero alternations in Hungarian, in *Proceedings of the Annual Meeting of the Berkeley Linguistics Society 31*, Berkeley Linguistics Society.

Adelaar, Willem (1984), 'Vowel length and the classification of Quechua dialects', *International Journal of American Linguistics* 50, 25–47.

Adelaar, Willem and Pieter Muysken (2004), *The Languages of the Andes*, Cambridge University Press, Cambridge.

Adu-Amankwah, David (2003), *Asante-Twi Learners Reference Grammar*, NALRC Press, Madison, WI.

Akinlabi, Akin (1996), 'Featural affixation', *Journal of Linguistics* 32, 239–289.

Alderete, John (1999), Head dependence in stress-epenthesis interaction, in B. Hermans and M. van Oostendorp, eds, *The Derivational Residue in Phonological Optimality Theory*, John Benjamins, Amsterdam, pp. 29–50.

Alderete, John (2001a), 'Dominance effects as transderivational anti-faithfulness', *Phonology* 18, 201–253.

Alderete, John (2001b), *Morphologically Governed Accent in Optimality Theory*, Routledge, New York.

Ali, Mohammed and Andrzej Zaborski (1990), *Handbook of the Oromo Language*, Franz Steiner Verlag, Wroclaw.

Álvarez, José (2005), Vocalic mora augmentation in the morphology of Guajiro/Wayuunaiki, in *Proceedings from the Eighth Workshop on American Indigenous Languages (2005)*, Santa Barbara Working Papers in Linguistics, vol. 16.

Álvarez, José and Alicia Dorado (2005), 'Derivación de verbos estativos duales en guajiro/ wayuunaiki', *Saber* 17, 174–186.

Anderson, Stephen R. (1992), *A-Morphous Morphology*, Cambridge University Press, Cambridge.

Anttila, Arto (2002), 'Morphologically conditioned phonological alternations', *Natural Language and Linguistic Theory* 20, 1–42.

Archangeli, Diana (1991), 'Syllabification and prosodic templates in Yawelmani', *Natural Language and Linguistic Theory* 9, 231–284.

Arensen, Jon (1982), *Murle Grammar*, University of Juba.

Arndt-Lappe, Sabine and Birgit Alber (2012), Templatic and subtractive truncation, in J. Trommer, ed., *The Morphology and Phonology of Exponence: The State of the Art*, Oxford University Press, Oxford.

Artiagoitia, Xabier (1993), Syllable structure in Modern Basque and in Proto-Basque, in J. Hualde and J. Ortiz de Urbina, eds, *Generative Studies in Basque Linguistics*, John Benjamins, Amsterdam.

Bakovic, Eric (2011), Opacity and ordering, in J. Goldsmith, J. Riggle, and A. Yu, eds, *The Handbook of Phonological Theory* (2nd edition), Wiley Blackwell, Oxford, pp. 40–67.

Bals Baal, Berit Anne, David Odden, and Curt Rice (2012), 'An analysis of North Saami gradation', *Phonology* 29, 165–212.

Bank, Sebastian and Jochen Trommer (2015), Learning and the complexity of ø-marking, in M. Baerman, D. Brown, and G. G. Corbett, eds, *Understanding and Measuring Morphological Complexity*, Oxford University Press, Oxford, pp. 185–204.

Bank, Sebastian and Jochen Trommer (to appear), Paradigm learning and subanalysis complexity, in *Proceedings of CLS 48*.

Banksira, Degif (2013), 'Chaha labialization and palatalization as coalescence', *Brill's Annual of Afroasisatic Languages and Linguistics* 5, 159–190.

Bat-El, Outi (2002), 'True truncation in Colloquial Hebrew imperatives', *Language* 78, 651–683.

Becker, Michael and Kathryn Flack (2011), The emergence of the unmarked, in M. van Oostendorp, C. J. Ewen, E. Hume, and K. Rice, eds, *The Blackwell Companion to Phonology*, Wiley Blackwell, Malden, MA, chapter 58.

Beckman, Jill (1998), Positional Faithfulness, PhD thesis, University of Massachusetts at Amherst.

Beesley, Kenneth R. (2000), 'A note on phonologically conditioned selection of verbalization suffixes in Aymara', Technical Report, Xerox Research Centre Europe.

Bell, Arthur (2003), 'Gemination, degemination and moraic structure in Wolof', *Working Papers of the Cornell Phonetics Laboratory* 15, 1–68.

Bender, Byron W. (1968), 'Marshallese phonology', *Oceanic Linguistics* 7, 16–35.

Bender, Byron W. (1974), 'Parallelisms in the morphophonemics of several Micronesian languages', *Oceanic Linguistics* 12, 455–477.

Bensoukas, Karim (2001), Stem Forms in the Nontemplatic Morphology of Berber, PhD thesis, Rabat: Mohamed V University.

Benua, Laura (1997), Transderivational Identity: Phonological Relations between Words, PhD thesis, University of Massachusetts.

Berkley, Deborah Milam (2000), Gradient Obligatory Contour Principle Effects, PhD thesis, Northwestern University.

Bermúdez-Otero, Ricardo (1999), Constraint Interaction in Language Change: Quantity in English and Germanic, PhD thesis, University of Manchester.

Bermúdez-Otero, Ricardo (2001), 'Underlyingly nonmoraic coda consonants, faithfulness, and sympathy', Ms. University of Manchester, online available at http://www.bermudez-otero.com/DEP-mora.pdf.

Bermúdez-Otero, Ricardo (2012), The architecture of grammar and the division of labour in exponence, in J. Trommer, ed., *The Morphology and Phonology of Exponence: The State of the Art*, Oxford University Press, Oxford, pp. 8–83.

Bermúdez-Otero, Ricardo (in preparation), *Stratal Optimality Theory*, Oxford University Press, Oxford.

Besnier, Niko (1987), 'An autosegmental approach to metathesis in Rotuman', *Lingua* 73, 201–223.

Bickel, Balthasar (1998), 'Rhythm and feet in Belhare morphology', Ms., University of California, Berkeley, available online at ROA 287.

Bickel, Balthasar and Johanna Nichols (ongoing), 'Autotyp, developing an international network of typological linguistic databases', http://www.spw.uzh.ch/autotyp/.

Blevins, Juliette (1994), 'The bimoraic foot in Rotuman phonology and morphology', *Oceanic Linguistics* 33, 491–516.

Bowers, Norman (1996), *Hidatsa Suprasegmentals. A Phonological Analysis of a Siouan Native North American Language*, University of Idaho Press.

Boyle, John (2007), Hidatsa Morpho-syntax and Clause Structure, PhD thesis, University of Chicago.

Briggs, Lucy Therina (1976), Dialectal Variation in the Aymaran Language of Bolivia and Peru, PhD thesis, University of Florida.

Broadbent, Sylvia (1964), *The Southern Sierra Miwok Language*, University of California Press.

Broadwell, George A. (1993), 'Subtractive morphology in Southern Muskogean', *International Journal of American Linguistics* 59(4), 416–429.

Broadwell, George Aaron (2006), *A Choctaw Reference Grammar*, University of Nebraska Press.

Broselow, Ellen, Su-I Chen, and Marie Huffman (1997), 'Syllable weight: Convergence of phonology and phonetics', *Phonology* 14, 47–82.

Brown, Jason (2004), Some tonogenetic properties of Upriver Halkomelem, in L. Harper and C. Jany, eds, *Proceedings of the 7th Annual Workshop on American Indigenous Languages*, Santa Barbara Papers in Linguistics, vol. 15, Santa Barbara, CA, pp. 40–48.

Brown, J. C. (2003), Floating moras and features in Southern Sierra Miwok, in 'Proceedings from the sixth Workshop on American Indigenous Languages'.

Buckley, Eugene (1998), 'Iambic lengthening and final vowels', *International Journal of American Linguistics* 64, 179–223.

Burzio, Luigi (2000), Cycles, non-derived-environment-blocking, and correspondence, in J. Dekkers, F. van der Leeuw, and J. van de Weijer, eds, *Optimality Theory: Phonology, Syntax, and Acquisition*, Cambridge University Press, Cambridge.

Burzio, Luigi (2011), Derived environment effects, in M. van Oostendorp, C. J. Ewen, E. Hume, and K. Rice, eds, *The Blackwell Companion to Phonology*, Wiley Blackwell, Malden, MA, chapter 88.

Bye, Patrik (2006), Subtraction, optimization, and the combinatorial lexicon, Ms., University of Tromsœ, CASTL.

Bye, Patrik and Paul de Lacy (2008), Metrical influences on fortition and lenition, in J. B. de Carvalho, T. Scheer, and P. Ségeral, eds, *Lenition and Fortition*, Mouton de Gruyter, Berlin, pp. 173–206.

Bye, Patrik and Peter Svenonius (2012), Non-concatenative morphology as epiphenomenon, in J. Trommer, ed., *The Morphology and Phonology of Exponence: The State of the Art*, Oxford University Press, Oxford, pp. 426–495.

Byrd, Dani (1993), Marshallese suffixal reduplication, in J. Mead, ed., *Proceedings of the 11th West Coast Conference on Formal Linguistics*, CSLI Publications, Stanford, CA.

Caballero, Gabriela (2011), 'Morphologicallly conditioned stress assignment in Choguita Rará-muri', *Linguistics* 49, 749–790.

Caha, Pavel and Tobias Scheer (2008), The syntax and phonology of Czech templatic morphology, in A. Antonenko, J. Bailyn, and C. Bethin, eds, *Annual Workshop on Formal Approaches to Slavic Linguistics: The Stony Brook Meeting 2007*, University of Michigan, pp. 68–83.

Cairns, Charles E. (1976), Universal properties of umlaut and vowel coalescence rules: implications for Rotuman phonology, in A. Juilland and A. Juilland, eds, *Linguistic Studies Offered to Joseph Greenberg: Volume 2: Phonology*, Anma Libri, Saratoga, CA, pp. 271–283.

Callaghan, Catherine (1987), *Northern Sierra Miwok Dictionary*, University of California Press.

Campbell, Lyle (1997), *American Indian languages: The Historical Linguistics of Native America*, Oxford University Press, New York.

Campos-Astorkiza, Rebeka (2003), Compensatory lengthening as root number preservation: Codas in Eastern Andalusian Spanish, in E. Hajicová, A. Kotešovecová, and J. Mírovský, eds, *Proceedings of the Seventeenth International Congress of Linguistics*, Matfyzpress and MFF UK, pp. 1–11.

Campos-Astorkiza, Rebeka (2004), Faith in moras: A revised approach to prosodic faithfulness, in K. Moulton and M. Wolf, eds, *Proceedings of NELS 34*, GLSA, Amherst, MA, pp. 164–174.

Carando, Agustina (2009), A moraic account of Korean tense consonants, Ms., Graduate Center, CUNY.

Cerrón-Palomino, Rodolfo (2000), *Lingüística aimara*, Centro de Estudios Regionales Andinos "Bartolomé de Las Casas", Cuzco, Peru.

Cerrón-Palomino, Rodolfo (2008), *Quechuamara: estructuras paralelas del quechua y del aimara*, Plural Editores: PROEIB Andes, La Paz, Bolivia.

Chen, Chun-Mei (2006), A Comparative Study on Formosan phonology: Paiwan and Budai Rukai, PhD thesis, University of Texas at Austin.

Christaller, J. G. (1964), *A Grammar of the Asante and Fante Language*, Gregg Press, Ridgewood, NJ.

Churchward, C. M. (1940), *Rotuman Grammar and Dictionary*, Australasia Medical Publishing Co. [Repr. 1978, AMS Press, New York.], Sydney.

Clements, George N. (1985), 'The geometry of phonological features', *Phonology Yearbook* 2, 225–252.

Clements, George N. and Beth Hume (1995), The internal organization of speech sounds, in J. Goldsmith, ed., *The Handbook of Phonological Theory*, Blackwell, Cambridge, pp. 245–306.

Coler, Matt (2010), A Grammatical Description of Muylaq' Aymara, PhD thesis, Vrije Universiteit Amsterdam.

Crowhurst, Megan (1994), 'Foot extrametricality and template mapping in Cupeño', *Natural Language and Linguistic Theory* 12, 177–201.

Crum, Beverly and Jon Dayley (1993), *Western Shoshoni Grammar*, Boise State University, Boise.

Crysmann, Berthold (2004), 'An inflectional approach to Hausa final vowel shortening', *Yearbook of Morphology*, pp. 73–112.

Czaykowska-Higgins, Ewa and Marvin Dale Kinkade (1998), Salish languages and linguistics, in E. Czaykowski-Higgins and M. Kinkade, eds, *Salish Languages and Linguistics: Theoretical and Descriptive Perspectives*, de Gruyter, Berlin, New York, pp. 1–68.

D'Alessandro, Roberta and Marc van Oostendorp (2016), Abruzzese metaphony and the A eater, in F. Torres-Tamarit, K. Linke, and M. van Oostendorp, eds, *Approaches to Metaphony in the Languages of Italy*, Mouton de Gruyter, Boston, Berlin, pp. 349–368.

Davis, Stuart (2011a), Geminates, in M. van Oostendorp, C. J. Ewen, E. Hume, and K. Rice, eds, *The Blackwell Companion to Phonology*, Wiley Blackwell, Malden, MA, chapter 37.

Davis, Stuart (2011*b*), Quantity, in J. Goldsmith, J. Riggle, and A. Yu, eds, *The Handbook of Phonological Theory (2nd edition)*, Wiley Blackwell, Oxford, pp. 130–140.

Davis, Stuart and Gina Torretta (1998), An optimality-theoretic account of compensatory lengthening and geminate throwback in Trukese, in P. Tamanji and K. Kusumoto, eds, *Proceedings of NELS 28*, GLSA, Amherst, MA, pp. 111–125.

Davis, Stuart and Isao Ueda (2002), 'Mora augmentation processes in Japanese', *Journal of Japanese Linguistics* 18, 1–23.

Davis, Stuart and Isao Ueda (2005), The typology of mora augmentation, *Proceedings of LP 2005*.

Davis, Stuart and Isao Ueda (2006), 'Prosodic vs. morphological mora augmentation', *Lexicon Forum* 2, 121–143.

de Lacy, Paul (2012), Morpho-phonological polarity, in J. Trommer, ed., *The Morphology and Phonology of Exponence: The State of the Art*, Oxford University Press, Oxford.

Dench, Alan (1995), *Martuthunira: A Language of the Pilbara Region of Western Australia*, Pacific Linguistics C:125, Canberra.

Derbyshire, Desmond (1979), *Hixkaryana*, North Holland Publishing Company, Amsterdam.

Derbyshire, Desmond C. (1985), *Hixkaryana and Linguistic Typology*, Summer Institute of Linguistics.

Dolphyne, Florénce Abena (1996), *A Comprehensive Course in Twi (Asante)*, Ghana University Press.

Dressler, Wolfgang (2000), Subtraction, in G. Booij, C. Lehmann, and J. Mugdan, eds, *Morphologie. Ein internationales Handbuch*, Walter de Gruyter, Berlin, pp. 581–587.

Dyen, Isidore (1965), *A Sketch of Trukese Grammar*, American Oriental Society, New Haven, CT.

Elfner, Emily Jane (2006), Contrastive syllabification in Blackfoot, in D. Baumer, D. Montero, and M. Scanlon, eds, *WCCFL 25*, Cascadilla Proceedings Project, Somerville, MA, pp. 141–149.

Elmendorf, William and Wayne Suttles (1986), 'Pattern and change in Halkomelem Salish', *Anthropological Linguistics* 2, 1–35.

England, Nora (1971), Aymara verbal derivational suffixes, Master's thesis, University of Florida.

England, Nora (1983), *A Grammar of Mam*, University of Texas Press, Austin.

Ettlinger, Marc (2008), Input-Driven Opacity, PhD thesis, University of California at Berkeley.

Finley, Sara (2009), 'Morphemic harmony as featural correspondence', *Lingua* 119, 478–501.

Fitzgerald, Colleen (1997), O'odham Rhythms, PhD thesis, University of Arizona.

Fitzgerald, Colleen (2009), 'Proliferating prosodies in Tohono O'odham Reduplication(s)', Seventeenth Manchester Phonology Meeting, May 30, 2009.

Fitzgerald, Colleen (2012), 'Prosodic inconsistency in Tohono O'Odham', *International Journal of American Linguistics* 78, 435–463.

Fitzgerald, Colleen and Amy Fountain (1995), 'The optimal account of Tohono O'odham truncation', Ms., University of Arizona.

Fitzpatrick, Justin (to appear), 'A concatenative theory of possible affix types', Papers from EVELIN I, online available as lingbuzz/000662.

Flack, Kathryn (2007*a*), The Sources of Phonological Markedness, PhD thesis, University of Massachusetts, Amherst.

Flack, Kathryn (2007*b*), 'Templatic morphology and indexed markedness constraints', *Linguistic Inquiry* 38, 749–758.

Freeland, Lucy Shepard (1951), *Language of the Sierra Miwok*, Waverly Press, Baltimore.

Fukazawa, Haruka (1999), Theoretical Implications of OCP Effects in Feature in Optimality Theory, PhD thesis, University of Maryland at College Park.

Galloway, Brent (1993), *A Grammar of Upriver Halkomelem*, University of California Press, Berkeley, CA.

Gess, Randall (2011), Compensatory lengthening, in M. van Oostendorp, C. J. Ewen, E. Hume, and K. Rice, eds, *The Blackwell Companion to Phonology*, Wiley Blackwell, Malden, MA, chapter 64.

Geytenbeek, Brian and H. Geytenbeek (1971), *Gidabal Grammar and Dictionary*, Australian Institute of Aboriginal Studies, Canberra.

Glinert, Lewis (1989), *The Grammar of Modern Hebrew*, Cambridge University Press, Cambridge.

Gnanadesikan, Amalia (1997), Phonology with Ternary Scales, PhD thesis, University of Massachusetts, Amherst.

Goldrick, Matthew (2000), Turbid output representations and the unity of opacity, in A. Coetzee, N. Hall, and J. Kim, eds, *NELS 30*, GLSA, Amherst, MA, pp. 231–245.

Goldsmith, John A. (1976), Autosegmental Phonology, PhD thesis, Massachusetts Institute of Technology.

Golla, Victor (2011), *California Indian languages*, University of California Press, Berkeley, CA.

Golston, Chris and Richard Wiese (1996), 'Zero morphology and constraint interaction: subtraction and epenthesis in German dialects', *Yearbook of Morphology 1995*, pp. 143–159.

Goulet, Jean Guy and Miguel Angel Jusayú (1978), *El idioma guajiro: sus fonemas, su ortografía, y su morfología*, Universidad Catolica Andres Bello Centro de lenguas indigenas.

Gouskova, Maria and Kevin Roon (2008), Interface constraints and frequency in Russian compound stress, in J. Reich, M. Babyonyshev, and D. Kavitskaya, eds, *Proceedings of the 17th Meeting of Formal Approaches to Slavic Linguistics*, Michigan Slavic Publications, Ann Arbor, MI, pp. 49–63.

Greenberg, Joseph H. (1963), Some universals of grammar with special reference to the order of meaningful elements, in J. H. Greenberg, ed., *Universals of Language*, MIT Press, Cambridge, MA, pp. 58–90.

Grimes, Stephen (2002), Mora augmentation in the Alabama imperfective: an optimality theoretic perspective, Ms., Indiana University, online available at http://pweb.ldc.upenn.edu/~sgrimes/papers/alabama.pdf.

Grimes, Stephen (2010), Quantitative Investigations in Hungarian Phonotactics and Syllable Structure, PhD thesis, Indiana University.

Grimes, Steve (2002), Morphological gemination and root augmentation in three Muskogean languages, Ms., Indiana University.

Hale, Ken (1973), Deep-surface canonical disparities in relation to analysis and change: an Australian example, in T. Sebeok, ed., *Current Trends in Linguistics, vol. XI*, Mouton de Gruyter, The Hague, pp. 401–458.

Hale, Kenneth (1965), 'Some preliminary observations on Papago morphophonemics', *International Journal of American Linguistics* 31, 295–305.

Hale, Mark (2000), 'Marshallese phonology, the phonetics-phonology interface and historical linguistics', *Linguistic Review* 17, 241–257.

Hall, Christopher (2000), Prefixation, suffixation and circumfixation, in G. Booij, C. Lehmann, and J. Mugdan, eds, *Morphologie. Ein internationales Handbuch*, de Gruyter, Berlin, New York.

Hall, Nancy (2011), Vowel epenthesis, in M. van Oostendorp, C. J. Ewen, E. Hume, and K. Rice, eds, *The Blackwell Companion to Phonology*, Blackwell, Malden, MA, chapter 67.

Halle, Morris (2003), Infixation versus onset metathesis in Tagalog, Chamorro and Toba Batak, in *Ken Hale: A Life in Language*, MIT Press, Cambridge, MA, pp. 153–168.

Hansson, Gunnar Olafur (2001), Theoretical and Typological Issues in Consonant Harmony, PhD thesis, University of California, Berkeley.

Hardman, M. J., J. Vásquez, with L. Briggs, J. D. Yapita, N. England, and L. Martin (2001), *Aymara: compendio de estructura fonológica y gramatical*, Instituto de Lengua y Cultura Aymara.

Hardman, Martha J. (2001), *Aymara*, LINCOM.

Hardy, Heather and Timothy Montler (1988a), 'Imperfective gemination in Alabama', *International Journal of American Linguistics* 54, 399–415.

Hardy, Heather and Timothy Montler (1988b), Alabama radical morphology: H-infix and disfixation, in W. Shipley, ed., *In Honor of Mary Haas: From the Haas Festival Conference on Native American Linguistics*, Mouton de Gruyter, New York, pp. 377–409.

Harley, Heidi and Maria Flores Leyva (2009), 'Form and meaning in Hiaki (Yaqui) verbal reduplication', *International Journal of American Linguistics* 75, 235–74.

Harris, John (2011), Deletion, in M. van Oostendorp, C. J. Ewen, E. Hume, and K. Rice, eds, *The Blackwell Companion to Phonology*, Wiley Blackwell, Malden, MA, chapter 68.

Harris, John and G. Lindsey (1995), The elements of phonological representation, in J. Durand and F. Katamba, eds, *Frontiers in Phonology*, pp. 34–79.

Hart, Michele (1991), The moraic status of initial geminates in Trukese, in *Proceedings of the 7th annual meeting of the Berkeley Linguistics Society*, BLS, pp. 107–120.

Haspelmath, Martin (2002), *Understanding Morphology*, Arnold, London.

Haugen, Jason (2005), Reduplicative allomorphy and language prehistory in Uto-Aztecan, in B. Hurch, ed., *Studies on Reduplication*, de Gruyter, Berlin, pp. 315–350.

Haugen, Jason (2008), *Morphology at the Interfaces. Reduplication and Noun Incorporation in Uto-Aztecan*, John Benjamin, Amsterdam.

Haugen, Jason and Cathy Hicks Kennard (2008), 'Morphological moras and morphological doubling theory', paper given at the LSA Annual Meeting, San Francisco.

Hawkins, John A. and Gary Gilligan (1988), 'Prefixing and suffixing universals in relation to basic word order', *Lingua* 74, 219–259.

Hayes, Bruce (1989), 'Compensatory Lengthening in moraic phonology', *Linguistic Inquiry* 20, 253–306.

Hayes, Bruce (1990), Precompiled phrasal phonology, in S. Inkelas and D. Zec, eds, *The Phonology-Syntax Connection*, University of Chicago Press, Chicago, pp. 85–108.

Hayes, Bruce (1995), *Metrical Stress Theory: Principles and Case Studies*, University of Chicago Press, Chicago.

Hayes, Bruce (1999), Phonological restructuring in Yidiɲ and its theoretical consequences, in B. Hermans and M. van Oostendorp, eds, *The Derivational Residue in Phonological Optimality Theory*, John Benjamin, Amsterdam, pp. 175–205.

Heilig, Otto (1898), *Grammatik der ostfränkischen Mundart des Taubergrund*, Breitkopf und Härtel, Leipzig.

Heine, Bernd (1981), *The Waata Dialect of Oromo*, Dietrich Reimer Verlag, Berlin.

Hendricks, Sean Quillan (1999), Reduplication without Template Constraints: A Study in Bare-consonant Reduplication, PhD thesis, University of Arizona.

Henri, Fabiola and Anne Abeillé (2008), Verb form alternations in Mauritian, in *Proceedings of the HPSG08 Conference*.

Hill, Jane and Ofelia Zepeda (1992), 'Derived words in Tohono O'odham', *International Journal of American Linguistics* 4, 355–404.

Hill, Jane and Ofelia Zepeda (1998), 'Tohono O'Odham (Papago) plurals', *Anthropological Linguistics* 40, 1–42.

Hinton, Leanne (1994), *Flutes of Fire, Essays on California Indian Languages*, Heyday Books, Berkeley, CA.

Hohulin, Lou and Michael Kenstowicz (1979), 'Keley-I phonology and morphophonemics', *South-East Asia Linguistic Studies* 4, 241–254.

Horwood, Graham (2001), Antifaithfulness and subtractive morphology, Ms., Rutgers University, available as ROA 466-0901.

Horwood, Graham (2002), Precedence faithfulness governs morpheme position, in L. Mikkelsen and C. Potts, eds, *Proceedings of WCCFL 21*, Cascadilla Press, Somerville, MA, pp. 166–179.

Hualde, José (1990), 'Vowel lengthening in Basque', *Folia Linguistica* 24, 269–288.

Hualde, José (1991), 'Unspecified and unmarked vowels', *Linguistic Inquiry* 22, 205–209.

Hualde, Jose (2012), *Basque Phonology*, Taylor and Francis, New York.

Hualde, José and Jon Ortiz de Urbina (2003), *A Grammar of Basque*, Mouton de Gruyter, Berlin, New York.

Hulstaert, G. (1938), *Praktische Grammatica van het Lonkundo (Lomongo) (Belgisch Kongo)*, De Sikkel, Antwerpen.

Hurch, Bernhard (2005), *Studies on Reduplication*, Mouton de Gruyter, Berlin.

Hyde, Brett (2011), Extrametricality and non-finality, in M. van Oostendorp, C. J. Ewen, E. Hume, and K. Rice, eds, *The Blackwell Companion to Phonology*, Blackwell, Malden, MA, chapter 43.

Hyman, Larry (1982), The representation of length in Gokana, in *Proceedings of WCCFL 1*, Cascadilla Press, Somerville, MA, pp. 198–206.

Hyman, Larry (1985), *A Theory of Phonological Weight*, Foris Publications, Dordrecht.

Hyman, Larry (2009), Perfective, pluractional, and progressive aspect formation in Leggbo, in S. G. Obeng, ed., *Topics in Descriptive and African Linguistics*, LINCOM, pp. 5–28.

Inkelas, Sharon (1990), *Prosodic Constituency in the Lexicon*, Garland Publishing, New York.

Inkelas, Sharon (1995), The consequences of optimization for underspecification, in *NELS 25*, pp. 287–302.

Inkelas, Sharon (1999), Exceptional stress-attracting suffixes in Turkish: representation vs. the grammar, in R. Kager, H. van der Hulst, and W. Zonneveld, eds, *The Prosody-Morphology Interface*, Cambridge University Press, Cambridge, pp. 134–187.

Inkelas, Sharon (2014), *The Interplay of Morphology and Phonology*, Oxford University Press, Oxford.

Inkelas, Sharon (to appear), The morphology-phonology connection, in *Proceedings of BLS 34*, Berkeley Linguistic Society.

Inkelas, Sharon, C. Orhan Orgun, and Cheryl Zoll (2004), The implications of lexical exceptions for the nature of grammar, in J. McCarthy, ed., *Optimality Theory in Phonology: A Book of Readings*, Blackwell Publishers, Oxford, pp. 542–551.

Inkelas, Sharon and Cheryl Zoll (2005), *Reduplication: Doubling in Morphology*, Cambridge University Press, Cambridge.

Inkelas, Sharon and Cheryl Zoll (2007), 'Is grammar dependence real? a comparison between cophonological and indexed constraint approaches to morphologically conditioned phonology', *Linguistics* 45(1), 133–171.

Itô, Junko (1988), *Syllable Theory in Prosodic Phonology*, New York: Garland Publishing.

Itô, Junko and Armin Mester (1990), The structure of the phonological lexicon, in Natsuko Tsujimura, ed., *The Handbook of Japanese Linguistics*, Blackwell, Malden, MA, pp. 62–100.

Itô, Junko and Armin Mester (1998), Sympathy theory and German truncations, in P. S. of Japan, ed., *On'in kenkyuu Phonological Studies*, Katakusha, Tokyo, pp. 51–66.

Itô, Junko and Armin Mester (2003), Weak layering and word binarity, in T. T. Takeru Honma, Masao Okazaki, and S.ichi Tanaka, eds, *A New Century of Phonology and Phonological Theory. A Festschrift for Professor Shosuke Haraguchi on the Occasion of His Sixtieth Birthday*, Kaitakusha [Reprint of Weak Layering and word binarity. Santa Cruz, CA: UC Santa Cruz. LRC Working Paper 92-9.], Tokyo, pp. 26–65.

Itô, Junko and Armin Mester (2009), The extended prosodic word, in B. Kabak and J. Grijzenhout, eds, *Phonological Domains: Universals and Deviations*, Mouton de Gruyter, Berlin, pp. 135–194.

Jaggar, Philip (2001), *Hausa*, John Benjamin, Amsterdam.

Jurgec, Peter (2012), 'Morphological locality', poster, given at Manchester Phonology Meeting 20.

Ka, Omar (1994), *Wolof phonology and morphology*, University Press of America, Lanham, MD.

Kager, René (1999a), Consequences of Catalexis, in H. van der Hulst and J. van der Wiejer, eds, *HIL Phonology Papers*, The Hague: Holland Academic Graphics, pp. 269–298.

Kager, René (1999b), *Optimality Theory*, Cambridge University Press, Cambridge.

Kawahara, Shigeto (2004), Locality in echo epenthesis: Comparison with reduplication, in *Proceedings of NELS 34*, pp. 295–309.

Kawahara, Shigeto (2007), 'Copying and spreading in phonological theory: Evidence from echo epenthesis', *UMOP: Papers in Optimality Theory* 32, 111–143.

Kaye, Jonathan, Jean Lowenstamm, and Jean-Roger Vergnaud (1985), 'The internal structure of phonological elements: a theory of charm and government', *Phonology Yearbook* 2, 305–328.

Kenesei, István, Robert M. Vago, and Anna Fenyvesi (1998), *Hungarian*, Routledge, London.

Kennard, Catherine Hicks (2004), 'Copy but don't repeat: The conflict of dissimilation and reduplication in the Tawala durative', *Phonology* 21, 303–323.

Kennedy, Robert (2002), 'Stress and allomorphy in Woleaian reduplication', *Proceedings of the Texas Linguistic Society* .

Kenstowicz, Michael (2005), Paradigmatic uniformity and contrast, in L. J. Downing, T. A. Hall, and R. Raffelsiefen, eds, *Paradigms in Phonological Theory*, Oxford University Press, Oxford, pp. 145–169.

Kenstowicz, Michael and Charles Kisseberth (1977), *Topics in Phonological Theory*, Academic Press, New York.

Kim, Yuni (2003), 'Vowel elision and the morphophonology of dominance in Aymara', Ms., UC Berkeley.

Kimball, Geoffrey (1985), A Descriptive Grammar of Koasati, PhD thesis, Tulane University, New Orleans.

Kimball, Geoffrey D. (1991), *Koasati Grammar*, University of Nebraska Press, Lincoln and London.

Kiparsky, Paul (1968), Linguistic universals and linguistic change, in E. Bach and R. Harms, eds, *Universals in Linguistic Theory*, Holt, Rinehart, and Winston, New York, pp. 170–210.

Kiparsky, Paul (1973), Abstractness, opacity, and global rules, in O. Fujimura, ed., *Three Dimensions of Linguistic Theory*, Tokyo: TEC, pp. 1–135.

Kiparsky, Paul (1991), 'Catalexis', Ms., Stanford University.

Kiparsky, Paul (1993), Blocking in nonderived environments, in *Studies in Lexical Phonology*, Vol. 4 of Phonetics and Phonology, San Diego: Academic Press, pp. 277–313.

Kiparsky, Paul (2000), 'Opacity and cyclicity', *The Linguistic Review* 17, 351–67.

Kiparsky, Paul (2003), Syllables and moras in Arabic, in C. Féry and R. van de Vijver, eds, *The Syllable in Optimality Theory*, Cambridge University Press, Cambridge, pp. 147–182.

Kiparsky, Paul (2011), Compensatory lengthening, in C. Cairns and E. Raimy, eds, *Handbook on the Syllable*, Brill, Leiden, pp. 33–69.

Kisseberth, Charles (1970), 'The treatment of exceptions', *Papers in Linguistics* 2, 44–58.

Klein, Thomas B. (2005), 'Infixation and segmental constraint effects: UM and IN in Tagalog, Chamorro, and Toba Batak', *Lingua* 115(7), 959–995.

Klokeid, Terry Jack (1976), *Topics in Lardil Grammar*, MIT, Cambridge, MA.

Ko, Eun-Suk (1998), A two-root theory of Korean geminate consonants, in E. van Gelderen and V. Samiian, eds, *Proceedings of WECOL 98*, Department of Linguistics, University of Fresno, CA.

Ko, Eun-Suk (2010), Stress and long vowels in Korean: Chicken or egg, first?, in *Japanese Korean Linguistics 17*, CSLI Publications, Stanford, CA, pp. 377–390.

Kosa, Loredana (2006), An argument for process-based morphology: subtractive morphology in Tohono O'odham (Uto-Aztecan), Master's thesis, Simon Fraser University.

Kula, Nancy (2008), 'Derived enviroment effects: A representational approach', *Lingua* 118, 1328–43.

Kurisu, Kazutaka (2001), The Phonology of Morpheme Realization, PhD thesis, University of California at Santa Cruz. ROA 490-0102.

Ladd, Robert, Bert Remijsen, and Caguor Adong Manyang (2009), 'On the distinction between regular and irregular inflectional morphology: Evidence from Dinka', *Language* 85, 659–670.

Landerman, Peter (1997), Internal reconstruction in Aymara and Quechua, in J. H. Hill, P. J. Mistry, and L. Campbell, eds, *The Life of Language: Papers in Honor of William Bright*, Mouton de Gruyter, Berlin, pp. 35–57.

Landman, Meredith (2002), Morphological contiguity, in A. Carpenter, A. Coetzee, and P. de Lacy, eds, *Papers in Optimality Theory II: University of Massachusetts-Amherst Occasional Papers in Linguistics*, GLSA, Amherst, MA.

Langdon, Margaret (1970), *A Grammar of Diegueño. The Mesa Grande dialect*, University of California Press Berkeley, CA.

Levin, Juliette (1985), A Metrical Theory of Syllabicity, PhD thesis, MIT, Cambridge, MA.

Lewis, M. Paul, Gary F. Simons, and Charles D. Fennig (2014), *Ethnologue: Languages of the World, Seventeenth Edition*, SIL International. Online version: http://www.ethnologue.com.

Liberman, Mark and Alan Prince (1977), 'On stress and linguistic rhythm', *Linguistic Inquiry* 8, 249–336.

Lieber, Rochelle (1992), *Deconstructing Morphology*, University of Chicago Press, Chicago.

Lin, Yen-Hwei (1987), Theoretical implications of Piro syncope, in J. McDonough and B. Plunkett, eds, *NELS 17*, pp. 409–423.

Lin, Yen-Hwei (1993), Sonority and postlexical syllabicity in Piro, in C. Canakis and J. Denton, eds, *CLS 28*, pp. 333–344.

Lin, Yen-Hwei (1997a), Cyclic and noncyclic affixation in Piro, in G. Booij and J. van de Weijer, eds, *Phonology in Progress—Progress in Phonology*, Holland Academic Graphics, The Hague, pp. 167–188.

Lin, Yen-Hwei (1997b), 'Syllabic and moraic structures in Piro', *Phonology* 14, 403–436.

Lin, Yen-Hwei (1998), On minor syllables, in O. Fujimura, B. D. Joseph, and B. Palek, eds, *Proceedings of LP '98*, pp. 163–183.

Lin, Yen-Hwei (2005), Piro affricates: Phonological edge effects and phonetic anti-edge effects, in J. van de Weijer and M. van Oostendorp, eds, *The Internal Organization of Phonological Segments*, Mouton de Gruyter, Berlin, New York, pp. 121–152.

Lloret, Maria-Rosa (1991), 'Moras or skeletal units? a question of parametric variation', *Catalan Working papers in Linguistics, Universitat Autónoma de Barcelona*, pp. 149–165.

Lombardi, Linda (2002), 'Coronal epenthesis and markedness', *Phonology* 19, 219–251.

Lombardi, Linda and John J. McCarthy (1991), 'Prosodic circumscription in Choctaw morphology', *Phonology* 8, 37–71.

Lubowicz, Anna (2010), Infixation as morpheme absorption, in S. Parker, ed., *Phonological Argumentation: Essays on Evidence and Motivation*, Equinox, London.

Lupardus, Karen Jacque (1982), The Language of the Alabama Indians, PhD thesis, University of Kansas.

Marantz, Alec (1982), 'Re reduplication', *Linguistic Inquiry* 13, 483–545.

Martin, Jack (1988), 'Subtractive morphology as dissociation', *Proceedings of WCCFL 7* pp. 229–240.

Mason, John Alden (1950), *The Language of the Papago of Arizona*, Philadelphia, University Museum, University of Pennsylvania.

Mathiot, Madeleine (1973), *A Dictionary of Papago Usage, 2 vols.*, Bloomington, Indiana.

Matteson, Esther (1954), 'Piro phonemes and morphology', *Kroeber Anthropological Society Papers* 11, 17–59.

Matteson, Esther (1965), *The Piro (Arawakan) Language*, University of California Press, Berkeley, CA.

Matthews, Peter H. (1974), *Morphology*, Cambridge University Press, Cambridge.

Matthews, Washington (1873), *Grammar and Dictionary of the Languages of the Hidatsa*, Cramoisy Press, New York.

McCarthy, John (1979), Formal Problems in Semitic Phonology and Morphology, PhD thesis, Massachusetts Institute of Technology.

McCarthy, John (1981), 'A prosodic theory of nonconcatenative morphology', *Linguistic Inquiry* 12(3), 373–418.

McCarthy, John (1983a), Consonantal morphology in the Chaha verb, in M. Barlow, D. Flickinger, and M. Wescoat, eds, *Proceedings of WCCFL* 2, SLI, pp. 176–188.

McCarthy, John (1983b), A prosodic account of Arabic broken plurals, in I. Dihoff, ed., *Current Trends in African Linguistics*, Vol. 1, Foris, Dordrecht, pp. 289–320.

McCarthy, John (1988), 'Feature geometry and dependency: A review', *Phonetica* 43, 84–108.

McCarthy, John (1993), Template form in prosodic morphology, in E. A. Smith, and L. Stvan, eds, *Papers from the Third Annual Formal Linguistics Society of Midamerica Conference*, IULC Publications, Bloomington, IN, pp. 187–218.

McCarthy, John (1996), 'Faithfulness in prosodic morphology & phonology: Rotuman revisited', ROA 110.

McCarthy, John (1999), 'Sympathy and phonological opacity', *Phonology* 16, 331–399.

McCarthy, John (2000a), Faithfulness and prosodic circumscription, in J. Dekkers, F. van der Leeuw, and J. van de Weijer, eds, *Optimality Theory: Phonology, Syntax, and Acquisition*, Oxford University Press, Oxford, pp. 151–189.

McCarthy, John (2000b), Harmonic serialism and parallelism, in M. Hirotani, A. Coetzee, N. Hall, and J. Kim, eds, *NELS 30*, GLSA, Amherst, MA, pp. 501–524.

McCarthy, John (2000c), 'The prosody of phase in Rotuman', *Natural Language and Linguistic Theory* 18, 147–197.

McCarthy, John (2003a), 'Ot constraints are categorical', *Phonology* 20, 75–138.

McCarthy, John (2003b), Sympathy, cumulativity, and the Duke-of-York gambit, in C. Féry and R. van de Vijver, eds, *The Syllable in Optimality Theory*, Cambridge University Press, Cambridge, pp. 23–76.

McCarthy, John (2007a), Derivations and levels of representation, in *The Cambridge Handbook of Phonology*, Paul de Lacy, Cambridge, pp. 99–117.

McCarthy, John (2007b), *Hidden Generalizations: Phonological Opacity in Optimality Theory*, London: Equinox.

McCarthy, John (2007c), 'Slouching towards optimality: Coda reduction in OT-CC', *Phonological Studies (Journal of the Phonological Society of Japan)* 7, 89–104.

McCarthy, John (2008a), *Doing Optimality Theory*, Blackwell, Malden, MA.

McCarthy, John (2008b), 'The gradual path to cluster simplification', *Phonology* 25, 271–319.

McCarthy, John and Alan Prince (1986/1996), 'Prosodic morphology 1986', Technical Report 32, Rutgers University Center for Cognitive Science, 1996. Available online at: http://works.bepress.com/john_j_mccarthy/.

McCarthy, John and Alan Prince (1990), 'Foot and word in prosodic morphology: The Arabic broken plural', *Natural Language and Linguistic Theory* 8, 209–283.

McCarthy, John and Alan Prince (1993a), 'Generalized alignment', *Yearbook of Morphology* pp. 79–153.

McCarthy, John and Alan Prince (1993b), Prosodic morphology. Constraint interaction and satisfaction. ROA 485-1201.

McCarthy, John and Alan Prince (1994*a*), The emergence of the unmarked: Optimality in prosodic morphology, in *NELS 24*, GLSA, Amherst, MA, pp. 333–379.

McCarthy, John and Alan Prince (1994*b*), Prosodic morphology, in J. Goldsmith, ed., *A Handbook of Phonological Theory*, Basil Blackwell, Oxford, pp. 318–366.

McCarthy, John and Alan Prince (1995), Faithfulness and reduplicative identity, in J. Beckman, L. Dickey, and S. Urbanczyk, eds, *UMOP*, GLSA, Amherst, MA, pp. 249–384.

McGarrity, Laura W. (2008), Nonuniformity of coda weight in Kuuku-Yaʔu, in A. W. Farris-Trimble and D. A. Dinnsen, eds, *IUWPL6: Phonological opacity effects*, IULC Publications, Bloomington, In, pp. 55–70.

McGregor, William (2003), 'The nothing that is, the zero that isn't', *Studia linguistica* 57(2), 75–119.

McLaughlin, John (1982), Two or three (or four) points about adverbs and aspect in Central Numic (Uto-Aztecan), in *Kansas Working Papers in Linguistics*, University of Kansas. Linguistics Graduate Student Association.

Mel'cuk, Igor (1991), Subtraction in natural language, in M. Grochowski and D. Weiss, eds, *Words are Physicians for an Ailing Mind*, Sagner, München, pp. 279–293.

Mester, Armin (1990), 'Patterns of truncation', *Linguistic Inquiry* 21, 478–485.

Michelson, Karin Eva (1983), A Comparative Study of Accent in the Five Nations Iroquian Languages, PhD thesis, Harvard University.

Miestamo, Matti (1973), *Standard Negation: The Negation of Declarative Verbal Main Clauses in a Typological Perspective*, Mouton de Gruyter.

Miller, Amy (1999), *A Grammar of Jamul Diegueño*, UMI, Ann Arbor, MI.

Miller, Amy (2001), *A Grammar of Jamul Tiipay*, Mouton de Gruyter, Berlin.

Mithun, Marianne and Hasan Basri (1986), 'The phonology of Selayarese', *Oceanic Linguistics* 25, 210–254.

Molina, Felipe (1999), *Hippocrene Standard Dictionary Yoeme-English, English-Yoeme*, Hippocrene books, New York.

Moravcsik, Edith A. (1977), *On Rules of Infixing*, Indiana University Linguistics Club, Bloomington.

Muller, Jennifer (1999), A unified mora account of Chuukese, in S. Bird, A. Carnie, J. D. Haugen, and P. Norquest, eds, *Proceedings of WCCFL 18*, Cascadilla Press, Somerville, MA, pp. 393–405.

Munro, Pamela and Charles Ulrich (1984), Structure-preservation and Western Muskogean rhythmic lengthening, in *Proceedings of WCCFL 3*, Stanford Linguistic Association, pp. 191–202.

Mutonyi, Nasiombe (2000), *Aspects of Bukusu Morphology and Phonology*, UMI, Ann Arbor, MI.

Nespor, Marina and Irene Vogel (1986), *Prosodic Phonology*, Foris Publicatios, Dordrecht.

Newman, Paul (2000), *The Hausa Language: An Encyclopedic Reference Grammar*, New Haven: Yale University Press.

Newman, Stanley (1932), 'The Yawelmani dialect of Yokuts', *International Journal of American Linguistics* 7, 85–89.

Nichols, Johanna, Alena Witzlack-Makarevich, and Balthasar Bickel (2013), 'The AUTOTYP genealogy and geography database 2013 release', http://www.spw.uzh.ch/autotyp/.

Nicklas, Thurston Dale (1974), *The Elements of Choctaw*, UMI, Ann Arbor, MI.

Nies, Joyce (1986), *Diccionario Piro*, Ministerio de Educación, Lima.

Nishiguchi, Sumiyo (2007), 'Bimoraic filter and sonority sensitive syllable contact in Dasenach imperfective', *Research in African Languages and Linguistics* 7, 43–58.

Nishiguchi, Sumiyo (2009), The prosodic morpheme in Dasenach, in C. G. Häberl, ed., *Afroasiatic Studies in Memory of Robert Hetzron: Proceedings of the 35th Annual Meeting of the North American Conference on Afroasiatic Linguistics (NACAL 35)*, Cambridge Scholars Publishing, Newcastle.

Noonan, Michael (1992), *A Grammar of Lango*, Mouton de Gruyter, Berlin, New York.

Noske, Roland (1985), Syllabification and syllable changing processes in Yawelmani, in H. van der Hulst and N. Smith, eds, *Advances in Nonlinear Phonology*, Foris, Dordrecht, pp. 335–361.

Odden, David (1988), 'Anti antigemination and the OCP', *Linguistic Inquiry* 19, 451–475.

Okello, Betty Jenny (2003), *Some Phonological and Morphological Processes in Lango*, UMI, Ann Arbor, MI.

Orgun, Cemil Orhan (1996), Sign-based Morphology and Phonology with Special Attention to Optimality Theory, PhD thesis, UC Berkeley.

Owens, Jonathan (1985), *A Grammar of Harar Oromo (Northeastern Ethiopia)*, Buske, Hamburg.

Pagotto, Louise (1992), 'Constraints on causativization in Marshallese: The case for actor conservation in Oceanic languages', *Oceanic Linguistics* 31, 251–266.

Park, Indrek (2012), A Grammar of Hidatsa, PhD thesis, Indiana University.

Paster, Mary (2006), Phonological Conditions on Affixation, PhD thesis, University of California, Berkeley.

Paster, Mary (2010), 'The verbal morphology and phonology of Asante Twi', *Studies in African Linguistics* 39, 77–120.

Paster, Mary and Yuni Kim (2011), 'Downstep in Tiriki', *Linguistic Discovery* 9, 71–104.

Pater, Joe (2000), 'Nonuniformity in English stress: the role of ranked and lexically specific constraints', *Phonology* 17(2), 237–274.

Pater, Joe (2006), The locus of exceptionality: Morpheme-specific phonology as constraint indexation, in L. Bateman, M. O'Keefe, E. Reilly, and A. Werle, eds, *Papers in Optimality Theory III*, GLSA, Amherst, MA, pp. 259–296.

Pater, Joe (2009), Morpheme-specific phonology: Constraint indexation and inconsistency resolution, in S. Parker, ed., *Phonological Argumentation: Essays on Evidence and Motivation*, Equinox, London, pp. 123–154.

Pater, Joe and Andries Coetzee (2005), 'Lexically specific constraints: gradience, learnability, and perception', *Proceedings of the 3rd Seoul International Conference on Phonology* pp. 85–119.

Payne, David L. (1991), A classification of Maipuran (Arawakan) languages based on shared lexical retentions, in D. C. Derbyshire and G. K. Pullum, eds, *Handbook of Amazonian Languages*, Mouton de Gruyter, Berlin, pp. 355–499.

Pertsova, Katya (2007), Learning Form-Meaning Mappings in Presence of Homonymy, PhD thesis, UCLA.

Picard, Marc (2004), '/s/-deletion in Old French and the aftermath of compensatory lengthening', *French Language Studies* 14, 1–7.

Piggott, Glyne L. (1995), 'Epenthesis and syllable weight', *Natural Language and Linguistic Theory* 13, 283–326.

Popjes, Jack and Jo Popjes (2010), Canela Krahô, in D. C. Derbyshire and G. K. Pullum, eds, *Handbook of Amazonian Languages*, Mouton de Gruyter, Berlin, pp. 128–199.

Poser, William (1989), 'The metrical foot in Diyari', *Phonology* 6, 117–148.

Prince, Alan (1990), Quantitative consequences of rhythmic organization, in M. Ziolkowski, M. Noske, and K. Deaton, eds, *Parasession on the Syllable in Phonetics and Phonology*, Chicago Linguistic Society, Chicago, pp. 355–398.

Prince, Alan and Bruce Tesar (2004), Learning phonotactic distribution, in R. Kager, J. Pater, and W. Zonneveld, eds, *Fixing Priorities: Constraints in Phonological Acquisition*, Cambridge University Press, Cambridge, pp. 245–291.

Prince, Alan and Paul Smolensky (1993/2002), 'Optimality theory: Constraint interaction in generative grammar', [first circulated as Prince & Smolensky (1993) Technical reports of the Rutgers University Center of Cognitive Science], ROA 537-0802.

Pulleyblank, Douglas (1986), *Tone in Lexical Phonology*, Reidel, Dordrecht.

Raimy, Eric (2000), *The Phonology and Morphology of Reduplication*, Berlin and New York, Mouton de Gruyter.

Reh, Mechthild (1993), *Anywa Language*, Rüdiger Köppe Verlag, Köln.

Revithiadou, Anthi (1999), Headmost Accent Wins: Head Dominance and Ideal Prosodic Form in Lexical Accent Systems., PhD thesis, LOT Dissertation Series 15 (HIL/Leiden Universiteit), Holland Academic Graphics, The Hague.

Revithiadou, Anthi (2007), Colored turbid accents and containment: A case study from lexical stress, in S. Blaho, P. Bye, and M. Krämer, eds, *Freedom of Analysis?*, Mouton De Gruyter, Berlin, New York, pp. 149–174.

Rice, Keren and Peter Avery (1989), 'On the interaction between sonority and voicing', *Toronto Working Papers in Linguistics* 10, 65–92.

Ringen, Catherine and Robert Vago (2011), Geminates: Heavy or long?, in C. Cairns and E. Raimy, eds, *Handbook of the Syllable*, Brill, Leiden, pp. 155–169.

Robinett, Florence (1955a), 'Hidatsa I: Morphophonemics', *International Journal of American Linguistics* 21, 1–7.

Robinett, Florence (1955b), 'Hidatsa II: Affixes', *International Journal of American Linguistics* 21, 160–177.

Robinett, Florence (1955c), 'Hidatsa III: Stems and themes', *International Journal of American Linguistics* 21, 210–216.

Rose, Sharon (1997), Theoretical Issues in Comparative Ethio-Semitic Phonology and Morphology, PhD thesis, McGill University.

Rose, Sharon (2007), Chaha (Gurage) morphology, in A. Kaye, ed., *Morphologies of of Asia and Africa*, Eisenbraums, Winona Lake, Indiana, pp. 399–424.

Rose, Sharon and Rachel Walker (2004), 'A typology of consonant agreement as correspondence', *Language* 80(3), 475–532.

Rosenthall, Sam and Harry van der Hulst (1999), 'Weight-by-position by position', *NLLT* 17, 499–540.

Round, Erich (2011), 'Word final phonology in Lardil: Implications of an expanded data set', *Australian Journal of Linguistics* 31, 327–350.

Rubach, Jerzy (1986), 'Abstract vowels in three-dimensional phonology: The yers', *The Linguistic Review* 5, 247–280.

Saba Kirchner, Jesse (2007), Cleaning up the scraps: a new look at Kwak'wala m'u:t reduplication, in A. Kaplan and D. Teeple, eds, *Phonology at Santa Cruz 7*, University of California at Santa Cruz.

Saba Kirchner, Jesse (2010), Minimal Reduplication, PhD thesis, University of California at Santa Cruz. ROA 1078-0610.

Saba Kirchner, Jesse (2013), Reduplicative exponence and minimal reduplication, in J. Trommer, ed., 'New theoretical tools in the modeling of morphological exponence', Special issue of *Morphology*, 227–243.

Saba Kirchner, Jesse (in press), 'Minimal reduplication and reduplicative exponence'.

Sagey, Elizabeth (1986), The Representation of Features and Relations in Non-linear Phonology, PhD thesis, MIT.

Salanova, Andrés Pablo (2004), 'Subtractive morphology in Mẽbengokre', Ms., University of Ottawa, available online at http://aix1.uottawa.ca/~asalanov/Docs/ initial-truncation.ps.

Salanova, Andrés Pablo (2007), Nominalization and Aspect, PhD thesis, MIT.

Salanova, Andrés Pablo (2011), Relative clauses in Mẽbengokre, in R. van Gijn, K. Haude, and P. Muysken, eds, *Subordination in Native South American Languages*, John Benjamins, Amsterdam, pp. 45–78.

Samek-Lodovici, Vieri (1992), A unified analysis of crosslinguistic morphological gemination, in P. Ackema and M. Schoorlemmer, eds, *Proceedings of CONSOLE 1*, Holland Academic Graphics, The Hague, Utrecht, pp. 265–283.

Samko, Bern (2011), 'Compensatory lengthening in Harmonic Serialism', qualifying paper, UCSC.

Samuels, Bridget (2010), 'The topology of infixation and reduplication', *The Linguistic Review* 27, 131–176.

Sapir, David (1969), *A Grammar of Diola-Fogny: A Language Spoken in the Basse-Casamance Region of Senegal*, Cambridge University Press, Cambridge.

Scheer, Tobias (2001), 'The key to Czech vowel length', Handout from the Formal Description of Slavic Languages 4.

Scheer, Tobias (2004), *A Lateral Theory of Phonology. Vol 1: What is CVCV, and Why Should It Be?*, Berlin: Mouton de Gruyter.

Scheer, Tobias (2011), Slavic yers, in M. van Oostendorp, C. J. Ewen, E. Hume, and K. Rice, eds, *The Blackwell Companion to Phonology*, Blackwell, Malden, MA, chapter 122.

Schuh, Russel G. (1989), Long vowels and diphthongs in Miya and Hausa, in P. Newman and R. Botne, eds, *Current Approaches to African Linguistics*, Foris, Dordrecht.

Segel, Esben (2008), 'Re-evaluating zero: When nothing makes sense', *Skase Journal of Theoretical Linguistics* 5(2), 1–20.

Seiler, Guido (2008), 'How to do things with moras: variation and change of quantity alternations across Upper German dialects', Paper presented at the International Morphology Meeting, Vienna.

Selkirk, Elisabeth (1986), 'On derived domains in sentence phonology', *Phonology* 3, 371–405.

Selkirk, Elisabeth (1991), A two-root theory of length, in E. Dunlap, J. Padgett, E. Dunlap, and J. Padgett, eds, *University of Massachusetts Occasional Papers in Linguistics 14: Papers in Phonology*, GLSA Publications, Amherst, MA.

Selkirk, Elizabeth (1995), The prosodic structure of function words, in *Papers in Optimality Theory*, Vol. 18 of *University of Massachusetts Occasional Papers*, University of Massachusetts, Amherst, MA, pp. 439–469.

Shaw, Jason (2009), Compensatory lengthening via mora preservation in OT-CC: Theory and predictions, in A. Schardl and M. Walkow, eds, *NELS 38*, GLSA, Amherst, MA, pp. 323–336.

Sheffer, Hadass (1995), 'Visibility and abstract form: Evidence from spirantization in Modern Hebrew', *University of Pennsylvania Working Papers in Linguistics* 2.2.

Sherer, Tim D. (1994), Prosodic Phonotactics, PhD thesis, University of Massachusetts at Amherst.

Shetler, Joane (1976), *Notes on Balangao Grammar*, SIL.

Siptár, Péter and Miklos Törkenczy (2000), *The Phonology of Hungarian*, Oxford University Press, Oxford.

Sloan, Kelly Dawn (1991), Syllables and Templates: Evidence from Southern Sierra Miwok, PhD thesis, MIT.

Smirnova, M. (1985), *The Hausa Language: A Descriptive Grammar*, Routledge & Kegan Paul, London.

Smith, Jennifer (2002), Phonological Augmentation in Prominent Positions, PhD thesis, University of Massachusetts, Amherst.

Smith, Jennifer (2008), Markedness, faithfulness, positions, and contexts: Lenition and fortition in optimality theory, in J. B. ao de Carvalho, T. Scheer, and P. Ségéral, eds, *Lenition and Fortition*, Mouton de Gruyter, Berlin, pp. 519–560.

Spaelti, Phillip (1994), Weak edges and final geminates in Swiss German, in M.Gonzàlez, ed., *Proceedings of NELS 24*, GLSA, Amherst, MA, pp. 573–588.

Spaelti, Phillip (1997), Dimensions of Variation in Multi-pattern Reduplication, PhD thesis, University of California at Santa Cruz.

Spencer, Andrew (1986), 'A non-linear analysis of vowel-zero alternations in Polish', *Journal of Linguistics* 22, 249–280.

Sprouse, Ronald L. (1997), 'A case for enriched input', Handout of a presentation at TREND, 3, available online as ROA 193.

Staubs, Robert, Michael Becker, Christopher Potts, Patrick Pratt, John McCarthy, and Joe Pater (2010), *OT-Help 2.0. software package*, University of Massachusetts Amherst, Amherst, MA.

Steins, Carsten (2000), How to account for non-concatenative phenomena in a morpheme-based theory, in B. Stiebels and D. Wunderlich, eds, *Lexicon in Focus*, Akademie-Verlag, Berlin, pp. 105–122.

Stemberger, Joseph and Barbara Bernhardt (1998), 'Contiguity, metathesis and infixation', *Proceedings of the WCCFL 17*, CSLI Publications, Stanford, CA, pp. 610–624.

Steriade, Donca (1982), Greek Prosodies and the Nature of Syllabification, PhD thesis, MIT.

Stiebels, Barbara and Dieter Wunderlich (1999), 'Second stems in Hungarian nouns', *The Linguistic Review* 16, 253–294.

Stonham, John (1994), *Combinatorial Morphology*, John Benjamin, Amsterdam.

Stonham, John (2007), 'Metathesis as prosodic repair', *Studies of Phonetics, Phonology and Morphology* 13, 3–24.

Stroomer, Harry (1987), *A Comparative Study of Three Southern Oromo Dialects in Kenya*, Buske, Hamburg.

Stump, Gregory T. (2001), *Inflectional Morphology*, Cambridge University Press, Cambridge.

Sye, Anand (2009), 'The short and long form of verbs in Mauritian Creole: functionalism versus formalism', *Theoretical Linguistics* 18, 61–97.

Szigetvári, Péter (2011), The skeleton, in M. van Oostendorp, C. J. Ewen, E. Hume, and K. Rice, eds, *The Blackwell Companion to Phonology*, Wiley Blackwell, Malden, MA, chapter 54.

Szypra, Jolanta (1992), 'Ghost segments in nonlinear phonology: Polish yers', *Language* 68, 277–312.

Tesar, Bruce and Alan Prince (to appear), Using phonotactics to learn phonological alternations, in *Proceedings of the 39th Regional Meeting of the Chicago Linguistics Society*.

Tesar, Bruce and Paul Smolensky (2000), *Learnability in Optimality Theory*, Cambridge, MA: MIT Press.

Thompson, David (1976), A phonology of Kuuku-Ya'u, in P. Sutton, ed., *Languages of Cape York*, Australian Institute of Aboriginal Studies, pp. 213–235.

Tola, Wako (1981), The Phonology of Mecha Oromo, PhD thesis, Addis Ababa University.

Topintzi, Nina (2006), 'A (not so) paradoxical instance of compensatory lengthening: Samothraki Greek and theoretical implications', *Journal of Greek Linguistics* 7, 71–119.

Topintzi, Nina (2008*a*), 'On the existence of moraic onset geminates', *Natural Language and Linguistic Theory* 26, 147–184.

Topintzi, Nina (2008*b*), 'Weight polarity in Ancient Greek and other languages', *The Proceedings of the 8th International Conference on Greek Linguistics*, pp. 503–517.

Topintzi, Nina (2010), *Onsets: Suprasegmental and Prosodic Behaviour*, Cambridge University Press, Cambridge.

Topintzi, Nina (2012), 'Compensatory lengthening', invited talk at the 20th Manchester Morphology Meeting, Manchester, 24th–26th May 2012.

Torres-Tamarit, Francesc (2012), 'Compensatory lengthening and opaque gemination in harmonic serialism', talk given at the OCP 9.

Tosco, Mauro (2001), *The Dhaasanac Language*, Rüdiger Köppe Verlag, Köln.

Tranel, Bernard (1991), 'CVC light syllables, geminates and moraic theory', *Phonology* 8, 291–302.

Trommer, Jochen (2010), 'Paradigmatic generalization of morphemes', *Linguistische Arbeits Berichte Leipzig* 88, 227–246.

Trommer, Jochen (2011*a*), 'Phonological aspects of Western Nilotic mutation morphology', Habil, University of Leipzig.

Trommer, Jochen (2011*b*), Phonological sensitivity to morphological structure, in M. van Oostendorp, C. J. Ewen, E. Hume, and K. Rice, eds, *The Blackwell Companion to Phonology*, Wiley Blackwell, Malden, MA, chapter 103.

Trommer, Jochen (2012), ø-exponence, in J. Trommer, ed., *The Morphology and Phonology of Exponence: The State of the Art*, Oxford University Press, Oxford, pp. 326–354.

Trommer, Jochen and Eva Zimmermann (2010), 'Generalized mora affixation', talk given at the 18th Manchester Morphology Meeting, Manchester, 20th–22th May 2010.

Trommer, Jochen and Eva Zimmermann (2014), 'Generalised mora affixation and quantity-manipulating morphology', *Phonology* 31, 463–510.

Udoh, Imelda Icheji (2004), 'Ghost consonants and lenition in Leggbo', *Journal of West African Languages* 31, 47–63.

Ulrich, Charles Howard (2003), *Choctaw Morphophonology, 1986*, UMI, Ann Arbor, MI.

Ulrich, Charles W. (1993), 'The glottal stop in Western Muskogean', *International Journal of American Linguistics* 59, 430–441.

Urbanczyk, Suzanne (1998), A-templatic reduplication in Halq'eméylem, in K. Shahin, S. Blake, and E. Kim, eds, *WCCFL 17*, CSLI Publications, Stanford, CA, pp. 655–669.

Urbanczyk, Suzanne (2011), Root-affix asymmetries, in M. van Oostendorp, C. J. Ewen, E. Hume, and K. Rice, eds, *The Blackwell Companion to Phonology*, Wiley Blackwell, Malden, MA, chapter 104.

Urquía Sebastían, Rittma and Stephen A. Marlett (2008), 'Yine', *Journal of the International Phonetic Association* 38, 365–369.

Ussishkin, Adam (2000), The Emergence of Fixed Prosody, PhD thesis, University of California, Santa Cruz, Santa Cruz, CA. Reproduced and distributed by SLUG Pubs, Department of Linguistics, University of California, Santa Cruz, CA 95064.

Ussishkin, Adam (2003), Templatic effects as fixed prosody: the verbal system in Semitic, in J. Lecarme, J. Lowenstamm, and U. Shlonsky, eds, *Research in Afroasiatic Grammar III*, John Benjamins, Amsterdam, pp. 511–530.

Ussishkin, Adam (2005), 'A fixed prosodic theory of nonconcatenative templatic morphology', *Natural Language and Linguistic Theory* 23(1), 169–218.

Vamarasi, Marit (2002), *Rotuman*, LINCOM, München.

van de Weijer, Jeroen (1992), 'Basque affricates and the manner-place dependency', *Lingua* 88, 129–147.

van Oostendorp, Marc (1995), Vowel Quality and Phonological Projection, PhD thesis, Katolieke Universiteit Brabant.

van Oostendorp, Marc (2003), 'Comparative markedness and containment', *Theoretical Linguistics* 29, 65–75.

van Oostendorp, Marc (2004), 'Crossing morpheme boundaries in Dutch', available online at ROA 655 0404.

van Oostendorp, Marc (2005), 'Expressing inflection tonally', *Catalan Journal of Linguistics* 4(1), 107–127.

van Oostendorp, Marc (2006), 'A theory of morphosyntactic colours', Ms., Meertens Institute, Amsterdam, available online at http://egg.auf.net/06/docs/Hdt.

van Oostendorp, Marc (2007a), Derived environment effects and consistency of exponence, in S. Blaho, P. Bye, and M. Krämer, eds, *Freedom of Analysis?*, Mouton de Gruyter, Berlin, pp. 123–148.

van Oostendorp, Marc (2007b), 'Restricting repairs', Ms. online available at http://www.vanoostendorp.nl/pdf/toomanyrepairs.pdf.

van Oostendorp, Marc (2007c), 'Stress as a prefix in Modern Greek', talk given at OCP 4, online available at http://www.vanoostendorp.nl/pdf/moderngreek_ocp04.pdf.

van Oostendorp, Marc (2008), 'Incomplete devoicing in formal phonology', *Lingua* 118, 1362–1374.

van Oostendorp, Marc (2012), 'Stress as a proclitic in Modern Greek', *Lingua* 122, 1165–1181.

Vaux, Bert (2002), 'Consonant epenthesis and the problem of unnatural phonology', talk presented at Yale University 16th September 2002.

Walker, Douglas C. (1970), Diegueño plural formation, in *Linguistic Notes from La Jolla 4*, University of California, pp. 1–16.

Walker, Rachel (1998), Nasalization, Neutral Segments, and Opacity Effects, PhD thesis, UC Santa Cruz.

Walker, Rachel (2000*a*), Long-distance consonantal identity effects, in R. Billerey and B. Lillehaugen, eds, *WCCFL 19*, Cascadilla Press, Somerville, MA, pp. 532–545.

Walker, Rachel (2000*b*), 'Nasal reduplication in Mbe affixation', *Phonology* 17, 65–115.

Walker, Rachel (2000*c*), Yaka nasal harmony: spreading or segmental correspondence?, in L. Conathan, J. Good, D. Kavitskaya, A.Wulf, and A. Yu, eds, *BLS 26*, Berkeley Linguistic Society, Berkeley, CA, pp. 321–332.

Walker, Rachel and Bella Feng (2004), A ternary model of morphology-phonology correspondence, in V. Chand, A. Kelleher, A. J. Rodriguez, and B. Schmeiser, eds, *Proceedings of WCCFL 23*, Cascadilla Press, Somerville, MA, pp. 787–800.

Walter, Mary Ann (2007), Repetition Avoidance in Human Language, PhD thesis, MIT.

Weber, David John (1947), *A Grammar of Huallaga (Huánuco) Quechua*, University of California Press, Berkeley, CA.

Weber, David John (1996), *Una gramática del Quechua del Huallaga (Huánuco)*, Instituto Lingüístico de Verano, Lima.

Weeda, Donald (1992), Word Truncation in Prosodic Morphology, PhD thesis, University of Texas at Austin.

Wilkinson, Karina (1988), 'Prosodic structure and Lardil phonology', *Linguistic Inquiry* 19, 325–334.

Willson, Heather (2002), Marshallese reduplication. Ms., UCLA.

Willson, Heather (2003), 'A brief introduction to Marshallese phonology', Ms., UCLA.

Wolf, Matthew (2005), An autosegmental theory of quirky mutations, in *Proceedings of the 24th West Coast Conference on Formal Linguistics*, pp. 370–378.

Wolf, Matthew (2007), For an autosegmental theory of mutation, in L. Bateman, M. O'Keefe, E. Reilly, and A. Werle, eds, *UMOP 32: Papers in Optimality Theory III*, GLSA, Amherst, MA, pp. 315–404.

Wolf, Matthew (2009), Mutation and learnability in optimality theory, in A. Schardl, M. Walkow, and M. Abdurrahman, eds, *Proceedings of the 38th Annual Meeting of the North East Linguistic Society*, GLSA, Amherst, MA, pp. 469–482.

Wolff, Ekkehard (1993), *Referenzgrammatik des Hausa*, Hamburger Beiträge zur Afrikanistik, Münster, Hamburg.

Yearley, Jennifer (1995), Jer vowels in Russian, in J. Beckman, L. Walsh Dickey, and S. Urbanczyk, eds, *Papers in Optimality Theory*, GLSA Publications, Amherst, MA, pp. 533–571.

Yeh, Shih-chi (2008), Suffixal reduplication in Paiwan, in *Proceedings of CLS 44*, Chicago Linguistic Society, Chicago, pp. 225–238.

Yoon, Junghyoe (2008), 'Mora augmentation in Korean noun subcompounding', IULC Working Papers online.

Yu, Alan C. L. (2002), 'Understanding infixes as infixes', talk, given at NAPhC 2.

Yu, Alan C. L. (2003), The Morphology and Phonology of Infixation, PhD thesis, UC Berkeley.

Yu, Alan C. L. (2004), Toward a typology of compensatory reduplication, in *Proceedings of WCCFL 24*, Cascadilla Proceedings Project, Somerville, MA, pp. 397–405.

Yu, Alan C. L. (2007), *A Natural History of Infixation*, Oxford University Press, Oxford.

Yun, Gwanhi (2006), 'Comparative faithfulness: evidence from compensatory lengthening in Bantu', *Studies in Phonetics, Phonology and Morphology* 12, 339–360.

Zec, Draga (1988), Sonority Constraints on Prosodic Structure, PhD thesis, Stanford University.

Zec, Draga (1995), 'Sonority constraints on syllable structure', *Phonology* 12, 85–129.

Zewen, François-Xavier Nicolas (1977), *The Marshallese Language. A Study of its Phonology, Morphology and Syntax*, Reimer, Hamburg.

Ziková, Markéta (2013), 'Templatic lengthening in Czech: Diminutives', talk, given at the FDSL 10.

Zimmermann, Eva (2009), Metathesis without Reordering, Master's thesis, University of Leipzig.

Zimmermann, Eva (2011), 'Cluster restrictions in Yine: a non-derivational approach', Ms., University of Leipzig.

Zimmermann, Eva (2013a), 'Non-concatenative allomorphy is generalized prosodic affixation: The case of Upriver Halkomelem', *Lingua* 134, 1–26.

Zimmermann, Eva (2013b), 'Vowel deletion as mora usurpation: the case of Yine', *Phonology* 30, 125–163.

Zimmermann, Eva and Jochen Trommer (2012), Portmanteaus as generalized templates, in V. Renner, F. Maniez, and P. J. L. Arnaud, eds, *Cross-disciplinary Perspectives on Lexical Blending*, Walter de Gruyter, Berlin, pp. 233–258.

Zimmermann, Eva and Jochen Trommer (2013), The linearization of morphological weight, in F. Heck and A. Assmann, eds, *Rule Interaction in Grammar*, Vol. 90, University of Leipzig, pp. 123–161.

Language index

Subject index